Cycle Europe

20 Tours, 12 Countries

Jerry Soverinsky

MBI

First published in 2004 by MBI, an imprint of MBI Publishing Company, Galtier Plaza, Suite 200, 380 Jackson Street, St. Paul, MN 55101-3885 USA

MBI titles are also available at discounts in bulk quantity for industrial or sales-promotional use. For details write to Special Sales Manager at Motorbooks International Wholesalers & Distributors, Galtier Plaza, Suite 200, 380 Jackson Street, St. Paul, MN 55101-3885 USA.

ISBN 0-7603-1869-7

On the front cover 1: If I had a dime for every time I had to check my map in front of a fifteenth century church, I'd be a rich man. *Jerry Soverinsky*

On the front cover 2: Often, the best way to escape paying for hotel room incidentals is to hop on your trail bike and coast down a mountainside. *Grindelwald Tourism*

On the back cover: The Swiss mountain biking itinerary reaches into the most spectacular areas of the country, filled with dramatic, awe-inspiring scenery. *Jerry Soverinsky*

Edited by Amy Glaser
Designed by Mandy Iverson

Printed in China

796.64
SOV
7/04

Dedication

This book is dedicated, in heartfelt gratitude, to the person who signs me to my next book or other significant writing project.

CONTENTS

ACKNOWLEDGMENTS

Very special thanks go to Howard Horowitz and his group of marketing specialists, whose dedicated work enabled my company to get its feet off the ground in 1990.

Thanks also to all the guests who have traveled with my company and offered input into improving my itineraries, and whose suggestions I tried to incorporate into my trips (unless the ideas were dumb).

Thank you to the dozens of outstanding guides with whom I've had the pleasure of working, who worked tirelessly over many weeks on end in demanding and high-pressure environments. You represented my company in the most professional way, and your insightful comments enabled my company to grow and continually improve.

Thank you to Dennis Pernu and the people at MBI, who allowed this project to proceed. Thank you, Amy Glaser, for your very attentive editorial eye, and for your insightful suggestions that no doubt spared me from several defamation lawsuits.

Thank you to the following people and organizations who generously allowed reprints of their photos: Niels Povlsen, Shannon Development, Cork-Kerry Tourism, R. Gerth and Ticino Tourism, Ghent Tourist Office, Colchester Borough Council, the Highlands of Scotland, Visit Scotland, Perthshire Tourist Board, Gloucestershire Tourism, J.C. Carbonne and Ville D'Aix, Servizio Turistico Associato Assisi, Kandersteg Tourismus, Grindelwald Tourism, VVV Gouda, National Tourist Office Luxembourg, Lausanne Tourism, and T.I.P. Delft.

And finally, no thanks to seven of my company's previous travelers whom I consider to be Class-A, Number-One, Schmucks: Dan Trangloroffoley, Susan Borelskim, Leon O'Juelst, Tim Jimbowolor, Farina Baxter-Muffin, Francerino Steinmangoldbaum, and Sledgey.

PART 1

INTRODUCTION

BICYCLE TOURING, FOOTNOTES IN HISTORY

During a recent trip to my dentist, while waiting to be examined, I passed the time by browsing a back issue of AJONASAEC (Archaeology Journal of North and South America Excepting Canada). After wading through the endless swimwear ads (bravo Time Warner!), I finally came upon a substantive article. Written by Russian scientists in Mobile, Alabama, the scholarly piece unearthed evidence that several hundred thousand years ago, two Cro-Magnon men had taken part in a very basic form of bicycle touring. Using what was referred to at the time as the *turshlot* (from the Cro-Magnon *tur* meaning "bi" and *shlot*, meaning "cycle"), they set out to ride these primitive two-wheeled machines from the area that today is Schaumburg, Illinois, to the Lincoln Park area of Chicago. However, their journey was cut short when one of the riders lost his map (Windy City), and during a heated discussion between the two adventurers, a pack of dinosaurs ate them.

Predating the previously recognized invention of the bicycle by some 400,000 years, the scientists' assertion understandably created chaos among the journal's seven subscribers. After a quick Internet search later that day, I discovered that the scientists' article, though heavily footnoted, never gained acceptance among conventional archaeologists. (A few grad students at the University of Essex, just outside Colchester, England, enthusiastically embraced the findings and nicknamed themselves The Turshlotians. They were mocked by their classmates, decided to disband, and later formed an anti-cricket movement that to this day is still active, though also ridiculed.)

Regardless of your leanings, it remains incontrovertible that bicycle touring stirs up passion and debate across all segments of society, oblivious to gender, race, or social accomplishment. Bicycle touring is not just a passing fancy, such as the step aerobics of the new millennium. No, bicycle touring is much more than that. Bicycle touring is adventure. Bicycle touring is travel. Bicycle touring is adventure travel.[1]

I started bicycle touring 18 years ago with a job guiding teenagers on trips through the U.S. and Europe. It was an unplanned summer job; I only knew that I had to get away from the chicken-cleaning factory (my hands! my hands!). I had ridden a bicycle since kindergarten (not non-stop, but you get the idea), yet I was never one of those fanatics who memorized professional racing stats or prattled on about the latest cycling components. I couldn't repair anything technical, either. The only thing mechanical I felt confident enough to attempt was inflating the tires, which I neglected most of the time anyway. I liked to bike, as did any caffeine-drinking teenager, and that was about it.

I applied for the tour guide position on a whim, and because I fit the camp's leadership criterion (willing to accept an unreasonably low salary), they hired me.

There was nothing exceptionally poetic about my first bicycle tours. I didn't witness a litter of puppies born under a Provencal sunset. I didn't hear an Alphorn while cycling into Switzerland. And I never heard an Irish farmer singing in Gaelic. Instead, I was a camp counselor who got paid to travel, who used to sneak off at night with my co-counselor to drink beer because the European bartenders never asked for my proof of age (pretty heady stuff when you're a 19-year-old American). All things considered, it seemed like a pretty good deal, and I spent the next two summers bicycle touring. My arthritic chicken-cleaning hands were gaining some much-needed rest, and I was slowly gaining an appreciation for cultures about which I previously knew very little.[2]

I should stop for a moment and clarify things. Despite my intrigue and affection for this new world of adventure, I wasn't (and still am not to this day) one who whines on about how our society short-changes itself because we don't carry baskets on our heads or wash our laundry in mountain streams (like so many of the Parisians that we see on television). I grew up in suburban Detroit and now live in Chicago, so cycling through Europe was—and is—a great opportunity to escape a traffic-jammed, television-marathon lifestyle to experience life at a more deliberate pace.

About 10 years ago, I was guiding a group of college students on a tour through France and Luxembourg and staying in rural campgrounds along the way. We were in a small town in the French Ardennes, and I awoke early and walked into town (a good 30 feet from the campground). There was a *Salon de Thé*, or Tea Room, that also served as the town's *boulangerie* (bread shop), *patisserie* (pastry shop), and *fabrique du mobilier* (furniture factory). It was just after 6 a.m. and the shop-keeper was unlocking her store's front door, allowing the thick, inviting aroma of fresh bread to drift through the village's lone street. It was all the encouragement I needed, so I entered the salon and ordered an espresso and nine croissants.

---

[1] Some would assert that all bicycle touring is adventure travel. Syllogistic reasoning would then deduce that while some adventure travel is hiking, that not all adventure travel is therefore bicycle touring. But all hiking is definitely bicycle touring, while only some bicycle touring is racquetball.
[2] Nothing.

This is how *not* to look like a cyclist:

(1) Leave helmet on at all times, especially while eating;

(2) Collar shirt (Izod, no less!);

(3) Sugar cone (instead of the much cooler waffle variety);

(4) Money pouch the size of a toaster oven—unzipped.

Jerry Soverinsky

Between sips of an extraordinarily rich coffee, I exchanged small talk with the proprietor and felt encouraged when she complimented my French.[3] A few weary locals popped in and out of the shop, purchasing breads, end tables, and other morning staples. Almost everyone mentioned something about France's World Cup performance the previous night—a loss—and shook their heads in mild disgust.

As I was starting my seventh croissant, a young girl about six years old entered the shop. She was wearing pajamas and slippers, as she walked lazily to the counter. The shopkeeper greeted her courteously in a tone that was consistent with how she had welcomed her other adult patrons.

The young girl was tired, but her request was confident and matter-of-fact: "*Deux baguettes l'ancienne et quatre croissants.*" Two loaves of bread and four rolls. She handed the shopkeeper a bill, the shopkeeper handed her change and the order, and the girl exited the shop as inconspicuously as she had entered.

[3] A rule of thumb when testing your foreign language skills: Be the first to take control of a conversation and pose everything in the form of a yes or no question. That way, you can understand the immediate answer to your question, and anything else that you pick up along the way is a bonus.

The North Sea Bike Path: Come for the Koffie, Stay for the Appelpunt. *Jerry Soverinsky*

Just another transaction at the *Salon de Thé*. But the simplicity of the exchange and the unassuming nature of both participants were something I had never encountered. The closest U.S. parallel I can remember took place at an Indiana McDonald's rest stop a few years earlier, when the manager stormed into the McPlayground™ and yelled at the nine-year-olds for not taking off their shoes. He even used the word "impudent," which prompted the kids to giggle. One of the mothers took issue with his choice of words, apparently thinking he had said "impotent."

I finished my croissants, ordered three more for the road, and headed back to the campground, thinking to myself that this was indeed a great day.

After I finished my undergrad studies, I headed to law school, unsure in which direction to head. A "D+" in Property pretty much clarified things for me, and I decided that my future as a lawyer was dim at best. I think it was during the series finale of *Jake and the Fatman* (the counterfeiting episode when Jake's friend is killed) that I decided to start my own company, guiding travelers on bicycle through Europe. After much trial and error, CBT Tours was founded (an interesting concept: you're walking down the street, trip over some glass—look! CBT Tours), a company I have owned since 1989. Since then, I have hosted thousands of travelers on European bicycle tours and personally guided close to 100 trips. This book is a compilation of some of my favorite tours, ones that will take you into the smallest and most charming areas of Europe, hopefully leading to your own very rich and rewarding experiences.

Bicycle touring through Europe has awarded me with innumerable first-hand encounters such as the one in the French Ardennes, and each one has had a way of tugging at my arm, forcing me to stop for a minute and reassess my priorities, while reminding me that there is more to life than fast food restaurants, HBO pay-per-view, and Nintendo.

Not that I'm willing to give up any of those. It's just nice to know that there are options.

WHY EUROPE?

There are four reasons to travel by bicycle through Europe (other voices espouse a more expansive classification system. One misleading analysis, originating in Canada, outlined 100 reasons, though they were working in a base$_2$ system, so we're back to the original 4). The reasons, in no particular order:

1. Europeans[4] make good coffee.

One major U.S. chain would have you believe their product is consistently superior. I would have to agree if, after consuming their basic drink, it is desirable to feel nauseous.

I favor a less unsettling coffee-drinking experience, and I routinely achieve this when drinking coffee in Europe. Perhaps their secret lies in the roasting process or the brewing procedure. Or maybe it's their Bopla cups. The fact remains that I *generally* find European coffee to be a rich and satisfying beverage, far better than what I'm *generally* accustomed to in the U.S. Plus, the European policy of including a cookie or chocolate with most orders? A very welcome touch. (Are you listening, Starbucks? Three bucks for a muffin?!)

Choose your travel companions carefully. These two arrived on my France tour as childhood friends and departed (in the words of the cyclist at right) "hating the stench of each other's shadow."

Jerry Soverinsky

2. Pastries everywhere!

If you take nothing else away from reading this book, other than the fact that I'm not wearing shoes, make it this crucial assessment: Europeans do pastries well. Very well.

Almost every European town supports a patisserie, a phenomenon that Americans would be well-served to replicate. In fact, a given European community may not offer adequate housing, employment, or living standards, but darned if they don't offer fine pastry, to which I say, "Well done."

So, if your Paris firm is relocating to North Korea because they've been caught dumping toxic waste into the local water supply, contaminating the

---

[4] *Continental* Europeans. My assertion excludes the coffees brewed by the British and Irish (unless you *prefer* your product diluted and overly acidic).

In 1984, France tried unsuccessfully to ride the coattails of the mega-hit *Ghostbusters* by producing its own transparent rip-off, *Avenay Val D'Or Busters*. It failed miserably in Europe, but achieved modest success in Singapore. *Jerry Soverinsky*

surrounding region and threatening the existence of all human life within a 20 kilometer[5] radius, and you're forced to move from your cozy seventeenth-century stone mansion into the Euro trailer park across the river, wondering where you'll ever find employment because you're 50 years old with a seventh-grade education and completely lack any marketable employment skills, fret not. Rest assured that your endless stream of socialist unemployment checks will still be able to buy you a daily *pain au chocolat.*[6]

3. The Pissoir

Leave it to the French to develop the pissoir, a brilliant plumbing innovation. Situated in cities and towns of all sizes, these open-air restrooms provide much-needed relief to waterlogged cyclists. Designed as a simple sewer grate with a modest horizontal plank shielding its patrons' midsections from surrounding traffic, they eliminate the need to intrude on restaurants (most of which are closed during morning and late afternoon hours) for use of their facilities. *Merci*, Monsieur Chirac!

4. European women sunbathe topless.
Nice.

WHY *NOT* EUROPE

As I mentioned in the opening pages, I'm not one to take my favorable European experiences and, by implication, disparage the United States. I'm a fiercely proud American. Although I enjoy traveling through Europe, THIS SHOULD NOT BE READ BY CONSERVATIVE TALK SHOW HOSTS TO SUGGEST THAT I'M OPPOSED TO TRAVELING THROUGH THE UNITED STATES.

On the contrary, I'm a strong advocate of U.S. travel. For those looking for specific reasons *not* to travel through Europe, here are the four essential reasons:

[5] 63,360 feet.
[6] Ding Dong or Ho-Ho.

1. Europeans make good coffee.

Since this is the only reason to make both the *Why Europe* and *Why Not Europe* lists, it bears explaining. While I'm addicted to the savory, rich flavor of European coffee, I end up consuming far too much caffeine. Therefore, I prefer the bitter, pungent offerings back here in the U.S. because I rarely drink it. Consequently, I also worry far less about my heart jumping into atrial fibrillation.

2. Vittel water tastes like crap.

I don't know who makes this cloudy bottled liquid, but it's by far the worst water I've ever consumed. During an exceptionally hot (104° F/40° C) ride through the Flemish countryside several years ago, I stopped at a rural market to purchase water for my group. The only product they offered was Vittel.

I bought a dozen bottles, but its objectionable taste prompted my guests to refuse it and opt instead for clinical dehydration. I cleaned my company van with the leftovers.

Since 1992, Luxembourg ice cream consumption has tripled, prompting one cabinet minister to beg for U.N. assistance: "This is no laughing manner (sic). Please help." *Jerry Soverinsky*

3. British money is too big.

The penny, five-pence, ten-pence, and twenty-pence coins are fine. Their sizes are manageable and well constructed. But the fifty-pence piece? Attach a handle and you've got yourself a sauté pan. And it's not even round!

Don't get me started on the paper currency. There's no uniform color scheme, the notes are various sizes, and the larger bills (twenty- and fifty-pound) won't fit in a wallet. When they're not being rejected at British shops ("Can't break a twenty, mate."), they can double as beach mats.

4. No Twizzlers.

Let's see, the U.S. exports Snickers, Milky Way, M&Ms, Twix, Kit Kat, Reese's, and a long line of other essential candies. But where's the strawberry Twizzlers? I came across Cherry Nibs late last year in the Czech Republic, but they're a poor substitute.

WHO SHOULD READ THIS BOOK

Most books have a specific, niche target audience. For instance:

Looking for a mid-life change, and you and your spouse are not averse to home repair while living out a fantasy? *Under the Tuscan Sun.*

Enjoy chicken baked with corn flake crumbs, reality television, and PTA meetings? *The Dummies' Guide to* [latest trend you read about in *People* magazine goes here].

Single female living in Chicago, angry at men, frightfully insecure, not too bright? *The Nanny Diaries.*

And so on.

This book is different. Sure, cyclists will find it an invaluable tool for planning a European trip, but others will benefit as well.

1. Jugglers

Whether you're a recent college graduate wishing to cycle Europe on a budget, or a retired dentist seeking the finest facilities and services, this book is for you. If you're skateboarding through Asia, South America, or Antarctica, you'll also pick up some useful travel tidbits here. If you're a homebody and have no intention of leaving your driveway, you'll enjoy hours of vicarious entertainment browsing through these pages.

2. Third World Diplomats

Any person whose language has Latin roots would be well served to buy and read this book. Regardless of your political affinity, I think you'll agree "this is without a doubt the best, most original work ever written in any language, in any time period, on any subject."[7]

3. Character Actors

If you don't want to visit Europe, or if you want to visit Europe but would never consider cycling, you should still buy this book. It just makes sense.

PRE-TRIP PLANNING

I know a few people who travel spontaneously as free spirits, never prearranging or reserving travel details prior to departure. In many cases, their vacation plans are determined last-minute, as was one friend's recent trip to Japan.

She's a schoolteacher and found herself bored during her spring break. Barely a day into her vacation, she found an unbelievable travel deal while browsing an Internet human genome site. Eight hours later, she was en route to Tokyo with a small knapsack holding only a few personal belongings and gum. Despite not making any hotel reservations nor obtaining any sightseeing or travel-related

---

[7] My grandmother.

information prior to departure, she thoroughly enjoyed her experiences in Japan, wandering the same two streets aimlessly by day and sleeping on park benches at night. A true explorer.

A sense of adventure is a must for any traveler,[8] but proper pre-trip planning will enable you to make the most efficient use of your time and money. It will also provide you with the greatest chance of meeting your travel expectations.

Group Tours

Group tours are not for everyone, but if you decide it's the right call for you, contact my company at 1-800-736-2453 from the U.S. and Canada, or +1-773-871-5510 from everywhere else on earth.[9]

When to Go

The ideal period to cycle through Europe is May 14 through May 24. Anything else and you're taking your chances.

Many travel books tell you to avoid traveling through Europe during the peak tourist months of July and August. To that I say, "More soup for me."

I'll provide background information under each tour regarding the weather that you can expect. It's up to you to decide what seems to be the most suitable environment.

Get yourself alone with a Belgian lace maker and prepare for some rib-ticklin' laughter. This woman had me laughing so hard, I nearly peed my pants!
Jerry Soverinsky

Level of Support

Most cycling guidebooks (all three of them) focus on self-contained cyclists whose bicycles are saddled with 90 pounds of gear. Bicycle purists (low-income cyclists) insist that this is the only way to travel, as it unifies man and machine in a central journey . . . blah, blah, blah.

I have traveled both self-contained and with full support (my luggage transferred from hotel to hotel). I can tell you that unless price is a factor (support is

---

[8] As is reliable diarrhea medicine.
[9] Shameless plug #1.

If you ask me, nothing beats camping in Europe. Except, of course, a nice hotel room.
Jerry Soverinsky

not free), or you're staying at facilities that won't provide safe storage for your belongings when delivered by third parties, there is little virtue in lugging your own gear, unless you're racked with personal guilt from a childhood trauma and this form of masochistic self-denial is somehow replenishing.

Those two "unlesses" are significant, and traveling with full support is not always a practical option. Transferring luggage between hotels that are 50 miles apart can cost up to $200. If you multiply this by a 7-day trip, your trip price is already $1,400, excluding hotels, food, and airfare. That's a pretty steep tag if you're traveling alone, regardless of your 401k.

If you're with a spouse or friends, this fixed support cost is allocated among all participants, so a group of four in the scenario above would share the $1,400 transfer cost. It's a huge difference and affordable for many more people.

Not all accommodations will accept luggage that is delivered to them. Municipal campgrounds, which are common throughout Europe, are frequently unattended properties where a manager might appear in the evening during a limited time frame to collect camping fees. During the rest of the day, there's no one available to accept and store bags.

Delivering luggage to hostels can also pose problems. I've stayed in hostels throughout Europe, and most are staffed by transient students with a high turnover rate. The random person who would be working when the bags were delivered would most likely not expect them. Would I then be able to find my bags when I arrived? Probably not. Additionally, many hostels are closed from the late morning to early afternoon, so delivery of the bags would encounter the same problem as at campgrounds: nobody home.

Some cyclists advocate self-contained travel because it provides for a much more challenging workout than cycling *sans baggage*. Silly. You want a physical test? Perform 50 push-ups at the end of your ride or curl your suitcase until you can't lift your arms. But don't attach everything you own to the back of your bicycle for the sake of exercise so that when you pop into a shop to buy a can of soda, you're neurotically peeking out of the store window to see if anyone is rifling through your bags.

Equipment and Clothing

I'm never surprised by what people will bring on a European trip and their justifications for doing so. I've seen thick, terry-cloth robes ("I wasn't sure if the hotel would provide towels), blenders ("Can't miss my morning smoothie"), horseshoes ("I like a spontaneous game"), and even a halogen floor lamp ("My eyes hurt when I read by dim-wattage bulbs"). No wonder there are long lines at airport x-ray baggage areas.

When newlyweds cycle through Switzerland, it's customary that at least one spouse cycles shirtless. *Jerry Soverinsky*

Bicycles

What kind of bicycle should you ride on your tour? There are a few factors to consider. First, what type of bike do you ride at home? Hybrid? Touring? City? Road? For most trips, I recommend riding the same type of bike to which you're accustomed. The only exception is the Swiss mountain bike tour, when you should ride a dedicated mountain bicycle[10] because you'll be traveling off-road for significant portions of the tour.

Cyclists who prefer racing bicycles should know that the roads in some countries, such as Ireland,

---

[10] As opposed to multi-purpose mountain bicycles, which double as steam mops.

England, and many European town centers, can be very rough. A road bike is perfectly suitable, but your ride may be somewhat uncomfortable over those stretches of coarse pavement. I tell my company's guests that they should purchase a slightly wider and aggressive tire tread for these areas. They make the ride more stable and comfortable.

Overall, your choice should be based on personal preference, and I recommend that you experiment at home before you leave.

Renting, Bringing Your Own

Renting a bike overseas is simple, and I list rental shops along each of the tours. However, *caveat rentor*, especially if you're American. European rental bikes can be pretty lousy.

Never heard of Cheetah brand? Minx? Double-Dare? Neither did I, until I saw them for rent at various European shops (think Wal-Mart rejects). If you're a serious cyclist, you should check out ahead of time the type of bicycle that will be available, or you might be seriously disappointed.

Keep in mind that in most instances, you'll need to return the bicycle to the rental shop at the end of your tour. This could be a travel inconvenience that you'd rather avoid.

Bags, Racks

If you're traveling the self-contained route, you'll need large, roomy panniers to transport your gear. Australian travelers, miraculously, seem to fit everything necessary into a mid-sized shirt pocket.

You'll need a sturdy rear rack for your bicycle, which will support your panniers, and these should all attach securely to your bicycle's frame (seatpost mounted rear racks, while great for day rides, are unsuitable for loaded touring). You should invest in a good set of waterproof pannier covers to protect them from onlooking spitters.

On all of my long-distance, self-contained rides, I've never opted for front panniers. That's a personal choice, I just don't think the extra weight in the front of my bicycle is comfortable. I'd rather have my steering unencumbered.

Packing Notes
Money

Almost every travel book advises that you buy a big, bulky waist pouch (money pouch, fanny pack, etc.) and wear it while traveling overseas. Besides creating the most unappealing fashion statement, its primary purpose seems to scream, "ROB ME!"

Isn't it enough that you've got sunscreen on your nose, an encyclopedic guidebook in one hand, and a video camera in the other? Now you've got to wear a suitcase around your waist, too? Save yourself the 20 bucks. Buy candy.

Whatever you use on a daily basis will work just fine in Europe.

A Packing Note for Canadians

If you're a Canadian citizen, you'll need to buy 40 Canadian flag patches and attach them to everything you own. Backpacks, duffle bags, suitcases, panniers, tires, hands, ears, etc., all should be affixed with a red and white maple leaf.

Why? Canadians are a fiercely proud people who strive to maintain the unique cultural qualities that so clearly distinguish them from their American neighbors.[11] They do this, of course, by shopping at their 107 Gap stores and 213 Wal-Marts, while eating Big Macs at their 1,300 McDonald's and drinking Slurpees at their 496 7-Elevens.

Fitness and Conditioning

The most common question I get from prospective travelers, besides, "What's J.Lo really like?" is "What kind of fitness level do I need to attain before arriving in Europe?" Here's a good guideline:

If you can bike 20 miles in Vermont, you'll be able to cover 33 kilometers in Holland. If you can bike 48 miles in the Ohio, you'll be able to cover 80 kilometers in Germany. If you can bench press 100 pounds in North Dakota, you'll be able to lift 220 kilograms in Italy. Please keep these numbers in mind when planning your trip.

Bicycle Repair Skills

Mechanical breakdowns are a legitimate concern for anyone traveling through a foreign country, especially for those untrained in bicycle repair. Certain countries provide extensive bicycle repair facilities and transportation systems to reach them while stranded, so even if you can't distinguish an allen wrench from an Ethernet cable, you can cycle reassured that even if your pedals disappear, you'll be able to find a replacement and a mechanic to attach them to your bicycle. Unless it's Sunday, when everything's closed. Then you're in trouble.

In a country like Scotland,[12] you can cycle for hours without passing a house, much less a bicycle shop, so you'll need to be somewhat more experienced in bicycle repair. I was far from a skilled mechanic when I started guiding tours, and I encountered several blips during my first few tours: a dented wheel in the British countryside; a shattered crank in Germany; and a shredded tire along the Belgium-Luxembourg border. In all of these instances, the breakdowns occurred without a bike shop in sight. With a little patience and a lot of alcohol, I endured the inconveniences, soliciting the generosity of locals to assist me.

[11] It's easy to spot a Canadian traveling through Europe (besides their omnipresent patches). When they approach a European, they always ask, "Do you have a tissue? My nose is funny," and they always end their conversations with, "Can you believe those Americans, eh?"

[12] Chad, for instance, is like Scotland.

Cycling solo through Europe can be a rewarding, introspective experience. Or it could suck. *Shannon Development*

Looking back, my positive interactions with those people far outweighed the relatively minor cycling interruptions. Bicycle shops for each day's ride, where available, are listed.

Repair equipment

The minimum repair equipment that you should bring is a frame pump, two extra tubes, and tire levers. These will enable you, or someone with bike repair skills, to repair a flat tire. I never use patch kits. They make a mess and I can't seem to ever get them to adhere properly. Besides, bike tubes are cheap (about $2 each).

If you're experienced with bike repair, you'll want to bring additional items: an adjustable wrench, screwdriver, and Dust Vac.

Maps and Books

It goes without saying that you should take this book with you on your tour. This will be your Bible, your sacred tome, and your key that unlocks the cultural subtleties in every European town. Buy an extra copy and pack it away in your suitcase in case you misplace one. It just makes sense.

I don't recommend buying any other book. None of them are well-written. They're all littered with factual errors and grossly overpriced. Take only *this* book with you.

You'll want to purchase country-specific maps for your tour (you could always find your way with just the cue sheets in this book, but I think it's easier to complement the directions with a detailed map). I'll mention the maps that I've found the most helpful under each individual itinerary.

Internet Research

If you don't have access to a computer, I'm assuming you've got more dire things to worry about than a European bike trip, like repairing your ship. I probably don't have to sell you on the Internet; I'm sure you'll agree any medium that offers photographs of Anna Kournikova eating garden vegetables is worthy of

If you will be arriving after 6 p.m., phone your hotel to alert them. It's embarrassing if they send an unneeded search party. *Cork-Kerry Tourism*

your attention. I'll provide you with detailed web addresses for each individual tour, which you can link to dozens of others as you coordinate your itinerary.

Keep in mind that the Internet is not an exhaustive research tool. But does anybody really like the taste of cilantro? And I might be crazy, but it just doesn't seem like kids today are good whistlers. Is the FCC aware that the Lifetime Channel shows 7 hours of *The Nanny* and *The Golden Girls* each day?

EUROPEAN MATTERS
Time

London is 2 hours ahead of Greenwich Mean Time,[13] which is 5 hours ahead of New York Time, 8 hours ahead of San Jose Time, 4-1/2 hours ahead of Newfoundland Time, and 6 hours ahead of Indiana Time, except in the summer when Indiana doesn't adjust for Daylight Savings Time.[14]

If you're traveling through Europe, I can think of only one reason that you'd even begin to care about what the time might be back in your hometown: Courtesy phone calls to family. To which I say, " Psshhhhh." Try this:

(RING . . . RING).

---

[13] Greenland's "claim to fame," the world's comparative time standard.
[14] You're independent, we get it.

(groggily) "H'lo?"

"Hi, Dad, 'sup?"

(groggily) "Huh?"

"Dad, it's me, Jerry. What's wrong? You sound tired?"

(fumbling sounds, muffled cursing)

"Are you out of your mind? It's four in the morning!"

"In the MORNING?! Oh, wow, this time change thing is really throwing me for a loop. I'm sorry."

(more fumbling)

"That's OK, it's OK. How's it going?"

You see what I did there? I deftly steered the conversation away from the time of day and onto my own sympathetic difficulty with understanding time zones. Before I knew it, my dad was already asking me about my trip. Forget about time changes and all that. Enjoy Europe. Call home when you want.

Electricity

About 45 percent of European towns are wired for electricity. It's never necessary that you purchase specialty adapters before using your equipment overseas. Just know that you'll destroy your appliances if you don't.

Most newer computers and cameras have internal voltage switches that will automatically adapt to the European standard of 220V[15] (as opposed to the far better 110V here in the U.S.), but your leaf blower may not. Check to see. You'll also need special plug adapters for your appliances because European outlets have funny holes.

You can purchase adapters at a number of shops. I stay away from the dedicated travel stores; their prices tend to be high. I opt instead for Radio Shack, where they still write invoices by hand, despite the fact that they're a specialty technology store.

Customs

You'll instantly know when you've met a native European: They'll bow and tie your shoes.[16] After this welcoming gesture, it's considered polite to place your right hand on that person's rib cage (either side, though left is generally considered to be a sign of desperation) and say, "Tumult."

A few other essential gestures that will allow you to quickly gain favor with your foreign hosts:

When you enter a restaurant, always leap and try to touch the top of the doorframe.

When calling your hotel's front desk to request more towels, always end the conversation with "I love you."

---

[15] Vitamins.

[16] Only when you're visiting *his* country. When he visits *your* country, he'll expect you to offer misleading road directions.

The worst day biking through Europe beats (by far) the best day answering customer service complaints for Northwest Airlines.
Ticino Tourism

When pitching a tent at a European campground, prior to inserting your stakes into the ground with your arms outstretched and in a falsetto voice, scream, "I like ice cream, yes, I do! I like ice cream, how 'bout you?!"

And finally, when invited for dinner at a European's home, remove your shoes before entering the house and hand them to your host SOLES UP (if the laces are pointing up, it's thought to be bad luck for local crops). When you're preparing to leave, as soon as your host returns your shoes, hold up your hand in a gesture of refusal, and say, "Keep them, the traction's shot." If the response is tasteful laughter, you'll know that they like you (yeah!). But if your host winks at you with either eye, you probably took the last piece of beef, which means you'll be up all night with heartburn.

Money

I haven't purchased travelers' checks in several years; I opt instead for my ATM card when traveling overseas. It's accepted in almost every town of appreciable size, and the exchange rate is far better than what I get from travelers' checks (about 2 to 5 percent better).

Visa and MasterCard are the two most common credit cards accepted overseas. American Express is accepted, but not as universally. Leave your Diner's Club, Discover, and Marshall Field's cards at home.

Under each tour description, I'll detail the currencies used. For a list of current conversion rates, check out www.fxtop.com.

Phone

Over the past several years, the cost of phoning internationally has decreased substantially. While in Europe, you have a few options:

1. Hotel calls

The only thing more expensive than the macadamia nuts in your hotel's minibar are hotel direct-dial phone calls. Unless your eyebrows have caught fire and you need urgent attention, opt for a phone card or cell phone (see below).

2. Phone cards

In the late seventeenth century, European phone card usage was relegated to the aristocracy and criminals. It wasn't until the fall of the Berlin Wall in 1991 that the masses gained access.

Initially, each country distributed its own phone cards, which were unique and functional only for its own public phones or from calls made from within its borders. For instance, if you bought a French telephone card, it was accepted only at French phones. This worked fine for travelers visiting only one country, but it required purchasing multiple phone cards for those who visited more than one country.

On November 20, 2002, all that changed.[17] Phone cards that were operational throughout Europe were introduced. By dialing a country-specific access code and supplied PIN,[18] you can now use the same phone card in multiple countries for rates that are as low as pennies a minute. The cards are accepted at most phones, including those in hotels. Keep in mind that if you're using the card from your hotel room, you might still have to pay for the local access call. Sometimes[19] these calls are complimentary, although there's usually a modest[20] fee.

Phone cards are sold at shops throughout Europe in a variety of denominations (Jewish, Christian, Catholic, and Muslim). You can even buy international cards prior to leaving the U.S. Check with your long-distance phone carrier to see if they offer ones that can be accessed from overseas. But be careful—some of the cards have very high initial minute access fees. So even if they promote calls for 2 cents a minute, that's not such a bargain if your connection fee is $17,000.

Cell phones

One of the truly great questions I receive from U.S. travelers headed to Europe: Can I bring my U.S. cell phone to Europe? To this I answer, "Of course you can, though it might not work."

Cell phones that accept SIM cards can be used in multiple countries and cell zones. If you buy a phone that accepts these cards (ask your vendor to make sure, they're very specific models), you're able to use them throughout Europe. The cards are available in multiple denominations (10 Euros, 25 Euros, etc.) and contain unique phone numbers that are activated within their coverage zones.

---

[17] November 20 is now a bank holiday throughout Europe, informally known as Phone Card Day (PCD). The week building up to PCD is one of the most festive throughout Europe when schools stage elaborate pageants, and municipal workers dress as push-button dialpads. For superstitious reasons, Estonia and Sweden celebrate PCD on November 21 every year whose last digit ends in "5."

[18] Punch In Numbers.

[19] Never.

[20] Exorbitant.

First Aid

Hospitals and clinics are located throughout all of the enclosed itineraries, and I detail facilities along each day's route.

If you have any medical concerns, I advise wearing a Medic Alert tag during your tour, which you can order from your local pharmacist or from Medic Alert at 888-633-4298/209–668-3333; www.medicalalert.org.

It's always helpful to know basic first aid and CPR before you depart. Your local fire department or Red Cross office should be able to provide you with certification classes available in your area.

Maps

I detail specific map recommendations for each of the enclosed tours, and you can order them prior to your tour or upon your arrival in Europe.

European maps vary dramatically in price. Czech maps, for instance, might cost $1 or $2, while Swiss maps might run $30. Neither map is superior to each other. That's just the Czech Republic and Switzerland.

You may also wish to obtain maps of the towns that you'll visit. These are much more difficult to find at home (unless home is in one of the towns), and your best bet will be to write the town's tourist board (I supply complete contact information under each tour).

Food

It's difficult to find Pop Tarts in Europe. Or a good corned beef sandwich. Or Spaghetti-Os. And of course, no Twizzlers there either (see *Why Not Europe*).

Despite these shortcomings, don't be dissuaded from visiting Europe. You'll find a variety of wonderful food items, each of them beckoning for your sampling.

Europeans have their own regional delicacies, so don't feel betrayed if your personal favorite is missing. For instance, while I find it odd that many Europeans don't eat peanut butter, I appreciate that the Italians introduced us to Nutella. Give and take.

I'm no vegetarian, but I stay away from meats that aren't already in my daily diet. Goat at Indonesian restaurants . . . probably OK, but not for me. Horse at French restaurants . . . don't think so. And cuddle fish . . . well, let's just say if cuddle fish is on the menu, order white rice and call it a night.

Some of my guests are game for anything, and I've always envied that type of culinary adventurism. Not really, but I tell them that I do. If you have a specific dietary requirement—i.e. 3 cups of soy nuts each day—you should bring these to Europe, clearly marked and in the manufacturer's unopened packaging. Don't expect to find a GNC or Whole Foods when you land in Europe.

A Note about Tourist Offices

It can get confusing trying to figure out which tourist office is responsible for your destination. For instance, if you're traveling to the Cotswolds in England, you can write the Stow-on-the-Wold Tourist Office (one of the cities along the route); or the Gloucestershire Tourist Board, the county where Stow is located; or the Heart of England Tourist Board, the region that covers Gloucestershire; or the Visit Britain office, which handles all travel to the United Kingdom.

If you're really ambitious, you could then write the European Tourist Office (handles all European countries); or Eastern Hemisphere Incoming (covers Europe, Asia, etc.); or Earth Tourism; or the Solar System Tourist Board (SSTB); or Visit Milky Way (formerly Milky Way Tourist Authority); and finally, the Cluster Tourist Authority, which includes the y-axis of the CVn I Cloud Group, but excludes the Mafei I Group. I've heard rumors of a small satellite office that covers the M83 group of galaxies, but I sent an email and never received a response (their server said to expect a response in 27 octodecillion light years). [21] A lot of choices, with a lot of useful information.

Claustrophobics fare poorly at late-night Belgian celebrations. *Ghent Tourist Office*

I'll list all appropriate tourist boards under each tour, and describe "Where am I?"—that is, the city, county, region, and any other geographical groupings that you're likely to come across in researching your destination.

The majority of overnight stops listed in this book have their own tourist offices. I detail the contact information under each daily itinerary.

---

[21] 27,000,000,000,000,000,000,000,000,000,000,000,000,000,000,000,000,000,000 light years (shelf life of a twinkie).

VIII. GETTING THERE AND AROUND

Planes
History of the Airline Industry

When I visited Europe for the first time, back in 1985, only government prop planes serviced the U.S.-Europe routes. Due to this noncompetitive monopoly, roundtrip prices were high and often topped $84,000 during peak travel months. The luxury of international travel was therefore accessible mainly to the upper class, and I usually found myself sharing passenger cabins with dukes, duchesses, and junk bond kings. They were fun times, to be sure (I still have your wool socks, Fergie, if you're reading this), but they exacted a heavy toll on my savings account.

In 1987, flight travel was deregulated, which meant that international flights were now extremely affordable. (Remember those $19 roundtrip fun fare flights from New York to London? Talk about Mardi Gras in the sky!). While my chances of rubbing elbows with foreign royalty were greatly diminished,[22] I was able to fly far more frequently to Europe, and my discretionary income was earmarked for other essential items, like candy.

"So I says to him, I says, 'That's not my glotchnik . . . it's a fupal!'" *Niels Povlsen*

Almost all of the enclosed 20 tours begin at or near major European airports, and I detail specific arrival/departure transfer information under each tour heading with information on accessing nearby airports and train stations.

Travel Agents: Buggy Whips of the Travel Industry

A few blocks from the Football Hall of Fame in Canton, Ohio, workers are busy putting the final touches on a long-overdue museum, one that pays tribute to the staple of twentieth century travel, the Travel Agent (it'll be easy to spot as you travel down I-77—look for the giant Chip Clip® with the phrase "I'm sorry, but I distinctly remember you requesting a windowless cabin next to the tap dance studio" emblazoned across its marble base).

---

[22] In September 1991, at an airport restroom in Manchester, England (turn right out of customs, left by the 3rd baggage carousel), I peed next to the Count of Gloucester. This was a chance encounter because his private charter was grounded due to circuitry problems.

Long before the Internet, travel agents were our bridges to the airline industry, the ones people turned to when booking airline tickets. You always had the option of phoning the airlines directly, but the majority of people delegated the entire ticketing process to their agents. In fact, I maintain that the whole concept of having an agent enabled the industry to flourish. Regardless of your social standing, there was something indulgent about working with an agent—and letting others know that you had obtained a dialogue with one. Interactions like the following were common across all segments of society, especially among entry-level blue collar workers:

"Hey, Joe, you and the lady wanna go to Jersey with me and Alice over Christmas?"

"Jersey . . . (whistles, impressed) looks like someone died and left you some dough, huh?"

"Nah, my agent's great, she'll get us a good rate."

"You've got an agent? (whistles, more impressed) Jeez."

"Yeah, Shirley. She's the best. I'll give her a call now."

"Better finish hosing down the puke from that sidewalk. Call when our shift's over."

For those too young to remember the travel agent's role and unable to get to Canton, you can still spot a few former agents sprinkled across the country. They're all 57 to 63 years old, slightly overweight, and when they venture outside, they're the ones clutching multiple Bloomingdale's bags (all stuffed with newspaper comics) mumbling "Damn computers!" as they stagger through busy intersections.

If you're not computer-savvy and if there are any travel agents left working at the time of this printing, you're of course free to consult one when purchasing an airline ticket. Be prepared to pay a special handling fee; many agents, struggling to make a living in the age of the Internet, may tack on $50 to 75 per ticket. It's a very fair price, considering that they'll do all of the legwork for you. And besides, when you tell your buddy at work that you're headed to Newark for Easter and he asks where you got your ticket, you can reply, "Got a great deal from my agent." You'll be the envy of the slaughterhouse.

Trains

It seems everybody who's traveled through Europe gushes as they recount an exciting train experience: "I met a German girl who's been to Maine!" "I made three new friends from Albania!" "I lost my virginity to a Dutch social worker!"

In response, I assert the following: One, they've been deceived—no German has ever stepped foot on Maine soil; two, something's fishy here—Albanians travel in groups of two or four, never odd numbers; and three, probably true.

Foreign farm workers get a kick out of tourists who demand they stop working and pose for a patronizing photo.
Niels Povlsen

While European train travel can have its social advantages, it's not necessarily cost-effective. Consider the following:

You're traveling with three friends around the South of France and decide that you want to cycle the Paris to Luxembourg itinerary detailed in this book (great choice!). You have three options[23] for getting from Nice to Paris: One, you can take the train, the ubiquitous travel mode for Europeans; two, you can fly between Nice and Paris; and three, you can rent a car. Let's look at each option separately.

Nice to Paris Transportation Costs[24]

Train: The cost for a 2nd class ticket between Nice and Paris is $105 (www.raileurope.com). Multiplied by 4 (you and your 3 friends), total cost for the journey is $420.

Flight: An economy one-way ticket between Nice and Paris, if purchased online, is approximately $97 (www.easyjet.com). Multiplied by 4 (you and your 3 friends), total cost for the journey is $388.

Car rental: The cost for a one-way compact car rental between Nice and Paris is approximately $192 (www.autoeurope.com). No need to multiply by 4, since you and your friends will all fit comfortably inside. But add in the cost of gas, about $80, and tolls (avoid tolls by taking smaller roads, though the trip duration will increase dramatically), about $70, for a grand total of $342. The train journey is the most expensive option!

Of course, this is just one travel itinerary; in many others, train travel is the least expensive and most convenient means for reaching your destination. Check around just to be sure and don't assume train travel is your only practical means for European travel.

You can purchase point-to-point rail tickets and extended passes from Rail Europe before departing for Europe at www.raileurope.com. However, you're likely to save a bit of money if you purchase point-to-point tickets directly from the issuing country. For instance, a 2nd Class Zurich to Bern ticket, if purchased

---

[23] Public transportation options. You could of course walk, skip, or crawl, too. All are addressed in my previous book, *The Imbecile's Guide to Walking, Skipping, and Crawling Between Nice and Paris.*
[24] Approximate prices based on current exchange rates at the time of this writing, 10:45 a.m.

directly from Rail Europe, costs $37 plus a $15 shipping/handling fee—$52. However, the same ticket, if purchased at the Zurich train station, costs 45 CHF, or $34 at today's conversion rate. That's an $18 savings.

Here are the appropriate website links for each country's train system:

Austria: http://public-transport.net/timetabl.htm

Belgium: http://www.b-rail.be/

Czech Republic: http://idos.datis.cdrail.cz/ConnForm.asp?tt=c&cl=E5

France: http://www.sncf.com/indexe.htm

Germany: http://reiseauskunft.bahn.de/bin/query.exe/en

Great Britain: http://www.nationalrail.co.uk

Ireland: http://www.irishrail.ie/home/

Italy: http://www.fs-on-line.com/

Luxembourg: http://www.cfl.lu/

Netherlands: http://www.ns.nl/domestic/index.cgi

Switzerland: http://www.rail.ch/index_e.htm

Make sure that the train/bus/rickshaw that you plan on taking accepts bicycles. Almost all do, although some exclude peak morning and evening rush periods as well as allocate specific cars for their transport. And almost all that do accept bicycles will charge an additional fee.

Cars

As mentioned briefly above under the train section, car travel is a practical, and often economical, means of traveling throughout Europe. I rent the majority of my company's European cars from Auto Europe (Phone: 800-223-5555; www.autoeurope.com), a company that works as the middleman for the major European rental companies (Auto Europe doesn't maintain its own fleet). Prices are competitive and it has flexible rental policies throughout most of Europe. A minimum 3-day rental is required, which means that if you're driving point-to-point for a day, you're better off booking directly through the car companies.

Barbecued wolf, South Bohemia, Czech Republic. Tastes like chicken!
Niels Povlsen

If your journey ends in a country other than the one where you rented your car, you'll more than likely incur a significant drop-off fee, which can total several hundred dollars. In these cases, train or air travel will probably provide better travel rates.

Buses

Depending on your travel destination, bus travel may be the only public transportation option for certain segments of your journey. If your cities aren't listed under the train timetables, try the European bus links below:

Austria: http://public-transport.net/timetabl.htm

Belgium: http://www.delijn.be/

Czech Republic: http://www.vlak.cz/ConnForm.asp

France: http://www.sncf.com/indexe.htm (includes bus information)

Germany: http://reiseauskunft.bahn.de/bin/query.exe/en (includes bus information)

Great Britain: http://www.nationalexpress.com/neh.cfm?w=800&j=1

Ireland: http://www.buseireann.ie/site/home/

Italy: http://www.italybus.it/orario.asp

Luxembourg: http://www.cfl.lu/f/bus/index.htm

Netherlands: http://www.9292ov.nl/ (an outstanding site that offers door-to-door tram, bus, and train recommendations for travel throughout Holland. Language is Dutch, but it's relatively easy to navigate)

Switzerland: http://www.rail.ch/index_e.htm (includes bus information)

What can be more inspiring than watching a true chef hard at work, laboring over his signature dish, and dripping sweat into your entree? *Niels Povlsen*

Taxis

Whenever I take a taxi in Europe, I ask the driver for an approximation of the fare before I depart. This is especially important on longer transfers, such as to/from a distant airport. While I provide taxi costs under the arrival and departure information for each tour, they're usually presented as a range, thanks to the vast fluctuations that drivers have been known to charge.

A Note About Getting your Bike to Europe and Back Home

Almost every airline transports bicycles, though an increasing number charge a fee ($80-$125 and up). Check with your airline to determine its policy. In order to transport your bicycle, I recommend using either a bicycle case or box.

Packing Your Bicycle for Airline Travel

You need to pack your bicycle properly for airline travel. If you're not mechanically inclined, visit your local bike dealer and ask him to package your bike for you. If he starts poking around and asking questions ("Where're you going?" "How long you goin' for?"), flap your arms quickly and scream, "I'm not unreasonable!" He'll get the point, especially if he's certified. Most shops will charge you a modest fee for packing your bicycle, $10 to $25. It's a valuable service, especially if they buy you lunch.

I recommend you ask the shop to show you the proper way to reassemble your bicycle upon landing in Europe. This should take about 15 minutes, and you should offer to marry his daughter.

Here's all you need to know to package your bike properly:

1. Place bike in box or case.

2. If lid does not close or parts of bike protrude from box/case, remove one item from bicycle.

3. Repeat steps 1 and 2 until everything fits inside the box/case.

What's the only thing that horses love more than grown children riding their backs? Wearing costumes, of course! *Niels Povlsen*

Unless you've got some bike repair experience, I don't advise fiddling around trying to pack your bicycle because you'll more than likely damage something. Take your bike to a shop. You and your bike will be much happier.

CYCLING SAFETY, ETIQUETTE, AND CONCERNS

No matter where you're cycling, don't antagonize motorists, even though they're always wrong. It makes things worse for other cyclists.

I always find it puzzling when a 120-pound cyclist verbally thrashes a passing motorist, regardless of how poor the motorist's driving etiquette. The cursing does nothing to educate the motorist on how to deal with cyclists. Instead, it provokes the driver to hate the cyclist, and by association, all other cyclists.

If a motorist cuts you off or passes you a bit too closely and if you're given the chance to confront him[25] (stopped at a red light or stuck in the same pottery class on Thursday nights), approach the motorist respectfully and inform him of his transgression. Don't patronize or scold him. Talk to him. Just remember that (in his mind) you represent all other cyclists that share the same road. Also understand that he's got a 4,000-pound machine that travels six times faster than a bicycle. You don't want to get him mad. After you leave, slash his tires when no one's looking.

Sides of the Road

There's only one thing that maintains a universal standard throughout the world—the width of a toilet paper roll. Everything else is a crapshoot. You've got differing phone jacks, electrical outlets, computer operating systems, bike tube valve stems, computer connection cables—the list is endless. It's therefore not surprising that Europeans drive on different sides of the road too (especially when leaving the pubs).

You'll travel along the right side of the road in all of the countries detailed in this book, except for England, Scotland, and Ireland, where you'll cycle along the left side. (In January 1967, Belgians experimented with cycling along the centers of roads. They decided to revert to the right-side standard only one month later, after 27,000 cyclists had been hit by cars.)

Make sure that you visualize the proper way to travel before setting out on your bicycle. Look left, right, up, and down when you reach an intersection, and pay careful attention when cycling through roundabouts . After an hour or two on the road, cycling along the left side will become second nature to you, and upon returning home to the U.S., you'll have to readjust for traveling along the right side.[26]

A good pair of owl gloves can fetch upwards of $700 on Austrian eBay. Robin Hood hat not included. *Niels Povlsen*

[25] Or her. It's not always men who drive like animals. It just makes the sentence reader easier (I don't like the "him/her" dual pronoun).
[26] Not really.

OFF YOU GO

When I arrived in Europe to guide my company's first trips, I thought I was sufficiently prepared. I was carrying 96 hotel confirmation letters, 43 detailed country and city maps, 9 reference letters from foreign consulates, and a carton full of condoms.

After landing at Luxembourg's Findel Airport, I rented my company's van at the neighboring car rental station and started my journey, eager to visit my first overnight stop, the Luxembourg youth hostel.

According to correspondence from the hostel, it was situated merely 7 kilometers from the airport, so I shifted my truck into fourth gear (novice manual transmission driver), glanced at my very detailed Luxembourg map, and started for the hostel. Everything appeared to be clear, and I was anxious to arrive, since I was hungry and in need of a shower.

Six hours later, I found the hostel. That's 7 kilometers, 4 miles, 6 hours.

I wish I could offer a plausible excuse for the delay. Road construction? Nope. Funeral procession? I wish. Seismic tremors? Would've been convenient. Unfortunately, I just got disoriented—and thereby lost.

What's my point? When you depart for Europe, take this book with you. Buy all of the maps that I recommend. Bring an organized binder filled with reservation confirmations, sightseeing brochures, and current event clippings. Forward your phones. Place vacation holds on your newspapers and mail. Brush up on your French. Practice your smirk. And finally, when you arrive in Europe, be prepared to endure some inconveniences because you're bound to lose your way on occasion. It's one of the adventurous aspects of foreign travel, which you'll curse at the time but remember fondly upon returning home. Or not.

You might remain livid every time you think back to your European trip, and in the future, never venture further than your neighborhood Dairy Queen. If so, try the Peanut Buster® Parfait. Delish.

IRELAN

ATLANTIC
OCEAN

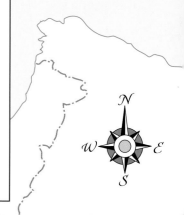

PART 2

THE TOURS

As some general background for all countries and regions that I discuss, it's helpful if you keep in mind that every European hates every other European, including himself.

It's true. Europeans are miserable, miserable, people; resentful of the centuries of wars that enslaved their ancestors and tried to annihilate their unique cultures.

But it's a subtle misery, which more closely resembles mild indigestion. It's the reason most Europeans don't smile,[27] and it shouldn't affect your trip. So if you see a Dutchman walking gingerly while rubbing his stomach, chances are that it has nothing to do with the meal he ate. He's just remembering the time in 1795 when French troops killed his great-great-great grandparents, stole their house, pillaged their business, enslaved their children, and taught French in their schools.

The French were of course ousted in 1813, when things in Holland generally improved. Until 1940, when German troops occupied his country and killed his grandparents, stole their house, pillaged their business, enslaved their children, and taught German in their schools.

The Germans were of course ousted in 1945, when things in Holland generally improved. Until the country relinquished Indonesia in 1949 and Suriname in 1975. So if you're not enthusiastically embraced when you first meet a European, don't be disappointed. It's not that they don't like you.[28] They've been through a lot.

U.K. and IRELAND

The United Kingdom is comprised of England, Scotland, Wales, and Northern Ireland. England, Scotland, and Wales form Great Britain, so you can just as easily say that the United Kingdom is comprised of Great Britain and Northern Ireland. The official name of the country is The United Kingdom of Great Britain and Northern Ireland, which is often abbreviated UKOGBANI, and pronounced "England."

---

[27] I tripped when walking across a market square in Paris and several passersby laughed, but amazingly, nobody smiled.

[28] It probably has *something* to do with it.

The island of Ireland is comprised of Northern Ireland and the Republic of Ireland. If someone says, "I'm going to Ireland," you can figure that they're visiting the Republic of Ireland, unless they say, "I'm going to Northern Ireland," in which case you'll say, "Oh, the United Kingdom," and they'll reply, "The UK, that's right," and you'll say, "Enjoy Ireland."

Cycling Overview

The terrain on the Cotswolds trip and Ireland itineraries are similar and what I'd describe as rolling. While there are some flat stretches, the majority of the rides are comprised of inclines generally all less than 6 percent for distances shorter than 1 mile. The Scotland trip is more challenging; there are several occasions where hills top 8 to 10 percent grades and exceed 2 to 3 miles in length.

For fathers, nothing beats an U.K. cycling trip with your eldest son. For sons, nothing fuels unbridled depression like an U.K. cycling trip with your dad. *Shannon Development*

Climate

Four words: take good rain gear. I know, I know, everyone says that, but there's a reason: it rains. A lot. The Scotland tour is an exception. Several years ago, upon reaching the top of a difficult mountain pass, there was hail and light snow. You really didn't need rain gear. You needed a parka and Sherpa guide.

Combining Tours

If you'd like to combine two or all three of the tours in this section, you can do so with relatively inexpensive air connections. Ryanair serves a direct route from Shannon Airport to London's Stansted Airport; there are public transportation shuttles that connect London's Stansted and Gatwick Airports; and easyJet flies between London's Gatwick Airport and Scotland's Inverness Airport. Current pricing is remarkably affordable:

Shannon-London's Stansted Airport: €45, or roughly $54.

Ryanair: www.ryanair.com; Phone: **+353 1 249 7851** (Ireland phone number)

The view from the top of Connor Pass (Dingle to Tralee) is truly special. If it's overcast, the entire view is compromised, in which case you might consider bypassing the difficult climb. *Jerry Soverinsky*

Bus Shuttle, London's Stansted Airport to Gatwick Airport: 23 pounds, or approximately $35. National Express Bus Company: http://www.nationalexpress.com/; Phone: 08705 757747 (+44 8705 757747).

London's Stansted Airport to Scotland's Inverness Airport: 12 pounds, or roughly $20. easyJet: www.easyjet.com; Phone: +0044 870 6 000 000 (England phone number).

Total transportation costs to connect all three itineraries is about $110.

Currency

Ireland has adopted the Euro (€), so if you're flying over from Italy, no need to stop at Thomas Cook, unless you prefer to give away money. Euro coins are divided into 100 cents and are available in 1, 2, 5, 10, 20, and 50 cent coins; and 1 and 2 Euro coins. Euro notes come in denominations of 5, 10, 20, 50, 100, 200, and 500 Euros. Euro coins offer individual member States' unique design on one side, but the coins are interchangeable throughout any of the Euro countries.

The United Kingdom has to date rejected the Euro and retained its Pound Sterling (£), and you'll find identically valued coins and paper currency in both

Once you navigate the winding descent from the Connor Pass, the remainder of the ride to Tralee is relatively flat, though it is still filled with beautiful countryside. *Jerry Soverinsky*

England and Scotland (their pictures differ, but the value is the same). England's money is freely accepted throughout Scotland, although many British stores will reject the Scottish currency, complaining, "It's not big enough."

Coins are divided into 100 pence (p) and are available in denominations of 1p, 2p, 5p, 10p, 20p, 50p (ridiculously big), £1, and £2. Notes are in denominations of £5, £10, £20, and £50. Scotland also distributes £1 and £100 notes.

Special Notes

If you're heading overseas and don't want to make the travel arrangements yourself and you can't get a hold of my company or me at 1-800-736-2453 from the U.S. and Canada, or +1-773-871-5510 from anywhere else on earth,[29] contact **Motion Europe**. It has London-based incoming operators, and they can help with your travel through the U.K. and Ireland. Motion Europe: Phone: 020 762 99777; fax: 020 762 99333; email: Mail@motion-europe.com. Ask for Luca or Sylvia, they're great people.

Travel Advice

There are a few vital travel tips that will keep you in good stead with your British, Scottish, and Irish hosts:

When sitting down to a meal with a Brit, never gesture—no matter your intimacy level—that he's got something caught in his teeth. More than likely, it's been there for years and he knows about it. Believe it or not, Brits prefer the delinquent dental reputation that they've worked so hard to cultivate and disdain the floss industry for its alleged Communist ties.[30]

When you hear Gaelic for the first time, don't say, "What?" This sounds similar to the Gaelic word meaning "pudgy." Say, "teal" instead; even if misunderstood, the Gaelic homonym means "try," the rugby version of "touchdown."

Scottish people wear a lot of sweaters. They like it when you touch their sleeves and say, "Oh, *that's* really nice. New?"

---

[29] Shameless plug #5.
[30] Never substantiated.

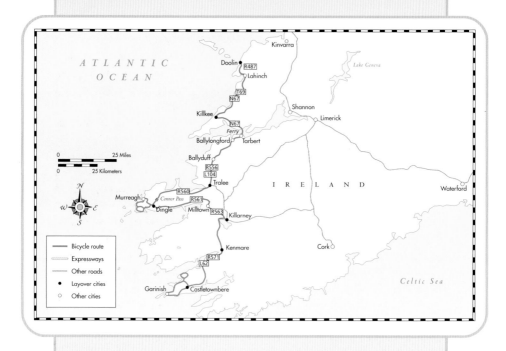

IRELAND'S Southwest Coast

This tour is consistently one of our company's most popular itineraries. It's filled with some of Europe's friendliest people, strikingly beautiful scenery, remote cycling routes along lightly traveled roads—all of the necessary ingredients for an outstanding tour.

One of the things I like best about Ireland, besides peat, is the opportunity to meet locals. Whether it's during the course of one of your daily rides or while sipping a pint of Guinness at a local pub, if you can open your mouth and make sounds, you're guaranteed[31] to interact with native Irishmen (not to be confused with Native Irishmen, brethren of Native Americans).

Tourist Information

The Irish Tourist Board (its official name is Tourism Ireland) is a wealth of information, and its website is detailed and comprehensive: http://www.tourismireland.com/. If you don't have access to a computer, when you've finished balancing your checkbook with an abacus, you can call them toll-free at 1-800-223-6470 (U.S.) or 0800 0397000 (U.K.).

---

[31] No guarantee.

The Ireland itinerary affords travelers an intimate look at nature's most extraordinary landscapes. And nothing compares to eating a synthetic energy bar in lieu of a banana while taking a mid-afternoon break. *Shannon Development*

When to Go

The best time to visit Ireland is between 2 p.m. and 4:15 p.m., CDT. Outside of those hours, it's tough to hail a cab.

I've cycled through Ireland as early as March and as late as October. On my seven-day March visit, it rained four times, but it was St. Patrick's Week so nobody seemed to notice. On the other hand, temperatures were in the high 40s or low 50s, which is a bit cool for many people. During my October trip, it rained six times out of eight, and while I wasn't wearing the St. Patty's weather blinders (whiskey), I didn't hear too many complaints from my tour participants.

Some of my July tours have been rain-free, although most experienced 1 to 3 days (out of 8 to 10 travel days) of precipitation.

Here's what you can expect:

KILLARNEY[32]

MONTH	AVERAGE HIGH (°F)	AVERAGE LOW (°F)	AVERAGE PRECIPITATION (IN)
JANUARY	52	32	6.6
FEBRUARY	52	34	4.8
MARCH	54	36	4.8
APRIL	57	37	3.0
MAY	63	43	3.5
JUNE	64	46	3.2
JULY	70	50	2.9
AUGUST	70	48	4.4
SEPTEMBER	66	46	4.9
OCTOBER	61	37	5.8
NOVEMBER	52	36	6.3
DECEMBER	52	36	6.3

[32] From http://uk.weather.com/.

The Healy Pass (Castletownbere to Kenmare) is not particularly steep, but why is European laser paper larger than its American counterpart? *Jerry Soverinsky*

Arrival and Departure
Air
CASTLETOWNBERE

From the U.S., Aer Lingus (800-IRISHAIR, www.aerlinguscom), Continental (800 231 0856, www.continental.com), and Delta (800 241 4141, www.delta.com) offer direct flights into Shannon and Dublin. However, you can also find connections with almost any major airline that stops in London, Amsterdam, Frankfurt, etc., en route.

This tour begins in Castletownbere, and the closest airport is Kerry's Farranfore, near Killarney. There are no direct flights into Kerry (it's a small airport, you can kick a soccer ball from one end to the other) and the two main commercial airlines that service it are Ryan Air (www.ryanair.com; flights via London Stansted and Frankfurt Hahn); and Aer Arann (+353 1 814 1058, www.aerarann.ie; flights via Dublin). Cork Airport offers slightly better ground transportation facilities than Farranfore, but it's further from Castletownbere.

For current airport information, check with the following:

Dublin: http://www.dub.aero; customer.relations-dublin@aer-rianta.ie;
   Phone: +353 1 8141111.

Shannon: http://www.snn.aero; marketing.shannon@aer-rianta.ie;
   Phone: +353 61 712000.

Some cyclists prefer the self-contained route, carrying all of their luggage attached to their body and bike, and describe the experience as "the only truly independent way to travel." Translation: I wish I wasn't poor. *Shannon Development*

Farranfore (Kerry): http://www.kerryairport.ie/; info@kerryairport.ie; Phone: ++353 (0) 66 9764644. **Cork**: http://www.ork.aero; feedback@corkairport.com; Phone: +353 21 4313131.

DOOLIN

The tour ends in Doolin, and the closest airport (by far) is Shannon. There's good bus service from Doolin so you can return from any of the above airports with straightforward transfers.

To and From the Airport
Taxis and Private Cars
TO CASTLETOWNBERE

You'll find taxis outside all of the major Irish airports. Approximate taxi rates for Ireland are 1.75 €/mile, so you can expect the following:

Dublin-Castletownbere: €350
Shannon-Castletownbere: €210
Killarney-Castletownbere:€ 75
Cork-Castletownbere: €140

The Muckross Gardens are a first-class welcome as you approach Killarney. *Cork-Kerry Tourism*

Finding a taxi outside Farranfore Airport is not always easy. Contact one of the following taxi services before you arrive:

Con Moran: Phone: 066 9764701;
Cell: 087 2538759.
John Brosnan: Phone: 066 7141184; Cell: 087 2601474.
Dan Corcoran: Phone: 064 36666; Cell: 087 2488757.
John Griffin: Phone: 066 9764846; Cell: 087 2315995.
Griffins Taxi: Phone: +353 066 9764846; www.kerrytaxi.com.
Shandon Cabs: Phone: +353 21 4505333.

Harrington's Mini-Bus Service: Phone: (027) 74265.
Donoughue's Mini-Bus & Coach Service: Phone: (027) 70007.
Glengarriff Cabs & Coach Hire: Phone: (027) 63060.

FROM DOOLIN

Plan on flying home out of Shannon, since this is the closest airport to Doolin. Expect to pay about €75-125 for the one-way lift.

Contact **Pat Keogh**; Newmarket-on-Fergus (close to Shannon Airport): Phone: 061 368833; patkeogh@pat-keogh.com; www.pat-keogh.com; or **Bunratty Chauffeur Service**: Phone: 061 362325; chauffeurireland@iegateway.net; www.chauffeurireland.iegateway.net.

Public Transportation

TO CASTLETOWNBERE

There are no direct public transportation links to Castletownbere. If you have some patience and are willing to change buses once or twice, you'll save quite a bit from the private car options. Bikes are allowed only if space permits (I've never encountered a problem), and the fixed cost on all Bus Eireann buses is €9 for each bicycle.

For the most current bus information, contact

Ireland is constantly upgrading its road network, and prominent cycling signage is becoming more common. Not that much assistance is needed. In many cases, there's only one road to follow.
Cork-Kerry Tourism

Bus Eiereann:
http://www.buseireann.ie/site/home/;
info@buseireann.ie;
Phone: +353 (01) 8366111.

From Shannon Airport
Buses from the Shannon Airport to Castletownbere transfer in Limerick, and either Cork or Killarney (depending on the time of year). The duration is about 7 hours, including layovers, and the cost is under €20. You can purchase tickets in the airport at the Bus Eireann desk.

From Dublin Airport
Bus service from the Dublin Airport to Castletownbere transfers in downtown Dublin and then in Cork. Total travel time is about 10 hours (including layovers) and the cost is under €30. You can purchase tickets in the airport at the Bus Eireann desk.

From Kerry Airport
From June 28 to August 30, bus departures

It's scenery such as this that has inspired some of western civilization's greatest poets. And some of the world's best Irish Whiskey producers, too. *Cork-Kerry Tourism*

leave **Killarney** at 3:45 p.m. and reach Castletownbere at 6:10 p.m. The approximate cost of the bus, one way, is €15.

From Cork Airport

Service is extended throughout most of the year from Cork, but in off-peak months, buses run only Mondays, Wednesdays, and Fridays. Total travel time is about 3 hours and costs €15.

FROM DOOLIN

At the end of your tour, keep things simple and fly from Shannon. It's an easy bus connection from Doolin (about 2-1/2 hours) and costs €12. The journey time to Dublin is at least 3 to 4 hours longer and more than double the cost. Check the Bus Eireann link above for current schedule information.

The downtown area of Castletownbere at rush hour. *Cork-Kerry Tourism*

Bike Rental

While many shops rent bicycles throughout Ireland, the quality may not be up to your standards. Check with the rental company to determine the brands they carry.

For rentals throughout Ireland, try:

Ireland Rent-a-Bike: Phone: (061) 416983; Fax: (061) 319 229; emeraldalp@eircom.net; www.irelandrentabike.com. They rent Trek bicycles for €70 per week and offer pick up and delivery throughout Ireland for €25 each way per bike.

Raleigh Rent-a-Bike (http://www.raleigh.ie/rent-a-bike.htm) touts itself as Ireland's oldest bike rental firm and they include dozens of locations throughout the country. One-week rentals, one way, cost €100. The nearest locations to Castletownbere are in Bantry and Glengariff. Expect to incur a delivery charge for the bicycle.

Kramer Cycles, Glengarriff Road, Glengariff; Phone: +353 (0) 27 50278; Fax: +353 (0) 27 50278; email: ckramer@eircom.net.

Jem Creations, Ladybird House; Glengariff; Phone: +353 (0) 27 63113; Fax: +353 (0) 27 63547; email: bikes@jemcreationsireland.com.

You can rent bikes directly in Castletownbere. Try the following:

Donegan's Spar Store, The Square, Castletownbere; Phone: (027) 70057 Fax: (027) 70138.

Murphy's Super Valu, Castletownbere; Phone: (027) 70020 Fax: (027) 70520.

From my experience, the bike quality at either of these markets is marginal. You'll want to confirm brand availability, which will determine your rental price. Both stores can also assist with pick up of the bicycles at the end of your tour.

Cycling Notes

You'll be cycling on the left side of the road in Ireland. Also, the distance signs are in miles, unless followed by a kilometer designation. Roads in Ireland are generally old and coarse. I recommend exchanging your high-pressure road tires for more forgiving touring tires.

Maps

Good: Michelin #405, *Ireland*, 1:400,000.
Better: Ireland West 2nd Edition, 1:250,000 and Ireland South 2nd Edition, 1:250,000. Published by The Director of the Ordnance Survey Office, Dublin.
Best: Ordnance Survey of Ireland Discovery Series Maps, 1:50,000. Map #s: 84, 85, 78, 79, 70, 71, 63, 64, 57, 51.

Accommodations Notes

I don't recommend camping in Ireland. Irish campgrounds are mostly caravan parks, and the abundant rain along the Southwest coast makes camping uncomfortable.

Speaking of whiskey, Scots insist that you distinguish between Scotch whisky and Irish whiskey, the latter which includes an "e" in its spelling. The Irish are concerned about more serious matters, such as who won the club football match. *Cork-Kerry Tourism*

Black Pudding

About 10 years ago, I visited a typical Irish restaurant (instead of peanut shells on the floor, there was sheep hair) in Killarney. Morris, one of my company's guests, expressed interest in a "real, authentic Irish meal." One of the other group members recommended the black pudding.

"I'm not sure what it is, but I've seen it on all the menus," he responded, and this seemed as good a suggestion as any.

"Jerry, what's black pudding?"

"Huh?" I replied, engrossed in a Guinness. My thoughts were elsewhere, running through the logistics of the following day, when I had appointments to give haircuts to all 44 of my group participants.

"Black pudding. What is it?" Morris wanted to know.

"Just get it, it's good," I reassured him. "It's got molasses, honey, some cumin. It's great. You'll love it."

I had no idea. It was one of my first European tours and I wasn't a very adventurous eater. Black pudding. It sounded like a good dessert. Who wouldn't like it?

Morris ordered the black pudding, and when it arrived, it didn't have the typical "molasses and honey" texture he expected. But tentatively, along with a few other group members, he tried it.

"There's no honey in this," cried one.

"It tastes like garlic. Ucch, I don't like it," moaned another, as she spit a piece into her napkin.

"It's weird," critiqued David, my vegetarian tour guide.

Morris found our waiter and asked, "What is this? It's not pudding."

The waiter laughed (more like a light chuckle). "*Black* pudding. You know, pig's blood."

Along the spectrum of what's acceptable for a vegetarian to eat, I suppose at the very far left you've got your poached salmon and broiled whitefish. Moving further to the right, you've got baked chicken; then barbecued chicken (you're moving fast to the right now); hamburgers; kosher hot dogs; shrimp; tacos;

ballpark hotdogs; and at the far end of the acceptability scale, you've got bacon, sausage, and boiled ham, and maybe even chopped liver.

But we're not done. Because way off the scale, miles to the right of boiled ham and chopped liver, you've got your pig's blood. Black pudding, or *blood* pudding, as it's more commonly known. It would've helped to have known that earlier.[33]

Background Notes and Information

Where Am I?

Country: Ireland
County: Cork
Region: Beara Peninsula
City: Castletownbere

Tourist Information

Beara Tourism and Development Association, The Square, Castletownbere, Beara, Co. Cork, Ireland. Phone/Fax: 00353 (0)27 70054; bearatours@eircom.net; www.bearatourism.com. This association offers detailed maps that can be downloaded free of charge from its site (a rarity, so take advantage). Its office is open only in the summer, and don't expect a quick reply from email inquiries.

If you can't find the tourist information you need on their website, you can also try www.bearainfo.com, which details businesses throughout the Beara Peninsula, and http://www.corkkerry.ie/, the official site for Cork-Kerry tourism.

Bike Shops

Donegan's Spar Store, The Square, Castletownbere; Phone: (027) 70057 Fax: (027) 70138.
Murphy's Super Valu, Castletownbere; Phone: (027) 70020 Fax: (027) 70520.

Sightseeing

Beare Island: The island was a former naval base and today it makes a perfect location to take an afternoon hike. There are several walks of varying distances, with detailed maps available in town. To reach the island, you must take a ferry (less than 15 minutes) from the center of Castletownbere. It runs every hour and costs €2.

Walking/hiking: There are several walking paths throughout the Peninsula. Details are available from the Beara Tourism website.

---

[33] For those wishing to sample this Irish and Scottish delicacy, you can order it via the Internet: http://www.scottishgourmetfood.co.uk/haggis_and_puddings.htm.

Dunboy Castle: The castle was built by the Puxley family, who made their fortune from the nearby copper mines in Allihies. There are nearby woods to explore on walks.

Dursey Island: This remote island can only be reached by cable car, a 15-mile ride from town. The cable car takes less than 10 minutes, and runs from 9 a.m. to 1 p.m., 2 p.m. to 5 p.m., and 6 p.m. to 8 p.m. (ask for exact return times before your departure). Arrive at least 15 minutes prior to departure.

Golfing, swimming, fishing, tennis, and various other **water sports** are also nearby. All of these activities are detailed on the Beara Tourism website.

Restaurants

Because Castletownbere is a fishing town, you'll find delicious, fresh fish at almost every restaurant. Try **Jack Patrick's** and **Murphy's**, which are both on Main Street. If you're staying at **Cametringane Hotel**, they also offer good dinner options. Two popular pubs are **McCarthy's** and **O'Donaghue's;** both are near the town center.

Luggage Transfers

C.T.B. Hackney: Castletownbere; Phone: 027 70736.
Martin Shanahan: Derrymihan West, Castletownbere; Phone: 027 70116.

CASTLETOWNBERE LOOP RIDE

Days 1 and 2: Castletownbere
Distance: 6 to 56 miles (several turnaround points en route).
Lunch Stops: It's best to bring a picnic lunch; markets are scarce, especially along the extended route. Allihies and Ardgroom offer limited facilities.
NOTE: *The entire route, including the extensions, is 56 miles. Very few of my company's participants have been physically able to complete the entire ride. It's not so much the distance (many had previously cycled century rides), but the jet lag, combined with the coarse Irish roads, that make for a very difficult ride. Set aside most of the day if you plan to ride the entire loop.*
Directions (miles): From the center of town, start cycling **WEST** in the direction of Dunboy Castle. You'll also find signs for the Casmetrigane Hotel. As you pass the hotel's driveway a few hundred yards ahead, you'll be on Shangrila Street and heading for Dunboy Castle.

After 1.5 miles, you can head **LEFT** for Dunboy Castle, a thirteenth-century castle destroyed in the Battle of Dunboy in 1602 (it closes at 4:30 p.m.; entry fee is €1).

After the castle, turn **LEFT** on the main road toward Allihies 11km, Ring of Beara, and the Beara hostel; at the fork 3/4 mile ahead, bear left (unmarked). You'll be cycling uphill.

At the bottom of the hill, follow signs **LEFT** for Allihies 10, Dursey 8, Ring of Beara, and Cathermore (distances are km). At the 10-mile mark for the day, you're riding along the coast. Be careful because the road narrows at many points.

When returning home from your Ireland cycling trip, as you're showing photos to your friends, start every sentence with: "You think it's pretty in the photograph, you should see it up close. You can't imagine, you just can't imagine!" People love that.
Cork-Kerry Tourism

After 12 miles, follow the road **LEFT** for Dursey 8km. After 15 miles, you have the option of heading **LEFT** for the Dursey Cable Car (unless you want to visit the nearby beach). New York is 5,200 kilometers away. It's 5 miles to the cable car from here. The car travels to Dursey Island, a renowned bird sanctuary and popular walking destination.

The cable car out to Dursey runs June, July, and August: Monday-Saturday, 9-1, 2-5, 6-8; Sunday, 4-5.

To continue: Retrace your path from Dursey and head for Allihies. At the 22-mile mark, head **LEFT** at the intersection for Allihies.

The ride is downhill and the water is on your left. After 24 miles, you can head for the Ballydonegan Beach and the Pier; otherwise, make the **RIGHT** for Allihies village to continue the route. In Allihies, there's a market open 9 a.m. to 9 p.m. daily. There are also four (!) pubs here. You can return to Castletownbere from this point, which would make a 30-mile loop for the day.

As you pass through the town, head **LEFT** for Eyeries 16km and the Ring of Beara (unless you want to return to Castletownbere 16km). Head **RIGHT** for Castletownbere 16km/Eyeries 8km after 25 miles. The road is steep, so be careful going downhill.

A few miles ahead, continue to Eyeries 4.5 miles (**BEAR RIGHT**). There's a market/post office in Urhan, open 9 a.m. to 6 p.m., Monday through Saturday.

After 33 miles, you can head **RIGHT** for Castletownbere 4-1/4 miles on the L62 and follow the signs the rest of the way; or head **LEFT** for Eyeries and the Ring of Beara on the L62.

To continue to the furthest extension of this ride: **BEAR LEFT** for the Ring of Beara. **NOTE:** *The Ring of Beara is a difficult portion to cycle, with narrow roads and steep climbs. At times, there's loose gravel. Extreme caution is advised. Also, because of the remoteness of the ride, bring extra tubes and a pump.*

Just up the hill at a stop sign, turn **LEFT** for the Ring of Beara and Eyeries 2. Through Eyeries, there's O'Sullivan's market. After 36 miles, head **LEFT** for the Ring of Beara. After 2 miles, head for Ardgroom. Continue to the Ring of Beara and the coast road. In Ardgroom, the market is open Monday through Friday from 9 a.m. to 5:30 p.m. and Saturday from 9 a.m. to 1 p.m.

Through Ardgroom, Castletownbere is 9-1/2 miles away on the L62. Follow signs for Castletownbere. You'll pass through Eyeries again at the 52-mile mark. Follow signs all the way back to Castletownbere.

There's a Super-Valu market on the corner of the major intersection in town.

Background Notes and Information

Where Am I?

Country: Ireland
County: Kerry
Region: Ring of Kerry
City: Kenmare

Tourist Information

Kenmare's Chamber of Commerce and Tourism offers detailed information about tourist and business services: Phone: +353 (0)64 42615; http://www.kenmare.com/; info@kenmare.com. Also try the Kenmare Business and Community Guide's site: http://www.neidin.net/index.html.

If you can't find what you're looking for, try the Cork-Kerry Tourism site: http://www.corkkerry.ie/detail.asp?memberID=5314.

Bike Shops

Finnegan's (rents bicycles), Henry Street, Kenmare; Phone: 064 41083; failtefinn@eircom.net; http://www.neidin.net/finnegan/.

Sightseeing

Heritage Center displays extensive information on the history of Kenmare. While here, don't forget to stop by the **Lace and Design Center** to view traditional lace making and purchase their finished products. It is open Monday through Saturday from 9:30 a.m. to 7 p.m. The local tourist office can provide you with maps of the **Kenmare Heritage Trail**, a self-guided walk that leads you through the town's major historical points.

Restaurants

An Leath Phingin is popular for Northern Italian food (35 Main Street; Phone: 064 41559). Also try The Lime Tree Restaurant (Shelbourne Street; Phone: 064 41225; benchmark@iol.ie), which is situated in an early nineteenth century building.

Luggage Transfers

Atlantic Cabs: Phone: 027-70116; Fax 70368; Cell 086-2461877; luganohouse@eircom.net.
Glengarriff Cabs: Phone: 353-27 63060; Cell 353-87-9730741.
Rock Island Cabs: Phone: 087-2877888.

CASTLETOWNBERE TO KENMARE
ROUTE NOTES

Day 3: Castletownbere to Kenmare

I used to combine this ride with the Kenmare-Killarney segment, though the 53-mile combined ride proved too difficult for the majority of my company's guests. During today's ride, you'll cycle the difficult Healy Pass, a climb that appears rather benign, but will definitely test your cycling strength.

Kenmare is a quaint Irish town set at the confluence of the River Roughty and Kenmare River. It was founded in 1670 and today is a popular crafts destination.**Distance:** 35 miles

Lunch Stop: Limited snacks are available at the top of the Healy Pass.

Directions (miles): At Castletownbere's town center, follow signs to Adrigole 16km to the **EAST**.

About 2 miles past Adrigole, there's a tiny market, Peg's, which is the last food stop until the top of the Healy Pass.

After 10 miles, turn **LEFT** for the Healy Pass 6, Lauragh 13, and Kenmare 39.

The Healy Pass is a gradual 3-mile climb that offers a tough physical challenge amidst wonderful Irish scenery. When you reach the top, there's a gift shop and small market.

As you descend from the Healy Pass, you're entering County Kerry. Be careful as you coast downhill, especially look out for loose gravel and oncoming traffic.

At the 18-mile mark (30 km), you have two choices: (1) the most direct route to Kenmare (saving two miles) with a challenging climb; and (2) the coastal route, two miles longer without the major climb.

Shorter Route, With Hill: At the Murphy's Irish Stout gas pump, make a ***RIGHT*** for Kenmare 15-1/4. Just ahead, turn ***RIGHT*** on the R571 to Kenmare 24km and keep following Kenmare signs.

Otherwise, for the ***Coastal Route:***

18.1: Just after the right turn at the Murphy's Irish Stout gas pump, turn **LEFT** toward Castletownbere 27, Ring of Beara.

18.3: Turn **RIGHT** toward Coast Road, Kenmare 27; continue on this road and follow signs for Kenmare.

25.2: T-intersection: turn **LEFT** to Kenmare 16km.

At 33.4 miles for the day, there's the N71 intersection (intersection of the two routes). To the right is Glengarriff and to the left is Killarney 33km, Kenmare 1km. Go **LEFT**. The route at this point is relatively flat.

You reach Kenmare at 35.2 miles (33.5 if you took the shorter route).

An Irish farmer walks into a pub with his dog and 12 sheep. The barkeep says, "Get those filthy things out of my pub." The farmer replies, "Things were much easier before the E.U." *Jerry Soverinsky*

City maps for your Ireland cycling trip are hardly necessary because there's usually only one or two streets to navigate. *Cork-Kerry Tourism*

Background Notes and Information
Where Am I?
Country: Ireland
County: Kerry
Region: Ring of Kerry
City: Killarney

Tourist Information
There are hundreds (four, actually) of sites that seem to be the official tourism site for Killarney, but all—as you probe deeper—are commercial sites that offer to assist with your reservations.

Killarney's official tourist office is located at the Town Hall (Phone: 064 31633; Fax: 064 34506) and its website is: www.corkkerry.ie/killarneytio. The office is open year-round and it has a wealth of information for any of your Killarney or Kerry County tourism needs. The website is poorly designed, so you might have better luck at one of the following: http://www.killarney.ie/; www.kerrygems.ie/places/killarney/index.html; or www.killarney-insight.com.

Bike Shops
Bishops Lane, New Street, Killarney, Co. Kerry; Phone: 064 31282; Fax: 064 20799; david@killarneycyclehire.com.

Sightseeing
Ross Castle: Situated on the shores of Lough Leane, this fifteenth century castle is a worthwhile afternoon destination. The castle is open daily from 9 a.m. to 6:30 p.m. in the summer, with slightly limited hours the rest of the year. Phone: 064 35851; Fax: 064 35852; rosscastle@ealga.ie; www.heritageireland.ie. The cost of the tour is €4.

Muckross House and Gardens: Less than 4 miles from Killarney, this nineteenth century mansion offers beautiful views of well-manicured gardens. It's home to a Kerry Folklife and History museum. Phone: 064 31440; Fax: 064 39192; mucros@iol.ie; www.muckross-house.ie. The cost is €5.5.

Killarney Riding Stables: One mile west of town on the R562, the riding stables offer tours in Killarney National Park and pays visits to Ross Castle and Ross Island. Phone: 064 31686; Fax: 064 34119;
krs@eircom.net; www.killarney-reeks-trail.com.

Gap of Dunloe: If you opt out of the extended ride, but want to see what the fuss is about, evening tours depart from town and pass through Moll's Gap. This remote path offers beautiful views of the evening sunset. Contact the O'Donaghue Brothers at The Old Weir Lodge: Phone: 064 31068;
Cell: 087 2390723; oldweirlodge@eircom.net.

Lake cruise: Departing from Ross Castle, these cruises offer fantastic scenery of Killarney National Park and the McGillicuddy Reeks Mountain Range. The last departure of the day is at 5:15 p.m.. Destination Killarney: Phone/Fax: 064 32638; destinationkillarney@eircom.net.

Restaurants
Wander the central area of town and stop in any of the numerous (and usually crowded) local restaurants for fresh seafood and meats.

Luggage Transfers
Finnegan's Coach and Cab Hire: Phone: 064 41491; Fax: 064 42636;
kenmarecoachandcab@eircom.net; http://www.neidin.net/finnegans/. Expect to pay €40 to €60 to transfer luggage to Killarney.

KENMARE TO KILLARNEY
ROUTE NOTES

Day 4: Kenmare to Killarney
Today's route offers two options, though I recommend the more difficult ride which passes through the Gap of Dunloe, a truly special area formed thousands of years ago during the last Ice Age.

If you plan on cycling the Gap of Dunloe, make sure you've got durable tires (high-pressure road tires might not cut it).

Almost every visitor to Ireland makes a stop in Killarney, the most popular Ring of Kerry destination. It's undoubtedly overcrowded in the summer months, but its extensive facilities and surrounding attractions make it a worthwhile destination.**Distance:** 20 to 26 miles
Directions (miles): At the four-way intersection in town, follow signs for Moll's Gap. You're heading also toward Killarney, Ring of Kerry, and Sneem.
> 0.3: follow the N71 to Killarney/Tralee; there will be an Esso gas station on your right. It's uphill until Moll's Gap.
> 6.0: At the top of Moll's Gap, there's a restaurant/shop.
> From Moll's Gap, there are two routes to Killarney: (1) the first route is the most direct and passes through the National Park, Torc Waterfall, and Muckross House and Gardens;

and (2) the second is more remote and passes through the Gap of Dunloe. Either route is great, but my groups prefer the Gap of Dunloe.

Direct Route: Total distance: 20 miles

Turn **RIGHT** for Killarney 22km and Tralee 54km. You're on the N71 road. Three miles later, you enter the Killarney National Park.

One mile later (10.0), there's a gift shop and café. At 16 miles, you'll pass the Torc Waterfall (on the right—a worthwhile stop). One mile ahead, you'll pass the Muckross House and Gardens (at the 16-mile mark for the day). There's a bike path on your left.

At 18.7, you reach a Maxol gas station. Just past the station, there's a Texaco station—you're on Muckross Road. Follow Muckross Road into town (another mile). Total distance: 20 miles.

Gap of Dunloe: Total distance: 26 miles

6.2: Turn **LEFT** for Sneem 24km and Catherdaniel 45km.

6.6: Turn **RIGHT** onto a smaller road, downhill, toward Black Valley Equestrian 9.5, Hillcrest Farmhouse 9, and Shamrock Farmhouse B&B 13.

NOTE: *This is a narrow road—use extreme caution. There are no guardrails.*

7.7: Stay on the main road (to the **RIGHT**); do not turn left onto a dirt road.

8.2: You'll cross a small bridge, then come to an intersection; turn **RIGHT** toward Hillcrest Farmhouse.

Just ahead, you'll come to an intersection; go **STRAIGHT** for the Gap of Dunloe (unmarked).

NOTE: *You can take a boat ride from here to Killarney (bikes accepted, too!). To do so, turn* **RIGHT** *at this turn for the Tangney's Boating Tour; 200 yards ahead (after the turn), turn* **LEFT** *for Tangney's Boat; at the Hillcrest B&B, the road becomes dirt—continue to the boats from here.*

13.8: Turn **RIGHT**, following signs for Gap of Dunloe, which you reach a few hundred yards ahead. There are beautiful views from here. The top of the hill comes at 15.3. Take your time on your descent; watch for vehicles, bicyclists, horses, and choppy roads!

18.8: You'll reach the bottom of the Gap of Dunloe (several places to eat here). Continue **STRAIGHT** past the Esso station on your right.

19.8: Turn **RIGHT** to Killarney 12km. Keep following signs for Killarney from here.

20.9: Cross a bridge, continue **STRAIGHT**.

22.2: T-intersection; turn **RIGHT** to Killarney 7 (there's a bike path to the right but also room on the left).

23.0: You'll pass the Golden Nugget Restaurant; continue **STRAIGHT** (you'll pass the same restaurant en route to Dingle).

25.2: At a roundabout, exit toward Town Centre West. You're on Port Rd.

25.8: Continue to the **LEFT** around the cathedral and into town.

26.3: At the stop sign, turn **RIGHT** toward Kenmare (N71); you'll be in the center of town.

I highly recommend a layover day in Dingle to give you the opportunity to explore some of the finest cliff scenery in Ireland.

Cork-Kerry Tourism

Dingle Background Notes
Where Am I?
Country: Ireland
County: Kerry
Region: Dingle Peninsula
City: Dingle

According to the Cork-Kerry website, **Dingle** (*An Daingean* for our Gaelic-speaking friends), is the westernmost town in Europe. It's hard to believe for those cycling the Dingle Peninsula loop ride, since you'll pass several little towns as you head west from Dingle. Bar bets aside, it's a great destination and the place where I first heard Gaelic spoken (you always remember your first time).

(I enter a shop in Dingle, two elderly men are chatting; the shopkeeper is helping a sheep give birth in the corner).

JERRY

Got any Hard Rock Café Dingle t-shirts? *Note to readers: for my niece.*

SHOPKEEPER

(rolling her eyes)

Kinda busy here gettin' this lamb out!

(She struggles a bit, the sheep fusses).

(I browse the store, and stop to hear two elderly Irish men in an animated discussion. The men continue for 20 to 30 seconds, and I strain to figure out what they're saying).

(They gesture "goodbye" toward the SHOPKEEPER, she looks up, with sheep blood on her shirt).

SHOPKEEPER

A good day, then.

(She nods toward them, they leave).

(Pause)

(I approach the SHOPKEEPER, silent. I stand over her, curious).

(Pause)

SHOPKEEPER

Can I help you?

(Pause)

Quality raingear is essential for your Ireland trip. *Jerry Soverinsky*

JERRY

I was just wondering . . . what language were those men speaking?

(A long pause. The shopkeeper studies me, then shakes her head in mild disapproval).

SHOPKEEPER

English.

JERRY

Oh. (pause) Good luck with the lamb.

It just goes to show you. Even if you think you're hearing Gaelic, it might still be English. Tough accents in Dingle.

Tourist Information

Dingle's tourist office is open year-round (The Quay; Dingle; Phone: 066 151188; Fax: 066 9151270; dingle@eircom.net ; www.corkkerry.ie/dingletio).

Like Killarney's website, Dingle's is part of the Cork-Kerry tourism site, which can be difficult to navigate. Also check www.dingle-peninsula.ie and www.kerrygems.ie/places/dingletown/index.html.

Bike Shops

Dykegate Street, Dingle, Co. Kerry; Phone: 066 9152311; dingwal@iolfree.ie.

Sightseeing

En route to Dingle from Killarney, **Inch Strand** is a 3-mile-long beach, which is a perfect spot for a mid-day lunch and seaside walk.

Horseback riding: For our equestrian lovers, riding a horse along the remote Dingle Peninsula trails is a great way to see the sites.

Contact Dingle Horse Riding for information; Phone: 66 9152199; Fax: 066 9152018; info@dinglehorseriding.com; www.dinglehorseriding.com.

A 12-mile ride to **Dunquin** will enable you to take a ferry out to the uninhabited Blasket Islands to admire the ancient forts that bear testament to historic occupations. Contact Blasket Island Boatmen for ferry information; Phone/Fax: 066 9156422; lorcinmotion@hotmail.com.

An archeological minibus tour of the Dingle Peninsula is a great way to gain a better understanding of the area's history. The best I've found is with Michael Collins, whose mother owns a popular B&B in town (Phone: 066 9151937/9151606). Tours leave daily at 11 a.m. and 2 p.m.; reservations are essential.

Restaurants

Try **Walker's Hole in the Wall Bar** (pub food), **An Cafe Liteartha** on Dykegate Street (for a light lunch in a cafe/bookshop), **Singing Salmon** on Strand Street, and **Greaney's** on Bridge Street (the last two for seafood). **Beginish** (Green Street) and the **Chart House** are mentioned in at least one publication as two of Ireland's 100 best restaurants.

Luggage Transfers

Diamruid Begley (from Dingle). Phone/Fax: 066 9151440.
Kerry Taxi (Killarney). Phone/Fax: 066 9764846; info@kerrytaxi.com; www.kerrytaxi.com.
Expect to pay €50 to €60 for transferring luggage to Dingle.

KILLARNEY TO DINGLE
ROUTE NOTES

Days 5-6: Killarney to Dingle; Dingle Layover
The first half of the Killarney-Dingle ride is relatively easy, but the route from Inch to Dingle can be challenging, depending on coastal winds.
   The highlight ride will be the layover day loop, because the Dingle Peninsula is filled with extraordinary scenery and ancient ruins.
   Distance: 41 miles
Lunch Stop: Inch
Directions (miles): Begin at the movie theater in Killarney, which is near East Avenue Road. (before a roundabout).

- From the movie theatre, follow signs to "All Routes" and "Town Centre;" continue toward "All Routes."
- 0.5: The cathedral will be in front of you; turn **LEFT**.
- 1.1: At a roundabout, turn **LEFT** toward Dingle (N86).
- 1.3: Shell gas station on the left; continue **STRAIGHT**.
- 2.4: Killarney Golf and Fishing Club.
- 3.1: Fossa. Just ahead, turn **RIGHT** for Milltown 13km, Dingle 54, and Aghadoe.
- Keep following signs to Milltown. Eight miles ahead (11 miles for the day), you reach Milltown (markets, stores). As you pass through the town, follow signs for the N70 to Tralee. Bear **RIGHT** (by a Shell one-pump gas station, which is on the left).
- 13.1: Follow the R70 road **LEFT** to Tralee, Dingle 48km, and Castlemaine 1 (not straight to Limerick on the 561). As you make the left, there's a Shell gas station on your right and a Stat gas station on your left. As you head through Castlemaine (stores, shops), follow the road **LEFT** for Dingle 45km and Annascaul 27km (do not head right for Tralee).
- 16.3 miles ahead is Boolteens Village (stores, shops). The route at this point is fairly flat without any major climbs. At the 25-mile mark for the day, you enter Inch. Head for the Inch Strand 3/4 and Dingle 15-3/4. The Inch Strand makes a good lunch stop.
- As you leave the Strand, Annascaul is 4km away.
- 29.4 miles: **LEFT** for Dingle 18km. Follow this road the rest of the way to Dingle. At the 34-mile mark, you can detour for Minard Castle and a stone circle.
- 40.6 miles: You reach Dingle.

DINGLE LOOP RIDE

Many of today's signs will be in Gaelic, though even the locals who speak English will be hard to understand—the accent is *that* thick. This is a great ride, one of my favorites of the tour.

Distance: 24 to 30 miles

Lunch Stop: Bring a packed lunch, markets are scare along today's route.

Directions (miles): At the main traffic roundabout in town, follow the brown sign for Slea Head Dr. (not right for Town Centre and Connor Pass). As soon as you turn, there's a supermarket. Go 100 yards, turn **LEFT** at the intersection.

1.0:, Turn **LEFT** for Sleigh Head Dr. and Dun Chaoin. You're following the 559 to Ceann Tra. It's 17 kilometers to Dun Chaoin.

You'll follow the coast—great views. There's a market in Ceann Tra. A 1/2 mile past Ceann Tra, bear **LEFT** at the fork. Keep following signs to Slea Head and Dun Chaon.

The ride is slightly uphill at points, but not very steep. Be careful at the 10-mile mark—the road turns briefly to stone.

12.0: Dun Chaoin. There's a B&B, but not much else. On your left (12.5 miles), notice the stone formations. There's also a turnoff here for the beach.

As you head for the north side of the peninsula, you go gradually uphill.

13.0: To the left is Dhun Chaoin and to the right is Kruger 1, Duncan Pottery 1/8, Blasket Center, and Potttery 3.5. To visit the Blasket Islands, make the **LEFT** and follow the signs to Blasket Island Boats, which leave every 30 minutes from 10 a.m. to 6 p.m., weather permitting. Otherwise, to continue along the route, continue **STRAIGHT** to Kruger 1.

16.0: Just past the Glean Dearb B&B (not far from the ferry turnoff), you'll see a brown sign left for Slea Head Drive—but turn **RIGHT** (*unless you want to extend the ride—see below*). There's no sign pointing toward An Daingean (Dingle), but you'll see it soon after you turn. It will read Ceann Tra 6 and An Daingean (Dingle) 13. You'll start a challenging 1/2-mile climb.

19.0: **LEFT** for An Daingean 8 (not right to Dun Chaoin). As you turn left, there's a church on the right. Keep following sings to An Daingean/Dingle.

24.0: **RIGHT** to Dingle. This road leads to the center of town.

EXTENDED RIDE Northern extension adds 6 to 7 miles.

From directions above: Instead of turning right, continue on Slea Head Drive as it curves **LEFT**.

16.2: Kruger's B&B (bar food) is to the left.

16.5: Begin an ascent for .5 miles

20.9: Ballyferriter—several shops, pubs, etc.

21.7: **RIGHT** toward Ceann Tra 6km/An Daingean 11km. Do not continue on Slea Head Drive.

24.6: Meet up with the R599; turn **LEFT** toward Daingean 6km.

28.7: Cross bridge, come to roundabout, turn right toward An Daingean.

28.9: Reach An Daingean and continue into town.

29.3: Veer **RIGHT** with the road, keeping water and the docks to your right.

29.4: Reach the roundabout in Dingle's town center.

Background Notes
Where Am I?
Country: Ireland
County: Kerry
Region: Shannon Region Tourism
(even though it's located in County Kerry)
City: Tralee

Tourist Information
Tralee Tourist Office (open year-round), Ashe Memorial Hall, Tralee, Co. Kerry; Phone: +353 66 7121288; Email: touristofficetralee@shannondev.ie; http://www.shannonregiontourism.ie/detail.asp?memberID=12773.

Bike Shops
Tralee Gas & Bicycle Suppliers, Strand St., Tralee; Phone: 066 7122018.
Tralee Bicycle Supplies, Tralee; Phone: 066 712 2018; Fax: 066 712 7960.

Sightseeing
Aquadome is an indoor water park that is open 10 a.m. to 10 p.m.
The **Blennerville Windmill** via **Steam Railway** is a working mill with exhibits and craft displays. The train departs Tralee's Ballyard Station at 2, 3, 4, and 5 p.m., with returns at 2:30, 3:30, 4:30, and 5:30 p.m.
Horseback riding: From Kennedy's Equine Centre (located 2 kilometers from town), 1 to 3 hour treks are offered. Call (066) 26453 for reservations.

Restaurants
Popular choices include: **Skillet** (Barrack Lane) for a wide selection of Irish fare; **Brat's Place** (Milk Market Lane) for vegetarian food; and **The Old Forge** (Church Street) for inexpensive, lighter fare.

Luggage Transfers
Diamruid Begley: Phone/Fax: 066 9151440.
Brown's Taxi: Phone: 066 9151259/087 260 6500; jbrownes@iol.ie; http://www.iol.ie/~jbrownes/.
Expect to pay 40 to 70 for transferring luggage to Tralee.

DINGLE TO TRALEE
ROUTE NOTES

Day 7: Dingle to Tralee

It seems that all[1] of the cycling guidebooks for Ireland mention the ride over the Connor Pass as a brutal, horrible ascent, suitable only for the fittest cyclists. Nonsense.

It's a challenging climb, but if you started the tour in Castletownbere, you should be in fine shape by now for the four-mile climb. Don't misunderstand, four miles is four miles (and not five miles or six miles), but the grade isn't overly punishing. On a clear day, you'll have great views of the surrounding countryside; but if the weather is overcast, much of your view will be lost, in which case you can bypass the climb by cycling via Anascaul.

Tralee is the largest city on this tour, and not coincidentally, my least favorite. It's not so large that it's unmanageable to navigate; it just lacks some of the charm of the smaller towns. In fact, on some of my custom tours, the groups opted to be transferred past Tralee. **Distance: 31 miles**

Lunch Stop: Camp or Tralee

Directions (miles):

Connor Pass

> Follow Dykegate Street north until it ends. Turn **RIGHT** at the end of the street, and then a **LEFT** just ahead to Tralee 31 and the Connor Pass. Bear **RIGHT** 200 yards ahead to the Connor Pass and Tralee.
>
> 4.5: You reach the top of the Connor Pass. Be careful on your descent; much of the road is without guardrails.
>
> 7.7: You reach the bottom. Follow signs to Tralee 35km (Tra Li).
>
> 13.0: There's a market on the right side of the road, open 7 days a week.
>
> 20: You reach Camp. Up the road, follow signs for Tralee 10.
>
> 20.5: There's a pub. Traffic increases as you approach Tralee.
>
> 29.0: You reach Blennerville. There is a windmill on your left as you pass through the town.
>
> 29.4: Just past the windmill, follow signs **RIGHT** to Tralee on the N86.
>
> 30.5: There's a roundabout. Follow signs to the town center.

Bypassing the Connor Pass

Follow the main road away from town and head for Anascaul and Tralee on the N86. Head back toward the Inch Strand, as from the previous riding day.

> 9.0: You'll see signs for Tralee and Annascaul on the N86; follow it **STRAIGHT**. Ahead about 200 yards, there's a sign for Annascaul. Drive through the town (shops, markets).
>
> 19.0: You reach Camp Village.
>
> 20.0: There's an intersection: Turn **RIGHT** and continue from the main directions.

---

[1] One.

Background Notes
Where Am I?

Country: Ireland
County: Clare
Region: Shannon Region Tourism
City: Kilkee

Tourist Information
Kilkee Tourist Office (open only during the summer), The Square, Kilkee, Co. Clare; Phone: +353 65 9056112; http://www.shannonregiontourism.ie/.

Sightseeing
Kilkee Heritage Gallery has a collection of artifacts from Kilkee's seafaring industries. Kilkee has a championship 18-hole **golf** course. www.kilkeegolfclub.ie.

Tennis is located within walking distance of the town center.

Walks, hikes: Kilkee has a rugged coastline that's perfect for afternoon walks. Take pictures of **George's Head** and **Diamond Rocks.** The 3/4-mile-long sandy beach offers great opportunities for **swimming** in Horseshoe Bay.

Restaurants
A local favorite is **Purtill's** on O'Curry Street. Also try the restaurant at **Halpin's Hotel,** along the main street.

Luggage Transfers
Pat Keogh Chauffeur Serve; Boheraroan; Newmarket on Fergus; Phone: 061 368833; patkeogh@pat-keogh.com; www.pat-keogh.com. Bunratty Chauffeur Service; Bunratty; Phone: 061 362325; chauffeurireland@iegateway.net; www.chauffeurireland.iegateway.net.

TRALEE TO KILKEE
ROUTE NOTES

Day 8: Tralee to Kilkee
The ride from Tralee to the Tarbert ferry is generally flat and uninteresting. If you stayed last night in Tralee, you might as well forge ahead since you won't save a ton of time electing a personal transfer.

Once across the River Shannon, the terrain becomes more challenging, but not any more so than the first few days of the tour.

Kilkee is not an overwhelming tourist destination for Americans, but it makes for a worthwhile cycling stop. Its seaside location is perfect for those wishing to relax on a well-kept beach, and its several miles of shoreline trails provide an inviting network to explore the area.
Distance: 45 miles
Lunch Stop: Ballylongford, Tarbert, Kilrush
Directions (miles): Start from the center of town:

    0.3: At a fork, head for Other Routes and Ballybunion (in front of you at this point is SOL Travel). You're on a narrow street, with Walsh Bros. Electrical Store on your right. It's busy as you head out. Follow the sign toward Listowel. Go past the turnoff for the RR Station.

1.16: Go **STRAIGHT** to Ballybunion 19-3/4 (instead of right to Listowel); go past the Texaco station and continue uphill until 2.7 miles.

5.4: You reach Abbeydorney; at the crossroads, go **STRAIGHT** to Ballybunion 14 and Ballyduff 8.

12.61: Go **STRAIGHT** to Ballybunion on the 551. It's a climb until Ballyduff at 12.8.

14.1: Ballyduff has markets and shops; at the end of town, turn **RIGHT** to Liston 8 and Ballybunion 9. As you turn, a Texaco station is on your right.

16.8: **RIGHT** to Listowell and Tarbert on the R554. As you cross the street, a sign says Listleton is 3km away.

18.9: Listleton; go **STRAIGHT** (actually, a quick right, then left) on the 552 to Tarbert. At the crossroads in town ahead at a Statoil station, go **STRAIGHT** to Tarbert 25km.

19.2: The road bears **LEFT**, and Tarbert is 16km away. Keep following signs for Tarbert.

24.9: Ballylongford has shops and markets. As you head through town, turn **RIGHT** for Tarbert 8.

29.4: Turn **LEFT** for the R550 car ferry.

30.8: Car ferry.

FERRY INFORMATION: *Every hour on the half-hour, 9:30 a.m. to 7:30 p.m., 2, 25 minutes.* As you exit the ferry, turn **LEFT** for the N67 to Kilrush 9km and Kilkee. Follow signs to Kilrush, which you'll reach at 37 miles. There are lots of markets, stores, and shops here. At the roundabout, turn **RIGHT** for Kilkee 13km. There's a bicycle shop in Kilrush as you leave the town. You're on the N67 heading for Kilkee. Follow signs to Kilkee, which you'll reach at 45 miles.

Background Notes
Where Am I?
Country: Ireland
County: Clare
Region: Shannon Region
City: Doolin

Tourist Information
There's no official local office, but you can obtain detailed information from Shannon Region Development: http://www.shannonregiontourism.ie/ and www.doolin-tourism.com.

Sightseeing
Doolin is famous for friendly, musical pubs. You'll love the charm of the locals, who are always willing to lend advice and an ear while you're working a draught.

As for the sites, below are some suggestions:

Hiking in the Burren is a great way to spend an afternoon. There are miles of trails that will lead you past historical churches, castles, and archaeological remains.

Aran Islands: A fantastic day of sightseeing awaits on these islands, just 8 miles from Doolin, where you'll find ancient remains and rugged landscape, ideal for exploration. You can board a ferry from the Doolin Pier to reach the islands.

Golf: Lahinch is home to one of Ireland's famous courses. Contact Lahinch Golf Club at (065) 81003. They also rent clubs.

Restaurants

For homecooked meals, the **Appletree Restaurant** serves complete dinners for less than €12. The **Doolin Deli** on Main Street is a great place for both groceries and sandwiches, and it is open until 9 p.m. For well-prepared seafood, the **Lazy Lobster** in the Upper Village is a good choice.

KILKEE TO DOOLIN
ROUTE NOTES

Day 9: Kilkee to Doolin

The **Cliffs of Moher** are, quite simply, the most impressive cliff scenery that you'll see on this tour.

Some guidebooks whine about the tourist "crush" and commercialism of the area, but I'm assuming their measuring stick is a desolate island. As far as five-star European natural attractions go, the Cliffs of Moher are probably as *un*touristy as it gets. There's no entrance fee to see them (there's a suggested donation on your way out, a very nice touch), a can of coke costs less than a buck at their snack shop, and there's not a Cliffs of Moher paperweight to be found. Instead, there's a handful of Irish musicians selling homemade recordings, but that's really it. You'll be left on your own to explore the miles of cliff scenery (by foot, not bike), marveling at the crashing surf and wondering whether your hotel's restaurant serves dill sauce with the salmon.

Contrast that to almost any town in Switzerland, where entrance fees are almost always obligatory, and every village and attraction has its name emblazoned on t-shirts, key chains, and toaster ovens. And there's no dill sauce, either..**Distance:** 38 miles

Lunch Stop: Milltown Malbay, Lahinch.

Directions (miles): From the center of town, head to the water and turn **RIGHT.** Follow signs to Milltown Malbay 30km. You'll also see signs for Lahinch 41km and Doonbeg 10km.

You're on the N67.

3.0: You reach Bealaha. There's a gas station/store on your left (Maxol).

6.0: You pass through Doonberg. Follow signs to Milltown Malbay 20km. Past Doonbeg, there's another market. Keep following the N67 to Milltown Malbay 17km (veering **RIGHT** at a fork).

As the road curves, follow it to Lahinch. You'll see a pink house with a straw roof at the 8-mile mark for the day. Less than a mile later, follow signs again for Lahinch and Milltown Malbay.

12.0: **LEFT** for Milltown Malbay 9km and Lahinch 21km. There are great views of the ocean here.

14.0: The road curves down to the water and there's a store (look for the 7-Up sign). The road curves right as you reach the water. Bear **RIGHT** as the road curves around (not left for Setting Sun restaurant and Bell Bridge House Hotel). There's no sign as you bear right, but you're following the main road.

17.0: Milltown Malbay (stores, shops, etc.). Head through the town and turn **LEFT** for Lahinch. 100 yards ahead, turn **LEFT** again for Lahinch 12km and Ennistymon 15km.

NOTE: *For a great one-mile detour, before reaching Miltown, just after you cross a small bridge, turn **LEFT** toward Coast Drive and Spanish Point Golf Course (the Bellbridge House Hotel is on the corner). Just after the turn, you'll enter Spanish Point. Continue with this loop which eventually (3 miles ahead) merges with the N67.*

Follow signs to Lahinch, which you reach after 27 miles. There are shops and markets, and the town is on the coast. Head through the town and follow the sign **LEFT** for Liscannor 3 on the L54; the road curves right and then you'll reach another turn a little ahead: turn left for the Cliffs of Moher 7km, Liscannor 4km, and Lisdoonvarnor 22km.

Keep following the road to the Cliffs of Moher. Liscannor comes at the 30-mile mark (a few stores and restaurants).

As you leave Liscannor, head for the Cliffs of Moher and the R478. After 32 miles, you reach the Cliffs of Moher.

When you leave the Cliffs of Moher, turn **LEFT** for Doolin 9km and Lisdoonvarna 12km. Follow the R479 **LEFT** for Doolin 3 miles ahead. As you turn, another sign reads that Doolin is 2km away. After 38 miles, you reach Doolin at a T-intersection.

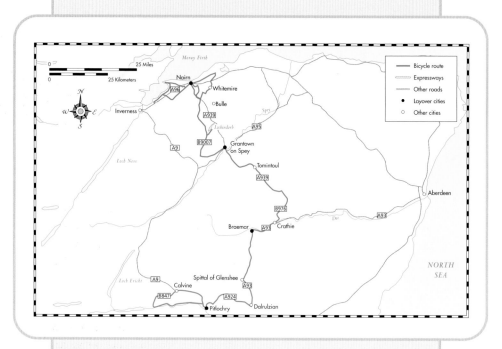

SCOTLAND'S Highlands

This tour offers unique insight into the rugged and natural beauty of the Scottish Highlands. You'll enjoy long stretches of open roads, dotted by centuries-old castles in a countryside blanketed by wild heather.

The Highlands offer a little bit for every taste. Whether you favor beaches or mountains, romantic solitude or active traveling, bustling towns or quaint villages, you'll find a little bit of all of these on this tour.

This tour has a very challenging itinerary; it is the most difficult of the three in this U.K./Ireland grouping. In addition to challenging terrain and distances, weather can play a significant factor. It's not uncommon for hail and sleet to beat down on your face as you reach the top of a pass, which happened during one of my recent group tours. I hired a motorcoach company to assist with the itinerary on two of the days because my guests were unable to ride—the weather was simply too harsh.

You'll begin your Scotland trip in Nairn, a quaint seaside village that's an ideal base for one or two layover rides. At night, grab a dram of whisky and a pita full of haggis and head down to the pier to reflect on the Highlands. *The Highlands of Scotland*

Tourist Information

The official Scotland National Tourist Board website is http://www.visitscotland.com/.

The site is geared to those who want broad information about Scotland, but you'll find more useful information under the regional and city sites, referenced below. You can also check out www.VisitBritain.org, the site that handles all of Great Britain. You can reach representatives by phone and email at 1-800-462 2748 (U.S.), 0131 332 2433 (U.K.); and travelinfo@bta.org.uk, info@stb.gov.uk.

When to Go

Due to some high-altitude climbs that can attract fierce winds and harsh rains (even hail), I recommend this ride only in July and August. Not that you'll be spared some of these weather extremes, but your chances for mild weather will be much greater. To help with your packing selections, here's what you can expect:

INVERNESS (Scotland)[34]

MONTH	AVERAGE HIGH (°F)	AVERAGE LOW (°F)	AVERAGE PRECIPITATION (IN)
JANUARY	43	36	2.0
FEBRUARY	43	34	1.6
MARCH	46	37	1.5
APRIL	50	39	1.5
MAY	55	45	1.8
JUNE	61	48	1.9
JULY	64	54	2.6
AUGUST	63	52	2.8
SEPTEMBER	57	48	2.3
OCTOBER	54	45	2.6
NOVEMBER	46	39	2.4
DECEMBER	43	36	2.1

[34] From http://uk.weather.com/.

While your Nairn layover rides are fairly undemanding, the horizon is dotted with challenging mountain climbs— your destination for the next few days. *The Highlands of Scotland*

Take good rain gear, expect the occasional rainstorm, and please be modestly competent at bicycle repair. There will be l-o-n-g stretches where you won't find any facilities along your rides.

Arrival and Departure
Air and Public Transportation
TO NAIRN

The trip begins in Nairn, which is about 20 miles from Inverness Airport (http://www.hial.co.uk/inverness-airport.html). There are daily flights into Inverness on British Airways (www.ba.com), easyJet (www.easyjet.com), and BMI (www.flybmi.com). You'll need to then take a taxi to Nairn (plenty outside the airport) or the 31-minute public bus ride (www.citylink.co.uk).

Got frequent flyer miles that will only get you into London? No problem. The 11-hour train ride from London to Nairn will make a minimum of 4 changes and costs about 100 pounds (www.nationalrail.co.uk).

FROM PITLOCHRY

The trip ends in Pitlochry, which is 70 miles from Edinburgh Airport (http://www.baa.com/main/airports/edinburgh/) and about 100 miles from Glasgow Airport (http://www.baa.co.uk/main/airports/glasgow/). You can take the 100-minute direct train from Pitlochry to Edinburgh (www.nationalrail.co.uk) for just over 12 pounds.

Private Transportation
TO NAIRN

If you want to prearrange private transfers, contact
TT Cabs: Firthview, Tomich by Beauly; Phone: 00 44 1463 783763; info@tartantaxis.com; www.tartantaxis.com; or
Tartan Taxis, Old Filling Station, Drumossie, Inverness Phone/Fax: 00 44 1463 233033; brian@tartantaxis.org; www.tartantaxis.org.

FROM PITLOCHRY

At the end of your trip, Elizabeth Yule can help you with private transfers from Pitlochry (Phone: 01796 472290; Fax: 01796 474 214).

The Scottish Highlands is a remarkable destination filled with dramatically rugged landscapes that are ideal for cycling. Facilities can be scarce along your route, so make sure you've got decent bike repair skills before setting out. *The Highlands of Scotland*

Bike Rental

You can rent bikes from **Highland Cycles**, 16 Telford Street, Inverness; Phone: 01463 234789, Fax: 01463 234789; and **Bikes of Inverness**, 39 Grant Street, Inverness; 01463 225965; enquiries@bikesofinverness.com.

Cycling Notes

Cycling in Scotland—at least the route that I describe—is an absolute joy. By joy, I don't mean gambling tables, fried foods, and Cinemax porn. Rather, joy as in absolutely quiet roads (to the point of being desolate in places), great scenery, and challenging rides.

Take plenty of food and water with you on every ride because facilities are scarce. In some instances, I've gone 30 miles without seeing a car, much less a store. Oh, and don't forget this is the U.K. You're cycling on the left side of the road.

Maps

Good: Michelin #401, *Motoring Map Scotland*, 1:400,000.
Much Better: Ordnance Survey Travelmaster 2, *Northern Scotland, Orkney & Shetland*, 1:250,000.
Best: Ordnance Survey Landranger Series, #'s 26, 27, 35, 36, 42, 43; 1:50,000.

Ode to Haggis

While the British are maligned as culinary delinquents, I believe the true honor goes to their northern brethren, the Scots. Case and point: haggis.

Haggis is a Scottish specialty that combines a sheep's windpipe, lungs, liver, and heart into a boiled, minced mess. They try to obscure this organ pureé with the euphemistic addition of something they call *beef suet*, but before you get too comfortable, it's not anything close to beef chop suey—we're talking kidney tissue here.

Just when you thought it couldn't get any worse, they wrap the mixture inside a sheep's stomach and then boil it for three hours (I'm assuming to make sure that the sheep is dead). So, the next time you hear the phrase *organic food*, double-check to see whether that's *organic* as in naturally grown, or *organic* as in containing organs. You need to know.

Background Notes
Where Am I?
Country: Scotland
Region: Highlands
City: Nairn

Tourist Information
The Highlands of Scotland Tourist Board, Peffery House, Strathpeffer, Ross-shire IV14 9HA; 01506 832 121; info@host.co.uk; www.highlandfreedom.com; www.cali.co.uk/HIGHEXP/Nairn/index.

Bike Shops
Highland Cycles, 16 Telford Street, Inverness; Phone: 01463 234789 Fax: 01463 234789.
Bikes of Inverness, 39 Grant Street, Inverness; 01463 225965; enquiries@bikesofinverness.com.

Sightseeing
Since 1858, the **Nairn Museum** (King Street) has been a popular cultural stop, thanks to its diverse international collection. The museum is open Monday through Saturday from 10 a.m. to 4:30 p.m. Phone (01667) 456791.

Since the fifteenth century, golf has been entrenched as a Scottish staple. For information on taking in a few holes, contact the **Nairn Golf Course** at (01667) 453208.

If fishing artifacts (think model boats) are your fancy, make the Nairn Fishertown Museum (Laing Hall, King Street) your late-afternoon rest stop. It is open Monday through Saturday from 10:30 a.m. to 12:30 p.m. and 2:30 p.m. to 4:30 p.m.

Bus Tours: Highland Country Buses offers trips to and from Inverness every half hour. Phone: (01463)-233371.

Nairn area tours, including tours to Loch Ness, leave daily from Nairn. Tickets and information are available at the Nairn Tourist Information Center; King Street, Nairn. Phone: (01667) 452753.

Along the Nairn loop rides, you'll pass:

Fort George: This well preserved, eighteenth century fortification is one of Europe's best (excellent espresso at its café!). It is open seven days a week from 9:30 a.m. to 6:30 p.m. Phone: 01667 462777.

Cawdor Castle: This fourteenth century castle exudes the Middle Ages with its drawbridge, tower, and extensive gardens. It is open seven days a week from 10 a.m. to 5:30 p.m. Phone: (01667) 404615.

Brodie Castle: Since 1160, the Brodie family has called this place home (curiously, no family member has ever been elected to the area's condo association). It's open Monday through Saturday from 11 a.m. to 5:30 p.m., and on Sunday from 1:30 p.m. to 5:30 p.m. Phone: (01309) 641371.

Culbin Forest: Extensive walking trails and off-road bike paths wind through this forest, located outside of Nairn. Keep an eye out for nesting osprey. Guided tours are available. Phone: (0870) 5143070.

Restaurants

The Longhouse (8 Harbour Street) has good seafood and traditional Scottish dishes. Stop at **Friar Tucks** (30 Harbour Street) for fish and chips, haggis, black pudding, and fried pizza. The **Claymore Hotel** (45 Seabank Road) offers standard hotel meals, accompanied by Monday night jazz sessions. Phone: (01667) 453705. The **Golf View Hotel** (63 Seabank Road), Nairn's five-star hotel, offers high-priced dinners in an upscale setting.

Luggage Transfers

Rank Radio Taxis, Ltd., 111 Academy Street, Inverness; Phone: 01463 220222; Fax: 01463 220303.

Central Taxis, Farraline Park, Inverness; Phone: 01463 222222; Fax: 01463 716404.

NAIRN LOOP RIDES

Days 1 and 2: Narin

You'll begin the trip in Nairn, a quaint seaside town (bigger than a village, smaller than a city) with relatively dry, temperate weather—as far as Scottish towns go. Facilities here are excellent, and I prefer the atmosphere to nearby Inverness, which though closer to the airport, is a bit too large for my taste.

Weather permitting, you can sun yourself at its popular beach and test your skill at one of its local golf courses.

NAIRN LAYOVER RIDE #1

Distance: 31 miles

Lunch Stop: Auldearn.

Directions (miles): 0.0: **RIGHT** out of the Tourist Office.

0.1: **RIGHT** at a roundabout for Aberdeen A96.

0.2: **STRAIGHT** through intersection (traffic light).

0.4: **LEFT** for Culbin Forest (large brown sign) on Lochloy Rd.

1.3: Culbin Forest entrance is on your left (one of two entrances).

2.2: **STRAIGHT** for Dyke 5 (Nairn 2 is behind you). The sign is on the right side of the road. Lochrdrum Stables is also here.

5.1: Continue **STRAIGHT**

NOTE: *The mileage assumed that you cycled in to the Culbin Forest and retraced your steps back out.*

5.8: **STRAIGHT** to Culbin Forest and Kintessack 2 (you can also turn right to Brodie Castle; after visiting the castle, if you returned to Nairn along the same path you have already traced, the ride for today will turn out to be 14 miles round-trip).

7.2: Culbin Forest entrance on your left. If you turn left to visit the forest, you reach the car park at 7.9

8.5: Return to the main road from the forest. Turn **LEFT.**

9.3: At an intersection, turn **RIGHT** for Dyke 1 1/4, Brodie 2 1/4 (straight is Wellhead Farm 1/4).

10.0: **RIGHT** to Dyke 1/2, Brodie 1 1/2 (there's a silo across the street).

10.4: You pass through Dyke (no food or stores).

10.9: Brodie Castle is on your right. It's open April through October. As you enter the grounds, you reach the car park at 11.5 miles (otherwise, take the left to Forres, Nairn). Mileage from here on assumes you entered the Castle grounds to the car park). There's a snack shop at the castle.

12.0: Exiting the castle, you reach the main road. Turn **LEFT** toward the entrance.

12.5: You reach the entrance once again (the driveway is a big loop); turn **RIGHT** for Forres and Nairn.

12.7: Cross over the A96 to Whitemire 2, Conicavel 2 (a **RIGHT** and then a quick **LEFT**).

13.3: **RIGHT** for Darnaway (straight is Berryley 3/4).

14.2: **LEFT** to Whitemire 2, Redstone 2 (you can also go **STRAIGHT** to Nairn 6 to finish the ride at 21 miles).

15.0: **RIGHT** for Whitemire 1/2.

15.7: Continue **STRAIGHT** (Whitemire 1/4 is left).

17.6: At an intersection, turn **LEFT** to Lethen 1 1/2 (straight is Auldearn 2 1/2, right is Brodie 3).

18.6: **STRAIGHT** to Lethen (Auldearn is right).

19.1: Telephone.

21.5: Unmarked intersection (actually the A939). Turn **RIGHT**.

23.1: **RIGHT** for Achavelgin Bed and Breakfast and a yellow sign "Afternoon Tea and Coffee."

23.4: Bear **LEFT** at an unmarked intersection (there are no real landmarks here, except for maybe a telephone pole with a triangular warning sign posted).

23.9: You see the water in the distance.

25.1: T-intersection (unmarked). Turn **LEFT** ("Give Way" yield sign is also there).

26.7: T-intersection, turn **LEFT**. You're in Auldearn (markets and shops).

26.8: **LEFT** for Cawdor on the B9101 and Cawdor Castle 6.

28.0: Unmarked crossroads; turn **RIGHT**. No other landmarks here. If you miss this turn, you'll eventually hit the A939, which you should follow toward Nairn.

29.3: T-intersection, unmarked; turn **RIGHT**. This is the A939.

29.7: **LEFT** to Inverness on A96.

29.8: Brown sign for Culbin Forest is on your right, Lochloy Road. Continue **STRAIGHT**.

30.0: **STRAIGHT** through the first intersection.

30.3: Turn **LEFT** for Inverness on the A96 road at the next intersection. This is King Street. The tourist center is on your left, just up the road, at 30.4 miles.

NAIRN LAYOVER RIDE #2

Distance: 30 miles

Lunch Stop: Pack picnic items. Otherwise, there's food at the Inverness Airport.

Directions (miles): 0.0: Turn **LEFT** out of the tourist office.

The dullest day cycling in Scotland beats the most exciting day watching PBS. *Visit Scotland Scottish Viewpoint*

0.2: **LEFT** on Waverly Road. Pass Lodgehill Road.

0.4: **RIGHT** to Cawdor 5 on the B9090 and Croy 7. The road is Cawdor Road.

0.5: **RIGHT** for Croy on the B9091.

2.3: Continue **STRAIGHT**.

2.8: At an unmarked turn (faded sign), bear **RIGHT**. It's almost immediately a winding road.

4.0: You reach the A96; turn **LEFT**.

4.7: Turn right toward Barmac (Ardersier).

5.3: At a yield sign, turn **LEFT** onto the B9092 (unmarked)

5.9: **RIGHT** for Upper Carse.

7.3: Continue **STRAIGHT** at a crossroads.

9.1: T-intersection; turn **RIGHT**. You reach Fort George at 9.3 (open Monday through Saturday, 10-6; Sunday, 2-6).

9.5: Leave Fort George by making a **LEFT** out of the parking lot.

10.6: You enter Ardersier (a few shops, markets, and stores).

11.4: **RIGHT** for Inverness 12km on the B9092.

11.7: **LEFT** at a T-intersection for Inverness 12km on the B9039.

13.8: There's a sign on your left for Inverness Airport 1/2. Continue **STRAIGHT** for Inverness 8km on the B9039.

15.6: **RIGHT** for Castle Stuart. Turn around and retrace your route.

17.3: **RIGHT** for Inverness Airport 1/2. The airport comes on your left at 17.8 (continue **STRAIGHT** unless you want a snack inside).

19.8: At a T-intersection (A96), turn **LEFT** for Aberdeen and then a quick **RIGHT** (less than 100 yards ahead).

21.0: You reach Croy. At a T-intersection, make a **RIGHT** and then a quick **LEFT** (the left comes at a store).

22.0: At a T-intersection (words are faded), turn **LEFT** (this is the B9091) for Nairn and Cawdor.

22.3: On the left side of the road, you see a sign for Nairn 7km. Traffic increases.

23.4: At a crossroads, continue **STRAIGHT** for Nairn 6km (you can also make a **RIGHT** on the B9090 for Cawdor Castle, 2 miles away—a worthwhile stop. Retrace your path to this point when you leave and add about 5 more miles to your route). It's an easy route, just follow the signs.

Keep following signs to Nairn.

29.1: **LEFT** at a T-intersection for Town Centre 1/2 on the B9090. You're on Cawdor Road and immediately go under an underpass. This road becomes High Street.

29.4: **LEFT** on Leopold Street. Turn right just ahead on the A96 for Aberdeen.

29.5: The tourist office is on your right.

Background Notes
Where Am I?
Country: Scotland
Region: Highlands
City: Grantown-on-Spey

Tourist Information
Grantown TIC, 54 High Street, Grantown on Spey PH26 3EH; 01479 872773; touristinfo@grantown.co.uk; www.grantown.co.uk.

Bike Shops
Grantown Dial a Bike, Phone: 07739 901 396 (handles rentals).
Logan's Bike Hire, Crann Tarra Guest House, High Street; Phone: 01479 872 197.

Sightseeing
Along today's ride, the ruined castle of **Lochindorb** sits undisturbed on a tiny island in a loch bearing the same name. It's not a lot to see, but it makes for a pleasant detour off the route.

Glenlivet, one of Scotland's most famous whiskey distilleries, is open Monday through Saturday from 10 a.m. to 5 p.m., and on Sunday from 11:30 a.m. to 5 p.m. To get there, head east along A95 until you come to the junction, then turn south. Phone: (01542) 783220.

The 150-year old **Glenfarclas** distillery, with its gift shop and visitor center, is open Monday through Friday from 9:30 a.m. to 5 p.m., Saturday from 10 a.m. to 4 p.m., and Sunday from 12:30 p.m. to 4:30 p.m. Phone: (01807) 500257.

Cardhu (from the Gaelic 'Black Rock') is one of the single malts that has long been included in the Johnnie Walker blends. The distillery is open Monday through Friday from 9:30 a.m. to 4:30 p.m., Saturday from 9:30 a.m. to 4:30 p.m., and Sunday from 11 a.m. to 4 p.m.

The nineteenth-century **Grantown Golf Club** course offers fine views of the neighboring Cromdale Hills. Phone: (01479) 872079.

The traditional art of fish smoking is on display at the **Spey Valley Smokehouse** (Achnagonalin, Grantown-on-Spey). It is open Monday through Friday from 9 a.m. to 5 p.m., and Saturday and Sunday from 10 a.m. to 1 p.m. Phone: (01479) 873078.

Restaurants and Nightlife
For fried food and bar-style meals, visit **Royal Fish Bar** (High Street) and **Ben Mhor Hotel** (High Street). The **Coppice Hotel** stocks over 100 malt whiskeys

at its cozy pub (the hotel is an excellent overnight choice too), and **Ardconnel House**: (Woodlands Terrace) offers well-reviewed French cuisine.

Luggage Transfers
Grantown Kabs: 15 Dulaig Court, Grantown-On-Spey Morayshire; Phone: 01479 873443.
Tran-Cabs: 41c High Street, Grantown-On-Spey; Phone: 01479 870011.

NAIRN TO GRANTOWN
ROUTE NOTES

Day 3: Nairn to Grantown on the Spey
Located on the Spey River, Grantown-on-the-Spey (Grantown if you're nasty) is a mid-eighteenth-century planned city (as opposed to London, which is a chaotic amalgamation of streets). Its rather drab, colorless buildings are nicely framed by tree-lined streets. It's a very popular Highlands destination, owing to its wild, outdoor scenery (think mountains and lush forests) and excellent salmon fishing. Its proximity to the Whiskey Trail is also a popular draw. Keep in mind that most distilleries offer their last tours at 4 p.m.

Several years ago, one of my company's tour guides paid a visit to a distant cousin, who lives close to Grantown. The cousin worked at one of the local distilleries and was complaining that his company had recently imposed a limit on its workers' complimentary take-home whiskey to a "stingy" 1.5 liters per week. That's roughly 48 one-ounce shots. Per week.

Distance: 41 miles
Lunch Stop: Carrbridge, Dulnain Bridge.
Directions (miles): 0.0: Turn **RIGHT** out of the tourist office.
  0.1: **RIGHT** at roundabout for Aberdeen A96.
  0.6: **RIGHT** for Grantown on Spey A939, 23.
  1.1: The road bears **LEFT** for Grantown on Spey 22.
  2.2: Continue **STRAIGHT** for Grantown on Spey 22 (this is the intersection with the **B9101**).
  5.3: **RIGHT** for Littlemill. There are also signs for a telephone and post office. After you turn, the Brae Lodge B&B is on your right.
  6.6: T-intersection (Littlemill points behind you); to the left you can see (look carefully) a triangular sign for Ford 1/2. Turn **LEFT.**
  6.8: Turn **RIGHT** at an unmarked turnoff; Meikleburn points to the right on an obscured sign. There's an orange gate at this junction, too.
  9.7: You reach an unmarked T-intersection (Meikleburn points behind you); turn **LEFT.**
  10.8: Continue **STRAIGHT** for Dulsie Bridge 1 1/4.
  13.6: **RIGHT** on B9007 for Carrbridge.
  17.2: *OPTIONAL TURNOFF.* **LEFT** for Lochindorb. A nice detour, with views of an island castle.
  19.8: Remains of the castle; retrace your route back to main road.
  22.8: Back at main road; turn **LEFT** onto the road.
  29.7: **RIGHT** for Carrbridge 1 1/2 on the A938. This is also a nice detour to a full-facility town (market, stores).

31.2: Carrbridge. Return to the route (from the 29.7-mile mark). You reach the intersection again at 33.7. Continue **STRAIGHT** for Grantown on Spey.

38.4: You enter Dulnain Bridge (shops, food); continue **STRAIGHT** for Elgin A95, Grantown on Spey 3, Tomintoul 7.

38.9: **LEFT** for Grantown on Spey (**B9102**), Tomintoul (**A939**), Elgin (**A941**), Keith A95.

40.7: Roundabout; follow the 11:00 position to Grantown on Spey B9102, Nairn, and Forres.

40.9: As you enter the town, the tourist office is at 41.5 (on your right), just past a set of lights.

Grantown on Spey Extended Route follows the B9102 (you can head out as far as you like, retracing your path to Grantown. This is preferable than looping around on the A95).

0: Turn **RIGHT** out of the tourist office.

0.5: **RIGHT** for Craiggellachie 24, Archies Town 19 on the B9102.

3.0: Continue along this road (to Knockandu).

5.0: On your left is Culfoiche More Farm (retracing your path from here will add 10 miles).

5.5: Uphill with great scenery.

8.1: You can retrace your path from here, cross the bridge to view a castle, or continue. This is an unmarked turn—to see the castle, turn **RIGHT** (you see a River Spey sign just after you turn right). To reach the castle, after you cross the bridge and continue uphill, turn **RIGHT** on the A95. You reach the castle at 10.6. Otherwise, if you continue straight, see below.

13.3: B9138 intersection (and Marypark 1). This would add 26 miles to your route if you back-tracked from here.

16.9: Ballindalloch Castle is along the A95: open daily from 10:00 a.m to –5:00 p.m. If visiting the castle, you'll only cycle on the A95 for a short distance. Retrace your route back over the water (from Marypark) and continue back to Grantown on the B9102.

Background Notes
Where Am I?
Country: Scotland
Region: Aberdeen and Grampian Highlands
City: Braemar

Tourist Information
Braemar TIC
The Mews
Braemar AB35 5YL
013397 41600
Braemar@agtb.org
www.braemarscotland.co.uk;
www.castlesandwhisky.com

Bike Shops

There is no bike shop in town. There's a mountain sports shop, **Mountain Supplies Braemar**, that may be able to help out in a pinch (Invercauld Road; Phone: 013397 41242; Fax: 013397 41496; email: braemar@freeheeldirect.com; www.freeheeldirect.com).

Sightseeing

The seventeenth-century **Braemar Castle** is the town's top tourist site. It's a fully furnished private home that includes an underground prison (talk about your "time-outs"). It is open from 10 a.m. to 6 p.m. daily except Friday. It is located north on the Aberdeen-Ballater-Perth Road. (A93).

Crathie Church is home to the Royal Family. Sunday morning services begin promptly at 11 a.m. It is located 9 miles east of Braemar on the A93.

Braemar Highland Heritage Center is next to the tourist office. Stop there for detailed information on local history. It is open daily (except Friday) from 9 a.m. to 6 p.m.

When you come upon a town in Scotland, load up on drinks and food. You never know when you'll come across another. *Colchester Borough Council, U.K.; www.visitcolchester.com*

Royal Lochnager is another fine representative of the Whiskey Trail. You can reach the distillery from Balleter or Crathie on the A93. It is open Monday through Saturday from10 a.m. to 5 p.m., and Sunday from11 a.m. to 4 p.m. Phone: (013397) 42273.

Creag Choinnich is a brisk 90-minute hike that will lead you to the top of this modest hill (1,765 feet), affording fine views of the valley below.

Linn of Dee (6 miles west of Braemar) is located along today's extended route (which is a great extension, by the way). This is a narrow gap along the River Dee.

Restaurants

Simple, local favorites include the **Invercauld Arms Hotel** and **Braemar Hotel.** Both serve traditional Scottish meals. Try the **Fife Arms Hotel** (Mar Road) for bar-style dishes.

Luggage Transfers

Ballater Taxis: Albert Hall, Station Square, Ballater Aberdeenshire;
Phone: 013397 55548.
C & J Nicol: 8 Viewfield Road, Ballater Aberdeenshire; Phone: 013397 55654.

GRANTOWN TO BRAEMAR
ROUTE NOTES

Day 4: Grantown to Braemar

Today's ride is the toughest of the tour and includes three challenging passes and the steepest road in Scotland. It was during this ride that one of my groups encountered a driving hail storm. Lesson learned: Check the weather forecast with your Grantown hotel staff before setting out. There are scarce facilities between Grantown and Braemar.

Distance: 47 to 67 miles

Lunch Stop: Tomintoul.

Directions (miles): 0.0: Turn **LEFT** out of the tourist office.

    0.1: **LEFT** at the light (onto Spey Avenue) for Torrintoul A939. There's an Esso Station on your left after you turn.

    0.5: Speybridge Roundabout: head for 12:00 position and Tomintoul (A939), Elgin (A941), Keith A95.

    0.8: **STRAIGHT** to Keith 95, Tomintoul (A939). There's a smokehouse on the corner.

    1.6: **RIGHT** to Tomintoul 13, Braemar 46 (A93). It's now uphill until about 2.2.

    5.6: Continue **STRAIGHT** for Braemar 41.

    9.0: Steep downhill (winding road). At 9.3: telephone.

    9.6: Tea room for snacks.

    9.8: Sign "Welcome to Moray." You begin a steep (20 percent!) climb until 10.6. Walk your bikes across cattle grids at 10.8.

    10.8: More cattle grids—careful.

    12.3: Continue **STRAIGHT** to Tominoul A939, Braemar (A93). This comes at the B9136 turnoff.

    12.5: Continue **STRAIGHT** to Tomintoul 2, Braemar 32. Begin an uphill until 13.2. There's a telephone after the Bridge of Brown.

    13.8: You enter Tomintoul (food).

    14.3: **LEFT** for Braemar A939 (A93), Dufftown (B9008).

    14.5: **RIGHT** for Braemar A939 (A93), Cockbridge, Lecht Ski Center. As you make the turn, Cockbridge 9, Braemar 30.

    19.9: Uphill (20 percent!).

    21.2: Top of the pass (Lecht Ski Center): Coffee and small snacks. Careful for another cattle grid!

    21.9: Downhill. At 23.1, there's a steep descent.

    23.6: You enter Lorgarff.

    23.9: **RIGHT** for Corgarff Castle (dirt road). Open daily 9:30 a.m. to 6:30 p.m., April through September, £2.50.

    24.3: After retracing your route from the castle, make a **RIGHT**.

    26.2: Coffee shop.

26.9, **RIGHT** for Ballater 12 A939 (A93), Braemar 19 (B976).

27.3: Uphill until 29.3, then a 2-mile very steep downhill until 31.8.

33.0: **RIGHT** for Balmoral 5, B976, Braemar 13 (A93).

38.0: **RIGHT** to Braemar A939 (this is a busy road—careful). Or (highly recommended): Turn **LEFT** and then a quick **RIGHT** for Balmoral Castle 1/2—and then retrace your route to continue to Braemar.

46.4: Entrance to Braemar Castle is on your right. Open daily (except Fridays) 10 a.m. to 6 p.m., £3.

46.9: Turn **RIGHT** to tourist office, which you reach at 47.1 The office is on your left.

Braemar Extended or Layover Route: To Linn of Dee.

0.0: Make a **LEFT** out of tourist office; follow brown and white sign to Linn of Dee.

0.1: Follow road **RIGHT** for Linn of Dee.

1.1: Uphill, with a river on your right (below).

5.3: Youth hostel on your right.

6.3: Linn of Dee; continue along the road (to free parking sign), as the road bears **RIGHT**.

7.1: Cattle grating.

9.8: Cattle grating.

10.4: Wooden bridge and paved road ends. Retrace your path to Braemar.

Background Notes
Where Am I?
Country: Scotland
Region: Perthshire
City: Pitlochry

Tourist Information
Pitlochry TIC
22 Atholl Road.
Pitlochry PH16 5BX
Phone: 01796 472 215
pitlochrytic@perthshire.co.uk
www.perthshire.co.uk

Bike Shops
Escape Route: 8 West Moulin Road, Pitlochry; Phone: 01796 473859.

Sightseeing
There's a glass-partitioned viewing area at the **Pitlochry Dam** that allows you intimate access to the salmon's journey to their spawning beds. Tours are offered daily from 10 a.m. to 5 p.m. Phone: (01796) 473152.

Scotland is continuously grooming an ever-expanding network of off-road cycling trails. The Scottish Tourist Board has reams of information that they'll be happy to send. *Perthshire Tourist Board*

Bell's **Blair Athol** (Perth Road, south of town) celebrated its 200th year producing popular single malt whiskeys in 1997. Tours are offered every half-hour during the summer. Phone: (01796) 472234.

The charming, stone-built **Blair Atholl** village makes for a worthwhile afternoon shop.

Blair Castle is located close to Pitlochry, and it proudly displays military artifacts from the castle's turbulent past.

Since the seventeenth century, Killiecrankie Pass has been a defensive military junction in the Central Highlands. It is open daily from 10 a.m. to 5:30 p.m. Phone: (01796) 481207.

Restaurants

For the standard Scottish bar grub and fried dishes, try **Ardchoille** (Atholl Road) and **McKay's House** (138 Atholl Road). The latter proudly serves haggis. Previous CBT participants loved the **Prince of India**, which serves modestly priced Indian dishes, and **il Pontevecchio** prepares the town's best Italian dishes.

BRAEMAR TO PITLOCHRY
ROUTE NOTES

Days 5-6: Braemar to Pitlochry; Pitlochry Layover
Set in the beautiful Tummel Valley, Pitlochry is surrounded by magnificent scenery, which has made it a popular tourist destination since the turn of the century. As late as 1880, Pitlochry's population was less than 400 until it was noted as a health spa—it's now home to roughly 2,500. Pitlochry is also known for Edradour and Bell's, its two local distilleries,.
Distance: 41 miles
Lunch Stop: Kirchmichael (at hotels)
Directions (miles): 0.0: Turn **RIGHT** out of tourist office onto the main road.
NOTE: You can also turn **RIGHT** toward Clunie Lodge and follow the river until the road merges with the A93 at 3.5 miles.
    0.1: **RIGHT** to Perth on A93 (Glenshee Rd.).
    7.5: Uphill.
    9.3: Glenshee Ski Resort (restaurant, toilets).
    9.6: Top of hill.
    9.8: "Welcome to Perth and Kinross" sign. Begin a 10 percent downhill for 2 miles with very few switchbacks. Check your brakes! Be careful! Watch for sheep! This is a very dangerous road because you can reach extremely high speeds.
    15.1: Continue **STRAIGHT** to Blairgowrie and Perth on the A93.
    20.2: **STRAIGHT** to Perth **A93** (after the turn, you see a sign for Blairgowrie 14, Perth 29). There's a pottery shop here, too.
    23.2: Coffee shop on your left.

23.5: **RIGHT** for Pitlochry 16, Kirkmichael 4 on the B950 (A924).

27.4: At a T-intersection (with a cross), **RIGHT** for Kirkmichael 1/4, Pitlochry 12, A924.

27.6: You enter Kirkmichael (market, food at hotels); continue **STRAIGHT**.

29.5: You enter Enochdu—no food here.

38.3: There's a sharp **RIGHT** turn. Follow the road for Pitlochry 2, and you'll pretty much continue downhill until the town.

39.0: You pass Pitlochry signs—though you are not there yet.

39.4: Moulin.

40.2: You are in Pitlochry. At the T-intersection, turn **LEFT** for Perth (A9).

40.5: **LEFT** toward the tourist office.

PITLOCHRY LOOP RIDE

Distance: 36 miles

Lunch Stop: Tummel Bridge, Blair Castle

Directions (miles): 0.0: **RIGHT** out of tourist office in the center of Pitlochry; head **STRAIGHT** through the town (toward the North, Inverness, (A9)).

0.8: **STRAIGHT** for Blair Atholl.

0.9: **STRAIGHT** for Killiecrankie, Tummel Bridge (not right for the A9).

1.2: **STRAIGHT** for B8019 (B8079), Blair Atholl.

2.2: You pass a campground.

2.7: **LEFT** for Queens View 4, Tummel Bridge 10 (brown sign).

3.7: Uphill until 4.7.

5.1: Sign: Tummel Bridge 8, B8019; uphill until 7.0.

6.8: Queen's View Lookout.

9.9: Restaurant.

13.1: Tummel Bridge (food).

13.6: **RIGHT** for Kinloch Rannoch 7 on B846 (left is Aberfeldy).

14.4: **RIGHT** for Trinafour 4, Calvine 10, and The North. Steep uphill until 17.0 (though a 2-mile downhill follows).

17.9: **RIGHT** for Trinafour 1, Struan 6, Calvine 7 (A9), B847.

18.3: Trinafour (only a telephone).

18.8: **STRAIGHT** for Calvine 5 1/2, B847.

24.1: Continue **STRAIGHT** (don't turn to Old Struan 1/2).

24.5: Calvine; turn **RIGHT** for Blair Atholl (B8079), Perth (A9). There's a gas station/shop after you turn.

25.7: **LEFT** for Blair Atholl B8079 (to the right is A9).

25.9: You immediately enter the hamlet of Bruar—with the House of Bruar restaurant at the corner.

28.7: You enter Blair Atholl (tea room and bookstore).

29.1: Blair Castle on your left. Fees are £6 for the castle, entrance to grounds is free.

29.3: Continue **STRAIGHT** (Old Blair 1 1/2 is to the left).

30.3: Continue **STRAIGHT** B8079 Killecrankie.

30.6: Continue **STRAIGHT** B8079 Killecrankie 1.

33.7: **STRAIGHT** for Pitlochry 2 on (A924), B8019.

35.2: **STRAIGHT** for Pitlochry A924.

35.5: **STRAIGHT** for Pitlochry.

35.9: You enter Pitlochry. The tourist center comes at 36.5 (on your left).

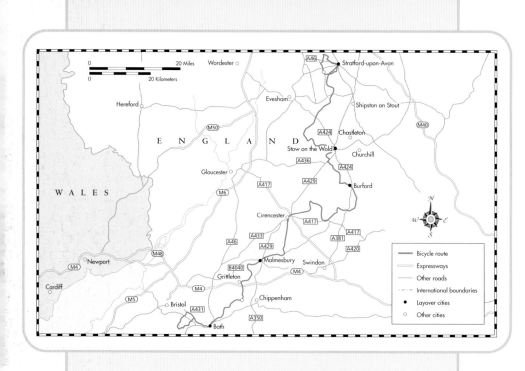

ENGLAND'S Cotswolds

This was the first overseas tour that I ever led, and it's a wonderful introduction to European cycling. The scenery is great, the roads are well-marked, and the people are friendly (except the brunette cashier at Bath's E-Z Market—would it have killed you to double-bag my rotisserie chicken?!).This is an ideal trip for cyclists of (almost) all abilities.

This route contains a delightful combination of rolling hills, soothing rivers, and charming villages. Because of its close proximity to London, it's easy to incorporate a big-city visit with countryside cycling (or some countryside cycling with a big-city visit), enabling you to enjoy a perfect balance of the urban and rural.

Tourist Information

The official National Tourist Office for Britain's website is www.VisitBritain.org. It's a massive site that contains thousands of links as you narrow down your travel preferences. You can also reach their representatives at 800 462 2748 (U.S.) or 888 847 4885 (Canada); travelinfo@bta.org.uk, britinfo@bta.org.uk.

Peddling dope on British streets is a felony. *Colchester Borough Council, U.K.; www.visitcolchester.com*

For detailed Cotswolds tourist information, check out the Gloucestershire website. The local contacts are extremely knowledgeable and helpful (Phone: 01452 425673; www.glos-cotswolds.com).

When to Go

This is a great trip for April through September, and even late March and early October will work well if you've got good fleece. It rains, as you can see below, so take solid rain gear (no ponchos). I've never had a trip unduly influenced because of weather extremes, though good beer at the end of each ride probably helped.

LONDON[35]

MONTH	AVERAGE HIGH (°F)	AVERAGE LOW (°F)	AVERAGE PRECIPITATION (IN)
JANUARY	45	36	2.4
FEBRUARY	45	36	1.4
MARCH	51	38	2.0
APRIL	55	41	1.7
MAY	62	47	1.8
JUNE	68	52	1.8
JULY	72	56	1.8
AUGUST	72	56	1.7
SEPTEMBER	66	52	1.7
OCTOBER	58	46	2.9
NOVEMBER	51	40	1.8
DECEMBER	47	38	2.3

[35] From http://www.usatoday.com/weather/resources/climate/worldcli.htm#l.

Arrival and Departure
Air

The Cotswolds trip begins in Bath, which is roughly 100 miles west of London. Like the saying goes, "If you can't figure out how to get to London, you can't figure out nothin.'"[36]

The British Airport Authority (BAA) website provides links to all of the major London Airports (Heathrow, Gatwick, Stansted): http://www.baa.co.uk/. There are tons of flights, both on traditional commercial airlines and the budget boutique carriers, that can bring you into London no matter your starting point. I don't have a personal favorite, but there is a Burger King at Gatwick if that helps with your decision. Also, be prepared for substantial customs delays at Heathrow and Gatwick due to current travel sensitivities.

Alternatively, Bristol Airport is only 15 miles from Bath and has service from a handful of international cities. Check out the Bristol Airport website for current schedules: www.bristolairport.co.uk and the easyJet website for airline deals: www.go-fly.com.

The tour ends in Stratford, which is 75 miles from Bristol and 100 miles from London. Any of the above airports would be convenient departure points.

For those whose big-city driving experiences are filled with nightmare encounters with hustling street people eager to squeegee your windshield for a buck or two, wait until you meet this aggressive shoeshine tandem while cycling through England.
Jerry Soverinsky

To and From the Airport
Taxi

TO BATH

There are hundreds of taxis outside of every London airport (and at least 14 outside the Bristol terminal). If you're starting from London, your cost will be steep—at least $200 with today's exchange rate. (Bath Taxis Phone: 01225 484488.)

Alternatively, if you want to arrange a private car or van for the journey, Motion Europe can help with the planning. (Motion Europe: phone: 020 762 99777; fax: 020 762 99333; email: Mail@motion-europe.com.)

FROM STRATFORD

Stratford has several private transport services that can help arrange for your post-trip departure. Try **007 Taxis** (Phone: 01789 414007), **Arrive in Style**

---

[36] My original saying. I mentioned it to a couple of people early last year.

(Phone: 01527 894875), or **The Open Road Classic Car Hire** (Phone: 01926 624891). Expect to pay at least $200 for a private transfer to London.

Public Transportation

TO BATH

Train: Upon your arrival into London, Bristol, or some other British airport, there are high-speed trains that regularly service Bath. Check out http://www.nationalrail.co.uk for details on your specific itinerary. Approximate times and prices are as follows:

Departure Airport	Duration	Cost (pounds)
Stansted	3h10	53
Gatwick	2h30	45
Heathrow	2h15	35
Bristol	1h00	9

Bus: If every penny counts and you can tolerate a slightly longer transfer, consider traveling by bus with National Express: www.nationalexpress.com. Approximate times and prices are as follows:

Departure Airport	Duration	Cost (pounds)
Stansted	5h10	26
Gatwick	5h30	19
Heathrow	5h40	24
Bristol	2h15	6

FROM STRATFORD

Use the above links for current time schedules and information. Expect to pay:

Train from Stratford

Departure Airport	Duration	Cost (pounds)
Stansted	4h00	35
Gatwick	3h27	30
Heathrow	4h27	30
Bristol	3h16	26

Bus from Stratford

Departure Airport	Duration	Cost (pounds)
Stansted	5h45	23
Gatwick	6h10	18
Heathrow	4h45	23
Bristol	3h40	18

Bike Rental

For my groups, I always use **Avon Valley Cyclery** (Phone: 01225 442442; Fax: 01225 446267; http://www.bikeshop.uk.com/). They're located in the railway

station and they've got a great selection of bikes. You can also try **John's Bikes;** (82 Walcot Street; Phone: 01225 334633); and **Total Fitness:** (9 Saracen St.; Phone: 01225 444164). Expect to pay about 75 pounds per week for a generic hybrid-style bicycle.

Cycling Notes

You'll be cycling on the left side of the road here, and pay special attention along the very small country roads. In many cases, high hedges obscure oncoming traffic and you need to look out for fast-moving cars (because they won't be looking out for you). Facilities are abundant along the route, and while you'll be hard-pressed to find a decent oatmeal cookie, bleached bread rolls are everywhere.

British condo associations are very strict about mailbox modifications. Most insist that owners find a way to incorporate the drops into centuries-old brick walls. *Gloucestershire Tourism, www.glos-cotswolds.com*

Maps

Good: Ordnance Survey Travelmaster 7, *Wales & West Midlands,* 1:250,000 (missing part of Bath ride).
Excellent: Ordnance Survey Landranger Series, #'s 150, 151, 172, 173; 1:50,000; and Ordnance Survey Touring Map 8, *The Cotswolds,* 1:63,360.

Accommodations Notes

British B&Bs, as mentioned in the introduction section, are not your typical Vermont-adultery-weekend type. Well, some are, but others are not.

Many bedrooms lack private facilities and are in desperate need of renovation. If you've found what you think to be too good of a deal, it probably is, unless you're just one of those lucky people who always seem to be called to shoot the half-court shot at NBA basketball games. Double-check to ensure that you'll receive what you expect.

Also, camping in the Cotswolds is very pleasant. The story below ($44) is my experience from camping in London. There is a difference.

There's no question that B&Bs in the Cotswolds can be quaint and charming (even regal, in this instance). But do your research because many are modest dwellings that might not meet your preconceptions. *Gloucestershire Tourism, www.glos-cotswolds.com*

London

First-time visitors to England should allow at least three full days for sightseeing in London prior to cycling. Contact the London Tourist Board for information to assist your visit:

Visit London
1 Warwick Row
London SW1
Phone: 020 7932 2000
Fax: 020 7932 0222
enquiries@visitlondon.com;
www.visitlondon.com

$44

I have two words of advice for those who wish to bike through Europe on the cheap: Don't camp in London. That's four words, actually, but it's still good advice.

In 1989, I began planning itineraries for my company's first season of tours to be held during the summer of 1990. I had determined that there was a need for van-supported, budget European bike trips in the marketplace, and I was committed to offer bargain-priced, fully serviced trips.

I could tell you that I had many long strategy sessions during that planning phase, drawing upon reams of scientific data and complex spreadsheet scenarios. The truth is, I took a bike ride one spring afternoon in May 1989, and when I returned home, my Cateye bike computer read 44 miles. I decided then that my trips would cost $44 per day. I had actually planned to ride 75 miles that day, but the 7 p.m. season finale of *Jake and the Fatman* prompted me to cut my ride short. So I settled for 44 miles and $44 per day. This was sound financial planning.

When I say that the trips were to be fully serviced, that meant that they were to be guided by two staff members, offer complete van support, private airport transfers, all accommodations, and at least half of the meals, all for $44 per day. This was my career path: Sound financial planning. Can you say, "Ramen noodles for life?"

Working backward from the $44 per day figure, I quickly (four months later) deduced that the tours would need to spend a majority of the nights at campgrounds, sprinkled with an occasional youth hostel. I finalized my itineraries

The Cotswolds countryside is rivaled only by its quaint buildings that demand your photo finger's constant attention. *Gloucestershire Tourism, www.glos-cotswolds.com*

that fall and quickly began promoting my company's first year of programs.

Not surprisingly, word spread about the $44 per day trips, and my first-year programs were remarkably well-attended. In fact, I had 16 people on my very first trip, an itinerary that began in London.

An old grade-school friend who was between jobs worked with me that summer, and the two of us arrived in London a week before the trip to acclimate ourselves and make final arrangements.

The London Municipal Campground was located (not any longer—it's now the site for a low-security prison), quite appropriately, in the lowest rent district of London. Think the Robert Horner homes and the location for the 1970s sitcom, *Good Times.*

Good Times. Any time you meet a payment . . . .

As we approached what I excitedly determined to be London's municipal campground (LMC from now on), we slowed to a stop so I could recheck the

The Cotswolds cycling itinerary leads you through an extensive collection of welcoming towns. Save time for a local draught, which is always better just after midday when the kegs are fresh. *Gloucestershire Tourism,www.glos-cotswolds.com*

map. My thoughts buried in my encyclopedic London A-Z map, I was furiously shaken by two men jumping on the hood of my minibus.

"Blah blah blah blah blah," the first one screamed, his hand outstretched. Very hard to understand a British beggar.

"Blah blah blah blah blah," his friend chimed in, his hand also reaching toward my driver's window. Tough accent to break.

They wanted money. I was in no mood to argue. I threw coins, Fig Newtons, and whatever I could find out the window. They evaporated off my car and pounced for the treats.

Good times, any time you need a friend. Good times, any time you're out from under. Not getting hassled, not getting hustled . . .

British stonewall-makers rarely have unscathed knuckles. When you find one, reassure yourself that you're in the presence of a true craftsman.
Gloucestershire Tourism,
www.glos-cotswolds.com

Finally, we reached the entrance and the first thing that caught my attention, right alongside the gravel road that linked the street with the LMC parking lot, was a gypsy woman and her infant son. The child was naked, and his mother was holding him at arm's length with her hands on the child's knees like he was a wishbone. The child, while being held in this airborne position, was relieving himself—that's relieving himself from the backside—along the entranceway. Not behind some bushes or down a drainage ditch. Immediately in front of my van. I stopped and idled the car while the child finished. I then proceeded to the parking lot. It was not exactly the welcome reception I had anticipated.

"Sov," my friend Bob laughed. "Welcome to London."

The campground setting was not what Americans would see as a traditional National Park atmosphere. More like a large gravel field with clotheslines. There was a thick stench of burning tires that seemed to hang in the air.

There were 20 or so aging camping caravans anchored to the lot, and I rarely saw human life emerge from their tin carcasses. Next to those were a dozen shabby tents that were crudely erected, and from these emerged an endless stream of travelers. I recognized them to be of human origin, but there was very little recognizable about their appearance. That is, their clothes, speech patterns, everything, was completely foreign.

The LMC was a harrowing introduction to foreign travel, and thankfully I had a lot of work to accomplish and was therefore somewhat distracted from the surroundings (years later, my psychiatrist would refer to this as denial).

Bob and I kept busy that week by finalizing reservations, orienting ourselves in London, and anticipating the arrival of the first group. I had a detailed schedule of tasks that we needed to complete, the last of which was to set up participant tents the day before their arrival.

We awoke that last "free" morning early. I heard something outside my tent that sounded peculiar (not like the car alarms and faint screams that had ominously become white noise by this point). I peeked my head outside my tent, but was comforted to find that it was only a goat. After a week at this LMC, it didn't seem that unusual. Denial.

The temperature that morning—May 14, 1990—was unseasonably cold. Forty-eight degrees, to be exact, with swirling winds. Not the greatest weather for setting up sixteen tents.

The two tents that Bob and I had used the previous few days were self-standing, so we didn't have to pound stakes into the ground to secure them (20 pounds of gear in each one did the trick). But the participant tents were "A-frames," which meant that in addition to being functionally useless, they needed to be staked into the ground. That would be a problem.

Keeping your head above water, making a wave when you can. Temporary lay-offs. Good times. Easy credit rip-offs. Good times.

It's difficult to pound aluminum stakes into gravel. Really difficult. After ruining the first 30 stakes, I took the subway into town and found a camping store where I bought a back-up supply of 300 stakes. Hustling back to the campground Bob and I re-attempted to set up the tents. I'm telling you, no matter how many stakes I ruined, I just could not pound aluminum stakes into gravel.

So I had an idea. A small field, clotted with four-foot wisps of rotted weeds, was about 50 yards east of the gravel lot. I commandeered my minibus and drove through the field for 20 or so minutes, matting down as much of the growth as I could. The ground accepted the stakes, the tents were set up, and the group arrived shortly after.

Our first afternoon and evening seemed to be going relatively well. Acute jetlag has a way of diminishing one's sense of their surroundings, so the complaints were muted at best. As I prepared my group's first dinner—pasta!—Jessie Brandon came running from the bathroom. She was upset, and she was wearing just a towel.

"My stuff's been stolen! I heard some lady run in and grab everything," she cried. "She stole my clothes, my entire duffel bag! All my stuff!"

This was a great B&B, and I especially enjoyed the copious breakfast. But why they're located next to a toy museum is beyond me. I was up all night, thanks to the constant clucking from the G'nip G'nop display that drove me nuts. *Gloucestershire Tourism, www.glos-cotswolds.com*

"This isn't happening," I thought. The trip was barely two hours old. What else could go wrong?

It started to rain.

While Bob took control of the dinner preparations, I searched in vain for the thief and questioned all who lurked in the area.

I returned to our site empty-handed and promised Jessie that I would take her into London in the morning for replacements. Thankfully, several of the other female participants pitched in and offered her temporary clothing and toiletries.

Scratching and surviving. Good times. Hanging in a chow line. Good times. . .

Bob wasn't faring too well with the spaghetti, especially since the sky was now heaving rain onto our unprotected community. Combined with gusts of wind and cold temperatures, an imminent dinner was not promising. I had no choice.

"Let's go, let's head into town," I said. "Forget the pasta." The group seemed relieved. An hour or so later—that's a 25 minute walk to the nearest tube station and a 35 minute train ride into town—we emerged at a hip, fashionable area of Central London. I had been there several times earlier in the week and knew that there were tons of restaurants in the vicinity. There was a cheap fish 'n chips place that I had in mind, but before I could mention it, one of the other participants noticed something else.

"Cool, Hard Rock Café!" he shouted.

"Gotta go there!" cried another.

A third and fourth soon chimed in. I didn't feel at that point that I had much room to maneuver. It was the first night of the trip. Someone had already been robbed. It was 48 degrees, raining, and my group was hungry. So we ate at the Hard Rock Café. Everyone loved it. After calculating the rate of exchange, the bill came to $735. The $44 per day was not looking good.

We returned to the campground later that night, and as we approached the back entrance of the grounds I nodded casually to the goat who had greeted me the morning before. He was with his friends, a group of six or seven. It was time for bed.

I didn't sleep well that night. I crunched numbers and tried to figure out how to recoup the $700 or so I had exceeded on the dinner budget. It was still dark when Joe Tablin shook my tent.

"The bikes are gone! Jerry, the bikes are gone!"

I jumped out of my tent (boxers, not briefs) and ran to where we had locked our bikes the night before. Was I still dreaming? Was it a nightmare? No, this was real. The tire stench was still in the air. It was still raining. And it was now 42 degrees.

Thankfully—ever the group leader optimist!—the entire locked mass of bikes was not stolen, but three bikes were in fact gone. Stolen. The trip was now 14 hours old.

The group slowly emerged from their tents over the next few hours and the collective mood was understandably low.

Bob helped me distribute breakfast to everyone. Although days before I was excited when my trip to Sainsbury's uncovered Kellogg's Corn Pops, it didn't turn out to be the power breakfast I had imagined.

I made a trip to the nearby police station where I reported the missing bikes. The clerk didn't offer much hope in recovering the bicycles, nor did I figure that he would. So that morning after the group went into London to sightsee, I took Jessie and the three bike-less participants into London to replace their belongings. I was inexperienced and I didn't figure on personal insurance or other means of self-protection, so I offered to pay for everyone's losses.

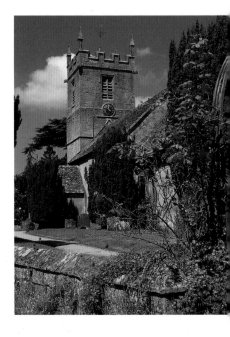

At the end of the day, a duffel-bag full of clothes and three bicycles later (after calculating the rate of exchange) came to $2,635. The $44 per day budget was not looking good.

Miraculously, the sun appeared that afternoon and my spirits lifted. The group was sightseeing, and we were to begin cycling the next day.

You wait anxiously for the clock to strike noon, just seven minutes away, because you know from experience that the Cotswolds clocks resonate with the soothing sounds of cool jazz. *Gloucestershire Tourism, www.glos-cotswolds.com*

While cycling through the Cotswolds, eating lunch alongside a village pond makes for an ideal break. Aren't you glad you left your Blackberry at home? *Gloucestershire Tourism, www.glos-cotswolds.com*

"So, there were a few opening-day glitches," I said aloud as I walked down Oxford Street. Things would get better. I visited a local pub that afternoon and ordered a beer, anxiously looking forward to a few minutes of solitude. The beer was warm, and it started to rain again.

Ain't we lucky we got 'em. Good times!

I remember dozing off to sleep that night because I dreamed of Ginger from *Gilligan's Island* and our seven children. Just as we were heading to Jamaica on our winter vacation, I heard a voice:

"Get out! Get out of here! Help! Help!"

Ginger vanished and I was back in London. The screams were real, and I leapt from my tent. A shadowy figure was running from Carla Hansen's tent, and Carla was crying as I ran to her.

"I was sound asleep and all of a sudden I heard this noise," she began. "This guy, I don't know who it was, he got in my tent and when I opened my eyes, he started taking off his clothes. I started screaming and he ran away."

Thankfully, he hadn't touched her. He had left when she started screaming, but it was nonetheless a horrifying ordeal. She and I stayed awake the rest of the night, probably too scared to sleep. Remarkably, the rest of the group remained asleep. I suppose the thunder and rain drowned out the majority of the commotion.

I returned to the police station very early the next morning with Carla. She seemed concerned that I was now on a first-name basis with the staff. They obtained the routine information about the crime, but the clerk didn't offer much hope in finding the offender.

I left London later that morning with my group. The majority of them were now battle-tough and weary, though the remainder of the tour fared mercifully better than its first two days, even if I had to make some last-minute changes. For example, the group campground dinners didn't all pan out and we visited several more restaurants in lieu of campground cooking. A few of the remaining campgrounds were so dilapidated (one didn't even exist) that I was forced to substitute cheap hotels instead.

Yes, I had a lot to learn about trip planning, but the group was remarkably good-spirited and seemed to enjoy their experience.

As I tallied the numbers, I was curious to know how close I would come to the $44 per day mark.

I lost just over $9,000.

Don't camp in London.

British cycling lanes are generally smooth, well-maintained asphalt. Be careful around tight corners; high hedges can obscure oncoming traffic. *Gloucestershire Tourism, www.glos-cotswolds.com*

Background Notes
Where Am I?
Country: England
Region: The South of England
County: Northeast Somerset
City: Bath

Tourist Information

Bath Tourism
Abbey Chambers, Abbey Church Yard
Bath BA1 1LY
Phone: 01225 477101
Fax: 01225 477787
tourism@bathnes.gov.uk
http://www.visitbath.co.uk/

Bike Shops

Avon Valley Cyclery: Phone: 01225 442442; Fax: 01225 446267;
http://www.bikeshop.uk.com/.
John's Bikes; 82 Walcot Street;
Phone: 01225 334633.
Total Fitness: 9 Saracen Street;
Phone: 01225 444164.

Sightseeing

Bath is a large city, and you can easily spend a full day exploring its local sites and cultural attractions.

Construction began at **Bath Abbey** just prior to the start of the sixteenth century, and if you're brave enough to fight your way through the tour bus crowds, it's a requisite visit.

Pulteney Bridge, nicknamed "Florence-on-Avon" (surrounded by tourist shops), is one of the most recognizable sites in Bath. It is open seven days a week.

Royal Victoria Park is Bath's version of Central Park. It's a much-appreciated oasis just outside the city center, and it's perfect for those who wish to escape the bustle of Bath.

Built over 2,000 years ago, the **Roman Baths Museum** is part of the most extensive remains in Bath (and Britain).

Victoria Art Gallery, Bath's city art gallery, houses the main permanent collection of British and European art, spanning the seventeenth century to the present day.

Considered by many to be the most beautiful street in Britain (no wonder eighteenth century aristocrats flocked here), **No. 1 Royal Crescent** is home to over 24 three-story houses, all finished in golden Bath stone.

Restaurants

Among the more popular with my company's guests are **The Hole in the Wall** (16 George Street), **The Moon and Sixpence** (6a Broad Street), and

Beaujolais (5 Chapel Row). All of these restaurants offer mid-priced entrees in warm, comfortable settings.

Luggage Transfers

Wilcombe Cars: 21 Greenacres, Bath; Cell: 07721 747921; Phone: 01225 422610; Evenings/Sundays: 01225-319959; enquiries@widcombe-cars.freeserve.co.uk; http://www.widcombe-cars.freeserve.co.uk/.

D C S Cars: 90 Meare Road, Bath; Phone: 07747 633234; www.taxis.uk.net.

BATH LOOP RIDE

Days 1 and 2: Bath

During its Roman occupation, Bath became famous for its comprehensive network of underground thermal baths, which seem to be the big tourist draw to the city. It's a fun destination, both by day and night, while also ideal as a springboard into Cotswolds cycling.

The layover Bath ride allows you the opportunity to stretch your legs on a very easy half-day bike route, following a dedicated waterway bike path. A cautionary note about British cycling: The British lanes are a wonderful system of paths that weave their way through the countryside. However, please be careful, especially around turns, because the high hedges can obscure oncoming cars.

Distance: 21 miles

Directions (miles): You'll cycle on the Bath-Bristol bike way to leave town.

Once on the bike path, continue 8km until you reach the Avon Railroad Station.

Enter the parking lot from the bike path and turn **RIGHT** going downhill to the main road, the A431.

Turn **RIGHT** onto the A431. Just after you take this turn, you'll cross under a bridge and the bike path.

5.3: Turn **LEFT** toward to Keynsham on the A4175. There's a side path on your right.

6.5: Enter Keynsham.

6.6: You cross over the A4 and head into town.

6.7: Turn **LEFT**.

6.8: Turn **RIGHT** at the Victoria Methodist Church.

7.3: The road will bear **RIGHT** and will turn into Carlton Road.

9.1: Turn **LEFT** toward Woollard 1 (small sign). Take the first **LEFT** after you fork toward Woollard 1. Take this first **LEFT** onto a smaller lane. This is a narrow lane with high hedges, watch for cars coming the other direction.

9.6: You'll begin a downhill; be careful of the narrow road. The road will veer **LEFT**, be careful, still going downhill.

10.5: You'll come to an intersection: Turn **RIGHT** (ignore the sign to the left for Hunstreten).

10.6: You'll cross a small bridge: On the other side, turn **LEFT** for Burnett 2, Stanton Prior 3, Bath 7.5, and Wells 16.5.

11.1: Veer **LEFT** for the Avon Cycleway.

12.4: Continue **STRAIGHT** to Middlepiece Lane.

12.8: You'll come to an intersection, turn **LEFT** following the Avon Cycleway sign.

13.8: You'll come to a T-intersection; **RIGHT** onto Manor road.

13.9: As the road ends, take another **RIGHT** onto the larger road (unsigned).

14.3: You'll come to another intersection; follow the bike sign to Mangots Field/Acon Cycleway **STRAIGHT** ahead. There's a car dealership to the right as you cycle across the intersection.

14.5: **RIGHT** onto High Street.

14.7: **LEFT** at the Bird in Hand pub. Continue back onto the bike path. Follow signs for Bath and retrace your route to the start at Victoria Park.

Background Notes
Where Am I?

Country: England
Region: The South of England, Cotswolds
County: Wiltshire
City: Malmesbury

Tourist Information

Malmesbury TIC
Town Hall, Market Lane
Malmesbury SN1 9BZ
Phone: 01666 823748
Fax: 01666 826166
malmesbury@northwilts.gov.uk; www.malmesbury.gov.uk;
www.visitnorthwiltshire.co.uk; www.visitwiltshire.co.uk.

Bike Shops

CH White & Son
51 High Street
Malmesbury
Open 9 a.m. to 1 p.m. Monday through Saturday; closed Sunday
Phone: 01666 822330
Fax: 01666 822330
Chwhite@Btinternet.Com; http://www.chwhite.btinternet.co.uk/.

Sightseeing

Malmesbury has retained many of its eighteenth century maze-like streets and alleys, which are connected by several footbridges that span the Avon and Ingleburn River tributaries.

Just over 500 years old, **Market Cross** reaches 40 feet high and prompts all who see it to say, "Hmmmm."

Built in the seventh(!) century, only fragments of the original **Malmesbury Abbey** remain.

Every bicycle book mentions a local (read: quirky) bicycle museum, and no doubt assumes that those interested in cycling must hold a deep curiosity for those tinkers who sacrificed so bravely, paving the way for today's Grip Shift and triple chainring components. For those curious to see a nineteenth century tricycle, as well as miscellaneous Malmesbury memorabilia, the **Athelstan Museum** next to the Town Hall is for you.

The **Abbey House Gardens** is located next to the Malmesbury Abbey. Here you'll find over five acres of impressive plants and flowers in one of Britain's most notable gardens.

Restaurants

Among the more popular Malmesbury restaurants, visit the **Kings Arms Restaurant** (High Street) for standard bar food and popular fish specials, and the **Cedar Room Restaurant** (Knoll House Hotel) for award-winning regional specialties (less formal options are available in its brasserie).

Luggage Transfers

Manor Taxis: Phone: 01666 575312.
Sapphire Private Hire: 1, Pear Tree Cottage; Phone: 01666 577774.
Manor Private Hire: Phone: 01666 575311

BATH TO MALMESBURY
ROUTE NOTES

Day 3: Bath to Malmesbury

Today's ride contains some fairly challenging climbs and passes a rich collection of picture-perfect towns. Enjoy the scenery, make time for a pastry stop, and don't forget to yell "Breakdance!" whenever you pass a redhead in the center of Malmesbury (a tradition I'll proudly take credit for starting in 1995).

Distance: 24 to 46 miles

Directions (miles): From the toll bridge just outside of town: Continue **STRAIGHT**, beginning an ascent on the other side of the bridge.

    0.1: Turn **RIGHT** at the intersection at the top of the hill.

    0.3: Reach Bath Easton, continue downhill into town.

    0.5: Pass through a traffic light and continue **STRAIGHT**.

0.7: You'll come to another traffic light; turn **LEFT**.

3.2: The road will veer **RIGHT**, follow signs toward Colerne1.5, Castle Combe 5.5. You reach Colerne at 4.1.

5.5: Turn right toward Thickwood 1/4/Euridge1/2 onto Thickwood Lane.

6.1: At a crossroads, continue **STRAIGHT** to Euridge.

7.3: You'll cross over a small bridge and come to a T-intersection; turn **RIGHT**.

7.9: Veer **LEFT** toward Biddestone, following it up and to the **LEFT**.

8.7: Turn **LEFT** at the intersection toward Church Road.

8.8: Turn **LEFT** following signs to Giddea Hall/Castle Combe.

9.0: Follow the road as it bears **RIGHT** toward Giddea Hall, you'll be on Yatton Road.

10.7: At a yield sign, turn **LEFT** onto the Street. The Bell Inn will be in front of you.

10.8: Veer **LEFT** toward Castle Combe on the B4039.

12.0: You reach Upper Castle Combe, continue **STRAIGHT**.

12.1: Follow the road veering **RIGHT** toward Burton 3/Chipping Sodbury 10 on the B3049.

12.4: Turn **LEFT** toward Castle Combe 1/2. This is a good place for a lunch stop.

12.5: Turn **RIGHT** toward Grittleton on a small road.

13.8: At the T-intersection, turn **LEFT** toward Luckington 4/Alderton 3/Grittleton 1.

13.9: Cross over the highway.

14.3: You reach Grittleton.

14.5: Stop sign: Turn **RIGHT** toward Hullavington/Stanton/Malmesbury.

17.1: Reach Hullavington.

17.8: Turn **LEFT** toward Norton 1/2/Sherston 4 1/2. Do not turn right toward Malmesbury 4/Chipenham 7.

19.2: Reach Norton.

19.3: Turn **RIGHT** toward Foxley 1 1/2/Malmesbury 4.

19.4: Turn **RIGHT** for Foxley 1 1/2/Malmesbury 4. You'll pass the Vine Tree Free House on your left just after the turn.

20.2: The road will veer **LEFT**.

20.5: Reach Foxley.

20.6: Turn **RIGHT** toward Malmesbury 2 3/4.

22.6: Reach Malmesbury (town limit sign).

22.9: At the yield sign, turn **RIGHT**.

23.0: At the intersection, arriving into town, turn **RIGHT**. Head for the town center and short-stay parking.

23.3: Turn **RIGHT** following signs to information and short-stay parking. These will bring you into the parking lot in the center of town.

Background Notes
Where Am I?

Country: England

Region: The South of England, Cotswolds

County: Oxfordshire

City: Burford

Tourist Information
Burford TIC
The Brewery, Sheep Street
Burford OX18 4LP
Phone: 01993 823558
Fax: 01993 823590
burford.vic@westoxon.gov.uk
www.oxfordshirecotswolds.org

Bike Shops
Giles Cycles: 1 Alvescot Road, Carteron; Phone: 01993 842396 (Note: This shop is 4 miles from Burford).

Sightseeing
Most of your free time can be spent wandering the streets of this most famous of Cotswolds towns. But if you're longing for culture, stop in to the **Tolsey Museum** in the fifteenth-century Tolsey Hall for a look at the town's charters and Tudor artifacts.

What British town is complete without its fifteenth-century church? In Burford, there's **St John the Baptist**, whose cruciform shape and octagonal spire is home to dozens of handcrafted artworks from centuries past.

Restaurants
The **Lamb Inn** is one of my groups' favorites and serves typical pub fare in the afternoon and more elaborate meals in the evening.

Luggage Transfers
Fairways Airport & Tour Cars: 12, Meadow End Fulbrook; Burford; Phone: 01993 823152.
Burford Business Class: 94, High St.; Burford; Phone: 01993 824337.

The most venerable British profession: Doctor? No. Lawyer? No. Ready? Gardener. *Gloucestershire Tourism, www.glos-cotswolds.com*

MALMESBURY TO BURFORD
ROUTE NOTES

Day 4: Malmesbury to Burford

Burford is one of the Cotswolds' most pristine and charming towns, seemingly lost in time with its fifteenth-century buildings, twelfth-century Norman church, and a central street (High Street) lined with old coaching inns.

Flowing just north of the town is the Windrush River. Its banks are lined with inviting walking paths, the perfect place to reflect on today's glorious ride during a late-evening stroll.

Distance: 50 miles

Directions (miles): 0.0: At the intersection of High Street and Oxford Street, turn **RIGHT** onto Oxford Street. The Whole Hog Food and Ale House will be in front of you.

- 0.4: Yield sign: Follow signs for "other traffic."
- 0.9: Just after you cross the River Avon, turn **RIGHT** onto Holloway Street.
- 1.1: You'll come to a yield sign at an intersection. Continue **STRAIGHT** across onto the bridle path.
- 2.6: Turn **LEFT** toward Charleton/Cricklade.
- 3.2: Turn **RIGHT** toward Cricklade 10 and Minety 5 on the B4040.
- 3.3: Follow the road as it veers **RIGHT** on the B4040 toward Cricklade.
- 3.6: Turn **LEFT** toward Crudwell and Hankerton (Vicarage Lane). You reach Hankerton at 4.4
- 4.7: The road will bear **RIGHT** and just past this, turn **RIGHT** toward Cricklade and Minety on Cloatley Rd.
- 7.0: You reach Upper Minety. At an intersection, turn **RIGHT** for Cricklade/Oaksey/S. Ford Keynes/Cirencester.
- 7.3: Turn **LEFT** toward Oaksey 2/S. Ford Keynes 3/Cirencester 7 1/2.
- 7.5: Continue **STRAIGHT** onto Crossing Lane, toward S. Keynes/Cirencester.
- 8.5: Turn **LEFT** toward S. Keynes/Cirencester.
- 10.5: Turn **RIGHT** toward Ashton Keynes 2/Cricklade 6.
- 14.4: Turn **LEFT** onto Somerford Road.

Entering Cirencester Head to the Brewery Car Park (short term parking). There are numerous shops and restaurants. To continue the route, retrace your path and go **LEFT** onto Ashcroft Road.

- 15.6: Turn **RIGHT** onto Cricklade Road.
- 15.9: Turn **LEFT** onto the Avenue.
- 16.1: Turn **LEFT** onto Pearly Road.
- 16.2: Turn **RIGHT** onto the larger road.
- 16.3: At a roundabout, continue **STRAIGHT** toward Burford on the B4425. Just after the roundabout, turn **RIGHT** onto London Road toward Ampney Crucis 2 1/2/Poulton 5/Fairford 8.
- 18.8: Turn **LEFT** toward Ampney Crucis. The turn is just before the Crown of Crucis Hotel.
- 19.7: Veer **LEFT** with the road. Just after you veer left, turn **RIGHT**. This will be an unmarked road, just past the curve and at the top of the ascent that leads to another smaller road.
- 20.1: Turn **RIGHT** at a T-intersection and yield sign.
- 22.4: Turn **LEFT** toward Bibury.
- 23.7: At the B4425, continue straight toward Ablington 1/Winson 1 3/4. Just at the bottom of a hill, turn **RIGHT** toward Ablington/Bibury 1 1/4.
- 24.9: Turn **RIGHT** toward Bibury 3/4, which you reach at 25.4.

25.6: The Swan Hotel will be to your left; turn **LEFT** toward Aldsworth 3 1/2/Burford 10 on the B4425.

26.0: Turn **RIGHT** toward Coln Street. Aldwyns 2 onto a lane.

28.0: Veer to the **RIGHT** toward Coln Street. Aldwyns/Fairford 4.

28.7: Quenington. As you top the hill, turn **LEFT** toward Southrop/Lechlade on Fowler's Hill Road.

30.9: Turn **LEFT** at a yield sign. There is a sign here pointing backward to Macarin Woods.

32.5: Bear right with the road heading toward Southrop 1/2.

32.9: Follow the road bending **LEFT** toward Southrop/Eastleach 1 1/2.

33.1: Turn **LEFT** toward Eastleach.

33.5: Continue **STRAIGHT** toward Eastleach 1/Burford 8.

34.3: Turn **RIGHT** toward Eastleach.

34.6: Turn **RIGHT** toward Filkins 2 3/4. You'll be cycling uphill, past a bench, and veering **RIGHT**. Just past the bench, the road will fork. Take the fork **RIGHT** toward Filkins.

35.4: Continue **STRAIGHT** toward Filkins 2.

36.8: Turn **RIGHT** toward Lechlade/Burford.

36.9: Turn **RIGHT** toward Filkins/Broughton Poggs.

37.2: Cross a small white bridge, follow the road **LEFT**.

37.3: **LEFT,** then quick **RIGHT**. The Lamb Inn Free House will be just to your left.

37.4: At the B4477, continue **STRAIGHT** toward Langford/Faringdon.

38.3: Langford. As you enter town, turn **LEFT** toward Broadwell 1/Kencott 1 1/2.

39.4: Kenkot.

42.1: Continue **STRAIGHT** to Holwell 1 on the single-track road.

42.7: Turn **RIGHT** toward Shilton/Burford.

43.1: Cross the A361, continue **STRAIGHT** toward Shilton.

44.6: Continue toward Shilton 1/4.

45.2: Cross the B4020. Continue **STRAIGHT**, following a sign for the Oxfordshire Cycleway.

46.2: Turn **LEFT**, following the Oxfordshire Cycleway signs toward Swinbrook 1 1/2/Witney 5 1/4.

46.5: A40 intersection; turn **LEFT**. This is a larger road and there will be heavy traffic. Follow the Oxfordshire Cycleway sign and head toward Cheltenham/Burford on the A40.

46.6: Turn **RIGHT** toward Swinbrook 1 on a single-track road. There will also be a sign for Oxfordshire Cycleway.

47.4: Turn **LEFT** toward Burford 2 1/4.

48.6: Turn **RIGHT** toward Burford 1 1/4, still following the Oxfordshire Cycleway signs.

49.3: Burford.

Background Notes
Where Am I?
Country: England
Region: Heart of England, Cotswolds
County: Gloucestershire
City: Stow-on-the-Wold

You wanna talk chutney salsa? Then you wanna talk Cotswolds. Delish.
Gloucestershire Tourism, www.glos-cotswolds.com

Tourist Information

Stow-on-the-Wold TIC
Hollis House, The Square
Stow-on-the-Wold GL54 1F
stowvic@cotswold.gov.uk
www.cotswold.gov.uk/tourism;
www.glos-cotswolds.com

Bike Shops

The closest shops are **Hartwell's** (High Street, Bourton-on-the-Water, 3.5 miles away; Phone: 01451 820405); and Country Lanes Cycle Centre (Station Car Park, Moreton-in-Marsh; 4.4 miles away; Phone: 01608 650065; cots@countrylanes.co.uk; www.countrylanes.co.uk).

Sightseeing

Among the town's sites, notice the fourteenth-century cross in the bustling **Market Square** (dozens of popular pubs and cafés surround it today) and its well-preserved stocks where guilty parties were publicly humiliated centuries ago. Over the past 20 to 30 years, Stow has developed a reputation throughout Britain for offering fine antiques. Among its 60 or so dealers, stop by **Huntington's** (Church Street), one of England's largest antiques dealers.

Restaurants

For dinner, stop by the **Grapevine Hotel and Restaurant** (Sheep Street) for mid-priced international dishes, or **Stow Lodge Hotel and Restaurant** (The Square) for savory homecooked specialties.

Luggage Transfers

F John's Private Hire: 51 Little Normans Longlevens, Gloucester; Phone: 01452 385050; bookings@jphcars.co.uk; http://www.jphcars.co.uk/.
Ian Swallow: 07775 876888 (Cell).
First Associated Taxis: 5 Coney Hill Road, Gloucester; Phone: 01452 523523.

BURFORD TO STOW-ON-THE-WOLD
ROUTE NOTES

Days 5 and 6: Burford to Stow-on-the-Wold; Stow-on-the-Wold Layover
Today's route leads you past many of the Cotswolds' most scenic towns and villages, including Barrington, Rissington, Bourton-on-the-Water, and the Slaughters (Upper and Lower). It's such an enchanting area that you can easily spend two days here, taking advantage of the Stow layover ride.

    Once a prosperous wool trading center, Stow-on-the-Wold retains much of its ancient charm and is a popular tourist spot for Cotswolds visitors.

Distance: 17 to 43 miles

Directions (miles): Turn **LEFT** onto High Street, heading uphill. Just ahead (approximately 150 yards), turn **RIGHT** onto Sheep St.

    0.5: Turn **RIGHT**. This turn is unmarked, but it will come just at the end of a stone wall before you head uphill.

    2.4: Little Barrington.

    3.1: Turn **RIGHT** at the T-intersection. There will be a red phone booth as you make the turn.

    3.3: Just past the Fox Inn, veer **RIGHT** toward Great Barrington 1/4/Rissingtons.

    3.5: Great Barrington.

    3.8: Bear **LEFT** toward Little Rissington 4 1/2/ Bourton-on-the-Sea 6.

    6.0: Turn **LEFT** toward Great Rissington 1/2/ Bourton-on-the-Sea 3.

    8.5: Turn **LEFT** toward Bourton-on-the-Sea 1 1/4.

    8.6: Bourton-on-the-Sea (several shops, restaurants, markets).

    10.1: Turn **RIGHT** onto Meadow Way.

    10.3: At a roundabout, turn **LEFT**.

10.6: Turn **RIGHT** toward Stow on the A429.

10.9: Turn **LEFT** toward the Slaughters (hotels, restaurants). The turn will be just before an Esso Gas Station.

11.2: Lower Slaughter.

11.5: Bear **LEFT** toward Upper Slaughter 1 and go over a small bridge. Follow the water through town.

12.1: Continue to the **RIGHT** toward Upper Slaughter 1/4/ Cheltenham 15.

12.3: Turn **RIGHT** toward Upper Slaughter/Lower Swell 2.

14.0: Turn **LEFT** toward Lower Swell 1/2/Stow-on-the-Wold 1 1/2.

14.4: Turn **RIGHT** toward Stow 1 on the B4068.

15.3: At the bottom of a hill, turn **RIGHT** toward Upper Swell/Stow 1 on the B4077.

16.6: As you enter Stow, follow signs to town center.

STOW-ON-THE-WOLD LOOP RIDE

Distance: 26 miles

Directions (miles): 0.0: Wells Lane behind the Royalist Hotel; turn **LEFT** onto Digbeth Street. Just ahead, turn **RIGHT** at a fork by a red post box for Maugersbury 5.

0.5: Turn **RIGHT** at T-intersection for Maugersbury.

0.6: Turn **LEFT** at crossroads.

0.8: Turn **RIGHT** at end of village loop.

1.0 Turn **RIGHT** at crossroads for Bledington 3/Kingham 5.

2.6: Take the **RIGHT** fork sign toward Icomb 1.5.

4.3: Turn **LEFT** for Rissington 3/Burford 8.

5.3: Turn **LEFT** at crossroads toward Swindon A424.

5.8: Turn **LEFT** for Church Westcote/Gawcombe.

9.8: Turn **RIGHT** on B4450 for Chipping Norton 5/ Kingham 1.

12.3: Turn **LEFT** for Ch. Norton 3.

13.5: Turn **LEFT**, tiny fork, for Cornwall.

13.6: Turn **LEFT** at unmarked T-intersection, continue downhill.

15.7: Turn **RIGHT** at crossroads sign posted Chastleton.

16.2: Cross the A436 sign toward Chastleton 1.

19.3: Turn **LEFT** on the A44 toward Eversham/Moreton in Marsh.

20.0: Turn **LEFT** on a small road toward Evenlode 2.

21.0: Turn **LEFT** for Evenlode 1/Broadwell 3.

22.0: Reach Evenlode and follow signs to Broadwell.

24.0: Turn **RIGHT** then left for Stow-on-the-Wold 1 1/2.

24.1: **LEFT** to Stow-on-the-Wold 1 1/2.

25.2: Turn **LEFT** on the A429 for Stow, then follow town center sign.

25.7: Town center.

Background Notes
Where Am I?
Country: England

Region: Heart of England, Shakespeare Country, Cotswolds

County: Warwickshire

City: Stratford-Upon-Avon

Parks abound in the Cotswolds, which are welcoming retreats where you can rest your weary legs. *Colchester Borough Council, U.K.; www.visitcolchester.com*

Tourist Information
Stratford-Upon-Avon TIC
Bridgefoot
Stratford-Upon-Avon
Warwickshire CV7 6GW
Phone: 01789 293127
Fax: 01789 295262
stratfordtic@shakespeare-country.co.uk; www.shakespeare-country.co.uk

Bike Shops
Clarke's Cycles: Guild Street, Stratford; Phone: 01789 205057.
Rockingham's Cycle Store: 2 Market Hill, Southam; Phone: 01926 812685.

Sightseeing
Owing to its claim as the birthplace to William Shakespeare, Stratford has evolved into a culturally rich city with several sightseeing opportunities.

Although **Shakespeare's Birthplace** is a replication of the 1564 Shakespeare home, here you'll find extensive background information on the world's greatest playwright.

The **Holy Trinity Church** is the burial site of William Shakespeare.

Continuing with the Shakespearean theme, **Anne Hathaway's Cottage** is a 12-room Tudor farmhouse where Shakespeare's bride-to-be resided until 1582. (This is the bedroom where she slept, this is the table where she ate, this is the spoon she might have used . . ..)

Harvard House (High Street) is the most elaborate house in Stratford and former home to Katherine Rogers, John Harvard's (founder of the college that bears his family name) mother.

Restaurants

For fairly upscale dining, try **The Boathouse** (Swan's Nest Lane), which sits alongside the River Avon and provides a gondola service to transport its patrons to the Royal Shakespeare Theatre performances. There's also the **Box Tree Restaurant** (located in the Royal Shakespeare Theatre), one of Stratford's best, with views of the Avon and a fairly expensive menu of regional specialties.

Local pubs abound, and you can share a pint where the famous previously tread. Try **The White Swan Inn** (Rother Street), Stratford's oldest building and former resting spot of Shakespeare.

Nightlife

The **Royal Shakespeare Theatre** is perched alongside the River Avon, and this internationally renowned complex serves as the launching pad for The Royal Shakespeare Company's productions (they're usually transferred to London within the year). Advance reservations are strongly recommended. Phone: 01789 403434; info@rsc.org.uk; www.rsc.org.uk.

STOW-ON-THE-WOLD TO STRATFORD-AVON
ROUTE NOTES

Days 7 and 8: Stow-on-the-Wold to Stratford-Upon-Avon; Stratford-Upon-Avon Layover
You'll pedal anxiously today for Stratford, birthplace of Shakespeare and an important cultural destination today. Your tour's last bike ride finishes along a dedicated bike path, following a dismantled railroad track up to Stratford's town limit.0.0: Begin in square near library/tourist office/parking lot; turn **LEFT** on A429.

0.2: Turn **RIGHT** for Lower Swell.

1.0: Lower Swell.

1.1: Turn **RIGHT** toward Upper Swell. Head toward Guiting Power 6.

4.7: Turn **RIGHT** toward Snowshill.

9.4: Veer **LEFT** toward Snowshill.

10.0: Turn **RIGHT** toward Chipping Campden 5.

10.8: Turn **LEFT** toward the Broadway Tower County Park 1 1/2.

11.0: Turn **LEFT**.

12.6: At an intersection with the A44, continue **STRAIGHT** for Picnic Area and Saint Bury 2.

13.4: Turn **LEFT** toward Saint Bury 1 1/2/Willersey 1 3/4.

14.0: Turn **RIGHT** toward Chipping Campden 2 1/4/Mickelton 5. Veer **LEFT** and continue toward Chipping Campden 1 3/4/ Mickelton 4 1/4.

16.2: Turn **LEFT** toward Evesham/Stratford (B4081) B4632.

16.3: Take the **RIGHT** fork toward (B4081) Stratford/Mickleton 2/Hidcote 3.

16.5: Turn **RIGHT** toward Hidcote Boyce 1/Hidcote Bartrim 1 3/4.

17.9: Turn **LEFT** toward Hidcote Bartrim 1 3/4/Mickelton 2 1/2.

18.7: Turn **LEFT** to Mickelton 1 (just before the gardens).

19.5: Turn **RIGHT**. Just after the turn, you'll come to a roundabout. Exit the roundabout toward Stratford on the B4632.

20.1: At a roundabout, exit **LEFT** toward Stratford on the B4632.

20.7: Continue **STRAIGHT** toward Long Marston.

21.7: Continue **STRAIGHT** toward Welford-on-Avon.

22.6: Long Marston. Continue **STRAIGHT** toward Long Marston 1/4/Welford 2 1/2.

23.1: There will be a BT phone booth to the left. Turn **RIGHT** onto Wyre Lane and **RIGHT** at a fork 0.2 miles ahead.

23.4: You reach the bike path, which leads into Stratford. Turn **LEFT** onto the bike path. Follow the path until it reaches Stratford, then cycle toward the town center. It's an additional 8 miles to finish the ride from here.

Most towns welcome visitors to their Sunday morning church services. Cyclists, do everyone a favor, though, and leave your spandex shorts at home. *Gloucestershire Tourism,* *www.glos-cotswolds.com*

STRATFORD-UPON-AVON
LOOP RIDE

These directions begin from the car park in town.

0.0: Turn **RIGHT** out of the car park. Veer **RIGHT** with the road toward Weston 3/4/Welford 1 1/4.

1.3: **RIGHT** at a T-intersection toward Welford 1/4/Barton 3.

2.6: **RIGHT** at a T-intersection with the B439 toward Stratford. Just after this turn, take a quick **LEFT** toward Binton 1/2.

4.2: Turn **LEFT** toward Temple Grafton 3/4/Bidford 4.

4.9: Just after the church, turn **RIGHT** onto Croft Lane (Haselor 1 3/4).

6.1: Cross the A46.

7.0: Turn **RIGHT** toward Walcote 1/4/Aston Cantlow 2.

7.8: Continue **STRAIGHT** onto Mill Lane; continue **STRAIGHT** toward Aston Cantlow 1 1/4/Wilmcote 2 3/4.

8.9: Turn **RIGHT** onto Brook Road toward Billesley 1 3/4/Wilmcote 2 1/2/Stratford 7.

9.7: Turn **LEFT** toward Wilmcote 1 1/4/Mary Arden's House/Leisure Drive.

10.9: To visit Mary Arden's House, turn **LEFT** onto The Green toward Mary Arden's House/Stratford 4/Henley 7. Otherwise, continue **STRAIGHT**.

11.7: Turn **LEFT** toward Stratford 4/Anne Hathaway's Cottage 2.

13.1: Cross over the A46.

13.2: At a yield sign, turn **LEFT** toward the town center on the A422.

13.7: Turn **RIGHT** onto Church Lane toward Shottery 1/2/Anne Hathaway's Cottage 1/2.

14.1: At a roundabout, turn **RIGHT** to visit Anne Hathaway's Cottage. To return to the route, come back to this roundabout and follow signs for Town Centre.

FRANCE

I love cycling in France. The geography is varied and offers endless opportunities for exploration. The roads are some of the best in Europe, with clear and omnipresent signage, and the people are some of the friendliest (?!) in Europe, who maintain a deep respect for cyclists, except those who insist in rehashing old *Facts of Life* episodes.

The tours in this section are some of my favorites and offer diverse scenery and cultural highlights. Bon voyage!

Cycling Overview

The terrain on the Dordogne trip is challenging, but not overwhelming, and cyclists of moderate ability should be able to complete all of the rides. Some walking may be necessary, but a triple chain ring should enable you to tackle the longer climbs.

The South of France tour is one of this book's most challenging itineraries and you must be in very good cycling shape to attempt the ride. There are few flat stretches, and most days include climbs of 2 to 4 miles in length.

At French markets, the plaid shopping cart is the fashion rage. Are you watching, Madison Avenue? *Niels Povlsen*

The oppressive summer heat adds to the difficulty of the Dordogne and South of France tours. I urge you to avoid these tours in July and August, when the sun can make the rides torturous. The latest I've offered the Dordogne trip is the first week in July, and temperatures routinely reached the upper 80s and lower 90s. The same goes for the South of France trip. In fact, temperatures topped 100 degrees for several days this past summer. Ouch.

The Loire Valley trip is for cyclists of all abilities and is designed to offer a brief but culturally rich introduction to French cycling. If you're looking for an intense workout, this tour won't be for you. Instead, the focus is on visiting the most interesting places in an area known for its castles, food, and wine.

Nothing says snoozeville to your friends at home like a photo album full of castles. Author's tip: You'll attract much more interest if you throw in an occasional shot of dead birds. *Niels Povlsen*

Tourist Information

The French Government Tourist Office is a wealth of information, and its web-site is detailed and continually updated: http://www.franceguide.com/. You can download brochures, link to specific regions, and have a grand ol' time browsing through a well-designed site. If you've got any further questions, you can reach contacts directly at the following:

U.S.:
Phone: 410–286-8310
Fax: 00 1 212 838 78 55
Email: info.us@franceguide.com
U.K.
Phone: 09068 244 123 (60p/min at all times)
Fax: (020) 7493 6594
Email: info.uk@franceguide.com

Cycling in a foreign environment can be intimi-dating, especially when traffic increases. Walk your bike, if necessary, until the congestion subsides. *Niels Povlsen*

France's Dordogne abounds with culinary treats. Unfortunately, this dish sucked. *Niels Povlsen*

Climate

For the Dordogne and South of France trips, make sure you have good sunscreen. That's a must because the sun will beat down on you without the filter of cloud cover.

The Loire Valley trip is an exception and temperatures are usually moderate throughout the summer. Take good rain gear because it rains often.

Combining Tours

If you'd like to combine the tours in this section, you can do so with convenient rail connections. France's national train system, SNCF, maintains an excellent website with detailed ticketing information available in French and English (http://www.sncf.com/indexe.htm). When you consult its schedules, under *Seating Preferences*, click on *Add Preferences* to select trains that accept bicycles.

The Dordogne and Loire trips can be easily reached by train with multiple connections throughout the day. The only difficult connection is the South of France tour, since its starting-point city is not served by either train or bus. However, it's a modest taxi ride from the Nice Airport or train station, and it's even cheaper from nearby Grasse or Vence. See the individual tour descriptions for detailed information on arriving and departing.

Currency

France has adopted the Euro (€), so if you're flying from Ireland, there's no need to stop at an American Express Currency Exchange.

Travel Advice

Keep these important travel tips in mind as you're cycling through France:

• Don't be offended that your French hosts rarely smile. They're not happy.

• Confirm with your butcher the source of his "famous" paté.

• Avoid Vittel, Volvic, and Badoit bottled waters. They suck.

• Breakfast in France is not a big deal. A croissant and coffee is typical fare, so don't expect oatmeal and bacon. On the other hand, demand that your wait-staff sing when they bring your order.

• Buy a *pain au chocolat* at a local patisserie. When no one's looking, smoosh the pastry in your right hand and morph the roll into a condensed chocolate treat. Then, pop the entire ball in your mouth and savor the delicate flavors. Chew twice, then swallow. Know what? It's fun!

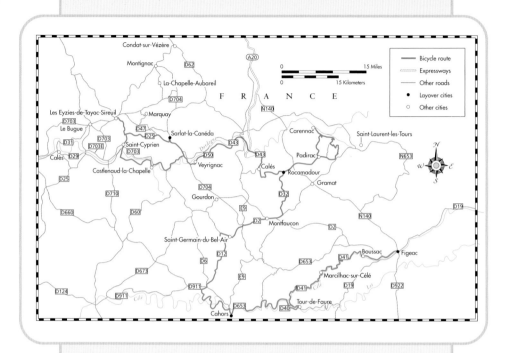

DORDOGNE & SOUTHWESTERN FRANCE

The Dordogne is a land frozen in time (favorite TV show of the locals? *Mannix*). It's an area where both history and nature peacefully coexist with its prehistoric caverns that perfectly complement its seemingly endless stretches of tranquil, picturesque scenery. The challenging landscape (this area is not flat!) leads you past dense pockets of fragrant woods, gushing rivers and streams, majestic cliffs, and remarkable impressions of prehistoric humanity. Food and wine connoisseurs will love this trip because the area overflows with scrumptious food and drink—savory rewards at the end of each cycling day. This tour incorporates the most important and impressive towns of this area at a pace that allows ample time to intimately explore its abundant sites and treasures.

When to Go

You can enjoy this trip from early April through late October, although some of the smaller towns can feel deserted before May. Temperatures during July and August are brutally hot, and unless you feel comfortable in 90-plus temperatures, stick to the spring and fall. Cycling through the end of October is certainly possible and very pleasant, but the days become quite short as November approaches.

Below is a rough guideline of what you can expect for climate on this tour:

BORDEAUX[37]

MONTH	AVERAGE HIGH (°F)	AVERAGE LOW (°F)	AVERAGE PRECIPITATION (IN)
JANUARY	49	36	3.0
FEBRUARY	52	38	2.5
MARCH	57	40	2.6
APRIL	61	43	2.6
MAY	67	50	2.8
JUNE	73	55	2.6
JULY	79	59	2.1
AUGUST	79	59	2.3
SEPTEMBER	74	54	2.8
OCTOBER	64	48	3.4
NOVEMBER	56	41	3.5
DECEMBER	50	38	3.4

Arrival and Departure
Air

Bordeaux and Toulouse airports offer the closest connections, but when you include airport transfer times (there are no direct U.S.-Bordeaux or U.S.-Toulouse flights, so you'll need to transfer in Paris or another European city) it can be just as quick to take a fast train from Paris (assuming you were able to find a direct flight into Paris). You'll have no trouble finding flights into either one of the Paris airports. Detailed flight information for both Charles de Gaulle and Orly airports (Paris' two main airports) can be found at www.adp.fr. You'll find information for Bordeaux and Toulouse airports at:

Bordeaux Merignac Airport:

http://www.bordeaux.aeroport.fr/.

Toulouse Blagnac Airport:

www.toulouse.aeroport.fr/fr/default.asp.

To and From the Airport
Taxi

If you're wealthy enough to take a taxi from Paris to Sarlat or Figeac, you might as well hire a helicopter. It'll be quicker and you'll arrive in time for lunch.

---

[37] From http://www.usatoday.com/weather/climate/europe/france/wbordeux.htm.

This used car dealership in southwestern France was surprisingly quiet when I arrived. I'm told it's best to avoid weekends, when business is brisk. *Niels Povlsen*

Taxis from Bordeaux to Sarlat will run about 220 Euros. A reliable local contact is **Taxis Eric Faugere** (Phone: 0553 29 87 89; taxi.eric.faugere@wanadoo.fr). Expect to pay at least 100 Euros more from Toulouse. From Figeac, contact **Taxi Luc Jean Michel** (Phone: 0565 50 00 20; Fax: 0565 14 11 84); or **Taxi Claude Busson** (2 Avenue, Jean Jaures; Phone: 0608 42 38 24).

Public Transportation

France's train system, SNCF, provides a detailed, up-to-date website with pricing and schedules (www.voyages-sncf.com). Plan on the following times and prices for transferring to Sarlat:

TO SARLAT

Airport	Travel Time	Cost (Euros)
Paris (either airport)	5h25	51
Bordeaux	2h45	20
Toulouse	4h15	24

FROM FIGEAC

Airport	Travel Time	Cost (Euros)
Paris (either airport)	5h25	51
Bordeaux	2h45	20
Toulouse	4h15	24

Bike Rental

Need a bike for your trip? Stop by **Christian Chapoulie** (4 Avenue de Selves, Sarlat; Phone: 0553 59 06 11; Fax: 0553 30 25 44). He's open year-round and rental bikes start at €11 a day or € 55 per week.

Cycling Notes

Thanks to this tour's abundance of rich, duck-related food products, you'll need to pedal most of the hills to avoid obtaining the classic LVCFA (Las Vegas Charter Flight Ass).[38] Be sure to take some bubble wrap or a couple of thick t-shirts along your daily rides. They make great wine bottle protectors for the local vintages you're sure to purchase.

Maps

Michelin #75, *Bordeaux, Perigueux, Tulle*; 1:200,000; and Michelin #79, *Bordeaux, Agen, Montauban*; 1:200,000.

Accommodations Notes

There are loads of campgrounds and hotels in almost every price category. Make sure to book early, especially if you're heading over in the summer. Popular hotels tend to fill quickly.

Background Notes
Where Am I?

Country: France
Region: Aquitaine
Department: Dordogne
City: Sarlat-la-Caneda

The French have more castles per-capita than any country in the world. Just a guess, but probably true. *Niels Povlsen*

---

[38] Remember your weekend trip to Vegas in 1998? How tough was it to reach your airplane's restroom with one of the other passengers standing in the aisle? Now you know what I'm talking about.

English Translation: The Dordogne. Don't be discouraged, not all French signage is this confusing. *Niels Povlsen*

Tourist Information

Sarlat Office de Tourisme
Rue Tourny
Sarlat 24203
Phone: 0553 31 45 45
Fax: 0553 59 19 44
info@ot-sarlat-perigord.fr
www.ot-sarlat-perigord.fr
(French)

Bike Shops

Christian Chapoulie: 4 Avenue de Selves, Sarlat;
Phone: 0553 59 06 11;
Fax: 0553 30 25 44.

Sightseeing

Grottes de Lascaux is the most important (or at least the most famous) prehistoric site in Europe. Four boys discovered the cave in 1940 while searching for their lost dog. A replica of the caves, **Lascaux II**, was built in 1983, as a result of extensive damage to the original caves. *NOTE: Tickets must be purchased in Montignac, next to the tourist office. The caves are located 17 miles north of Sarlat in Montignac (closest train station—Condat, 6 miles north of Montignac). I usually arrange for my groups to stop at the caves en route from the airport. You can do the same if you're hiring a private driver; otherwise, you can contact **Taxis Eric Faugere**; Phone: 0553 29 87 89;* taxi.eric.faugere@wanadoo.fr. *He's a very reliable local driver who can take you to/from the caves.*

Cathedrale St-Sacerdos is a sixteenth-century cathedral that replaced its twelfth-century ancestor.

Maison de la Boetie, Sarlat's most significant architectural building, was built in the early sixteenth century and was the 1530 birthplace of Etienne de la Boetie, a writer who is thought to have been an inspiration for Rousseau.

Restaurants

Sarlat is filled with dozens of lively cafés and restaurants. Among my guests' favorites are the **Hotel de la Madeleine** (1 pl. de la Petite Rigaudie), which offers daily specials that incorporate fresh, local products; the **Le Regent Brasserie** (pl. de la Liberte) offers savory duck dishes; and **Le Quatre Saisons** (Cote de Toulouse) features a duck-heavy menu.

The Dordogne is famous for its duck dishes. If you're a fan of duck (as opposed to a duck fan—animal preservationist, or a Mighty Ducks fan/Anaheim hockey supporter), you'll be happy like a pig for the duration of your tour. There's duck everything, at every meal. *Niels Povlsen*

Luggage Transfers

Taxis Eric Faugere; Phone: 0553 29 87 89; taxi.eric.faugere@wanadoo.fr.

SARLAT LAYOVER RIDE

Days 1 and 2: Sarlat

Surrounded by wooded hills, Sarlat preserves much of its centuries-old charm in a market-town atmosphere. Its winding medieval streets lead you through a vast collection of shops and stalls, many peddling a delicious assortment of locally produced foods. Your 28-mile, layover day ride is a virtual treasure trove of prehistoric sightseeing, including a visit to Les Eyzies de Tayac. *loop*.

Distance: 54km (34 miles)

Directions (kilometers): This ride begins at the central post office.

    0.0: Follow the signs to Gourdon, Bergerac, and Cahors on the Rue Emile Faure.

    1.0: At the roundabout, turn **RIGHT** on the D46 toward Bergerac (under the bridge).

    1.5: Turn **RIGHT** for Meyrals on the D25 (small, quiet road).

    7.2: Intersection; continue **RIGHT** on the D25 toward Meyrals (left is the C6).

    17.5: Turn **LEFT** to St. Cyprien 4 on the D48 (right is Les Eyzies 6).

Otherwise, for a great detour to Les Eyzies:

    ***RIGHT** to Les Eyzies 6 on the D48.*

    *23.5: Intersection with the D47. Turn **LEFT** toward the Les Eyzies Centre/Autre Sites/Monuments.*

    *24.0: In Les Eyzies on the D47. To continue the route, turn **LEFT** on the D706 toward Campagne. To join the main route, follow the D35 to D49 to D48 to D50 to D53, meeting with the main route at Parc Josephine Baker on the D53 (32.0km on the main route).*

    20.1: Follow this road into St. Cyprien.

21.5: Intersection; turn **RIGHT** toward the Centre Ville and then follow the "toute directions" signs.

22.0: Roundabout; exit onto the D48 toward Siorac/Bergerac/Berbiguieres/Marnac.

22.6: Cross the D703.

25.2: The road will very briefly turn to dirt as you travel between cornfields and cow pastures.

26.3: Turn **RIGHT** at an unmarked intersection.

27.3: At the roundabout, turn **LEFT** toward Envaux/Les Milandes.

29.3: Envaux.

32.0: **STRAIGHT** on the D53 toward Chateau de Castelnaud/Autre directions. On your left is the Parc de Loisirs Josephine Baker.

36.7: Turn **LEFT** following *autre directions* and cross the river.

37.8: Turn **RIGHT** toward La Roc Gageac 2.5 (or detour left toward Parc du Chateau de Marqueyssac 1 to visit Marqueyssac Garden).

42.9: Turn **LEFT** toward Sarlat 10 and Vitrac 2.5.

45.7: Turn **RIGHT** on the D703 toward Cingle de Montfort.

48.5: Montfort. Turn **LEFT** toward Sarlat la Caneda (uphill).

51.5: The road curves right near soccer fields.

53.5: **LEFT** at the yield sign.

54.2: Reach the roundabout with the fountain and turn **RIGHT** toward centre ville.

Background Notes
Where Am I?
Country: France
Region: Midi-Pyrenees
Department: Lot
City: Rocamadour

Tourist Information
Rocamadour Office de Tourisme
Maison du Tourisme
Rocamadour 46500
Phone: 0565 33 22 00
Fax: 0565 33 22 01
rocamadour@wanadoo.fr
www.rocamadour.com

Bike Shops
The tourist office rents bicycles (see address information above) and can offer very limited supplies. The closest bike shops are in Souillac, 12 miles from town:

The worst day cycling in the Dordogne beats the best day taking the #151 bus down Chicago's Michigan Avenue. *Niels Povlsen*

Carrefour du Cycle: 23 Avenue du General de Gaulle, Souillac; Phone: 0565 37 07 52.
Copeyre: Quercyland, Souillac; Phone: 0565 32 72 61.

Sightseeing

Rocamadour's streets are lined with buildings that date to the twelfth century. Spread out among four levels, you'll find (1) the valley below the Cite; (2) the medieval Cite (full of shops, cafes, etc.); (3) the level above the Cite that features the chapels; (4) and the plateau 500 meters above the valley with fourteenth-century chateau L'Hospitalet (the area just east of the plateau along the D32 is a bustling tourist area). There's a cable car, open from 8 a.m. to 8 p.m., that connects the upper and lower levels.

The main street of the **Cite** is connected to the chapels and plateau above by the Grand Escalier (223 steps). In the Cite, you'll find the **Chapelle Notre Dame**, home to the smoke-blackened Black Virgin.

L'Hospitalet offers a wonderful view of the Cite below from its chateau ramparts. You can listen to an audio guide and enjoy a birdseye view of the city.

The Grotte des Merveilles (next to the tourist office) displays stalactites and prehistoric drawings. It is open from 10 a.m. to 2 p.m., and 3 p.m. to 6 p.m.

Luggage Transfers

Andre Floch Taxis: Blanat 46500 Rocamadour; Phone:: 0565 33 63 10.

SARLAT TO ROCAMADOUR
ROUTE NOTES

Days 3 and 4: Sarlat to Rocamadour; Rocamadour Layover

The route from Sarlat snakes along the Dordogne River, offering miles of wonderful scenery, including the Grottes de Lacave and its extensive network of caves. The view as you approach Rocamadour is truly impressive. With its castle ramparts reaching high into the sky, Rocamadour's collection of medieval buildings clings precariously to the top of a limestone cliff. Your layover day ride visits the Gouffre de Padirac, a massive collection of cave galleries whose limestone walls were carved by a subterranean river.

Distance: 63.5

Directions (kilometers): 0.0: Begin at the post office in the middle of Sarlat. Follow signs for Gourdon, Bergerac, and Souillac. This will put you on the Rue Emile Faure, then Rue de Cahors, then Rue Gabriel Tarde.

1.4: At the roundabout with a fountain in the center, follow the sign **LEFT** toward Complexe Sportiv de la Caneda. As you go under the bridge, turn **RIGHT** for Etrier de Vitrac. This will put you on the Ave. Edmond Rostand. Continue on this street as it becomes Ave. Docteur Bossel.

2.8: Turn **LEFT** on Rue Jacques Anquetil.

3.3: There is no road sign here, but this is the Avenue de la Caneda. Turn **RIGHT**.

4.5: Turn **LEFT** toward Montfort (downhill), and then turn **RIGHT** at the next sign for Montfort (there will be a soccer field to your left).

7.5: Turn **LEFT** on the D703 for Carsac 2/Cingle de Montfort.

10.1: You can turn **LEFT** here and see a twelfth-century church.

10.5: Turn **RIGHT** on the D704 toward Grolejac 3/Gourdon 17/Carlux 11.

10.6: Go under a bridge to an intersection with the D703. Turn **RIGHT** to Cahors 62/Grolejac 4/Gourdon 16. This stretch of road can be busy, so be careful.

13.4: In Grolejac, there is a grocery store on the right that's open 8:00 a.m. to 12:30 p.m. and 3:30 p.m. to 7:30 p.m.

13.5: Just ahead, turn **LEFT** onto the D50 toward Veyrignac 2.5 and the Chateau de Fenelon.

15.6: Veyrignac.

19.2: Continue **STRAIGHT** on the D50 out of Ste. Mondane.

20.8: Ste. Julien de Lampon. Boulangerie here.

22.2: Intersection, continue **STRAIGHT** on the D50 toward Le Roc 7/Mareuil 5.

32.4: There will be a fork in the road, continue to the **RIGHT** (unmarked) (left will be the D255 to Souillac 3).

36.1: Turn **LEFT** on the N20.

36.4: As you enter Souillac, turn **RIGHT** toward Pinsac 4.5 and the Chateau de la Treyne on the D43.

42.9: Follow the D43 **STRAIGHT** for Grottes de la Cave 4/Rocamadour 14.

45.4: Turn **RIGHT** toward Cales 4 on the D23 (or to visit the cave: turn left toward Grottes de la Cave 1.5/Rocamadour 12. Retrace your steps to this intersection to continue).

49.5: Turn **LEFT** on the D673 toward Moulin de Cougnaguet/Rocamadour 13.

63.5: As the road curves left and the valley is in front of you, turn **RIGHT** toward Le Chateau. Follow the road to Rocamadour and the town center.

ROCAMADOUR LOOP RIDE

Distance: 64 km

Directions (km): 0.0: Begin at the tourist office on the D673. Take the D673 toward Brive 55 (green sign)/Grfe. de Padirac.

13.0: Padirac. You can turn **LEFT** to visit Gfre. de Padirac on the D90. To continue: Turn **RIGHT** on the D673 toward St. Cere 14/Bretenoux 14/Chateau de Castelnau 12.

15.1: Intersection with the D14, continue **STRAIGHT** on the D673 toward Autoire 6.

17.7: Turn **LEFT** on the D38 toward Autoire la Cascade 3.

20.5: Reach Autoire (good lunch spot). A few hundred yards ahead, turn **LEFT** on the D135 toward Loubressac 5 (this is a 180-degree left turn).

23.0: Segonzac (no facilities).

24.0: Intersection, continue **STRAIGHT** to Loubressac 2.

25.8: Loubressac.

26.0: Turn **RIGHT** on the D118 toward Grfe. de Padirac/Rocamadour/Chateau de Castelnau.

27.1: Turn **RIGHT** on the D14 toward Bretenoux 7/Chateau de Castelnau 6.

30.0: Intersection, turn **LEFT** on the D30 toward Bretenoux 4/Carennac 7/Chateau de Castelnau 2. The D30 runs along the river, you can cross at 2 points to visit Castelnau. Follow the D30 with the river to your right toward Gintrac 3.

33.8: Reach Gintrac and continue **STRAIGHT** to Carennac.

40.6: Turn **LEFT** on the D3 (smaller road) toward Magnagues 2.

42.3: Turn **RIGHT** for Padirac.

44.0: Turn **RIGHT**, unmarked.

44.1: Turn **RIGHT** for Padirac.

46.6: **LEFT** on the D90 toward Gfre. de Padirac 2.

48.4: Gfre. de Padirac.

48.6: Roundabout, exit at 12 o'clock toward Souillac 37/Rocamadour 14. Follow the D90 for Padirac.

51.0: Intersection in Padirac; turn **RIGHT** on the D673 toward the A20 Paris (blue sign)/Souillac 31/Rocamadour 13/Alvignac 6.

57.4: Alvignac.

64.1: Return to the tourist office.

Background Notes
Where Am I?
Country: France
Region: Midi-Pyrenees
Department: Lot
City: Cahors

French towns are a potpourri of bustling markets that are spread evenly throughout the week. Looking for an autographed first edition of *Le Petit Prince*? You'll find it here, along with basil. *Niels Povlsen*

Tourist Information
Cahors Office de Tourisme
Place Francois Mitterand
Cahors 46000
Phone: 0565 53 20 65
Fax: 0565 53 20 74
cahors@wanadoo.fr;
www.tourisme-lot.com;
www.mairie-cahors.fr

Bike Shops
Cycles C7: 117, Blvd. Leon Gambetta;
Phone: 0565 22 66 60; Fax: 0565 22 56 95.

Sightseeing
There are many popular sites as you wander the medieval streets of Cahors.

The **Cathedrale St-Etienne** (Pl. Chapou) is a sixth century, fortress-like church that has endured a long history of invasions.

As you round the corner, the leaves rustling in the background like a classical symphony, the landscape unfolds, and there before you winds the mighty Dordogne, a sweeping river that carves its way through the sumptuous landscape. "Honey! Check this out!" you scream to your spouse, who's cycling ahead. "It's fabulous!" *Niels Povlsen*

Musee Henri Martin (Rue Emile Zola) displays paintings of Southwestern France landscapes. It is open Monday through Saturday from 11 a.m. to 6 p.m. and Sundays from 2 p.m. to 6 p.m.

The **Pont Valentre** bridge was built in the fourteenth century and has six arches and three towers. It is a prime example of European medieval defense architecture (EMDA).

Maison Henry IV (R. St-Urcisse, Phone: 05 65 35 04 35) is the sixteenth-century private residence of Henry IV. It is open from 10 a.m. to 12 p.m., and 2:00 p.m. to 5:30 p.m. You can shop for regional food products at Les Halles (Pl. Galdemer), a festive market that offers the very finest produce, meats, poultry, and wines. It is open daily (except Mondays) from 8:00 a.m. to 12:30 p.m. and 3:00 p.m. to 7:00 p.m.

The **Musee de la Resistance** (Espace Bassieres) offers insight into the World War II French Resistance. It is open daily from 2 p.m. to 6 p.m.

Restaurants

Auberge du Vieux (Rue St. Urcisse) is very popular for fish specialties; **L'Avapagous** (134 Rue Saint Urcisse) is famous for both duck and fish entrées; and **Le Lamparo** (76 Rue Clemenceau) is the place to go for a bustling local atmosphere.

Luggage Transfers

Taxi David: 83, Rue D. Bergougnoux;
Phone: 0565 22 34 34.
Taxi Union: 62, Quai Verrerie;
Phone: 0565 22 60 60.
Allo Taxi: 742, Chem. Junies;
Phone: 0565 22 19 42.

ROCAMADOUR TO CAHORS
ROUTE NOTES

Day 5: Rocamadour to Cahors

The ride from Rocamadour is quite challenging and leads you to the Lot River and the medieval town of Cahors. For more than 2,000 years, Cahors has produced its own wine, a spirited vintage which gracefully complements any meal (well, maybe not your morning coffee and baguette, but a late-morning brunch for sure). Your layover ride visits the Grottes de Pech Merle, yet another striking cave housing 20,000-year-old (yawn) prehistoric art.

Distance: 80 km

Directions (km): 0.0: Begin at the Tourist Office on the D673. Take the D32 down to the city.

1.4: Turn **LEFT** on the D32 toward La Valee.

1.8: Turn **LEFT** to Couzou 5/ Cahors 56 on the D32.

7.2: Couzou.

7.5: Intersection; continue **STRAIGHT** on the D32 toward Carlucet 7/Cahors 52.

8.7: Turn **RIGHT** toward Carlucet 6/Cahors 51/on the D32.

16.4: **RIGHT** on the D50.

18.3: **RIGHT** on the D1.

20.8: Turn **RIGHT**; pass under a bridge.

23.4: **LEFT** for Montfaucon 25 on the D10.

25.5: **RIGHT** on the D2 St. Germain du Bel Aire 12/Mont Faucon 5/St. Cirq Lapopie 46.

25.6: Stay on the D2 to St. Germaine 12 (to the **RIGHT**).

29.3: Continue on the D2.

32.3: Turn **LEFT** onto the N20.

33.5: Turn **RIGHT** on the D23 toward St. Germaine 5.

37.3: St. Germaine du Bel Air (restaurant/boulangerie).

41.2: Turn **LEFT** on the D12 to Cahors 31/St. Denis 13.

53.7: Turn **LEFT** on the D12 toward Cahors 17.

54.3: St. Denis-Cactus.

54.8: Turn **RIGHT** on the D12 toward Cahors 17.

57.6: Follow road toward Cahors 15 on the D12.

62.2: Turn **RIGHT** on the D142 to Espere 5.

64.0: Turn **RIGHT** on the D145 toward Luzech 12/Les Berges de Caix.

64.1: Turn **LEFT** on the D240 toward Douelle 4/Caillac 1 Eglise Romane/Chateau Lagrazette.

65.2: Turn **LEFT** on the C5 toward Douelle (this road will take you through the vineyards where you can visit the Chateau Lagrazette to taste and purchase wine).

67.7: Follow the D12 to the **RIGHT** toward Douelle 1.

67.6: Turn **LEFT** on the D8 for Cahors 11.

77.0: Cahors.

78.0: Continue **STRAIGHT** at the roundabout.

79.2: Turn **LEFT** and cross over the Pont Valentre. On the other side of the bridge, turn **RIGHT** and take the first **LEFT** on the D8. This will be Rue G. Sindou. Turn **LEFT** on the D8 toward the Centre Ville/Gare SNCF.

In eerily realistic replications that would make Madame Tussaud blush, the Dordogne musea proudly display remnants of their region's ancestors. You'd swear the eyes were following you!
Niels Povlsen

HOMO ERECTUS (PITHEC.
moins 1,7 millions d'années à 100 000 ans

Background Notes
Where Am I?
Country: France
Region: Midi-Pyrenees
Department: Lot
City: Figeac

Tourist Information
Figeac Office de Tourisme
Pl. Vival
Figeac 46102
Phone: 0565 34 06 25
Fax: 0565 50 04 58
figeac@wanadoo.fr
http://www.quercy-tourisme.com/figeac/index.html

Bike Shops
Cycles Lacoste: 4 Rue Ste. Marthe; Phone: 0565 34 60 92.

Sightseeing
Next to Lascaux, **Grotte du Pech Merle** is the premier prehistoric cave with extensive paintings and engravings.

Cabrerets is set in a dramatically impressive position against a background of rocky cliffs where the Sagne and Cele rivers meet.

While in **Figeac**, be sure to visit its **Old Quarter**, which displays historical exhibits of its turbulent past. For further historical insight, there's **Portrait d'une Ville** (5 Rue de Colomb), a permanent exhibition that offers lectures on Figeac's past. It is open daily from 10:00 a.m. to 12:30 p.m. and 3:00 p.m. to 7:00 p.m. in the summer.

La Domaine du Surgie is Figeac's leisure park and nautical center. The park offers trampolines, miniature golf, and a swimming pool.

Restaurants

You'll find tasty, local dishes at **La Puce a l'Oreille** (Rue St. Thomas) and **La Spinx Brasserie-Restaurant** (7 pl. Carnot). Both restaurants are reasonably priced.

CAHORS TO FIGEAC
ROUTE NOTES

Day 6: Cahors to Figeac

Today's ride visits the Cele valley, tracing a route through Bouzie and its hidden fortress. You'll next visit the Grotte du Pech Merles, reinforcing once again that yes, this area is famous for its caves. Finally, you'll reach Figeac, a charming medieval town blanketed with fourteenth-century, half-timbered houses (can you imagine the heating bills?), providing the ideal backdrop and sendoff from a fairy-tale week of cycling.

Distance: 84 km.

Directions (km): 0.0: The Hotel de France, taking the Ave. Jean Jaures to G. Sindou. Turn **LEFT** at the river on the D108 toward Figeac.

    1.5: **STRAIGHT** toward Figeac on the D653.

    4.0: Continue **STRAIGHT** to Figeac/St. Cirq Lapopie. Take the bike path to the **RIGHT**.

    6.2: Laroque des Arcs.

    8.3: Lamagdelaine.

    11.3: Savanac.

    16.7: Vers; continue **STRAIGHT** on the D653 toward Figeac 55.

    16.9: Turn **RIGHT** at the roundabout on the D662 toward St. Gery 5/St. Cirq Lapopie 20.0: You'll cross a bridge.

    21.3: St. Gery.

    30.8: Turn **LEFT** on the D41 to Caberets 4/Grottes de Peche Merle 7.

    34.7: Continue **STRAIGHT** on the D41 toward Figeac 50. To visit the Grottes de Peche Merle, turn **LEFT** and the caves are 3km away.

    43.4: Sauillac s/ Cele.

Some B&Bs are more basic than others. This one here, in France's Dordogne, requires a primitive water gathering process before showering. Yet, the rates are cheap and there's a waiting list. *Niels Povlsen*

49.8: Marcilhac s/ Cele (on the Cele River); Figeac is 33km away. Boulangerie/patisserie here.

53.6: St. Sulpice.

59.4: Brengues.

72.3: Boussac.

77.5: Turn **RIGHT** on the D208 to Figeac.

79.7: Continue **STRAIGHT** toward Figeac.

80.9: Figeac.

81.2: Roundabout; continue following signs toward Figeac Centre.

82.2: Continue following signs to centre ville until 83.3.

83.3: Go **STRAIGHT** following the green signs for Rodez and Decazeville. The N140 to Centre Ville/Office du Tourisme is on the left.

When cycling with friends, make sure you fan out across the road and block the access of motorized traffic. Motorists find formations such as these beautiful. *Niels Povlsen*

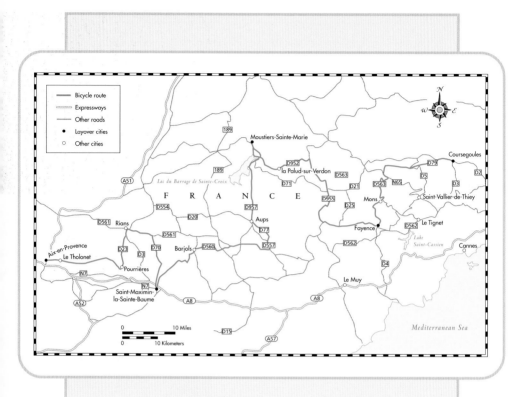

COTE D'AZUR & SOUTHERN FRANCE

This is one of my favorite tours because it combines wonderful mountain scenery with some of the friendliest people in Europe. In fact, for those who mutter the clichéd, "the French are rude," I invite them to visit this area of France. It will change your mind and send you scurrying to buy Pimsleur French tapes.

You can easily combine this trip with a pre- or post-trip visit to the Cote d'Azur beaches, a wonderful way to balance your visit.

A particular point of interest along this route is the magnificent Gorges du Verdon (see the ride into Moustiers), one of the most spectacular natural sites in Europe, though also one of the least known (to foreigners—the locals certainly know about it, they're just not telling).

Europeans use a comma where Americans would place a period, and a question mark wherever we use an exclamation point (the latter is a current events commentary).
Niels Povlsen

When to Go

April through June and late August through October are prime months for cycling this tour. I've braved the heat as late as the second week in July, and it was too much. Keep in mind that during April and May, some of the campgrounds are almost desolate. This can be great for catching a good night's sleep, but not so convenient if you're looking for the campground market to be open late at night (it most likely will not). Here are the temperatures and rainfall you can expect for the region:

NICE [39](Cote d'Azur):

MONTH	AVERAGE HIGH (°F)	AVERAGE LOW (°F)	AVERAGE PRECIPITATION (IN)
JANUARY	55	42	3.0
FEBRUARY	55	43	2.9
MARCH	58	46	2.9
APRIL	61	49	2.5
MAY	67	56	1.9
JUNE	74	62	1.5
JULY	79	67	0.7
AUGUST	80	68	1.2
SEPTEMBER	75	63	2.6
OCTOBER	68	56	4.4
NOVEMBER	61	48	4.6
DECEMBER	56	43	3.

Arrival and Departure
Air

Nice Airport is the closest arrival airport, and Marseille is best for your departure. You'll find information for Bordeaux and Toulouse airports at:

Aeroport Nice Cote d'Azur: http://www.nice.aeroport.fr.

Marseille Marignane Airport: http://www.marseille.aeroport.fr/.

[39] http://www.usatoday.com/weather/climate/wnice.htm.

To and From the Airport
Taxi
TO COURSEGOULES
There's no direct transfer information to Coursegoules, so a taxi or private car company is your best bet. Expect to pay €60 to €80 for the 60-minute transfer.

Taxis are bountiful outside the Nice airport, but if you prefer to have someone waiting for you at the airport with your name on a cardboard sign, here are a few local companies that provide private services:

Auto Nice Transport: Phone: 0492 29 88 80; Fax: 0492 29 88 81; auto-nice-transp.t@wanadoo.fr.

S.A.M. Autocars: Phone: 0493 54 14 49; Fax: 049 54 32 97; lucwengersam@aol.com.

FROM AIX-EN-PROVENCE
It's only 20 miles from Aix-en-Provence to the Marseille Airport, and you can pre-arrange your transfer with several companies:

Compagnie Autocars de Provence: Phone: 0442 97 52 10; Fax: 0442 97 52 11; cap@transdev.fr.

Taxi Radio Aixois: Phone: 04 42 27 71 11; Fax : 04 42 38 81 27; taxisradioaixois@wanadoo.fr.

Public Transportation
TO COURSEGOULES
There is no public transportation service into Coursegoules. Vence, 8 miles from Coursegoules, is the closest town with a bus station. You'll make one transfer during the 1 hour and 45 minute trip, and including the taxi ride to get you to Coursegoules, you'll pay between €30 and €40 total for the transfer. For information, check out www.sncf.com.

FROM AIX-EN-PROVENCE
There are very good public transportation options that connect Aix and Marseille Airport. Total transfer time, station to station, is 1 hour and 30 minutes and costs roughly €15 (www.raileurope).

Bike Rental
The nearest bike shop to Coursegoules is in Vence, 8 miles away:
Vence Motos; 7 avenue des Poilus; Phone: 0493 58 56 00; Fax : 04 93 58 57 34; gabardcvision@aol.com; http://www.pays-vencois.com/vencetousterrains/index.htm.
Rental prices start at €100 per week.

American cyclists blow billions of dollars every year on dedicated cycling gear. French cyclists do just fine in housecoats. *Niels Povlsen*

Cycling Notes

Mistrals are very dangerous, gale-force winds that can strike this southern France area. Two of my groups have experienced their fierce high speeds and destructive forces. They can occur year-round, though they're most commonly experienced in the winter and spring. If your local hosts caution you about approaching strong winds (some can reach speeds of 100 miles per hour), *do not* set out on your ride and attempt to chronicle the meteorological phenomenon on your handicam. Wait out the storm inside your hotel, and only after the winds have subsided should you dare continue your itinerary.

Maps

Michelin #245, *Provence Cote d'Azur*, 1:200,000.

Accommodations Notes

Coursegoules is a tiny village, and Fayence is a fairly small town, so don't expect a wide assortment of hotel choices. On the other hand, if you can do without the mundane frills that go with the more luxurious properties (in-room Internet service, a Toblerone-stocked minibar, chambermaids wearing Chanel No. 5), then you'll do just fine at the towns' family-run establishments. They all seem to gush with personal attention and warmth, which more than compensates for their modest facilities.

Une Pizza Marguerite

I love this area of France. The people are some of the warmest of any that I've met in Europe, and they always seem eager to meet Americans.

Several years ago, I was traveling off-season on a 6-day trip that was jammed with appointments to conduct research for a new tour. I arrived at the Nice airport after an 8-hour trans-Atlantic flight, which was followed by a 4-hour layover in the Frankfurt airport, which was then followed by a 90-minute flight to Nice. Needless to say, I was tired.

I rented my car and drove to three hotel inspections, and then I drove groggily to my Alpes Maritime hotel (the region where this tour begins).

After checking in to my pension, I was both exhausted and starving. Being the *chazer*[40] that I am, I decided to head out in search of food instead of a pillow. *Can't go to bed hungry*, I thought to myself, as I spotted a lone pizzeria with vertical beads serving as its door in my village's town square.

I entered the pizzeria and was immediately overwhelmed by its warmth and smell. Lining the back wall of the room was a rustic fireplace oven with a man in his fifties arranging coals in preparation for that evening's meals. He stopped his work when I entered and immediately assessed me to be a foreigner.

"*Oui, monsieur?*" he asked. Yes, sir?

In passable French, I explained to the man my purpose for visiting the area, that I was quite hungry after a long day of traveling, and then asked whether I could buy a pizza.

The man was intrigued by my story and background; he enthusiastically set out to create my dinner. First he kneaded some dough, flipping it expertly into the air to create just the right thickness. Next he dipped a slightly bent ladle into a bucket of tomato sauce and spread it liberally onto the dough. He sprinkled just the right amount of cheese onto the sauce—not too much, but not too little—and finished it off with a gentle toss of oregano.

All the while, he's busy chatting with me and I'm enjoying the opportunity to exercise my limited French skills. He placed the pizza into the fireplace oven and a quick 3 to 4 minutes later, he assessed it to be fully cooked. As he extracted the pizza from the oven with a large pizza spatula, it looked and smelled great. The man was very excited now, as he looked at me and sensed that I was indeed pleased with his creation. He placed it into a cardboard box, and just before he closed the lid, he looked to me once more for reassurance that he had done well.

Just as I'm gushing in French over how great it looked, a huge smile spread over his face and a thick puddle of happy drool fell from his lips onto the pizza. He then closed the box, oblivious to his emotional leakage, and handed me my dinner.

So where are we? It's 6:30 in the evening in a tiny French village. I'm in the area's only restaurant, holding a 12-inch pie that smells wonderful and looks great, except that I know it's also serving as a coaster for this French pizza man's spit. I've been awake just over 36 hours, am starving, and OCD nightmares are flashing through my mind.

I paid the man, thanked him profusely, walked 10 minutes until I was well past the town limits, found a dumpster outside a sewer construction project, and dumped the pizza. I then returned to my hotel, ate a Powerbar, and called it a night.

[40] Pig.

Background Notes
Where Am I?
Country: France
Region: Provence-Alpes-Cote d'Azur
Department: Alpes Maritimes
City: Coursegoules

Tourist Information
Mairie de Coursegoules (no official tourist office)
36, Rue Clastre
Coursegoules 06140
Phone: 0493 59 11 60
Fax: 0493 59 13 31
www.pays-vencois.com;
www.pays-accueil-provence06.net/coursegoules1.html;

Bike Shops
The nearest bike shop to Coursegoules is in Vence, 8 miles away:
Vence Motos; 7 avenue des Poilus; Phone: 0493 58 56 00; Fax : 04 93 58 57 34;
gabardcvision@aol.com;
http://www.pays-vencois.com/vencetousterrains/index.htm.

Sightseeing
Hiking and cycling are the main activities. Stop by the mayor's office for hiking maps of the area.

Luggage Transfers
Taxi Lionel: Pl. du Grand Jardin; Vence; Phone: 0609 28 55 36;
taxislionel@cote.azur.fr.

No, she just passed, maybe two or three minutes ago . . . Uh-huh, uh-huh . . . Well, you can probably catch her if you get going. Yes, I agree, a great ass. *Niels Povlsen*

DAY 1: COURSEGOULES ARRIVAL

Day 1: Coursegoules to Fayence

Coursegoules is a tiny village set at the base of Mount Cheiron, which offers fantastic views of the Cote d'Azur countryside. Despite not being served by public transportation routes, I love the village and have always started my group tours here. There's only one campground and one hotel, and both are simple but great. There's a local who will even provide English-language tours of the village for a modest fee.

The surrounding mountains make an ideal place to explore by foot and you can pick up hiking information from the mayor's office (don't stop by before noon because he's also the mailman).

Background Notes

Where Am I?

Country: France
Region: Provence-Alpes-Cote d'Azur
Department: Var
City: Fayence

Tourist Information

Fayence Tourism
Pl. Leon Roux
Fayence 83440
Phone: 0494 76 20 08
Fax: 0494 39 15 96
Ot.fayence@wanadoo.fr
www.mairiedefayence.com;
www.fayence.com;
www.paysdefayence.com

Bike Shops

The closest shop is in Callian, 6 miles away:
Spit Bikes: 83440 Callian; Phone: 0494 76 06 76; Fax: 0494 76 42 27;
spit-bikes@wanadoo.fr.

Sightseeing

Along today's ride you'll pass **Callian**, which offers breathtaking views of the surrounding countryside, all from the convenience of its main square. Nearby is **Montaroux**, home to dozens of talented artisans and craftsmen who live in quaint seventeenth-century homes. From Montaroux, you can extend your ride another 20 miles by visiting **Lake St. Cassien**, a worthwhile swimming stop.

Your south of France trip finishes in Aix-en-Provence, the grand capital of Provence and a wealth of cultural activity. *Carbonne, JC; Ville D'Aix*

While in **Mons**, ask directions for the 30-minute walk to the **Siagnole Springs**, the site where converging springs form the Siagnole River. Mons also makes a perfect lunch spot; its main square (Place St. Sebastian) offers unimpeded views over the Siagne and Siagnole Valleys.

Fayence is a dramatically beautiful little village and is home to many craftsmen. Its Old Town is a condensed collection of perilously steep streets teeming with 200-year-old houses.

Restaurants

Castellaras is a Michelin-rated restaurant, about 5 kilometers from town. Reservations are necessary (Phone: 0494 76 13 80). If you'd rather stay in Fayence, try **Restaurant Le Provencal** or **Restaurant des Arts**. Both serve regional specialties. For something light and quick, there's a snack shop and pizzeria in the village center.

Luggage Transfers

Allo Taxi Andre: Phone: 0494 76 95 19.
Taxi Troin; Phone: 0494 76 20 95..

COURSEGOULES TO FAYENCE
ROUTE NOTES

Days 2 and 3: Coursegoules to Fayence; Fayence Loop Ride

Your next two rides border the Pre-Alps region known as Haute-Provence, a tranquil area that is ideal for cycling. You'll pass dozens of sleepy French villages set in the midst of a lush, green plateau before reaching Fayence, a romantic town set between the mountains and sea.

Distance: 50 km.

Lunch Stop: Andon, Mons

NOTE: *Green signs indicate highways—no biking allowed.*

Directions (km):

From the center of the village by the boulangerie, head toward the post office (you are going sharply downhill); at the crossroads (.3km), turn right to Greolieres 12, Vence 17.

- 1.4: D2: Very sharp **RIGHT** to Greolieres 12 and Thorenc 24.
- 8.8: Turn **RIGHT** for Greolieres on the D2 (all uphill until you reach the town).
- 9.7: Keep going **STRAIGHT** to Thorenc 16 and Greolieres 2 (left is Cipieres).
- 10.9: Greolieres; turn **LEFT** to centre ville. After passing through Greolieres, turn **LEFT** on the D79 toward Andon.
- 23.6: At a small fork, turn **LEFT** for Andon. Ahead 100 yards, turn **RIGHT** on the D79 toward Andon RN 85.
- 26.1: Andon (a market and restaurant). Turn **RIGHT** at the roundabout just ahead toward Caille 6; continue following signs to Caille.
- 31.9: Turn **LEFT** to Caille, RN85, and Grasse.
- 32.3: Caille.
- 33.5: **LEFT** on the D79 toward Grasse (RN 85).
- 34.0: **LEFT** on the N85 toward Grasse.
- 37.5 **RIGHT** on the D563 toward Mons (narrow road and is missing guardrails in places—careful). It is up and down climbing from here for the next 10 km.
- 49.8: You enter Mons, a great lunch spot. Turn **RIGHT** on the D563 toward Fayence. Follow the D563 until you reach Fayence at 63.8.

Background Notes
Where Am I?

Country: France

Region: Provence-Alpes-Cote d'Azur

Department: Alpes de Haute Provence

City: Moustiers Sainte Marie

This was overheard while touring the palace alongside an AARP group from West Bloomfield, Michigan: "It's nice, I guess, but not for me. I mean, look at this crown molding. It must be 200 years old!"
Carbonne, JC; Ville D'Aix

The South of France itinerary is filled with difficult ascents during every ride.
Carbonne, JC; Ville D'Aix

Tourist Information

Office de Tourisme
Rue de la Bourgad
Moustiers 04360
Phone: 0492 74 67 84
Fax: 0492 74 60 65
moustiers@wanadoo.fr
www.ville-moustiers-sainte-marie.fr/indexot.htm

Bike Shops

Holiday Bikes: Route Salles; 04360 Moustiers Sainte Marie; Phone: 0492 74 60 00;
Fax: 0492 74 63 03. Try also Riez Motos in Riez, 15 kilometers from Moustiers:
0492 77 84 22.

Sightseeing

If you're spending a layover day in Moustiers (strongly recommended), you have
several sightseeing options.

If you'd like to keep active, there are several self-guided walking trail tours that traverse both the north and south sides of the Verdon. The tourist office can even help arrange a local guide, if you'd rather not go it alone.

In nearby **Les Salles Sur Verdon**, tennis and golf are both offered, and your hotel can call ahead for reservations.

Contact Mr. Stepien at 0494 70 22 60 if you'd like to go **horseback riding**.

Back in Moustiers, the **Musee des Faiences** is a local museum that features prime examples of the town's *faienceware* (pottery) from centuries past.

While you're searching for that elusive chai tea, wander off to the Romanesque church of **Notre Dame de Beauvoir** (rebuilt in the twelfth and fourteenth centuries), which is accessible by footpaths.

Luggage Transfers
Taxi de L'Etoile: Phone: 04 92 74 66 87 / 06 07 37 33 78; taxi.etoile@wanadoo.fr.

FAYENCE TO MOUSTIERS
ROUTE NOTES

Day 4: Fayence to Moustiers

Today's ride is the most spectacular of the trip, as you'll visit the Gorge du Verdon, a wondrous canyon with cliffs reaching 2,300 feet.

Along the way, you'll pass Seillans, one of the many towns that painter Max Ernst called home (he also called all brunette women "Mommy"). You'll find a sprawling network here of cobblestone streets, along with remnants of its ancient castle.

Next, you reach Bargemon, the ancient stronghold bordering the Provence region. Grab an apple[2] at a local market and snap pictures of its ancient castle ruins and twelfth-century Roman gateway, a perfect way to break up your ride.

Moustiers is situated in a truly spectacular setting, with a lively mountain stream and towering limestone cliffs clearly marking its borders. It's also the perfect spot to plan a rest day, as the ride from Fayence is physically very challenging.

Distance: 86 km.

Lunch Stop: Comps s/ Artuby.

Directions (km): Head through the town. At the bottom of the hill, turn **RIGHT** for Seillans 5 and Bargemon 18.

> 5.0: Turn **LEFT** on the D19 for Bargemon; this takes you into Seillans.
>
> 17.3: Bargemon. At the fountain in the center of Bargemon, follow signs for Compes 20, Gorge du Verdon 20. Bargemon has several markets and shops. A few hundred yards ahead, turn **LEFT** for Comps and Gorge Du Verdon on the D19.
>
> 22.4: Turn **RIGHT** on the D955 to Comps-S-Artuby;
>
> 36.4: Comps-S-Artuby (markets and restaurants); as you cycle through the town, follow signs

[2] Please pay for it.

to La Bastide, Castellane, Gorges du Verdon, and Rive Droite. You want to follow the Rive Droite on the D955 for Moustiers—not the rive gauche (left bank) to Aiguines; 200 meters ahead, turn **LEFT** for Castellane on the D955.

41.4: In Jabron, turn **LEFT** on the D955 for Castellane and the Gorge Rive Droite. There's a small restaurant/snack bar on your left just past this turn.

48.2: Continue **STRAIGHT** for Castellane. Left would take you to Trigance (twelfth-century church there). It's an additional 3.5km roundtrip to visit the village.

51.2: Soleils. Soon after, you'll enjoy a 4km downhill.

54.0: Turn **LEFT** for Moustiers 33, Rougon, La Palud 13, and Gorge du Verdon Rive Droite. You'll climb almost the entire way to Lapoint Sublime (from 54.5km to 60km). There will be a snack bar on your right as you reach the top of the climb.

58.5: Lapoint Sublime. Moustiers is 27km away on the D952 (rolling terrain).

67.0: La Palud. You'll continue uphill for the next 3km, before enjoying an 8km downhill.

83: Turn **RIGHT** on the D952 for Moustiers, 3km.

85.4: You reach the main roundabout in Moustiers.

Background Notes
Where Am I?
Country: France
Region: Provence-Alpes-Cote d'Azur
Department: Var
City: St. Maximin la Ste. Baume

Tourist Information
Office de Tourisme
Hotel de Ville
Saint Maximin la Sainte Baume 83470
Phone: 0494 59 84 59
Fax: 0494 59 82 92
office.tourisme.stmaximin@wanadoo.fr
www.stmaximin.enprovence.com

Bike Shops
Fun Cycles: Phone: 0494 78 06 86.

Sightseeing
Along today's ride, you'll first reach **Villecroze** and its grottes, underground caves that provide cool shelter from the oppressive summer heat. These are a stones-throw from its waterfall and rose garden, and both are very worthwhile stops.

You'll next pass **Aups**, the site of more castle ruins and home to a small modern art collection. And then there's **Tourtour**, an absolutely wonderful village, set among green woods and buttressed by (ho-hum!) still more castle ruins. The southeast corner of the village affords beautiful vistas of the Argens and Nartuby valleys that extend (on clear days) to the Luberon Mountains.

You'll also pass **Cotignac**, a small village known for its honey, oil, and wine production (several shopping opportunities). While here, notice the sixteenth-century Romanesque church and bell tower.

The next stop is **Barjols**, notable for its 25 fountains (and the question to this very famous *French Jeopardy* answer: "This town's locals are never thirsty."). And finally, you reach **Saint Maximin la Sainte Baume**, a cozy French town with a lively main square and ancient basilica. Pay a visit to its **Old Quarter**, lined with fourteenth-century arcades and the former location of a Jewish ghetto.

Luggage Transfers
Philippe Atti: 276 Chem. Argerie; Phone: 0494 78 08 06.

MOUSTIERS TO
ST. MAXIMIN LA STE. BAUME
ROUTE NOTES

Day 5: Moustiers to St. Maximin la Ste. Baume
Today's ride winds through several very charming villages, all teeming with life and character. It's far less taxing than the ride into Moustiers, but you'll still work up a sweat. The last portion of the ride eventually levels off somewhat, but be careful—traffic increases as you approach St. Maximin.
Distance: 85 km.
Lunch Stop: Aups.
Directions (km): From the main roundabout in town, turn **LEFT** on the D952 toward Castellane/Draguinan/Gorges du Verdon.

> 1.9: **STRAIGHT** for Les Salles/Aups/Draguinan on the D957.
> 9.0: Continue **STRAIGHT** for Les Salles 3, Aups 23, and the D957.
> 26.7: **STRAIGHT** for Aups 7 on the D957.
> 33.8: **LEFT** for Aups. Coast downhill into the village (stores, shops).
> 35.9: **RIGHT** for Sillans on the D22.
> 43.5: Sillans la Cascade. The path to the waterfall is to the left, the village center is to the right. The D560 road continues to Barjols.
> 61.0: Barjols (markets, shops). Just ahead, continue **STRAIGHT** for St. Maximin.
> 80.0: You reach St. Maximin (outskirts). Follow signs all the way to St. Maximin on the D560.
> 85.0: You reach the main square.

Background Notes
Where Am I?
Country: France
Region: Provence-Alpes-Cote d'Azur
Department: Bouches du Rhone
City: Aix-en-Provence

Tourist Information
Office de Tourisme
2, Pl. du General de Gaulle
Aix-en-Provence 13605
Phone: 0442 161 161
Fax: 0442 161 162
infos@aixenprovencetourism.com
www.aixenprovencetourism.com

Bike Shops
La Route Bleue: 5, Pl. de Narvik; Phone: 0442 27 92 34.
Cycles Zammit: 27, Rue Mignet; Phone: 0442 23 19 53.
La Rotonde: 2, Ave. des Belges; Phone: 0442 26 78 92.

Feel like a break from your rock-hard bike seat? There are tons of great hiking itineraries available throughout the area. Stop by any local tourist office for information.
Carbonne, JC; Ville D'Aix

Sightseeing

Along much of today's route, you'll ride alongside **Mt. Ste. Victoire**, a limestone mountain range and site to an ancient battle between Marius and the Teutons. Incidentally, Marius won. Whatever.

You'll also pass the **Cross of Provence**, a huge white cross perched at the top of rocky cliffs. You can hike to the top, where you'll find the seventeenth-century Notre Dame de Ste. Victoire.

You should plan on a full layover day in Aix-en-Provence. Hone your people-watching skills along **Cours Miradbeau**, a street lined with restaurants, shops, boutiques, and cafes.

Musee des Tapisseries houses seventeenth and eighteenth-century tapestries. It is open Wednesday through Monday from 9:30 a.m. to 12 p.m. and 2 p.m. to 6 p.m.

Cézanne's studio (at 9, Avenue Paul Cézanne) provides insight into the artist's former home and workplace. It is closed on Tuesdays.

Restaurants

Aix-en-Provence is a thriving, bustling city, teeming with restaurants in every price category. Most are centered around the **Place de Cardeurs** and **Rue Van-Loo**.

ST. MAXIMIN LA STE. BAUME TO AIX-EN-PROVENCE
ROUTE NOTES

Day 6: St. Maximin to Aix-en-Provence

Today's ride leads to Aix-en-Provence, the ancient capital of the Provence region and a popular destination for those visiting the South of France. It's a city that gracefully incorporates both old and new elements; the Old Town is filled with cobblestone streets and centuries-old homes, alongside modern residential and commercial developments.

Go through a roundabout just ahead as you pass over the highway. Immediately after you cross over the highway, turn **LEFT** onto a tiny road for Esparron and St. Martin on the D70. Follow signs to Esparron (2.2)

Follow the D70 all the way to Esparron.

As you reach Rians, follow signs toward St. Maximin 23 on the D3.

31.0: Turn **RIGHT** for Pourrieres on the D23.

36.5: You reach Pourrieres (markets, shops); follow signs to Aix-En-Provence and Marseille. At the end of the town, turn **RIGHT** on the D623 to Puylobier.

50.2: As you reach Puylobier, turn **RIGHT** on the D17 for St. Antonin. There are mountains on your right.

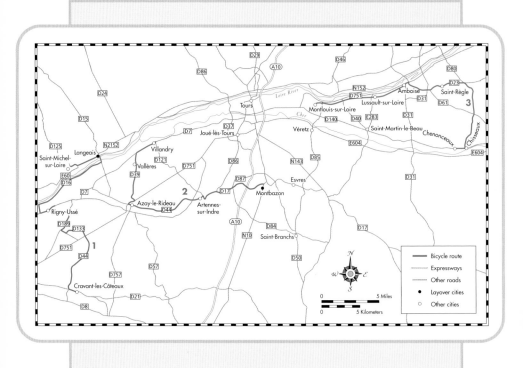

LOIRE VALLEY, an Introduction

This is a very easy five-day trip. It's perfect for those who arrive in Paris to close a business deal and find themselves with a few leisure days to spare.

I designed this trip several years ago for two extraordinarily wealthy families (traveling on business), who sought the very finest in food, lodging, and culture. It's a wonderful trip and a great introduction to European cycling.

I approach this chapter a bit differently from the other tours; I include the identical hour-by-hour itinerary that I used for my clients, as well as the same luxury hotels. You're of course free to opt out of any of the sightseeing stops, but I guarantee[41] that if you participate in all of the cycling routes and guided tours, you'll have experienced a wonderful introduction to the Loire Valley.

When to Go

Temperatures are cycle-friendly April through October, though you'll probably find April and May to be a little wet for your comfort zone. The chart below should give you a good idea of what to expect with temperatures and precipitation:

---

[41] No guarantee.

PARIS[42]

MONTH	AVERAGE HIGH (°F)	AVERAGE LOW (°F)	WET DAYS
JANUARY	43	34	20
FEBRUARY	45	34	16
MARCH	51	38	18
APRIL	57	42	17
MAY	64	49	16
JUNE	70	54	14
JULY	75	58	13
AUGUST	75	57	12
SEPTEMBER	69	52	14
OCTOBER	59	46	17
NOVEMBER	49	39	17
DECEMBER	45	36	19

The French take meticulous care in the presentation of their communities, an inviting atmosphere that makes French cycling some of the best in Europe. *Niels Povlsen*

Arrival and Departure
Air

Plan on flying in and out of Paris at the start and finish of your tour. You can find detailed flight information for both Charles de Gaulle and Orly at www.adp.fr.

To and From the Airport
Taxi

Taxis are plentiful outside of both Paris airports, but it will cost several hundred dollars for the direct two-hour journey to reach Tours. A more practical choice is to take the TGV between Paris and Tours, and then find a local taxi at the Tours train station (dozens eagerly await your entry) to take you to your starting hotel. Your Montbazon hotel staff can help arrange for the 9-mile shuttle back to the Tours train station at the end of your tour so you can meet your TGV train back to Paris.

---

[42] http://www.usatoday.com/weather/resources/climate/wparis.htm.

The Loire Valley route leads you past an endless collection of centuries old chateaux, an important reminder of France's aristocratic past. *Niels Povlsen*

Public Transportation

France's train system, SNCF, provides a detailed, up-to-date website with pricing and schedules: www.voyages-sncf.com. You can also purchase tickets in advance from Rail Europe: www.raileurope.com. The 51-minute, high-speed train costs $51 ($40 if you take the slower 2 hour, 30 minute-train).

Bike Rentals and Luggage Transfers

Amster Cycles in Tours is a reliable source for a very good bike selection and outstanding service. Phone: 0247 61 22 23; Fax: 02 47 61 28 48; amstercycles@wanadoo.fr; http://perso.wanadoo.fr/amstercycles/.

Cycling Notes

As mentioned above, this tour is slightly different from the others in that a complete daily itinerary is provided for all rides, including sightseeing stops. The roads are almost all along very small, lightly traveled paths that wind through the most interesting terrain in the region.

Background Notes
Where Am I?
Country: France
Region: Centre
Departments: Indre et Loire
City: Tours and surround area

Tourist Information
Office De Tourisme De Tours
78-82 Rue Bernard Palissy
37042 Tours
Phone: 033 2 47 70 37 37
Fax: 033 2 47 61 14 22
info@ligeris.com
http://www.ligeris.com/
Loire Valley Tourism
crtl.centre@crtlcentre.com
http://www.visaloire.com/accueil.php?lang=en

There's no better metaphor for the separation of classes that existed in Renaissance France than the view from behind a castle's wrought iron gate. *Carbonne, JC; Ville D'Aix*

Maps

Very Good: Michelin #232, *Pays de Loire*; 1:200,000.
Excellent: IGN TOP 100 #'s 25 and 26; 1:100,000.

Accommodations Notes[43]

While the turn-by-turn directions each begin from expensive chateaux properties, you can still cycle the identical itineraries while substituting less expensive hotels.

LOIRE VALLEY ITINERARY

Day 1

Noon to 3 p.m.: Arrive at the Tours train station and meet your local guide, who will escort you on a 3-hour walking tour of the city's best sites. To reserve a local guide, contact the Tours Tourist Office: 0247 70 37 37; info@ligeris.com. Expect to pay $150 to $200.

3:30 p.m.: Meet back at the station and take a taxi to your first night's hotel, Chateau Rochecotte.

7:00 p.m.: While you're deciding on which vintage matches well with your veal entrée in your hotel's tastefully decorated dining room, reconfirm that your rental bikes will be delivered tomorrow morning. **Amster Cycles**: 5 Rue Du Rempart; Phone: 0247 61 22 23; amstercycles@wanadoo.fr; http://perso.wanadoo.fr/amstercycles/.

Day 2

7:30 a.m.: Breakfast

9:00 a.m. to 11:30 a.m.: Cycle from Chateau Rochecotte to Chateau d'Usse.

Directions: Leave the Chateau from the parking lot.

0.3: (dirt) Road intersects with a paved road. Turn **RIGHT**.

4.2: Turn **RIGHT** onto the D71 toward Les Essards 4.

5.3: Turn **RIGHT** toward La Rouchouze 4/Pont Boutard 1.

5.7: Turn **RIGHT**.

6.1: Yield sign; turn **LEFT** and head downhill.

8.2: Turn **RIGHT** at a fork in the road.

13.0: Turn **RIGHT** as the road bears right.

13.3: Enter Langeais on the C9.

13.7: Yield sign; turn **LEFT** to centre ville.

14.1: Turn **RIGHT** at a stop sign.

15.0: The entrance for the Chateau.

15.5: Stop sign; Turn **LEFT** onto the D257 toward Azay le Rideau.

16.4: Turn **RIGHT** onto the D16 toward Brehemont/Rigny-Usse/Chateau du Usse. After the turn, the Loire River will be to your right.

20.7: Reach Brehemont (markets, shops) on the D16.

26.1: Continue **STRAIGHT** on the D16.

29.1: Turn **LEFT** on the D7 toward Rivarennes 5/Azay Le Rideau 15.

29.3: There will be a parking lot on both sides of the street for the Chateau.

Total distance: 29.3km.

---

[43] For more comprehensive listings and alternates, see http://langeaiscastel.free.fr/cadreacceuil.htm (Langeais) and http://www.gaf.tm.fr/fr/france/hotels/centre/indreetloire.php (Montbazon).

11:30 a.m. to 1 p.m.: Privately guided tour of the Chateau D'Usse. Contact the chateau via Phone: 0247 95 54 05 or Fax: 0247 95 54 05 to arrange the guide.
http://www.tourisme.fr/usse/e_index.htm.

1:45 p.m. to 4:30 p.m.: Cycle from Chateau D'Usse to Pallus winery.

Directions: Turn **RIGHT** onto the D7 heading toward town.

1.2: Turn **RIGHT** toward Eglise Notre Dame and Chambre D' Hotes.

1.8: Turn **LEFT** toward Eglise Notre Dame.

1.9: Turn **RIGHT** toward Eglise Notre Dame on Rue des Fougeres.

2.0: The Eglise de Notre Dame will be in front of you.

3.9: Turn **LEFT** onto Rue de Saint Benoit.

6.2: Turn **LEFT** onto the D133 toward Zone Industrielle. Continue following the D133 through the Zone Industrielle.

9.9: Cross the D751 and head **STRAIGHT** toward Cravant Les C./Vieille Eglise Cravant.

18.3: Cravant Les Coteaux.

18.7: Turn **LEFT** toward L'Ilebouchard on the D21.

20.4: Turn **RIGHT** into the Pallus winery entrance.

Total distance: 20.4km or 12.6miles.

4:30 p.m. to 5:30 p.m.: Wine tasting at the Pallus winery. To reserve a tour:
Le Syndicat Des Vins De Chinon; Impasse Des Caves Painctes; 37500 Chinon; Phone: 0247 93 30 44; Fax: 0247 93 36 36; Http://Www.Chinon.Com/Vignoble/Contacts.Asp.

5:30 p.m.: Transfer to the Chateau D'Ártigny, your resting spot for the remainder of the tour. This is one of the finest lodging destinations in the Loire Valley, and with advance notice, your hosts will gladly help arrange a pick up for you and your bike from the Pallus winery.

8:00 p.m.: Dinner in your hotel's scrumptious dining room is a treat and a welcome reward at the end of your busy day.

Day 3

7:30 a.m.: Breakfast.

9:00 a.m. to 11:30 a.m.: Cycle from your hotel to Chateau Azay le Rideau.

These directions begin from the front of the Chateau D'Artigny (with the Chateau at your back).

0.0: front of the Chateau D'Artigny.

0.5: **RIGHT** on Rue de la Poiteviniere.

3.0: **LEFT** at the yield sign. Just ahead, take an immediate **RIGHT** onto Rue Dubuisson.

4.0: Turn **LEFT** on the D87 toward Sorigny.

5.9: Turn **RIGHT** onto the D84 for Sorigny 3.5/Ste. Maure De T. 20.

9.0: Veer **LEFT**.

9.1: Turn **LEFT** onto Rue des Girardieries.

10.9: Turn **RIGHT** (unmarked).

12.1: Turn **RIGHT** at a stop sign.

13.8: Turn **LEFT** onto the D17.

14.3: Turn **LEFT** onto the D17 toward Azay de R.

15.5: Veer **RIGHT** onto the D84 toward Maison Medicale.

22.7: Azay Le Rideau. Follow signs to the Chateau and Centre Ville.

23.1: The Chateau Azay Le Rideau will be on your left.

Total distance: 25.4 kilometers or 15.7 miles.

11:30 a.m. to 1 p.m.: Guided tour of the Chateau Azay Le Rideau. Contact the chateau to arrange a private guide: Phone: 0247 45 42 04; Fax: 0247 45 26 61; expect to pay $100 to $200.

1:45 p.m. to 4:00 p.m.: Cycle from Azay le Rideau to Villandry.

Directions: 0.0: As you leave the chateau, turn **RIGHT** on the D84. Follow signs toward Chateau Sache.

0.5: As the road veers right, turn **LEFT** (up a hill) toward Maison de Repos du Plessis.

0.8: **LEFT** at an unmarked intersection.

2.2: **LEFT** toward *Toutes Directions* onto Route de Frogeraies.

3.5: **LEFT** at the D751 intersection.

3.6: **RIGHT** at Chateau Eau du Gerfaut. The road just ahead turns briefly to packed dirt.

4.8: **RIGHT** at a fork toward Legerfaut.

4.9: Turn **RIGHT** on the C301 (unmarked) toward Bonzai.

8.3: Valleres.

10.1: **RIGHT** on the D7 toward Villandry 3.5.

10.2: Just as you cross over a small bridge, turn **LEFT**.

10.9: **LEFT** at a fork; just ahead, RIGHT. The Loire River will be to your left.

15.0: Veer **LEFT**, following signs to Villandry.

15.2: Turn **LEFT** toward Villandry.

17.3: **LEFT** at a stop sign.

17.5: Chateau and gardens to the right.

Total distance: 17.5 kilometers or 10.9 miles.

4:00 p.m.: Reach Villandry and self-guided tour.

Chateau Villandry; Phone: 0247 50 02 09; Fax: 0247 50 12 85; info@chateauVillandry.com; www.chateauVillandry.com

5:30 p.m.: Transfer to your hotel (pre-arrange with your hotel staff).

7:00 p.m.: Dinner.

Day 4
Breakfast

9 a.m.: Transfer from the Chateau D'Artigny to the Chateau Chenoceau.

10 a.m. to 11 a.m.: Privately guided tour of the Chateau Chenonceau. To arrange a tour: Château de Chenonceau; 37150 Chenonceaux; Phone: 0247 23 90 07; Fax: 0247 23 80 88; chateau.de.chenonceau@wanadoo.fr; http://www.chenonceau.com/indexENG.html.

11 a.m. to 12:30 p.m.: Cycle from Chateau Chenoceau to Le Clos Luce.

Directions: 0.0: Turn **RIGHT** from the parking lot. Just ahead the road will fork; turn **RIGHT** toward town.

0.2: Turn **RIGHT** toward Chisseaux/Montrichard on the D40.

2.1: Turn **LEFT** onto the D80 toward Souvigny de Tne. 10.

12.1: Turn **LEFT** onto the D23 toward St. Regle/Amboise. Just ahead, take another **LEFT**, still continuing toward St. Regle/Amboise.

17.6: Turn **RIGHT** onto a small road.

18.2: Stop sign and intersection with the D31. Cross this road and turn **LEFT** on a smaller road.

19.8: Turn **RIGHT** onto the D61.

20.8: Turn **RIGHT** for Clos-Luce.

Total distance: 21.3 kilometers or 13.2 miles.

12:30 p.m.: Arrive at Le Clos-Luce and self-guided tour.

Le Close Luce
2, r. du Clos-Lucé
37400 Amboise
Phone: 02 47 57 62 88
http://www.vinci-closluce.com/

What photo album isn't complete without a trite landscape filled with sunflowers? Yes, yes, it's pretty. Turn the page.

Niels Povlsen

2 p.m. to 4 p.m: Cycle from Le Close Luce to Monluis wine tasting

Directions: 0.0: From the front gates of the Clos-Luce, turn **RIGHT** traveling downhill.

> 0.2: You'll pass the two parking lots to your **LEFT**.
> 0.4: Stop sign; continue **STRAIGHT** onto Rue de la Commanderie.
> 0.8: Stop sign; turn **RIGHT**.
> 3.0: Turn **RIGHT** onto D83, then a quick **LEFT** onto Avenue de la Grille Doree.
> 4.5: Just ahead, follow the road bearing **RIGHT** to Lussault s/L.
> 5.7: Follow signs to L'Ormeau Vigneau on the C300.
> 6.4: Reach Lussault sur Loire on the C300.
> 6.6: Yield sign; continue **STRAIGHT** on the "Route des Montlouis."
> 9.4: Vineyards of Montils.
> 9.7: Turn **RIGHT** for Dominique Moyer.
> 11.7: Turn **RIGHT** onto Rue des Aitres.
> 11.9: The winery will be on your left.

Total distance: 11.9 kilometers or 7.4 miles.

Arrange a private tasting at Domaine de le Taille aux Loups. Phone: 0247 45 11 11; Fax: 0247 45 11 14. Alternatively, you can email the Montlouis town hall for information and reservations: 6 place François Mitterrand; Phone: 0247 45 85 85; mairie@ville-montlouis-loire.fr.

> 5:30 p.m.: Transfer to the Chateau D'Artigny.
> 7:00 p.m.: Dinner.

Day 5

> 6:00 a.m.: Champagne breakfast and a private balloon ride with an English-speaking guide.

NOTE: *The tour can begin from the chateau.*

France Montgolfieres

La Ribouliere

41400 Monthou sur Cher

Phone: 0254 71 75 40; Fax: 0254 71 75 78

reservations@franceballoons.com; www.franceballoons.com

Prices begin from 380/couple.

8:30 a.m.: Return from balloon ride.

10:30 a.m.: Transfer to the gare in Tours.

ITALY

It's funny,[44] but when a prospective client calls my company at 1-800-736-2453 from the U.S. and Canada, or +1-773-871-5510 from anywhere else on earth,[45] to inquire about a tour—any tour—and I suggest Switzerland, most quickly respond, "Oh, I'm sure it's beautiful, but it's much too [mountainous/difficult/anti-American] for me." They then sneeze and follow up with, "But what about Italy?" Then I have to laugh, because if you must know, I'm being tickled.

But what about Italy? I love cycling through Italy. The roads are well-marked, the people are friendly, the food is outstanding, the accommodations can be excellent (though some can be real duds), and the scenery is beautiful. Breathtaking, in fact (not breathtaking as in "Where's my inhaler," but breath-taking as in *Sigh.*). However, it is not flat. At least the tours below are not.

I suppose there are flat sections in Tuscany and Umbria, but most that I have seen are along river roads that are heavily traveled by cars, trucks, and motor scooters, so they are unpleasant for cycling.

If you select any of the following three itineraries, it's important to be in very good physical shape prior to departing and be comfortable cycling up very long, steep ascents. You won't want to initiate yourself into hill riding on any of these tours because transportation lifts can be infrequent and expensive.

Cycling Overview

As mentioned above, the cycling on each of the Italy itineraries is difficult. That's a relative term, of course, so here are my guidelines to help you compare the effort necessary for the rides:

Activity	Effort
	(1=easiest, 100=most difficult)
Carrying a feather twenty feet across shag carpet—barefoot	1
Carrying a feather twenty feet across shag carpet—wearing boots	1.2
Opening a really tough pickle jar	3.9
Talking on the phone (no headset) while eating cereal	5
Performing a cartwheel, drunk	9
Having a good time while bowling	22
Telling your child he/she was adopted	38
Cycling Tuscany or Umbria itinerary (tie)	74
Americans only: Understanding the rules of cricket	81
Watching reruns of *The Nanny*	84
Americans only: Caring about understanding the rules of cricket	88
Cycling Il Mugello itinerary	92
Enjoying country music	94

---

[44] Not funny as in someone tripping over raisins, but funny as in curious. Not curious as in inquisitive, but curious as in odd. Not odd as in opposite of even, but odd as in peculiar. Not peculiar as in irregular, but peculiar as in funny. Not funny as in tripping over raisins, but funny as in curious.
[45] Shameless plug #6.

Local commentators predict that if left unchecked, Italy's goat population will overtake the country by 2014. *Niels Povlsen*

Tourist Information

The Italian State Tourist Board (ENIT) websites are www.italiantourism.com and www.enit.it. The ENIT site is particularly helpful and has links to provincial and regional sites. You can also reach its U.S. and U.K. offices direct at the following:

Italian Government Tourist Board: 630 Fifth Ave.; New York, NY 10111; Phone: 212 245 4822; Fax: 212 586 9249; enitny@italiantourism.com.

Italian State Tourist Board: 1 Princes St.; London W1B; Phone: 02007 3993562; 0207 3993564; italy@italiantouristboard.co.uk.

The Il Mugello itinerary is the most physically demanding route in this book. You'll encounter 10 to 18 percent grades along 5 to 8 mile climbs on a daily basis. *Jerry Soverinsky*

Climate

If you decide to cycle any of the Italy itineraries in this section during July or August, you might as well bring your mother-in-law along, since what you're really trying to do is punish yourself. It gets hot—really, really hot—along all of the itineraries, especially the Il Mugello trip, where you are climbing 8 to 10 miles each day. It's therefore best to avoid the months of July and August.

April through October is the ideal time period for all of the itineraries. The temperatures are pleasant, you'll be greeted with the occasional rain (not too often, but just enough to keep your tires from cracking), and you won't need to constantly search for shade.

As a general guide, for all three Italy trips, here's what you can expect:

FLORENCE, ITALY[46]

MONTH	AVERAGE HIGH (°F)	AVERAGE LOW (°F)	AVERAGE PERCIPITATION (IN)
JANUARY	51	35	2.8
FEBRUARY	54	37	2.7
MARCH	59	41	3.1
APRIL	66	46	3.1
MAY	74	52	2.9
JUNE	81	58	2.2
JULY	88	63	1.6
AUGUST	87	63	3.0
SEPTEMBER.	80	58	3.1
OCTOBER	70	50	3.46
NOVEMBER.	59	42	4.4
DECEMBER	51	36	3.6

Combining Tours

If you have three weeks of vacation time piled up, you can seamlessly combine all three of the Italy itineraries. Starting from Florence, you can either begin with the Il

Steep mountain cycling requires thorough stretching prior to and immediately after every ride. It never fails to draw European (and American) onlookers, either. *Jerry Soverinsky*

[46] http://www.usatoday.com/weather/climate/europe/italy/wflorence.htm.

Italy's small towns are seemingly lost in time, and its ancient traditions preserved in an atmosphere of rustic comforts. *Niels Povlsen*

Mugello or Tuscany trip—both leave directly from the city center. However, if conditioning is an issue, I suggest starting with the Tuscany trip. By the time you've reached Il Mugello two weeks later, your legs should be adequately acclimated to the hilly terrain.

The Tuscany tour ends where the Umbria itinerary begins, so no need to schedule a transfer between the two itineraries. Finally, the Umbria tour ends in Assisi, which makes a very easy train connection (2 hours, 30 minutes, $27; www.raileurope.com) back to Florence, the start of the Il Mugello tour.

Currency

Italy has adopted the Euro (€), so if you're traveling over from France, no need to seek a currency exchange (unless you'd like to visit some of the wackiest bank clerks in Europe!).

Florence

You can spend as much time as you like sightseeing in Florence before or after the Italy itineraries below. The Florence Tourist Office can provide you with tons of helpful information:

Agenzia per il Turismo di Firenze
Via A. Manzoni, 16
Firenze 50121
Phone: 055 23320
Fax: 055 2346286
info@firenze.turismo.toscana.it; apt@firenzeturismo.it
www.firenzeturismo.it

Travel Advice

If you're a female cyclist, I advise against traveling solo. A few of my company's female guests, in isolated incidents, were harassed by testosterone-charged Italian males. Thankfully, none of them were physical confrontations, but all were uncomfortable, aggressive assaults that left the women very shaken. Not to suggest that this only happens in Italy, but it's the only country among those that my tours visit where I've ever encountered the problem.

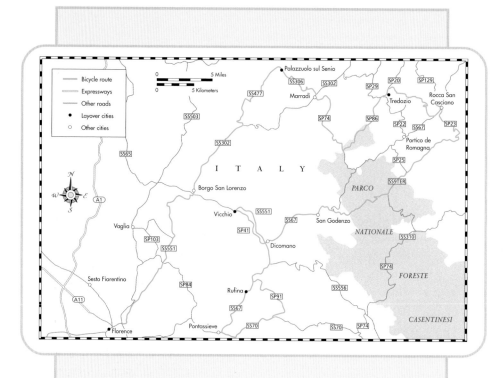

ITALY'S Il Mugello (North of Florence)

This is the most challenging trip in this entire book—hands, feet, arms, legs, knees, and elbows down. It's absolutely grueling and you'll encounter monstrously difficult climbs each and every day. Yet, if you're in great shape and not afraid to tackle 4- to 8-mile climbs, then you'll absolutely love this itinerary.

There are some other things to consider with this tour. You won't visit any significant cultural cities, there aren't many accommodation choices along the way, don't count on finding bike shops along the route (i.e., make sure you can handle routine bike repairs), and not many locals speak English. What you *will* find is extraordinary forested-mountain scenery, lightly traveled roads, homemade grappa, and an area that's nearly devoid of tourists, even though it's just a few miles outside of Florence.

You must bring a generous supply of water on every ride because there are long stretches that lack facilities.

Arrival and Departure
Air
The Florence airport is the best choice for your arrival and departure, although many international carriers service nearby alternates Bologna and Pisa. You'll find complete airline timetables at the following:

Florence: http://www.aeroporto.firenze.it/.
Bologna: http://www.bologna-airport.it/.
Pisa: http://www.pisa-airport.com/.

Italians are fiercely proud of their coveted reputation as the world's best pizza makers. And don't forget the world's best pizza deliverers, too, owing considerable deference to their reliable Vespas. *Jerry Soverinsky*

Taxi and Public Transportation
TO FLORENCE
Florence's **Amerigo Vespucci Airport** is less than 5 miles from the city center. A taxi can transport you to your hotel in less than 15 minutes and will charge €20 to €30. Otherwise, you can take a public SITA bus that will drop you at the downtown coach station (piazza Stazione) for €4.

If you're traveling from Bologna or Pisa, travel time from each is under 90 minutes and the bus/train combo will cost between €5 (Pisa) and €8 (Bologna): www.trenitalia.com.

FROM RUFINA
Trains run directly from Rufina to Florence in under 35 minutes and cost €2.05: www.trenitalia.com. From Florence, you can take a bus or taxi back to the airport.

Alternatively, you can take a taxi from Rufina directly to the Florence Airport. Budget €80 to €100 for the 45-minute journey.

If you want to reserve a private car and driver for your inbound or outboard journey, contact NewTours: Phone: 055 3361.308; Fax: 055 3361350; H.Williams@newtours.it; www.newtours.it.

Bike Rentals
I've worked with Florence by Bike for many years, and it provides solid, reliable rental bicycles. Florence by Bike: Phone: 055 488 992; Fax: 055 488 992;

info@florencebybike.it; http://www.florencebybike.it/. Prices start at €126 a week for hybrid bicycles. Pick-up and delivery is also available.

Cycling Notes

Take copious amounts of water with you every day. You won't find any roadside lemonade stands in the middle of your 8-mile climbs. Please make sure that you're addicted to mountain ascents. You'll need that energy to complete these extremely difficult rides.

Maps

Touring Club Italiano *Toscana, Carta Turisti*ca; 1:200,000.

Luggage Transfers

I recommend working with your hotels for this tour's luggage transfers. Communication within Italy can be difficult and I always find it easier to eliminate extra contacts.

Background Notes
Where Am I?

Country: Italy
Region: Tuscany
Province: Firenze
Area: Mugello
City: Palazzuolo Sul Senio

Tourist Information

Ufficio Turistico
Piazza E. Alpi, 1
Palazzuolo Sul Senio 50035
Phone: 055 804625
Fax: 055 8046461
www.palazzuolo.it

Italian butcher shops are not for the faint-hearted, and you shouldn't expect courtesy poultry decapitations. You want a chicken? You gotta look it in the eyes first. *Niels Povlsen*

Bike Shops

The closest shops are in Borgo San Lorenzo, 21 miles away. Visit the following:
Mugello Bike & Sport: 3 V. Beato Angelico; Phone: 055 8458713; and
Il Ciclismo di Formigli: Viale Pecori Giraldi 58; Phone: 055 8495422.

Sightseeing and Restaurants[47]

Along today's ride you'll pass through **Le Caldine**. Don't blink because you might miss the fifteenth-century convent of La Maddalena on the right side of the road. It's now a hospice run by two friars, but you're welcome to stop by to see several Fra Bartolomeo paintings in its chapel. It is open from 10 a.m. to 12 p.m. and 4 p.m. to 6 p.m.

The next town is **L'Olmo**, which has a few trattorie; and at the top of the steep climb is the summit of **Vetta Le Croci** (pizzeria Las Vegas is near the top). After a water bottle break, you'll descend into the **Mugello** region.

The Mugello extends on both sides of the Sieve River. It has been a summer destination for Florentians since the fourteenth century and is richly decorated with wooded hills, flowing landscapes, and centuries-old churches and villas. It's also the birthplace of the Medici family.

While snacking in **Borgo San Lorenzo**, stop by its twelfth-century church and look at its hexagonal bell tower.

Palazzuolo Sul Senio was ruled by the Ubaldini[48] until 1362, when it came under Florentine control. In the center, stop by its local museum and its seventeenth-century church and gardens.

For dinner, stop by **Locanda Senio** for regional dishes.

FLORENCE TO PALAZZUOLO SUL SENIO
ROUTE NOTES

Days 1 and 2: Florence to Palazzuolo sul Senio

The first year I offered this trip, it was nearly 90 degrees when we began this first ride. Since nearly half of the first 18 miles are uphill, it made for a brutal challenge (mile 18 was only our lunch stop—there was still a decent afternoon climb ahead of us).

Borgo san Lorenzo is the most significant of the Mugello area towns, and one that served as a throughway for most of the twentieth centuries' armies making their way south to Florence. As such, it's known its share of destruction (not counting the severe damage it suffered during a 1919 earthquake), but has rebounded to be a well-developed capital for the Mugello Valley.

You'll spend the night in Palazzuolo sul Senio, a mountain village divided by the river Senio. Up until the Tosco-Romagnola road was opened in the middle of the nineteenth century, it was largely isolated from the rest of Italy.

Distance: 40 miles

NOTE: *Leaving Florence is logistically easy, but I recommend departing early in the morning because you'll want to avoid the crush of morning traffic. In Italy blue signs are OK for biking; green signs are highway signs.*

---

[47] For this tour's daily rides, I'm combining these two sections since the information is very limited.
[48] No relation to the [Harry] Houdinis.

Directions (miles): Head to the main train station (Stazione) and follow blue signs for Bologna on the S65; you're on Spartaco Lavaginni at 0.8 miles; traffic is heavy; look for signs for Via Faentina on the S302.

At Plaza D. Liberta, follow blue signs to Bologna; you're now on Viale Don Giovanni Minzoni. Get in the right lane as you turn; follow signs for the S302 to Faentina and Fiesole.

1.1: Turn **RIGHT** for Faentina on the S302 and Fiesole; go over a bridge which curves left and turn **LEFT** past the Tam gas station for S302 and Via Faentina.

You're now on Via Passavanti; at a stop light ahead, keep going **STRAIGHT** for Faentina and S302. Just ahead, turn **LEFT** on Via Madonna Della Querce for S302 and Faentina.

2.3: You cross a river; turn **RIGHT** toward Via Faentina on Via Francesco Caraciolo.

The road curves left and becomes Via V. Cuoco; keep following signs for Via Faentina and S302 until the intersection ahead, where you'll turn **RIGHT** for Via Bolognese S65 and Borgo S. Lorenzo.

2.9: Veer **RIGHT** for Fiesole and S. Domenico until you reach a stop sign; then turn **RIGHT** for Fiesole and S. Domenico. Immediately after (you're along the river), turn **LEFT** for Borgo S. Lorenzo 25 (blue sign).

5.8: Reach Caldine and begin a steep uphill for the next 3.4 miles.

9.5 to 14: Steep downhill.

15: Reach Faltona; keep heading toward Borgo S. Lorenzo.

18.2: Turn **LEFT** for Borgo S. Lorenzo (good lunch stop); follow Tutti Direzzione to the **RIGHT** as you enter the town. Follow the 302 road through the town, toward Palazzuolo sul Senio 31 km and Maradi. Begin an uphill as you leave the town—for 8 (!) miles.

22.6: Reach Ronta (restaurants)—still climbing.

26.7: Razzuolo.

30: Just past Razzuolo, turn **LEFT** for Palazzuolo Sul Senio 16 on the S477 (right is Marradi and Faenza). There's a café as you turn. You're heading uphill for another 1.5 miles. You reach the top at 32.7.

NOTE: *This is a very tough stretch, from Borgo S. Lorenzo to 1.5 miles past this intersection.*

38.4: Reach Acquadalto (Cordalto). Markets and shops.

40.2: Palazzuolo sul Senio.

When a Mugellan local invites you to dinner for a chance to view his wine cellar, you willingly accept. Where else can you taste 300-proof "wine"?
Jerry Soverinsky

Background Notes
Where Am I?
Country: Italy
Region: Emilia Romagna
Province: Forli
City: Tredozio

Tourist Information
Ufficio Turistico
Via dei Martiri
Tredozio 47019
Phone: 0546 943937
Fax: 0546 943921
http://www.emiliaromagnaturismo.it/territor/ricerca.asp?idloc=345

Bike Shops
The closest shop is in Rocca San Casciano, 10 miles away:
Nonsolomoto Di Fabbrica Roberto
Via Saffi 34
47017 Rocca San Casciano
Phone: 0543 960433

Sightseeing and Restaurants
Along today's ride you'll pass through **Marradi**, which lies at the border of the Tuscany and Emilia Romagna provinces. It came under Florentine control in the fifteenth century and was captured during WWII by the Nazis. It's a great place for a late-morning snack (if you're lucky enough to visit during a market day, try the rotisserie chicken), with its variety of markets, stores, and shops.

San Benedetto in Alpe is a logical lunch stop, and here you'll find a good collection of small restaurants, cafés, and markets. This is also the town where a very large majority of my company's guests required a shuttle. The ride to this point is very difficult, and the thought of more climbs leading to Tredozio proved too daunting.

For dinner, try **Mulino San Michele** (6 Via Perisauli; Phone: 0546 943677) for classic Tuscan cuisine.

PALAZZUOLO SUL SENIO
TO TREDOZIO
ROUTE NOTES

Day 2: Palazzuolo to Tredozio

Today's ride offers more demanding climbs, and I recommend starting out early in the day to avoid the afternoon heat. The temperature reached 94 degrees along this route several years ago, and one of my company's guests went through eight (eight!) 1.5-liter bottles of water.

Distance: 36 miles

Directions (miles): From the center of town, turn **RIGHT** for Marradi 12. Start an uphill for the next 3.9 miles, a 7 to 8 percent grade.

    7.8: Marradi (many markets, stores, shops). Turn **RIGHT** for Firenze 64 and then a quick **LEFT** for S. Benedetto in Alpe. Begin another uphill—from 8.2 miles to 16 miles—a very tough stretch.

    18.6: Turn **RIGHT** for S. Benedetto in Alpe 6. It's a 3-mile downhill (no guardrails).

    21.6: Turn **RIGHT** at a slight fork toward Firenze and Forli (not left for Poggio); the road curves sharply and goes downhill.

    22.1: Turn **LEFT** for Forli 46.

    25.8: As you pass through Bocconi, head for Forli.

    28.2: Turn **LEFT** for Tredozio 13 and Modigliana 22. Follow this road all the way to Tredozio.

    32.1: Reach a tiny village; follow signs **LEFT** for Tredozio and Modigliana. Begin a descent.

    36.2: Tredozio.

Background Notes
Where Am I?

Country: Italy

Region: Tuscany

Province: Firenze

Area: Mugello

City: Vicchio

Tourist Information

Vicchio Tourism
Via Garibaldi, 1
Vicchio 50039
Phone: 055 8439220
Fax: 055 844275
Affair.generali@comune.vicchio.fi.it
www.comune.vicchio.fi.it/comune.html.

Bike Shops

The closest shops are in Borgo San Lorenzo, 5 miles away. Visit the following:
Mugello Bike & Sport: 3 V. Beato Angelico; Phone: 055 8458713
Il Ciclismo di Formigli: Viale Pecori Giraldi 58; Phone: 055 8495422.

Sightseeing and Restaurants

Along today's ride, **Dicomano** is a bustling market town with architecture dating back to the twelfth century.

Vicchio is no Graceland, but you'll find a monument dedicated to the early twentieth century painter Italo Vagnetti and the relatively new (2000) **Beato Angelico Museum** (on the Piazzetta Don Milani), which is filled with a diverse collection of Tuscan works. It is open Thursday through Sunday from 3 p.m. to 7 p.m. Finally, on the outskirts of town is a tiny manmade lake that is popular with local fishermen.

For dinner, try **La Casa di Caccia** (Roti Molezzano Nord; Phone: 055 8407629) for regional dishes in an idyllic setting.

TREDOZIO TO VICCHIO
ROUTE NOTES

Day 3: Tredozio to Vicchio

Today's ride poses still more physical challenges and focuses on the Valle di Sieve in central Mugello.

It was along this route several years ago that two locals chased down some of my company's guests and invited them to sample their homemade grappa. The Italians were genuinely impressed to see average cyclists venturing out into their very demanding terrain, and graciously presented Evian bottles full of their 80-plus-proof digestif to all who were willing to carry it. It was a festive reward for all who drank it later that night, a welcome nightcap to a memorable ride.

You'll spend the night in Vicchio, a small town with castle walls dating back to the fourteenth century. It's no stranger to devastation. Earthquakes destroyed much of the area in both 1798 and 1919, and the Nazis ravaged both the town and its citizens in 1944.

Distance: 80 kilometers

Directions (km): From the town center, head for Rocca S. Casciano 19. Follow signs all the way to Rocca, climbing steeply at points.

    10.0: Rocca.

    14.9: Turn **LEFT** for Forli 29; you then enter Rocca. As you head into town (markets, stores), turn **RIGHT** by the IP gas station; and then turn **RIGHT** for Scaliata S. Zeno (not left for Forli). You begin an uphill—10 percent for stretches.

    18.4: Bear **LEFT** for Galeana.

    25.8: **RIGHT** toward Premilcuore and Fantella.

    28.0: Fantella.

    34.5: Premilcuore (shops, markets); follow signs for Firenze 69 as you head through the town.

57.0: Turn **LEFT** for Firenze.
62.0: Godenzo (restaurants, bar).
66.0: San Bavello.
72.0: Dicomano (restaurants, stores). At the end of town, turn **RIGHT** for Bologna and Borgo S. Lorenzo.
79.5: Vicchio.

Background Notes
Where Am I?
Country: Italy
Region: Tuscany
Province: Firenze
Area: Montagna Fiorentina
City: Rufina

Tourist Information
Comunita' Montana Della Montagna Fiorentina
Via XXV Aprile No. 10
Rufina 50068
Phone: 055 839651; 055 839661
Fax: 055 8397760; 055 8396634
ced@comune.rufina.fi.it; segreteria@cm-montagnafiorentina.fi.it
http://www.comune.rufina.fi.it/;
http://www.cm-montagnafiorentina.fi.it/

Sightseeing
Today's route passes through **Dicomano** once again, a great place for a late-morning espresso and pastry.

You'll also pass through **Pontassieve**, a focal point of Chianti production. The town has many markets and shops with a good trattoria, **Girarrosto**, at Via Garibaldi 27.

Not far from Rufina is **Pomino**, where you'll find **Fattoria Pomino** (Phone: 055 8318810), a sixteenth-century farmhouse with an extensive wine cellar featuring vinsanto, which is owned by Marchesi Frescobaldi.

Since the eighteenth century, Rufina has earned its fame as a popular wine-growing center . Stop by **Museo della Vite e del Vino** for the full history of its wine production. Villa di Poggio Reale, Viale Duca della Vittoria 125. Phone: 055 8397932; museo@chiantirufina.it. It is open Tuesday through Saturday from 10 a.m. to 1 p.m. and 2 p.m. to 7 p.m.

For dinner, try **Girarrosto** for regional Tuscan fare. It's located four miles away in nearby Pontassieve (29 Via Garibaldi; Phone: 055 8368055).

VICCHIO to RUFINA
ROUTE NOTES

Day 4: Vicchio to Rufina
Today's ride, though still challenging, is perhaps the easiest of the trip. You can route your overnight to take advantage of the vast vineyards (both grape and olive) throughout the region. There are many upscale villas within just a few miles of Rufina, so those looking to pamper themselves will have many options.**Distance:** 43 kilometers

Directions (km): Retrace your route from the end of yesterday's ride and head for Dicomano.

    7.5: Dicomano. You are now on the S67. Head for Firenze and Pontassieve, not left on the S556 for Londa.

    27.7: Each S. Francesco.

Before you reach Pontassieve (many markets), turn **LEFT** for Vallombrosa and Arezzo.

    28.6: Turn **LEFT** on the S70 for Consumma, Poppi, and Vallombrosa. You start an ascent.

    34.6: Diacceto. Turn **LEFT** for Rufina 9.

    43.1: Rufina.

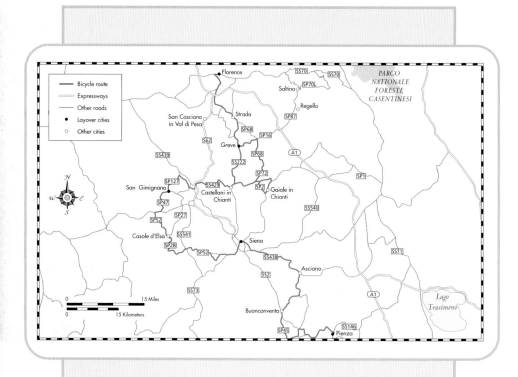

ITALY's Tuscany

The Tuscany trip is a very challenging itinerary that incorporates culturally rich tourist centers (Siena, San Gimignano, Florence) with the dramatic Tuscan countryside.

I can't promise that after visiting the area, you'll want to restore a villa (*Under the Tuscan Sun*), but I do guarantee[49] that you'll discover some of the warmest people and most beautiful scenery in Europe, filled with great food and wine at every stop.

Spend a few days pre- or post-trip sightseeing in Florence, a cultural mecca to visitors from around the world. Its collection of artwork is second to none, and it is home to the Renaissance art period, one of the most influential in the last 1,000 years.

[49] No guarantee.

Almost every Tuscan town of appreciable size has a church. Or at least a building with pretty stained glass windows. *Jerry Soverinsky*

Arrival and Departure
Air
The Florence airport is the best choice for your arrival and departure, although many international carriers service nearby alternates Bologna and Pisa. You'll find complete airline timetables at the following:

Florence: http://www.aeroporto.firenze.it/
Bologna: http://www.bologna-airport.it/
Pisa: http://www.pisa-airport.com/

Taxi and Public Transportation
TO FLORENCE
Florence's **Amerigo Vespucci Airport** is less than 5 miles from the city center. A taxi can transport you to your hotel in less than 15 minutes and will charge €20 to €30. Otherwise, you can take a public SITA bus that will drop you at the downtown coach station (piazza Stazione) for €4.

If you're traveling from Bologna or Pisa, travel time from each is under 90 minutes and the bus/train combo will cost between €5 (Pisa) and €8 (Bologna): www.trenitalia.com.

FROM PIENZA
Buses run from Pienza to Florence (one change) with a total journey time of 2 hours and 40 minutes (www.trainspa.it). Otherwise, contact **ABC Noleggio** for a private transfer (Phone: 0577 809007; info@abc-rent.com; www.abc-rent.com).

Bike Rentals
My top choice for renting reliable hybrid and road bicycles is with Florence by Bike (Phone: 055 488 992; Fax: 055 488 992; info@florencebybike.it; http://www.florencebybike.it/). Prices start at €126 a week for hybrid bicycles. Pick-up and delivery is also available.

You want to know the real way to ingratiate yourself to your Italian hosts? Take a large group of sweaty and smelly friends, block access to public sidewalks with scattered bodies and bicycles, pepper your conversations with cackling laughter, and leave trash and miscellaneous food crumbs behind after you leave. The result? Look how taken this shopkeeper (1) is with your effort. And wedging your napping friend into a nearby window sill (2) likely scored bonus points! *Jerry Soverinsky*

Cycling Notes

Compared to the rest of Western Europe, Italy's public transportation system is poor. This means that you should be a strong cyclist before you set out on this tour because support lifts will be difficult to find along the route.

I've hosted hundred of cyclists on this itinerary, from advanced beginners through expert, but the advanced beginners were considerably overmatched and spent a good deal of time in the company's support vehicle.

Italian rental bikes are sketchy at best. Try finding spoke replacements for their Depression-era wheels—not easy! *Niels Povlsen*

Maps

Touring Club Italiano *Toscana, Carta Turistica*; 1:200,000.

Background Notes
Where Am I?

Country: Italy
Region: Tuscany
Province: Firenze
Area: Chianti
City: Greve-in-Chianti

Tourist Information

Ufficio Turistico
Via Giovanni da Verrazzano 59
Greve in Chianti 50022
info@chiantichianti.it
www.comune.greve-in-chianti.fi.it/; www.greve-in-chianti.com

Bike Shops

Ramuzzi: Via Italo Stecchi 23; Greve; Phone: 055 853 037.

Sightseeing

The Chianti League consortium was established at the beginning of the thirteenth century as a defensive alliance to counter Siena's expansionist designs. A few hundred years later, Siena was absorbed by the Grand Duchy of Tuscany. The League's formal purpose was extinguished, but its more practical wine production was able to flourish. You'll pass the major Chianti League towns of **Greve**, **Castellina**, **Gaiole**, and **Radda** along the next few riding days.

Greve in Chianti developed in the Middle Ages as a market town, due to its position at the intersection of the old Via Chiantigiana Road.

Along the rides to and from Greve, you'll pass the eighth-century town, **Impruneta**, a traditional agricultural center famous for its cotto tile production. Its portrait of the Madonna (inside the basilica at Piazza Buondelmonti) is one of the town's most renowned treasures.

Montefioralle, a tiny village that is in walking distance from Greve, is the birthplace of the Vespucci family. There's a tiny trattoria here, **Taverna del Guerrino**, whose owner takes great pride in having been the host several years ago to Clint Eastwood (a vintage Dirty Harry glossy proudly hangs on its walls).

Continuing from Greve, you reach **Panzano**, whose parish church of San Leolino is typical of those found in the Tuscan countryside. Be sure to look at the remains of its ancient castle.

Shopping

There are several nearby farms and wine cellars that distribute the Chianti Classico wines. One of the most popular, **Castello di Uzzano** (Via Uzzano 5), offers tastes of its wine and extra-virgin olive oil. They also breed pure blooded Friesian horses. **Enoteca del Gallo Nero** (Piazza Santa Croce) offers an exhibit of the Classico wines and other local products.

Local meat specialties can be found at **Antica Macelleria Falorni** (Piazza Matteotti), which is renowned throughout Europe for its quality and selection. Stop by **Il Ferrone** (Via Chiantigiana 36) for the locally produced Florentine terracotta tiles.

Restaurants

Giovanni da Verrazzano (Piazza Matteoti); **La Cantina** (SS222); **Omero Casprini** (Passo dei Pecorari, Via G. Falcone); **Trattoria del Montagliari** (Panzano, Via Montagliari 29), and **Gallo Nero** (Via C. Battisti, 9) are among the popular and nearby favorites that serve tasty, homemade Tuscan dishes.

Luggage Transfers

Gemini Tours is a reliable firm for your next few days of luggage transfers. Ask for Eleanor; she speaks English (36 Via Mascaroni, Panzano; Phone: 055 852561; nologemini@tin.it).

FLORENCE TO GREVE IN CHIANTI
ROUTE NOTES

Days 1 and 2: Florence to Greve in Chianti
Leaving Florence is not technically difficult, but if you've spent just a few minutes near the city center, you'll understand that it's best to depart early in the morning and avoid the buzzing scooters and rickety Fiats that scream through its streets.

Today's ride is quite short—less than 20 miles—but it's always proved to be a more than adequate challenge for my company's guests. You'll enter the area known as Il Chianti, the only region authorized to produce the authentic Chianti Classico wine, the gallo nero (black rooster) its identifiable trademark. And you'll fall in love with the peaceful and friendly Tuscan countryside, its hills dotted with vineyards and olive groves.
Distance: 28 kilometers

Directions (km): 0.0: Begin at Piazza S. Maria Novella. Turn **RIGHT** into Via Dei Fossi; cross the bridge onto Via De'Serragli).

0.6: As you cross the bridge (Ponte alla Carraia), the street is called Piazza N. Sauro, which then turns into Via de Serragli.

    1.8: Porta Romana. Take the road uphill (Via Del Poggio Imperiale), which leads to Piazzola del Poggio Imperiale.

    3.1: At the Poggio Imperiale, turn **RIGHT** at di S. Felice a Ema

NOTE: *Go all the way to the palace until the road ends.*

    4.7: Follow the roundabout **LEFT** to Impruneta.

    6.8: Pozzalatico (there is a market on your left before the turn—look for the Tabacchi sign). At the church, turn **LEFT** to Impruneta. You begin a 3.3 kilometer climb uphill.

    11.5: Impruneta (many stores, shops, and restaurants). Follow the main road through the town.

    12.7: Turn **LEFT** to Greve 20km (not right to Siena) and Centro. As you head through the town, follow the next sign **RIGHT** to Greve (you are in the Centro, and Greve is 19km away at this point). As you head to Greve, you'll also see signs to Strada.

    13.2: You reach the piazza at Impruneta—check out Ristorante Bellavista for a snack.

    14.8: At an intersection, turn **LEFT** for Greve, Firenze, and Strada. You are heading downhill.

    17.6: **RIGHT** to Greve, 12km.

    17.9: You reach Strada in Chianti, with a bank, restaurant, and one or two shops. Head for Siena as you pass through the town.

    26.0: Castello di Verrazzano.

    27.7: You reach Greve in Chianti.

GREVE LOOP RIDE

The Greve loop ride visits the most important towns in Il Chianti. While not designed to be a pub crawl (I can tell you from experience, drinking wine while cycling under a Tuscan sun is not a wise combination), it's meant to lead you through a delightful collection of charming hill towns on a route that is generally lightly traveled.

Distance: 70 kilometers

Directions (km): 0.0: Take a **RIGHT** out of the piazza in the direction of Siena.

    6.2: Panzano.

    9.6: Take a **LEFT** at the fork for Radda in Chianti 11.

    11.3: Lucarelli

    19.9: Go **STRAIGHT** at a stop sign for Gaiole in Chianti 8 (also signed Siena and Montevarchi). Enter la villa.

    21.1: Take a **RIGHT** for Gaiole 7, Siena 32 (begin a descent).

    23.4: Commune di Gaiole in Chianti.

    27.2: Take a **LEFT** for Gaiole in Chianti and Montevarchi.

    29.2: Gaiole in Chianti. Follow the road through the village. Keep **STRAIGHT** as you leave Montevarchi.

    34.9: Take a **LEFT** for Radda in Chianti and Badia a Coltibuono (on your right just after you turn). Badia a Coltibuono is an Abbazia Vallombrosana from the eleventh century.

    41.0: Take a **RIGHT** and follow the road as it curves for Poggibonsi.

    41.7: La Villa.

    42.3: Take a **RIGHT** for Poggibonsi and Radda.

    42.4: Take a **RIGHT** for Lucolena and Badia Montemuro.

42.5: Careful! Fifteen percent downhill.

44.8: Begin a climb to 45.3 kilometers; after which, a descent.

45.9: Very steep climbing until 46.8.

53.8: Take a **RIGHT** for Lucolena.

NOTE: *You can also turn left here for Greve, shortening your ride by 4 kilometers.*

55.2: Lucolena.

59.1: Take a **LEFT** at a T-intersection for Strada 13 and Greve 10.

59.5: Dudda.

60.7: Take a **LEFT** and follow the road as it curves uphill for Greve in Chianti 8.

62.8: Top of the Sugame Pass; now downhill all the way to Greve.

69.1: Go **STRAIGHT** at a traffic light into the piazza.

Background Notes
Where Am I?
Country: Italy
Region: Tuscany
Province: Siena
City: San Gimignano

Tourist Information
San Gimignano Tourism
Piazza Duomo 1
San Gimignano 53037
Phone: 0577 940008
Fax: 0577 940903
prolocsg@tin.it
www.sangimignano.com

Bike Shops
Bellini Bruno: 41 Via Roma;
San Gimignano; Phone: 0577 940201; info@bellinibruno.com;
www.bellinibruno.com.
Autofficina Jolly: 10 Via di Fugnano; Phone: 0577 940575;
info@jolly-pentacar.com;
www.jolly-pentacar.com.

Sightseeing
San Gimignano has hardly changed since the Middle Ages when it was used as a throughway for pilgrims en route to Rome (not that anyone is still around

You'd be remiss if you failed to sample grappa during your Italian vacation. While some compare it to liquid fire, others are more compassionate and draw parallels to rubbing alcohol. No relation to the photo, except that there's a really good restaurant that serves grappa a few streets away from this church. *Servizio Turistico Associato Assisi*

from the Middle Ages to verify, but just an ongoing hunch by locals). After centuries of military conflict that engaged Tuscan families, only 14 of its original 72 towers remain as survivors.

Piazza della Cisterna, the town's main piazza, is surrounded by towers and palazzi (mansions). I love enjoying an early evening gelato (and mid-evening gelato, and late-evening gelato), people-watching, and reading comics here.

Torre Grossa is the highest tower in the town, and its the only one open for visitors to climb. The hours are 9:30 a.m. to 7:30 p.m. daily.

The Collegiata di Santa Maria Assunta, San Gimignano's largest church, houses Ghirlandaio's *Decoration Of The Chapel Of St Fina*, which is one of the great works of Renaissance painting. It is open from 9:30 a.m. to 12:30 p.m. and 3 p.m. to 6 p.m.

Museum of Sacred Art and the **Etruscan Museum** hold a wide range of art and archaeological artifacts from the area. Both museums are open daily, except Mondays, from 9:30 a.m. to 7:30 p.m.

Restaurants

Try **Pizzeria Peruca** (16 via Capassi) for pizza. More formal restaurants include **Dorando** (2 Vicolo dell'Oro) and **La Stella** (75 via Matteo). There are dozens of trattorie and pizzerie on or near Via San Giovanni. For dessert, **Gelateria di Piazza** (4 P. della Cisterna) serves the town's best gelato.

Luggage Transfers
Bianchi Girolamo: Phone: 0577 940499; 0577 940385.

GREVE IN CHIANTI TO SAN GIMIGNANO
ROUTE NOTES

Day 3: Greve to San Gimignano

The reviews of San Gimignano from my company's guests have been mixed. Some love the atmosphere of this picturesque hill town and its twelfth-century towers, while others grew tired of its omnipresent gift shops and tourist crowds.

I fall somewhere in the middle: I love the atmosphere of this picturesque hill town and its twelfth-century towers; and the omnipresent gift shops and crowds of tourists don't really bother me. Which is to say, both observations are accurate, so you need to decide for yourself how much of a buzzkill it'll be when you've passed your fourth consecutive store hawking San Gimignano boxer shorts (nice fit, I especially like the appropriately placed Bella Torretta).

Distance: 56 kilometers

Directions (km): 0.0: Take a **RIGHT** out of the piazza for Siena and Panzano.

    6.2: Go **LEFT** at Panzano. Follow the road as it curves for Siena.

    9.7: Take a **RIGHT** and follow the signs for Castellina and Siena.

    11.2: Take a **LEFT** and follow the road as it curves for Castellina and Siena.

    19.5: Go **RIGHT** at a crossroad for Poggibonsi (left is the center of Castellina).

    38.6: **LEFT** at a stop sign/t-intersection for San Gimignano, Volterra, and Certaldo.

    38.9: **STRAIGHT** past the AGIP station on your left. Don't take the right turn for San Gimignano. This is essentially a fork in the road; you're continuing straight, but it's the right fork.

    39.3: **RIGHT** for San Gimignano 11, Certaldo 11, and Empoli 40 onto Via XX Setttembre.

    40.1: **STRAIGHT** for Empoli (busy road).

    41.0: **LEFT** for San Gimignano 11 (there is a Superal store at this turn).

    42.2: **RIGHT** for Volterra and San Gimignano.

    42.2: **RIGHT**; IMMEDIATELY turn **RIGHT** again for Ulignano, Cusona, and Casaglia.

    43.4: **STAY RIGHT** for Cusona.

    48.1: **LEFT** at a stop sign for San Gimignano.

NOTE: *Make the right for the 4-kilometer detour to Certaldo, a very worthwhile stop.*

    55.6: San Gimignano.

Disobeying local cycling laws
can subject your bike to the
ultimate penalty: public hanging.
Niels Povlsen

Background Notes
Where Am I?
Country: Italy
Region: Tuscany
Province: Siena
City: Siena

Tourist Information
Siena Tourism
Via di Citta, 43
Siena 53100
Phone: 0577 280606
Fax: 0577 281041
aptsiena@siena.turismo.toscana.it
www.terresiena.it;
www.siena.turismo.toscana.it/homeuk.htm

Bike Shops
Centro Bici S.N.C.: Viale Toselli Pietro 110; Phone: 0577 282550.
DF Bike: Via Massetana Romana 54; Phone: 0577 271905.

Sightseeing
If you want to talk piazzas, there's none finer than the Piazza del Campo in Siena. This crescent-shaped medieval square, with its burnt-orange hues and Gothic town hall recall Siena's golden age from the thirteenth and fourteenth centuries.

The **Duomo** is a spectacular mix of sculpture, paintings, and Romanesque-Gothic architecture. It is open 7:30 a.m. to 7:30 p.m. Nearby, the **Museo dell'Opera del Duomo** houses important artworks including Duccio's *Maestà*. It is open 9 a.m. to 7:30 p.m.

In the center of the Piazza del Campo, you'll find **Palazzo Pubblico** (built in 1310) and its **Tower of Mangia**, available for climbing from 10 a.m. to 6 p.m. daily.

Siena's Museo Civico (in Palazzo Pubblico) is not to be missed because it houses masterpieces of Sienese art. It is open daily from 9:30 a.m. to 6:15 p.m. and on Sundays until 12:45 p.m.

Restaurants

Siena is famous for its *panforte*, a dense cake with honey, lemon, and almonds. Also try *ricciarelli*, soft almond cookies with powdered vanilla toppings. **Nannini** (Banchi di Sopra 22) is Siena's oldest pasticceria, and they make a mean panforte.

The more popular restaurants are **Antica Hosteria Cane e Gatto** (V. Pagliaresi 6), **Osteria le Logge** (V. del Porrione 33), and **De Carlo e Franca** (V. di Pantaneto 138 at Pispini). Save room for a gelato at **Bibo** (Via Banchi di Sotto 61), which serves sandwiches and lunch entrées.

Luggage Transfers

Radio Taxi: 0577 49222.
Taxi: Piazza Stazione; 0577 44504.

SAN GIMIGNANO TO SIENA
ROUTE NOTES

Day 4: San Gimignano to Siena

Cycling into Siena can be a daunting task because in addition to the unbearable traffic, as you're pedaling anxiously to reach the city center, children will try to hit you with soccer balls. Local tradition states that ". . . only when a [man/woman] has known the taste of a football[3] in the face will he truly be welcome as our guest."[4]

The traffic is definitely thick, and the city is definitely huge, so if you prefer a more tranquil hotel setting, you should arrange to stay outside the city, perhaps in nearby Sovicille, where there's frequent bus service to Siena well into the late evening.

Distance: 67 kilometers

Directions (km): 0.0: Go **RIGHT** out of parking lot #1 (parcheggio Montemaggio) for Siena, Poggibonsi, Volterra, Certaldo.

0.1: **RIGHT** at a stop sign for Siena, Poggibonsi, and Volterra (downhill).

0.5: Take the **FIRST EXIT** at the roundabout for Castel S. Gimignano and Volterra (still downhill).

12.4: Go **RIGHT** at a stop sign for Volterra 15. As you turn, you reach Castel S. Gimignano, a restaurant. You're now on the SS68.

15.5: Go **LEFT** for Casole d'Elsa and Ponsano.

23.0: Take a **RIGHT** for Casole d'Elsa 3 and Il Merlo.

23.4: Il Merlo.

25.4: Casole d'Elsa. The village is up ahead on the left. It's worth a visit.

26.5: Go **RIGHT** at a stop sign and head downhill. The sign is on your right, pointing to Radicondoli, Pomarance, Monteguidi, Mensano, and Pievescola. It's almost a 180-degree turn.

28.7: Follow the road **RIGHT** as it curves for Radicondoli, Larderello 34.

33.2: Follow the road **LEFT** as it curves for Mensano 2 and Radicondoli.

34.5: Follow the road **RIGHT** as it curves for Radicondoli.

36.2: Take a **LEFT** at a T-intersection for Siena, continue downhill.

40.7: Go **RIGHT** at a stop sign/T-intersection for Siena on the SS541.

[3] Soccer is known as football in Europe. And football is known as quilting.
[4] From *1,001 Wacky Siena Traditions*, page iv.

40.8: Turn **LEFT** for Sovicille, Ancaiano, and Pievescola.

42.0: Pievescola.

42.3: Turn **RIGHT** at a roundabout (statue in the middle) for Siena, Sovicille, and Ancaino.

47.2: Simignano.

51.7: Ancaiano.

53.0: Follow the road to the **RIGHT** as it curves for Palazzone. The sign is on your right, but it is obscured. Do not turn left for Piscialembita or Siena.

55.2: Go **STRAIGHT** for Sovicille

55.4: Sovicille.

55.9: Turn **LEFT** at a stop sign for Siena. Follow the road next as it curves **RIGHT** for Siena.

60.4: Go **LEFT** at a yield sign for Siena on a busy road.

63.0: Costalpino.

64.9: Costafabbri. Follow signs for Siena.

66.0: The road gets busier as you approach Siena.

66.4: Turn **RIGHT** at the roundabout for the Siena Centro sign. This puts you on Strada di Pascaia.

66.5: Follow the road as it curves **LEFT** for the Duomo. Follow your Siena map to your individual hotel.

Indigents seeking monetary donations are not relegated to American big cities. The larger Italian cities are rife with beggars.
Niels Povlsen

Background Notes
Where Am I?
Country: Italy
Region: Tuscany
Province: Siena
City: Pienza

Tourist Information
Pienza Tourism
Corso Rossellino, 59
Pienza 53026
Phone: 05787 49071
Fax: 0578 749071; 05787 17242
infopienza@quipo.it
www.infinito.it/utenti/ufficio.turistico

Bike Shops
Autofficina Valenti Alfiero: Via della Madonnina 28; Phone: 0578 748465.

Sightseeing
Pienza is the birthplace of the fifteenth century's Pope Pius II, who took a strong interest in developing Pienza into an aesthetically beautiful town (he commissioned Florentine architect Bernardo Rossellini for much of the design). You'll enjoy wonderful views of the Orcia Valley while sipping an espresso outside the Duomo, not caring a whit whether the Brinman file is up to date back at your office.

You can admire Rossellini's work in the **Piazza del Duomo**, which is home to its Duomo and Sienese school altarpieces. **Palazzo Piccolomini** provides insight into the Piccolomini family history.

Restaurants
Il Prato (Viale Santa Catarina 1) is one of Pienza's most respected trattorie. Also try **Trattoria Latte di Luna** (Via San Carlo 2) and **Osteria Sette di Vino** (Piaza di Spagna 1).

SIENA TO PIENZA
ROUTE NOTES

Day 5: Siena to Pienza
Your last riding day through Tuscany leads you to the attractive town of Pienza. The ride is not terribly taxing, with only a few modest climbs.
Directions (km): 0.0: Begin at the intersection of Via Antonio Lombardi and Via N. Orlandi, and turn **LEFT**.
  0.1: Go **LEFT** at a stop sign on Via N. Orlandi (you're heading southeast).
  2.0: Continue **STRAIGHT** and downhill past a stop sign.
  3.1: Go **LEFT** at a roundabout for the green Roma highway signs.
  3.3: Continue **STRAIGHT** through the roundabout, exiting toward green Roma sign.
  4.2: Agip station is on your left.
  4.3: Exit roundabout and follow green Roma sign.
  5.2: Turn **LEFT** and follow the green Roma sign at this busy intersection.
  7.3: Take the second roundabout exit marked Autostrada A1—a green sign. This takes you in
       the direction of the autostrada, not on it.
  7.7: Continue **STRAIGHT** and follow another green Roma sign.
  8.8: Turn **RIGHT** for Asciano.
  8.9: Taverne dÁrbia.
  9.8: Go **RIGHT** and follow a one-way arrow (straight ahead is no entry).
  10.4: Turn **RIGHT** for Asciano and you'll cross a bridge.

10.5: Arbia.

11.0: Continue **STRAIGHT** for Asciano. You'll continue following signs for Asciano for the next 17 km.

28.1: Go **RIGHT** on the SS2 at a T-intersection just before Asciano. Heading for Buonconvento 18, Abbazia di Monte Oliveto M. 10, Chiasure 10. You begin an ascent.

35.8: Head **RIGHT** for Buonconvento 9, Abbazia di Monte Oliveto M. 1

36.7: You can turn left to visit the Abbazia, a worthwhile stop. Otherwise, continue without turning.

44.8: Buonconvento.

45.3: Go **LEFT** at a stop sign for Roma 201.

47.6: Turn **RIGHT** for Montalcino.

57.2: Take a **LEFT** at a yield sign for Torrenieri and S. Querico dÓrica. DETOUR: you can turn right here to visit Montalcino, 1.2km away. Another worthwhile visit.

62.3: Continue **STRAIGHT** through an intersection for Torrenieri, S. Giovanni dÁsso, Siena, and Asciano.

62.9: Merge **LEFT** and join the SS2 road.

63.8: Exit for Torrenieri.

64.2: Continue **STRAIGHT** at a yield sign for Torrenieri.

64.6: Turn **RIGHT** at a stop sign (map reference 258).

65.0: Cross a bridge.

65.2: It's a steep uphill until 66.6

66.7: There's a steep downhill until 68.8. Be careful for loose gravel!

68.8: It's all uphill until 71.2

71.6: Take a **LEFT** at a yield sign and stop sign (away from S. Quirico center).

72.0: Turn **LEFT** for Pienza 9 (now on the SS146).

80.7: Pienza.

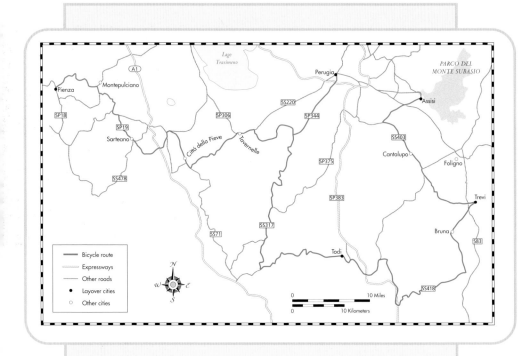

ITALY's Umbria

This is a wonderful trip and a perfect continuation from the Tuscany itinerary for those who can spare the extra week away from the office. The cycling is very challenging, with 2- to 5-mile climbs on every day's ride.

The route will take you through the most enchanting towns in the Umbrian region and give you the opportunity to intimately discover all of the area's cultural and gastronomic specialties.

Arrival and Departure
Air

The Florence airport is the best choice for your arrival and departure, though many international carriers service nearby alternates Bologna and Pisa. You'll find complete airline timetables at the following:

Florence: http://www.aeroporto.firenze.it/.
Bologna: http://www.bologna-airport.it/.
Pisa: http://www.pisa-airport.com/.

Continuing from Tuscany, you'll enter the Umbria region, a magnificent landscape ideal for cycling.
Servizio Turistico ssociato Assisi

Taxi and Public Transportation

TO PIENZA

From the bus station (piazza Stazione), you'll need to take two buses to reach Pienza: the #131 from Florence to Siena, and the #112 from Siena to Pienza. Total travel time is 3 hours and 25 minutes. You can find detailed schedules at www.trainspa.it.

If you want to reserve a private car and driver, contact **Ricci bus:** www.balzanabus.com; or ABC Noleggio: www.abc-rent.com. Expect to pay €150-200 for a one-way private transfer.

FROM ASSISI

Direct bus connections between Assisi and Florence last 2 hours and 30 minutes and cost €11. **SULGA** Phone: 0755009641; www.sulga.it; sulga@tecnonet.it.

Private taxis are considerably more expensive—you'll pay at least €185 for the door-to-door service. Contact one of the following:
Jacopi Claudio, Phone: 075812191, ascesi@ascesitour.it, www.ascesitour.it;
Cuppoloni Andrea, Phone: 075812777; ac.autonoleggio@virgilio.it
Baroni Autonoleggi via dell'Artigianato, Phone: 0758001855, Fax: 0758008504, baroni.autonoleggi@libero.it.

Bike Rentals

You can rent bikes from Pienza's **Valenti Alfiero** (Via della Madonnina 28; Phone: 0578 748465). However, when your trip ends, you'll need to return the bike to Pienza and then head back to Florence.

An easier solution is to rent your bike from **Florence by Bike**: Phone: 055 488 992; Fax: 055 488 992; info@florencebybike.it; http://www.florencebybike.it/. Prices start at €126 a week for hybrid bicycles. It will be a bit more convenient for returning the bike at the end of the trip and heading to the airport.

Cycling Notes

As I suggested for the Tuscany trip, you should be a strong cyclist before setting out because support lifts will be difficult to find along the route.

Maps

Touring Club Italiano *Toscana, Carta Turistica*; 1:200,000; and Touring Club Italiano *Umbria, Carta Regionale*; 1:200,000.

Background Notes
Where Am I?

Country: Italy
Region: Umbria
Province: Perugia
City: Perugia

Tourist Information

Perugia Tourism
Via Masi 9, Sangallo Palace Hotel
Perugia 06100
Phone: 0755736458
Fax: 07557 39386
info@sangallo.it;
info@iat.perugia.it
www.bellaumbria.net;
http://perugia.umbria2000.it/ciecm/ ;
http://perugia.umbria2000.it/ciecm/

Bike Shops

Casa del Ciclo: Via Pellas Fratelli 55; Perugia; Phone: 075 5729067.
Six miles from Perugia, there's **PuntoBici**: Via G.Brodolini; Ellera Di Corciano; Phone: 075 5181293; Fax: 075 5181295; puntobici@puntobici.com.

Sightseeing

Perugia is a thriving Umbrian town, and its medieval hill atmosphere is harmoniously in sync with its cosmopolitan shops and cafés.

Its main square, **Piazza IV Novembre**, is flanked on both sides by its impressive **Duomo** and thirteenth-century **Palazzo dei Priori**. The latter houses the finest Umbrian School paintings.

Restaurants

One of Perugia's more notable trattorie is **Cesarino** (Via della Gabbia 13), where you'll find traditional pastas and grilled meats. **La Taverna** (Via delle Streghe 8) and **Osteria del Bartolo** (Via Bartolo 30) are both popular with locals.

Luggage Transfers

Taxi Radio Taxi: Piazza Vittorio Veneto; Phone: 075 5004888.

PIENZA TO PERUGIA
ROUTE NOTES

Day 1: Pienza to Perugia

You'll begin your Umbria introduction with a visit to its bustling capital, Perugia. Despite its modern cultural importance (two universities and a commercial center), Perugia has preserved its medieval character with its narrow back streets and Etruscan walls. Sample the scrumptious Perugina chocolates, an indulgent local delicacy.

Distance: 107 kilometers

Directions (km): 0.0: Begin at the Hotel Corsignano (near the town center) and turn **RIGHT**.

0.1: Head **LEFT** for Montepulciano. Continue following signs for Montepulciano and Chianciano.

12.4: Montepulciano.

12.6: Turn **RIGHT** for Chianciano (also a green sign for Roma 1).

19.6: Chianciano Terme.

19.9: Go **RIGHT** for Chiusi. The road will curve left.

20.8: There will be an API gas station on your left.

21.4: Stay **LEFT** following signs for Perugia, Chiusi 12, and Sarteano 8.

21.6: You cross a tall bridge until 21.9km.

23.0: Go **STRAIGHT** through a roundabout for Sarteano.

23.9: Turn **RIGHT** for Sarteano 7 and Cetona 14.

25.1: It will be uphill until 29.3km.

29.3: Sarteano.

31.2: Continue **STRAIGHT** past a stop sign for Cetona 5.

31.5: Turn **RIGHT** for Cetona.

37.0: Cetona.

37.9: Go **STRAIGHT** past a stop sign. You're on the SS321.

40.6: Continue **STRAIGHT** for Chiusi Scalo 4.

44.2: There will be a Tamoil station on your left.

44.2: Turn **RIGHT** for Fabro.

51.2: There will be an IP gas station on your right.

51.3: Head **LEFT** at a stop sign for Citta della Pieve.

53.1: There will be a steep climb until 56.7km.

56.3: Citta dell Pieve.

56.7: Turn **RIGHT** at a stop sign for Perugia 40.

57.9: Go **LEFT** for Perugia 39. You're on the SS220.

72.6: Bear **RIGHT** for Perugia 24.

75.6: Turn **RIGHT** for Pietrafitta and Cibottola.

78.9: Pietrafitta, and a yield sign. Bear **LEFT**—and a steep ascent—for Cibottola. As the road curves right in the village, there is a gelateria on your left with a fountain in front of it. Just ahead the road narrows, and just beyond that, you'll turn **LEFT**.

79.6: After your **LEFT** turn, there will be a fruit/flower shop on your right and an open view of the landscape on your left.

80.2: Begin a steep descent.

81.6: Continue **STRAIGHT**. Do not turn right to Cibottola.

83.3: Turn **RIGHT** at a stop sign for Marsciano. There's an API gas station directly in front of you.

88.8: Go **LEFT** for Pila 7 and Perugia 11.5.

96.3: Pila.

100.4: Perugia. Continue **STRAIGHT**.

101.2: Begin following *Centro* signs (still **STRAIGHT**).

103.5: Follow the *Stazione/Centro* sign. This takes you through two underpasses. Continue following *Centro* signs as you travel uphill.

106.9: You'll reach the statue of A. Guissepe Garibaldi. Go through the arch and follow your city map to your individual hotel.

While lesser known to Americans than Tuscany, Umbria is no less inviting and is a region teeming with wonderfully rustic landscapes and culturally rich cities. *Servizio Turistico Associato Assisi*

A favorite joke among Umbrians making its way around the Internet: How many Tuscans does it take to screw in a lightbulb? Two. One to screw it in, and one to screw it up. Ouch. *Servizio Turistico Associato Assisi*

Background Notes
Where Am I?
Country: Italy
Region: Umbria
Province: Perugia
City: Todi

Tourist Information
IAT del Tuderte
Piazaza Umberto I, 6
Todi
Phone: 075 8943395
Fax: 075 8942406
info@iat.todi.pg.it
www.comune.todi.pg.it/

Bike Shops

Bike facilities along today's route are scarce. There is a shop in Spoleto, but that's 28 miles from Todi: **Scocchetti Cicli**: Via Marconi Guglielmo 82; Phone: 0743 44728.

Sightseeing

Todi, yet another remarkable Umbrian hill town, is perfect for a late-afternoon stroll. Its ancient streets all seem to offer majestic views of the valley below.

Its main piazza is the thirteenth-century Piazza del Popolo, buttressed by its **Duomo** and **Palazo del Commune** museum.

Restaurants

You'll enjoy typical Umbrian dishes at **Cavour** (Via Cavour) and **Ristorante Umbria** (Via San Bonaventura 13). The latter offers fine views from its picturesque terrace.

Luggage Transfers

Marconi Enia: Via Piana 23/b – Pantalla; Phone: 075 888235.
Mechella Giampiero: Via Terza di Firenzuola, 17; Phone 075 8944862.
Moriconi Dario: Loc. Ponte Rio, 233; Phone: 075 8989411.

PERUGIA TO TODI
ROUTE NOTES

Day 2: Perugia to Todi

Todi is an enchanting Umbrian town, tenaciously gripping the steep hillside upon which it rests, surrounded by a dense forest of olive trees that served as its natural defense system from centuries past. After a challenging day's ride, relax with a latte in its Piazza del Popolo, the perfect place to linger and reflect on your surreal surroundings.

Distance: 94 kilometers

Directions (km): 0.0: Begin at Porta San Costanzo. This is about 1.3km from the town center. As you head downhill, follow blue signs for Foligno and Todi, and green signs for A1 Firenze Roma.

0.9: Turn **RIGHT** at a traffic light onto Strada Tuderte.

1.4: You'll pass a sign indicating you're on the SS317.

4.0: You've left Perugia and are still heading downhill.

4.5: Bear **RIGHT** for Orvieto and Marciano. You're still on the SS317.

8.1: S. Martino in Colle.

9.5: Head **RIGHT** for Pila 4 and Castel del Piano 7.

13.5: Turn **LEFT** at a traffic light for Spina, Villanova, S. Biagio, and Badiola 3.

21.5: Go **LEFT** at a stop sign for Marsciano 11.5, Spina 1.5, and Mercatello 4.

22.1: Continue **STRAIGHT** for Marsciano 11 (left is Spina 1).

23.1: Exit roundabout for Marsciano 10. This will lead you downhill.

24.3: Turn **RIGHT** for Mercatello.

25.1: You'll cross the bridge.

25.4: Mercatello. Follow signs through the village for Migliano and San Vito in Monte.

31.6: Turn **RIGHT** at an intersection for Migliano.

32.5: Take a **LEFT** for S. Vito in Monte.

34.5: You'll begin a 10 percent ascent until 38.8.

38.8: San Vito in Monte.

40.6: Continue **STRAIGHT** for San Venanzo 10.

44.5: Continue **STRAIGHT** for Orvieto 35 and San Venanzo 6.

45.5: Turn **RIGHT** at a stop sign for Orvieto 31. You're on the SS317 and will bike uphill until 52.5.

48.0: Continue **STRAIGHT** for Orvieto 28.

50.3: Ospedaletto.

NOTE: *From here, there are several long ascents and descents, some as long as 10km.*

62.9: Colonnetta di Prodo.

63.5: Make an 180-degree **LEFT** turn at a stop sign for Todi on the SS79, continuing downhill.

69.6: Prodo. Continue following signs for Todi.

90.4: Turn **LEFT** at a stop sign for Todi 5.

90.7: Take a **RIGHT** for Todi 6 (yes, sign indicates 1km further than the previous sign. That's Italy.). You'll reach Pontecuti and follow the road signed for Todi.

92.1: Todi. Continue uphill.

93.9: Go **LEFT** and follow signs to *Centro*.

Background Notes
Where Am I?
Country: Italy
Region: Umbria
Province: Perugia
City: Trevi

Tourist Information
Palio dei Terzieri
Piazza Mazzini, 5
06039 Trevi
Phone: 0742 781150
Fax: 0742 781150
protrevi@protrevi.com
www.protrevi.com;
www.comune.trevi.pg.it/

Bike Shops
Scocchetti Cicli (11 miles from Trevi on Spoleto): Via Marconi Guglielmo 82; Phone: 0743 44728.

Climbing the bell tower in your Umbrian resting spot offers the best countryside views. Sorry, there are no elevators to the top. You'll need to make the climb yourself. *Servizio Turistico Associato Assisi*

Sightseeing

Most of Trevi's town life revolves around its central piazza, where you'll find its thirteenth-century town hall and civic tower. You can check out contemporary paintings at the **Flash Art Museum**, housed in the town's prestigious Lucarini residence. It is open 10 a.m. to 1 p.m. and 3 p.m. to 6:30 p.m. It is closed Mondays and Tuesdays.

Trevi's main square hosts an ongoing assortment of plays, musical performances, and gastronomic events during August. Several restaurants even offer dishes of centuries past, which is quite remarkable, as one would think 700-year-old dairy dishes would have gone bad by now.

Restaurants

Trevi has several intimate ristorante and trattorie that serve delicious Umbrian specialties. Among the more notable are **Da Pippo** (Via Sant'Angelo Nuovo); **Ristorante la Cerquetta** (Via Flaminia); **Pan di Zucchero** (Via Campo Reale 4); and **L'Ulivo** (Via Monte Bianco), 3 kilometers from Trevi in Matigge.

Luggage Transfers

Carlo Castellani: Via dei Trinci 38, Foligno; Phone: 0742 20300.
Taxi: Largo Carducci Giosue, Foligno; Phone: 0742 340790.

TODI TO TREVI
ROUTE NOTES

Day 3: Todi to Trevi

Today's ride leads you to Trevi, another spectacular hilltown with an approach framed by dense stretches of olive trees. It's a delightfully unaffected Umbrian destination, with winding, cobblestone streets that are enclosed within two sets of medieval walls.

Distance: 68 kilometers

Directions (km): 0.0: Begin from the Hotel Villaluisa, near the town center. Turn **LEFT** out of the hotel parking lot and then immediately bear **RIGHT** for Collevalenza. Continue on this road, following it as it curves left.

    5.9: Bear **LEFT** for Collevalenza and Massa Martana.

    6.0: Collevalenza.

    6.5: Continue **STRAIGHT** at a traffic light.

    9.8: Turn **RIGHT** for Massa Martana 3.

    12.6: Massa Martana.

    12.8: Turn **RIGHT** at a stop sign for Massa Martana Scalo.

    18.3: The road goes under railroad tracks.

    18.4: Head **LEFT** for M. Martana Scalo.

    20.3: Terni.

    20.5: The road goes under a highway.

    22.3: Acquasparta.

    23.5: Continue **STRAIGHT** at a stop sign for Spoletto.

    23.8: Turn **LEFT** for Spoletto 20. Go over railroad tracks

    24.1: The road goes under a highway. Follow signs for Spoletto over the next few kilometers.

    39.3: Baiano.

    46.2: Spoletto.

    46.5: There's a sign indicating just ahead that you'll turn left for Montefalco.

    46.7: Take a **LEFT** at a traffic light onto Via Marconi. It does not say Montefalco at the turn. This turn takes you over a small bridge.

    46.9: Turn **LEFT** at a stop sign for Montefalco.

    47.2: The road goes under a railway bridge. From 46.9km, the road is lined with businesses.

    48.1: Continue **STRAIGHT** at a traffic light for Montefalco.

    49.9: Go **STRAIGHT** at a yield sign for Montefalco.

    51.0: Maiano.

    56.1: La Bruna.

    56.6: Head **RIGHT** for Trevi.

NOTE: *Sign is faint, so look for the turn after you reach La Bruna.*

    58.0: Castel S. Giovanni.

    58.9: Turn **LEFT** for Trevi. It's a small, faded sign. If you get to a castle on the right side of the road, you've missed the turn.

61.0: Follow the road as it curves **RIGHT** for Trevi.

64.3: Take a **LEFT** at a stop sign for Flaminia and SS3 (straight is Cannaiola).

64.7: Turn **LEFT** at a stop sign, and then take an immediate **RIGHT** at a yield sign for Trevi 3.

65.3: Continue **STRAIGHT** at a traffic light on the SS3 for Trevi. Begin climbing into the city, following Trevi signs.

67.8: You'll see a sign for Pinacoteca and for Trevi Hotel. Take a **LEFT**.

68.1: Trevi.

Background Notes
Where Am I?

Country: Italy
Region: Umbria
Province: Perugia
City: Assisi

Tourist Information

Servizio Turistico Associato
Piazza del Comune, 22
Assisi 06081
Phone: 075 812534
Fax: 075 813727
info@iat.assisi.pg.it
www.umbria2000.it;
www.comune.assisi.pg.it/ita/index2.htm

Bike Shops

S. Maria Degli Angeli: Via G. Becchetti 31; Phone: 075 8042550;
angeluccicicli@libero.it.

Sightseeing

Despite its influx of daily crowds (thanks to its pilgrimage history), Assisi has managed to remain a remarkably picturesque and charming Umbrian town.

Make the **Basilica of San Francesco** your first stop (after the WC). It is the thirteenth-century church of St. Francis and pilgrimage destination for thousands of Assisi's annual visitors. It is open daily, but closed from 12 p.m. to 2 p.m. Walk to the nearby **Rocca Maggiore**, a fourteenth-century castle with majestic views of the Umbrian countryside below, and the **Museo Romano** (open daily from 10 a.m. to 1 p.m. and 2:30 p.m. to 5:30 p.m.), home to ancient Roman ruins.

Restaurants

Fine dining (not necessarily expensive) abounds in Assisi. Among the city's best, try **Fortezza** (Vicolo della Fortezza 2/b), **Da Erminio** (Via Montecavallo 19), **Frantoio** (Vicolo Illuminati), and **Umbra** (Piazza del Commune).

TREVI TO ASSISI
ROUTE NOTES

Day 4: Trevi to Assisi

This last Umbrian riding day leads you to the pilgrimage site of Assisi, a beautifully preserved medieval town overflowing with spectacular artworks and the most renowned restaurants in Umbria.

Distance: 52 kilometers

Directions (km): 0.0: Start at the central piazza, follow signs for Foligno, Spoleto, Roma, and Perugia.

- 0.1: Take a **RIGHT** for Spoletto at the fork (left of the fork makes a steep ascent).
- 0.5: Continue **STRAIGHT** at a stop sign and head downhill.
- 1.4: Make a sharp (almost 180-degree) **RIGHT** away from the sign facing you (pointing left for Spoleto). You're still going downhill at the turn. If you reach Bovara, you've missed the turn. As you turn right, you'll continue downhill and Trevi is in front of you. The turn is easy to miss.
- 1.8: Continue **STRAIGHT** and downhill for Borgo Trevi.
- 4.3: Make a quick **LEFT**, then a quick **RIGHT** (essentially straight) at the traffic light/stop sign, across the SS3, for Montefalco.
- 4.4: Turn **LEFT** at an intersection for Montefalco.
- 4.8: Take a **RIGHT** for Montefalco. This leads you on a bridge over the railroad tracks—the same road you approached Trevi on yesterday.
- 6.1: Cannaiola.
- 8.4: Turn **RIGHT** for Montefalco and Fabbri.
- 12.2: Bear **LEFT** for Montefalco.
- 12.6: Montefalco (outskirts).
- 12.9: Turn **RIGHT** toward Montefalco.
- 13.8: Go **LEFT** for Bevagna 8. DETOUR: You can turn right to visit Montefalco.
- 14.6: Bear **RIGHT** for Bevagna 6.
- 15.1: Montepennino.
- 15.4: There will be an Esso station on your right. You're heading downhill. Look carefully for the next turn.
- 15.9: Take a **LEFT** for Bevagna. It's a small sign. There's an Auto Accessori store at the turn.
- 19.4: Continue **STRAIGHT** at a yield sign for Foligno.
- 19.5: Bevagna.
- 20.3: Bear **RIGHT** for Foligno 10. Detour: Continue straight for centro to visit Bevagna, a highly recommended stop.
- 20.8: Turn **LEFT** for Bevagna and Cannara.
- 21.0: Follow the road as it curves **RIGHT** for Bettona and Perugia.
- 25.0: Cantalupo.
- 27.6: Continue **STRAIGHT** for Bettona 11.
- 34.9: Passagio.

35.1: Take a **RIGHT** at the roundabout for Bastia and Assisi. The sign is before the turn.

37.8: Costano.

39.3: Stay **RIGHT** for Assisi.

41.1: The road gets busier. Continue following signs for Assisi.

41.5: S.M. Angeli.

41.8: Bear **LEFT** for Assisi 4.

42.4: Continue **STRAIGHT** at a traffic light for Assisi.

42.7: Continue **STRAIGHT** and bear **LEFT** onto a smaller street. Otherwise, the road curves right here just past the basilica.

45.4: Take a **RIGHT** for Assisi 1. Follow signs for the Porta Nuova.

51.9: Assisi sign.

52.0: Turn LEFT at a T-intersection for Centro and Piazza Matteoti.

Your Umbria itinerary finishes in Assisi, a strikingly beautiful medieval town overflowing with spectacular artworks and the most renowned restaurants in the region. *Servizio Turistico Associato Assisi*

Hands-down, Switzerland is my favorite destination for outdoor sports. Its snow-capped mountains, picturesque villages, and well-maintained trails network make it the ideal destination for cycle touring. *Kandersteg Tourismus*

SWITZERLAND

Since 1993, I've spent every one of my vacations[50]—both summer and winter—in Switzerland. I absolutely love it there because it's paradise for those seeking outdoor action. Whether you like to bike, hike, mountain bike, walk, winter hike, ski, horseback ride, skip, handspring, or cartwheel, you'll find expertly maintained trails and an eager and attentive tourism staff to help plan your visit.

I briefly mention in the Italy section that many of my company's prospective guests have the perception that Switzerland is only for super-athletes, those fit to tackle a barrage of grueling Alpine ascents. This couldn't be further from the truth, unless they added, "But I hear they're real friendly there." More on that in a minute.

While Switzerland is filled with the most dramatically beautiful Alpine scenery in Europe, that doesn't mean that all roads lead only uphill. There's a fine network of moderate valley routes that make "The Best of Switzerland" route, below, suitable for cyclists of *almost* all abilities. Even inexperienced cyclists who find themselves overmatched will take comfort knowing that they are supported by Europe's most efficient and extensive transportation network.[51]

---

[50] Except for my Green Bay, Wisconsin, Binge Drinking Weekend (BDW) in June 1997.
[51] There's no real way to objectify that allegation, of course. But on another note, Swiss trains are the only ones in Europe where I feel comfortable enough to go number two.

Many people[52] nonchalantly dismiss the Swiss as rude and indifferent. I can't generalize for all Swiss, though my experiences have proved to be overwhelmingly positive, as much as in any other European country. The Swiss are not as outgoing and welcoming as the Irish, but they overcompensate with a very attentive and professional tourism industry. This means that while you're unlikely to strike up engaging conversations with Swiss locals, you'll receive almost instantaneous responses from your hotel reservation requests. [53]

Cycling Overview

It's no secret that the Swiss are Eco-friendly.[54] Their constant effort to expand and improve their very extensive national cycling network is a welcome sign for all cyclists. Road cyclists will find either dedicated cycling paths or wide, clearly delineated biking shoulders (usually separated from motorized traffic with bright, yellow lines). Mountain bikers will find a constantly expanding collection of packed-dirt trails and crude asphalt roads, all very well marked and maintained.

The Best of Switzerland tour can be cycled by cyclists of almost all abilities above the true novice level. Because the Swiss transportation is comprehensive and easily accessible during every day's ride (and very cycle-friendly), it's easy for those who want to cut short any day's ride to seek the assistance of a nearby bus or train.

The mountain biking tour is another story. While transportation lifts are still available throughout the route, the rides themselves are substantially more difficult than those on the road biking itinerary. Almost every mountain biking ride includes a 2- to 5-mile steep ascent, so you'll need to be in strong physical shape to complete the itinerary.

Tourist Information

Switzerland Tourism hosts a comprehensive tourist office website: www.myswitzerland.com. You can download maps, itineraries, historical information, and even recipes for Swiss specialties.

If you've got any further questions, you can contact representatives directly at the following:

U.S.:

Switzerland Tourism

Swiss Center

608 Fifth Avenue

New York, NY 10020

Phone: International Toll-Free 011800-100-200-30

Or U.S. only: 1-877-Switzerland

(1-877-794-8037)

Fax: (212) 262-6116

info.usa@switzerland.com

---

[52] My Uncle Ed and Aunt Mary.

[53] In one truly bizarre incident, I received confirmation for a Zurich hotel reservation three days before I sent the request!

[54] Several years ago, I was preparing to leave a Zurich campground with my company's cargo van. I started the ignition to warm the engine, knowing that the diesel van needed a bit of advance notice before chugging away. Apparently, 30 seconds of idling was a bit much for my camping neighbor, who reached into my car (the driver's window was rolled down) and shut off the ignition while I was sitting in the driver's seat!

U.K.
Switzerland Tourism
Swiss Centre
10 Wardour Street
London W1D 6QF
Phone: 00800 100 200 30; 020 7292 1550
Fax: 00800 100 200 31
info.uk@switzerland.com

Climate and When to Go

The road biking itinerary can be comfortably cycled May through October (expect colder and wetter extremes outside of July and August). You'll undoubtedly encounter rain no matter which month you visit, especially during your rides through the mountain ranges. Don't shy away from the summer period. I've hosted dozens of groups in July and August, and the weather was never too uncomfortable.

The mountain biking itinerary should only be cycled late June through mid-September. I suppose you could stretch it a bit and arrive in late May or late September (or even early October), but the spring thaw can affect trail conditions into early June, and early winter conditions can hit the Bernse Oberland in the early fall.

The temperatures and precipitation for Berne will serve as a good general guideline for both trips.

BERN[55]

Month	Average high	Average low	Wet days
JANUARY	36	27	15
FEBRUARY	40	29	13
MARCH	49	34	17
APRIL	54	39	17
MAY	64	47	18
JUNE	70	54	19
JULY	75	57	15
AUGUST	75	57	12
SEPTEMBER	68	51	12
OCTOBER	57	44	11
NOVEMBER	45	35	12
DECEMBER	38	30	12

[55] http://www.usatoday.com/weather/climate/europe/swtzlnd/wbern.htm.

The ugliest day in Switzerland beats the prettiest day on the slaughterhouse line at Tyson Foods. *Kandersteg Tourismus*

Combining Tours

It's an easy task to finish The Best of Switzerland tour and take the Lausanne train to Grindelwald for the Switzerland Mountain Bike Challenge. Travel time is just over 3 hours and a ticket, if purchased locally, costs 31 CHF. Swiss Federal Railways: http://www.rail.ch/index_e.htm.

Currency

Sorry, no Euros for the "neutral"[56] Swiss, who steadfastly hold on to their Swiss Franc. Therefore, if you're heading over from Italy or France, while many Swiss shops will still accept your Euros (and give you change back in francs), you'll receive a better exchange rate if you dump all your Euros at the nearest Swiss bank, forget about trying to get any of the bank tellers to smile, and obtain Swiss Francs.

You'll find abbreviations for the franc as both SFr or CHF, which can get confusing, because a famous Swiss cartoon heroine is named SFra, while her brother's name is CHFa. This is not to be confused with the large Swiss hamburger chain, SFRCHra.

Swiss Francs are broken down into 100 centimes. You'll find Swiss coins available in 1, 5, 10, 20, and 50 centime coins; and 1, 2, and 5 Swiss Franc coins. Swiss notes come in denominations of 10, 20, 50, 100, 200, 500, and 1000 Francs.

You can see current images of all Swiss coins and notes at the following: www.swissmint.ch/e/products/index.shtml (coins) www.snb.ch/e/banknoten/noten.html (notes).

Travel Advice

Take lots of money when traveling to Switzerland. It's not so much that the lodging is any more expensive than in the rest of Europe, but those darn trains and buses . . . well, you pay a high price for efficiency.

Food costs are also high. Switzerland is highly protective of local food products, and you won't find as many U.S. items on Swiss store shelves as you will in other European countries. The competition is not as strong, which means prices are almost always higher.

Take potato chips, for instance. I love a good chip with lunch, and Switzerland makes a really good paprika-flavored variety (think mesquite, though not as spicy). But that's all you'll usually find, just one Swiss brand. And at $2 or $3 a bag . . . well, sometimes I find myself reaching for the potato salad instead.

Luggage Transfer Notes

Most Swiss hotels can help coordinate your luggage transfers. In fact, in many cases the price is very modest. The Swiss railway system will transfer bags from one station to another throughout the country for only 10 CHF per bag. Your starting hotel can also coordinate with your destination hotel for retrieving the luggage when it arrives at their local station. It's a system that has worked very well for all of my Swiss custom trips where van support wasn't included. Make sure to ask your hotel before you depart; this can often help save you a lot of money, instead of hiring local taxis.

---

[56] Don't get me started.

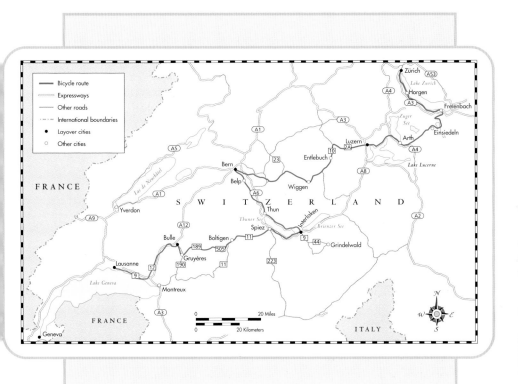

The Best of SWITZERLAND

Combining superb cycling with the highlights of traditional Swiss-German culture, this truly is a fantastic itinerary. There are two very difficult mountain passes, but with easily accessible transportation lifts, participants of almost all abilities can handle the rides.

Arrival and Departure
Air
Zurich (www.unique.ch),
Geneva (www.gva.ch), and
Basel (www.eurairport.com)
airports all receive regular service from throughout North American and Europe.

The trip begins in Zurich, so the logical gateway airport is in Zurich. For
your departure home, Geneva is closest to Lausanne (less than 40 miles), though
speedy train transfers can also whisk you back to Zurich or Basel.

A unique service to Switzerland's incoming visitors is the opportunity to check your luggage from your North American departure city all the way to your arrival city's train station. Cost for this extra service is $15 ($24 Canadian). Download the appropriate registration labels at http://www.raileurope.com/us/rail/passes/fly_rail_baggage.htm.

Similarly, when preparing to leave Switzerland, you can check your luggage all the way through to your final North American destination from 130 Swiss train stations—larger railway stations even issue boarding passes. Note: This service is not available to passengers on U.S. carriers, Air Canada, Air France, KLM, SAS, and Lufthansa.

Taxi and Public Transportation

TO ZURICH

Zurich's airport is a quick 15-minute ride into central Zurich. Expect to pay 50 CHF for the door-to-door service. You'll find dozens of taxis outside Zurich's arrival terminal.

Public transportation is simple and efficient, and the 11-minute direct train will cost you 7 CHF. www.sbb.ch

FROM LAUSANNE

From Lausanne, a taxi to the Geneva airport will run you 150 to 250 CHF and take just about an hour (both depend on your starting time and day of travel). Check out www.taxiservices.ch, where you can reserve a ride.

Alternatively, trains run from Lausanne to the Geneva Airport and the 43-minute journey costs 11.50 CHF. www.sbb.ch.

Bike Rentals

Switzerland offers one of the best and most efficient bike rental systems in Europe. You can pick up a city, mountain, or child's bicycle at one of over 100 rail stations throughout Switzerland and return it to any of the other participating stations (both Zurich and Lausanne offer staffed locations). Expect to pay 30 CHF per day for adult models http://www.rentabike.ch/.

Only in Switzerland would a public campground border a lake. This is the view from my tent at the Zurich municipal campground. *Jerry Soverinsky*

Cycling Notes

Not to harp on this, but don't be dissuaded from cycling in Switzerland for fear that it'll be one long, endless mountain. It's not. Granted, the scenery here is beautiful and mountains are plentiful, but the itinerary only traverses two major mountain passes. And with the assistance of an excellent public transportation network, you'll be able to cycle reassured and know that clean, safe support is almost always nearby.

There's so much to see and do in most of the overnight stops that you should allow for plenty of layover sightseeing days, especially in Luzern, Bern, and Interlaken.

Maps

Michelin #216, *Neuchatel-Basel-St. Gallen*; 1:200,000; and Michelin #217, *Geneve-Bern-Andermatt*; 1:200,000.

Zurich

First-time visitors to Switzerland should allow at least one full day for sightseeing in Zurich prior to cycling. Contact the Zurich Tourist Board for information to assist your visit:

Zurich Tourism
Hauptbahnhof
Zurich 8023
Phone: 01 215 4000; Fax: 01 215 4044
information@zuerich.com; www.zuerich.com.

Background Notes
Where Am I?

Country: Switzerland
Region: Central Switzerland
Canton: Luzern
City: Luzern

Tourist Information

Luzern Tourism
Bahnhofstrasse 3
Luzern 6002
Phone: 041 227 17 17
Fax: 041 227 17 18
luzern@luzern.org
www.luzern.org

Your ride up the Jaunpass will be your tour's most challenging ascent. When you reach the top, stuff yourself with Alpine Macaroni at the mountain restaurant and take a food-induced coma/nap. A perfect day.
Jerry Soverinsky

Bike Shops

Bike City: Hirschengraben 43;
Phone: 041 242 13 12.
Interbike Shop: Bireggstr. 35;
Phone: 041 361 01 71.
Velo Muller; Baselstr. 53;
Phone: 041 240 39 70.

Sightseeing

The tourist office in Luzern is located at Frankenstrasse 1. **Walking tours** leave from the tourist information office daily at 10 a.m. and 4 p.m. The tours last 2 hours and cost 15 SF.

Contact Schiffahrtsgesellschaft des Vierwaldstattersee at Werftestrasse 5 for **boat tours**. Phone: 041 40 45 40 for current times and prices.

You can rent pedalboats, sailboats, and motorboats near the train station. It's a great way to spend a sunny afternoon.

Visit the **Kappelbrucke** and its water tower.

The Wagner Museum (Wagnerweg 27) is open Tuesday through Saturday from 9 a.m. to 12 p.m. and 2 p.m. to 6 p.m. daily except for Sunday and Monday. It is open until 5 p.m. on Sunday and is closed Monday.

Mt. Pilatus is a 7,000 foot snow-capped mountain along the western part of Lake Luzern. To reach it, take a trolley from the train station to Kriens, where a cable car ascends the Frakmuntegg to 4,600 feet. From there, change cars to reach a peak of 5,500 feet. Finally, a short walk will take you to Esel, the center of Pilatus's many peaks. The current cost is about 75 SF.

Gletschergarten (Glacier Gardens) (Denmalstrasse 4) is a display of giant potholes and pits carved from the glacial ice that once covered Luzern some 20 million years ago. Look for the Lion Monument, which was carved in 1820 and dedicated to the Swiss soldiers who died in the French Revolution. It is open until 6 p.m.

Restaurants

Goldener Lower (Eisengasse 1), **Hotel Restaurant Waldstatterhof** (Zentralstrasse 4, offers vegetarian options), **Wilden Mann** (Bahnhofstrasse 30, offers a diverse menu in a tavern-like atmosphere), and **Galliker** (Schutzenstrasse 1) are the more popular restaurants for Swiss specialties.

Luggage Transfers

ABC Taxi: Phone: 041 2101010.
Alfons Steiner Taxi: Seestrasse 54; Phone: 041 3901533.

ZURICH TO LUZERN
ROUTE NOTES

Day 1: Zurich to Luzern

Today's itinerary begins with an easy ride along the Zurichsee, a crystal-clear lake dotted with lazy sailboats and steamers. You'll pedal anxiously for Luzern, the cultural center of Switzerland, where you should plan for a layover sightseeing day. Luzern has an enviable geographic location, nestled comfortably on the Vierwaldstatter See, a magnificent lake teeming with water sport activities and surrounded in the distance by spectacular snow-capped mountains.

Distance: 51 miles

Lunch Stop: Rothenthurn, Arth.

NOTE: *Swiss bicycle lanes are usually marked at the side of the road with yellow dashes, which separate the lane from automobile traffic. Also, green signs are for highways—no cycling allowed. The directions begin from the Zurich campground, 3 miles from the city center along the Southern edge of the Zurichsee.*

Directions (miles): Follow the bicycle path along the southern edge of the Zurichsee towards Pfaffikon. The Zurichsee is on your left, and you are riding on the 3-road. After less than 2 miles, you pass the Lindt chocolate factory on your right.

As you cycle along the 3-road, you'll pass Ruschlikon, Thalwil, Oberrieden, Horgen (following the road to Chur) and Wadenswil.

12.0: Richterswil. Keep following signs to Pfaffikon.

16.3: Pfaffikon.

16.7: Take a **RIGHT** toward Gotthard Schwyz and Einsiedeln.

NOTE: *If you pass an Elf gas station and a Peugeot dealer, you missed the turn.*

You can follow the 8-road until Schindellegi, but it's usually a very busy road. A better road (though slightly more difficult):

Follow the #9 bike route signs from Pfaffikon to Schindellegi. Immediately after your right turn, look for the #9 National Bike Path sign (points toward Einsiedeln). One-hundred yards ahead, turn LEFT, following the #9 sign. You'll also see an information sign indicating Zug 58 and Einsiedeln 20. You begin a very steep climb.

NOTE: *The climb from Pfaffikon to Altmatt is a challenging one. You can take the train from Pfaffikon, which greatly simplifies the ride. It eliminates almost all serious climbing and subtracts about 12 miles from the route.*

18.7: Follow signs for Feusisberg and Schindellegi onto Ruostelstrasse.

19.9: Feusisberg (Italian restaurant on the left. Bakery).

20.2: Pizzeria. A small market is on the left just past the pizzeria.

20.4: Continue **STRAIGHT** at an intersection toward Zurich 35.

21.1: Roundabout. Follow the blue signs to Einsiedeln.

21.7: Schindellegi.

22.1: Turn **LEFT** for Gotthard, Einsiedeln, and Schwyz.

21.9: There's a gas station. Follow signs to Schwyz and Einsiedeln.

22.9: You'll see a sign that says *Zentral Schweiz*. Ahead 300 yards, follow blue signs to Gotthard, Luzern, and Schwyz.

27.2: Rothenthurn (plenty of markets for a lunch stop).

28.7: Follow signs **STRAIGHT** for Luzern, Gotthard, and Schwyz. You're still on the 8-road.

30.0: You'll pass through Sattel. A half-mile later, turn **RIGHT** toward Arth. Ahead 100 yards, turn **RIGHT** for Luzern, Arth, and Steinerberg.

35.0: Goldau. A few 100 yards later, turn **RIGHT** for Zurich and Luzern.

36.2: As you pass through Oberarth, you'll reach a fork in the road. Follow the road **RIGHT** to Luzern.

37.5: Arth. Turn **LEFT** for Luzern (Zugersee will be on your right after the turn). Follow the bike path along the Zugersee.

41.0: Immensee. Bear **LEFT** at the intersection (across from the church).

41.4: At the top of a very short, steep climb, you reach an intersection. Turn **RIGHT**.

43.2: Kussnacht am Rigi. Turn **RIGHT** on the 2-road toward Luzern and Merlischachen.

43.5: Turn **LEFT** toward Luzern and Merlischachen (blue sign). At the traffic circle, exit **STRAIGHT** ahead for Meggen, Luzern, Merlischachen on the 2-road. Follow the 2-road the rest of the way to Luzern. You'll pass through Merlischachen and Meggen. The road goes downhill to lake level.

51.3 miles: Luzern.

The Swiss road biking itinerary has two very difficult climbs, but the remainder of the tour is manageable for cyclists of almost all abilities. *Jerry Soverinsky*

Background Notes
Where Am I?

Country: Switzerland
Region: Schweizer Mittelland
Canton: Bern
City: Bern

Tourist Information

Bern Tourism
Laupenstrasse 20
Bern 3001
Phone: 031 328 12 28
Fax: 031 328 12 99
info-res@bernetourism.ch
www.berne.ch

Bike Shops
Ski und Velo Center: Hirschengraben 7; Phone: 031 312 0031.
Velo Service Bern: Bollwerk 39; Phone: 031 311 6116.
VelokurierLaden: Lorrainestr. 6a; Phone: 031 333 0520.

Sightseeing
Visit the city's famous bears in their subterranean pit. It is open until 6 p.m. and is ideal for public viewing.

Arrive 4 minutes before the hour to see the famous live performance of the Clock Tower's figurines. Guided tours are given daily at 4:30 p.m.

Albert Einstein's House is located at 49 Kramgasse. The admission is free.

Bern is the capitol of Switzerland and you can visit the House of Parliament there. Tours are given on the hour from 9 a.m. to 12 p.m. and 2 p.m. to 4 p.m. The admission is free.

Kuntzmuseum (Hodelestrasse 8-12) features a collection of Paul Klee's works. It is open until 5 p.m. and closed Monday.

For shopping or browsing, visit the luxurious shops at Marktgasse and Spitalgasse.

For horseback riding, visit Reitsportanlage Eldorado at Gurtentali. Phone: 031 971 48 40 for reservations.

The ride from Luzern to Bern is long—62 miles—but it is relatively flat. If the distance still intimidates you, feel free to hop a train to boost you along. They're never more than a mile or two from your route throughout the day. *Jerry Soverinsky*

Restaurants

You'll find several reasonably priced restaurants along the Barenplatz and most have outdoor seating in the summer. Some popular favorites are Restaurant Brasserie Anker (Zeughausgasse 1; offers fondue), Klotzlikeller (Gerechtigkeitsgasse 62; great seafood), Le Mazot (Barenplatz 5; a traditional Swiss restaurant with fondue, raclette, and other specialties), Zum Rathaus (5 Rathausplatz; has been a Bern landmark since 1863; serves wonderful Swiss dishes), and Brasserie Zum Barnegraben (Muristalden 1).

Luggage Transfers

Baren Taxi: Weissenbuhlweg 6; Phone: 031 3711111; www.baerentaxi.ch.
Kombi Taxi: Phone: 031 332 2606; info@ktb-transporte.ch;
www.ktb-trasnporte.ch.

LUZERN TO BERN
ROUTE NOTES

Day 2: Luzern to Bern

Today's ride poses some short, challenging climbs, but always among spectacular scenery. If the 62-mile distance scares you, there are numerous train stations along your route, all of which can transport you quickly and efficiently to Bern.

I love Bern, the capital of Switzerland. It's a very charming, medieval city where I almost always include a layover sightseeing day.

Distance: 61 miles

Directions (miles): From the Luzern station, follow signs to Kriens and 2a signs. On the 2a road, follow signs to Bern, Littau, and Wolhusen. Follow the 2a road until it intersects with the 10-road. Do not turn off onto the 10-road when it is a green (highway) sign. Turn only when you see the blue 10-road signs.

13.0: You reach the 2a/10-road intersection. Turn **LEFT** for Bern. You'll soon see signs to Wolhusen, but there is no bicycle path, so stay to the side of the road. Follow the 10-road the entire way to Bern. Very easy directions.

15.0: You'll begin a 1.2-mile climb. While cycling along the 10-road, you'll pass Entlebuch (18.8), Hasle (20.3), Schupfheim (23.4—shops, markets), Escholzmatt (28.6), Trubschachen (34.5), Langnau (38.5), Grosshochstetten (46.3), Worb (51.7), Rufenacht (53.4), and Gumligen (57.1).

Continue to follow the 10-road to Bern; then to Zentrum, which leads to the town center.
61.0: Center of town.

There are as many local variations of the traditional Swiss fondue recipe as there are Belgians wearing monocles (a lot).
Bon appetit. *Jerry Soverinsky*

Background Notes
Where Am I?
Country: Switzerland
Region: Bernese Oberland
Canton: Bern
City: Interlaken

Tourist Information
Interlaken Tourism
Hoheweg 37
Interlaken 3800
Phone: 033 826 53 01
Fax: 033 826 53 75
mail@InterlakenTourism.ch
www.interlakentourism.ch

Bike Shops
Balmer Bike: Harderstr. 44; Phone: 033 822 42 28.
Free Motion GmbH: Aarmuhlestr. 1; Phone: 033 821 1440.

Sightseeing
There's no question that the journey up to **Jungfrau** is expensive, but if you can afford the 135 CHF ticket, it's a great excursion. Jungfrau is the highest rail station point in Europe and the views for most of the ride (except when you're completely underground) are spectacular. You can pick up the train from Interlaken East station.

The train ride to Harde Kulm has great views of Interlaken, the Thunersee, and Brienzersee. You can also pick up the train from Interlaken East train station.

You can visit Lauterbrunnen's immense waterfalls (Trummelbach) on the way to the Jungfrau.

Try hiking to the Ice Caves if you visit Grindelwald. It's an inexpensive choice, yet a great way to spend the afternoon. You can take the train to

Grindelwald from the East station for just a few dollars. A bus will take you to the caves (from Grindelwald), if you want to skip the 90-minute hike.

Outdoor tennis courts are located at Hoheweg 53.

The Hasler Riding Stables (21B Alpenstrasse) in Bonigen offers rides. Check also at the Voegeli Riding School (66 Scheidgasse) in Unterseen.

Paragliding (150-250 CHF.) is located in Unterseen, near Camping Manor Farm.

Sailing and windsurfing are located at Hotel Neuhaus, also near Camping Manor Farm.

During the summer, the William Tell pageant play in nearby Matten is presented in a 2,000-seat amphitheatre. Although the entire play is in German, you'll love the setting and production. Tickets range from 15 to 55 CHF and can be purchased through Tellburo at Bahnhofstrasse 5.

Restaurants

Among some of my groups' favorites are **Im Gade** (Hoheweg 70) for fresh fish and seasonal game specialties. They also offer a few tasty fondues.

Krebs (Bahnhofstrasse 4) has a casual terrace where you can sample seasonal Swiss specialties.

Luggage Transfers

Taxi Mader: Phone: 079 333 1060; taximaeder@gmx.ch.
ABC Taxi: Phone: 033 822 2700.
Alpenland Taxi: Phone: 033 8236060; a.taxi@gmx.ch.

BERN TO INTERLAKEN
ROUTE NOTES

Day 3: Bern to Interlaken

Your easy ride today follows the coast of the Thunersee, a picture-perfect lake in the spectacular Jungfrau region. Nestled between the Thunersee and Brienzersee, Interlaken is one of the most exciting travel destinations in all of Europe. I highly recommend spending at least one layover day in Interlaken, especially if you're an outdoor enthusiast. For whether you want to hang glide, river raft, hike to a group of ice caves, or take a full-day excursion to the top of the 3,454-meter Jungfraujoch, Interlaken is within easy access of all of these. While it has grown exponentially over the past dozen years (and thus attracts a large tourist crowd), such is the price to pay for location.
Distance: 54 kilometers
NOTE: *For the first half of today's ride (until Thun), you'll follow the #8 National bike path. Some parts are unpaved, hard-packed dirt.*

Directions (km): Begin at Bundesgasse and follow signs for Thun 30, Belp 9, and the #8 bike path. Follow this street to Kochergasse (casino is on your right), and bear **RIGHT**. You'll notice once again the bike path sign pointing to Thun and Belp.

0.4: Pass over the Kirchenfeldbrucke, bearing **RIGHT** at the end toward Thun and Belp on the #8 national bike path. Follow the road as it becomes Bernerstrasse.

Follow the #8 path and turn right on Aegertenstrasse. At the end of this street, turn **LEFT**, where you'll see the red bike path sign to Thun and Belp. This is also the #7 regional bike path. Follow this straight ahead.

Turn **RIGHT** onto Jubilaumsstrasse. This road veers to the left and eventually hits a T-intersection. Turn **LEFT** onto Tierparkweg and follow this toward Tierpark and the #8 national path. This road goes over a bridge and joins Sandrainstrasse, which you'll follow **LEFT**.

A few hundred yards ahead, turn **LEFT** on Seftigenstrasse.

3.3: Follow signs (at the roundabout) to Thun, Belp, and Munsingen. Less than 0.1 km ahead, turn **RIGHT** toward Thun and Belp onto Nesslerenweg.

4.8: You pass a farm and the road bears left. About 0.5 km later, turn **LEFT** toward Thun and Belp over a bridge. Immediately after the bridge, head **STRAIGHT** toward Thun and Munsigen along the #8 national path.

You'll eventually pass the airport, and soon thereafter, the road is packed dirt. From there, you need to keep following the Thun signs, which will eventually lead you to Thun.

The bike sign after the airport points **LEFT** to Thun 21km. The path is packed dirt for a short distance and then ends in a restaurant parking lot. Turn **RIGHT** just after the restaurant and follow the main road past cornfields. Continue **STRAIGHT** on this main road and look for notification of the #8 sign on electrical poles. Keep following #8 signs.

30.0: You'll reach the information kiosk in Thun. In the distance, you'll also see the Thun castle. Follow this out to the main road, and you'll be cycling parallel to the Aare River. Follow the blue sign **LEFT** to *Transit* at the T-intersection (do not turn right toward Interlaken). You'll be on Kyburgstrasse as you turn.

Turn **RIGHT** toward Gunten. The Thun Castle will be directly in front of you.

Just ahead at a roundabout, go **STRAIGHT** to Interlaken and Gunten, not right to Spiez. You'll be at Berntorplatz. Continue following signs to Gunten and Interlaken, which will take you along the north side of the Thunersee. As you follow this road, keep to the side by the bike path whenever possible.

51.0: You reach the Neuhaus Hotel (right side of the road). Across the street is a bike path that leads into Interlaken.

54.0: Interlaken.

Background Notes
Where Am I?
Country: Switzerland
Region: Pays de Fribourg
Canton: Fribourg
City: Bulle

Tourist Information
Bulle Tourism
Ave. de la Gare 4
Bulle 1630
Phone: 026 912 80 22
Fax: 026 912 88 83
tourisme@info-bulle.ch
www.info-bulle.ch

Bike Shops
Beaud Cycles: Route du Verdel 22; Phone: 026 912 2628.
Pythoud Cycles: Rue du Chateau-d'En-Bas 15; Phone: 026 912 3522.

Sightseeing
You can visit the **Gruyeres cheese factory**, which is open from 8 a.m. to 7 p.m., in nearby Pringy-Gruyeres.

The **castle** in Gruyeres is open from 9 a.m. to 6 p.m.

Moleson Village is four miles from Gruyeres. From there, you can ride a cable car up 6,565 feet for a fantastic view of the Gruyere countryside. It is open from 8:30 a.m. to 12 p.m., and 1:30 p.m. to 5:30 p.m.

Restaurants
The area's best restaurants are **Les Alpes** (Rue Nicolas Glass) for traditional Swiss dishes in a chalet setting; **Cheval Blanc** (16 rue de Gruyeres) for regional cuisine; and **De la Tour** in nearby La Tour de Treme (57, Rue Ancien Comte) for upscale, contemporary dinners.

Luggage Transfers
ABA Taxis: Ch. Des Prealpes 33; Phone: 026 912 2724.
Abado Taxi: Route de la Pala 118; Phone: 026 9127475.

INTERLAKEN TO BULLE
ROUTE NOTES

Day 4: Interlaken to Bulle
Today's ride is the most challenging of the tour and incorporates a 5-mile, 8 to 12 percent ascent up the Jaunpass, which straddles the German- and French-speaking regions of Switzerland (German at the base, French at the top). If you've managed to cycle this tour's previous rides

without transportation assistance, you should be in fine shape to handle this very tough climb. However, if you decide that the Jaun is too tough, coast back to the station in Boltigen and take a postal bus to the top.

Distance: 83 kilometers

Lunch Stop: Spiez, Boltigen, top of Jaunpass (try the Alpine Macaroni).

Directions (km):

0.0: From the train station, follow the red bike path sign for Thun and Spiez (the 8 and 9 national bike paths).

1.0: Turn **RIGHT** on the 6-road (blue signs) toward Bern, Thun, and Spiez.

1.6: You pass under the highway.

2.3: You again pass under the highway. Turn **RIGHT** toward Darligen and Spiez.

6.5: Turn **RIGHT** toward Leissigen on the 6- and 11-roads.

7.0: Leissigen. Continue **STRAIGHT**. Continue following the red bike path signs to Spiez (8 and 9 national paths). It occasionally merges with the main road.

15.6: Spiez. Continue following the main road.

16.7: Head **STRAIGHT** to Thun, Kandersteg, and Zweisimmen.

17.5: Turn **LEFT** toward Kandersteg, Adelboden, and Zweisimmen on the 8 and 9 bike paths. Continue following Zweisimmen signs until you reach Boltigen.

20.0: Wimmis.

21.7: Bear **LEFT** for Zweisimmen on the 11-road.

22.2: Turn **LEFT** in the direction of Zweisimmen on the 11-road. Continue following the 11-road until Boltigen.

43.0: Boltigen.

45.0: Take a **RIGHT** to Jaunpass. This will be the most difficult climb of your tour. Make sure you follow the sign for Jaunpass and Bulle; do not keep heading to Zweisimmen.

NOTE: *In Boltigen, there's a train station where a bus or train will take you from Boltigen over (or around) the Jaunpass to Bulle. The last bus leaves at 3:43 p.m., so plan your day accordingly.*

52.4: Car park, lookout point.

52.1: Jaunpass. You've reached the top.

53.5: A restaurant is on your right. Try the Alpine Macaroni—my favorite.

58.6: Jaun. Follow the blue signs to Fribourg and Bulle.

63.0: Im-Fang.

68.3: Charmey.

75.0: Turn **LEFT** to Bulle and Broc.

75.5 Turn **LEFT** to Bulle and Broc.

76.4: Broc.

77.3: Continue following signs to Bulle.

78.0: Roundabout; follow it **LEFT** to the chateau.

79.1: Epagny.

79.5: Roundabout; turn **RIGHT** to Fribourg and Bulle. There's also a green highway sign, and a sign for a motel and campground

80.1: Bulle campground (on your right) and the Motel De Gruyere on your left.

82.6: Center of Bulle.

Background Notes
Where Am I?
Country: Switzerland
Region: Lake Geneva
Canton: Vaud
City: Lausanne

Tourist Information
Lausanne Tourism
Ave. de Rhodanie 2
Lausanne 1000
Phone: 021 613 73 60
Fax: 021 616 86 47
beausoleil@lausanne-tourisme.ch
www.lausanne-tourisme.ch

Bike Shops
Cycles et Sports: Ave. d'Echallens 13; Phone: 021 624 2488.
Delacombaz Velos: Ave. William-Fraisse 10; Phone: 021 616 3859.

Sightseeing
Cathedral of Lausanne is one of Switzerland's most beautiful medieval church-es. Built in 1175, this gothic structure has two towers (225 steps) and beauti-fully decorated doors. It is open Monday through Friday from 7 a.m. to 7 p.m., Saturday from 8 a.m. and 7 p.m., and Sundau from 2 p.m. to 7 p.m.

    Musee Cantonal des Beaux-Arts is home to the Museum of Paleontology, the Geological Museum, the Archeology and Historical Museum, and the Zoological Museum. It is closed Monday.

    Olympic Museum (Quai d'Ouchy 1) provides a complete history of the Olympic Games since ancient Greece. It is open daily from 10 a.m. to 7 p.m.

Restaurants
Lausanne is home to many renowned Swiss restaurants. **La Table du Palace** (7, Rue Grand Chene), **San Marino** (20, Ave. de la Gare), **Le Saint Francoise** (5, Pl. Saint Francois), and **La Petite Grappe** (15, Cheneau de Bourg) are among the most popular.

BULLE TO LAUSANNE
ROUTE NOTES

Day 5: Bulle to Lausanne

The first part of today's ride starts out along fairly moderate terrain. You'll cycle up, then down, then up, then down again, but nothing too steep or difficult.

Six miles before Vevey, you'll begin a wonderful descent all the way to the shores of Lac Leman, a winding, hairpin-filled route that's dotted with acres of vineyards.

The last part of the ride follows a Swiss national bike path to Lausanne, a city that traces its roots to the Romans, but has managed to gracefully incorporate both the old and new into a bustling and energetic international destination.**Bulle to Lausanne Route Notes**

Distance: 33 miles

Lunch Stop: Vevey.

NOTE: *While there is a bike path part of the way en route to Vevey, it's difficult to follow and significantly more strenuous than the one below.*

> **Directions (miles):** 0.0: From the center of Bulle, cycle in the direction of Lausanne and Vevey, following blue signs.
>
> 0.3: Take a **LEFT** for Lausanne, Vevey, and Romont. Just ahead at a roundabout, head toward Leysin, Vevey, and Romont.
>
> 4.5: Turn **LEFT** to Vevey and Chatel St. Denis. Follow the blue signs, not the green signs, all the way to Vevey.
>
> 15.5: It's a downhill coast to Vevey. Eventually, you come to a T-intersection. Bear **LEFT**, followed by a **RIGHT** a few hundred yards ahead, toward Vevey-Centre.
>
> 20.5: You'll reach the train station (gare).
>
> To continue from Vevey to Lausanne, follow the #1 national bike path signs.
>
> Head down toward the water (Lac Leman) and look for the blue #1 national bike path sign.
>
> 27.0: Follow the road to the right to Lausanne on the #1 bike path. Keep following signs to Lausanne. You'll pass Villette, Lutry, Paudex, and Pruly.
>
> 32.0: You reach a blue sign; turn **LEFT** toward Ouchy (do not go straight toward Lausanne). There will be a sign for the Olympic museum and a red bike sign for Morges and Lausanne.
>
> 33.0: Lausanne.

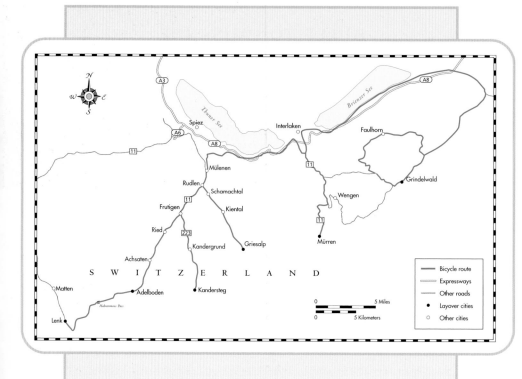

SWITZERLAND Mountain Bike Challenge

Bicycling magazine called this trip "One of the 50 Best Trips On Our Planet" (3/98), a generous compliment, though one I was sorry to learn did not carry with it a cash prize. This is, without question, a very challenging cycling itinerary set amidst my absolute favorite scenery in the world. While you'll encounter some extraordinarily steep ascents (several exceed 15 percent grades), you'll be rewarded many times over by the awesome views.

To complete this tour, you don't have to be a technical mountain biker, but you must be a strong rider. Every ride contains at least one (and in many cases three or more) challenging climbs, averaging at least 3 to 4 miles in length (some as long as 7 miles). Grades are almost all strenuously steep, with many grades exceeding 15 to 18 percent. You'll also tackle Europe's steepest paved road: a 2 kilometer, 28 percent grade. About 40 percent of the trails are single-track, the rest are an assortment of seldom-used Swiss farm paths.

I was eating lunch in a tiny town near Einsiedeln when a local boy, overheated from working the fields with his family, climbed onto this fountain for some much-needed refreshment. There aren't many things that can get me to put down a chocolate bar and reach for a camera. This was one of them.
Jerry Soverinsky

Arrival and Departure
Air

Zurich (www.unique.ch), Geneva (www.gva.ch), and Basel (www.eurairport.com) airports all receive regular service from North America and Europe.

The trip begins in Grindelwald, so either the Zurich or Geneva airport is convenient. For your departure home, Geneva is closest to Lenk (110 miles), though speedy train transfers can also whisk you back to Zurich or Basel.

A unique service for Switzerland's incoming visitors is the opportunity to check your luggage from your North American departure city all the way to your arrival city's train station. Cost for this extra service is $15 ($24 Canadian). Download the appropriate registration labels at
http://www.raileurope.com/us/rail/passes/fly_rail_baggage.htm.

Similarly, when preparing to leave Switzerland, you can check your luggage all the way through to your final North American destination from 130 Swiss train stations. Larger railway stations even issue boarding passes. Note: This service is not available to passengers on U.S. carriers, Air Canada, Air France, KLM, SAS, and Lufthansa.

Public Transportation
TO GRINDELWALD and
FROM LENK

Because this tour starts and ends in different cities that are quite far from the major Swiss airports, you should consider purchasing a Swiss Transfer Card that allows two one-way train trips—from Swiss airport to Swiss city and then back again, within one month—for a very reasonable $85: www.raileurope.com. This is far cheaper than purchasing two one-way tickets, Zurich-Grindelwald and Lenk-Geneva, which will run you about 50 percent more: www.sbb.ch.

Transfer time from Zurich to Grindelwald is 3 hours and 19 minutes; from Lenk to Geneva it is 3 hours and 40 minutes.

Private Transfers

Private transfers to Grindelwald from Lenk are expensive. You'll pay at least 450 CHF for either the Zurich to Grindelwald or Lenk to Geneva one-way service.

Grindelwald: **Oechslin & Graf Taxi**; Grindelwald; Phone: 033 853 62 61; Fax: 033 853 62 74; oechslin-graf@bluewin.ch; http://www.taxigrindelwald.ch/.

Lenk: **Gobeli Samuel**; Lenkstr. 61; 3775 Lenk; Phone: 079 6003366 and **Lenker Verkehrsbetriebe**; Rawilstr. 4; Phone: 033 7332525; Fax 033 7332838.

Bike Rentals

Switzerland offers one of the best and most efficient bike rental systems in Europe. You can pick up a city, mountain, or child's bicycle at one of over 100 rail stations throughout Switzerland and return it to any of the other participating stations. Both Grindelwald and Lenk offer staffed locations. Expect to pay 30 CHF per day for adult models http://www.rentabike.ch/.

You can rent high-quality mountain bikes from Mad House Bikes in Grindelwald (Phone: 033 853 59 69; mad-house@freesurf.ch).

Cycling Notes

This is a rigorous trip and you should be in very good cycling shape before you attempt the rides. You'll encounter severely steep climbs—up to 28 percent grades—sometimes without nearby support facilities.

Also keep in mind that mountain biking in Switzerland is not as rugged as in the U.S. The roads in Switzerland lead you past beautiful scenery, but the technical mountain bike obstacles to which you might be accustomed—logs, rivers, etc.—won't be nearly as common in Switzerland.

Maps

Kummerly and Frey, *Berner Oberland, Blatt/Feuille 6*; 1:60,000. This map covers the entire tour except for a small part on the ride from Grindelwald to Lauterbrunnen. Instead of purchasing this additional Swiss map (26 CHF), you can pick up the information from the Grindelwald Tourist Office.

Sightseeing Notes

I approach this chapter a bit differently from the others. Instead of separating the sightseeing attractions into a separate section, I note the stops along your ride with brief descriptions.

Restaurant Notes

Most of the restaurants along the route are quaint, Swiss restaurants that serve traditional, regional cuisine. If your hotel maintains a restaurant, ask for a half-pension supplement. These are usually very inexpensive dinner packages for hotel guests, sometimes as low as $8 to $10 for a 3-course meal.

Cycling Notes

I list altitude gains for each of the daily rides. This is vital, important information that should help you decide whether you're fit enough to complete the itinerary.

Background Notes
Where Am I?

Country: Switzerland
Region: Bernese Oberland
Canton: Bern
City: Grindelwald

Tourist Information

Grindelwald Tourism
Postfach 124
Grindelwald 3818
Phone: 033 854 12 12
Fax: 033 854 12 10
touristcenter@grindelwald.ch
www.grindelwald.com

Sightseeing

All of these are approachable via mountain bike.
Blue Ice Grotto is part of the Upper Grindelwald Glacier (Obere Gletscher). Your bike will get you only so close—you'll have to climb 900 stairs to get to the Grotto.

Once you're at the top of **First Mountain**'s 7,113-foot peak, enjoy a relaxing lunch at the

The worst day cycling in Switzerland beats the best day taking a Saturday morning calculus exam.
Kandersteg Tourismus

Swiss mountain biking can be very brutal. This sign ominously signals the beginning of the climb up to Griesalp, along the steepest paved road in Europe. Got a granny gear? You're gonna need it. *Jerry Soverinsky*

mountain restaurant before you descend back to Grindelwald.

Pfingstegg: If you're a bit tired from cycling, hop aboard an aerial cable car and ride to the top. It's also within hiking distance of the upper and lower Grindelwald Glaciers.

Restaurants

Informal Swiss restaurants abound throughout the village, and many are connected to tourist hotels. In the center of town, visit **Kreuz and Post**, **Adlerstube**, and **Alpli**. They are all located along Dorfstrasse and offer good-value Swiss meals.

Luggage Transfers

Oechslin & Graf, Taxi and Van Services: Phone: 033 853 62 61; Fax: 033 853 62 74; info@taxigrindelwald.ch; www.taxigrindelwald.ch.

GRINDELWALD LOOP RIDES

Days 1 and 2: Grindelwald
While Switzerland is my favorite holiday destination, I've spent more time in Grindelwald than anywhere else. This is a five-star outdoor resort destination and a perfect spot for anyone who likes to bike, hike, mountain bike, ski, winter hike, mountain climb . . . well, that about covers it for me. They have an efficient and helpful tourist office with staff who will ensure that all of your inquiries are answered promptly. While it can get busy in July and August (it's also one of the popular springboards for excursions to the Jungfrau), it's never affected my access to mountain trails, which are generally the least visited of their outdoor sites.
Distances: vary by route selected.
 Grindelwald is the number-one destination for Swiss mountain biking options, and its tourist office publishes a guide to local mountain biking, *Top Ten*, which details ten well-marked mountain biking trails beginning from its village. The publication, with detailed maps and route notes for all ten rides, is readily available from the Grindelwald tourist office, so I'll avoid reprinting the rides at length and instead summarize the ones that I think work best.
 All of the routes are indicated in pink/red, and there are other trails that connect with each (indicated in black, blue, and green).

Of the ten routes, the only one that you shouldn't choose for your Grindelwald layover days is number 5, because you'll be covering much of the route as you head for Lauterbrunnen.

Number 6 is the easiest (a relative term) and visits the Marmorbruch restaurant. You might start with this route to test your climbing since there's only a 170-meter altitude gain. If you like, you can lock your bikes at the restaurant and hike to Stieregg (the red dashed line on the *Top Ten* map), a wonderful hike that offers great views of the Unterer Gletscher. When you return to Marmorbruch, you can follow the blue or green trails instead of backtracking on the number 6 *Top Ten* route.

Number 8 is a great route and visits Kleine Scheidegg, the base camp for those who climb the Eiger. It's a very difficult 1,000-meter ascent, but the views from the top are extraordinary.

Numbers 1, 2, 3, and 4 also afford wonderful views. Number 4 in particular is unbelievably steep. In fact, I've hiked this many times and know it to be very difficult on foot. You could combine Numbers 2 and 4; however, I recommend cycling Number 2 (less steep than number 4) and continuing past the Waldspitz restaurant to Bachlager (alt. 1980 m. From there, you must walk/hike to First (good mountain restaurant). You'll then have a very steep descent all the way back down to Grindelwald.

Background Notes
Where Am I?
Country: Switzerland
Region: Bernese Oberland
Canton: Bern
City: Lauterbrunnen

Tourist Information
Lauterbrunnen Tourism
Lauterbrunnen 3822
Phone: 033 856 856 8
Fax: 033 856 856 9
info@lauterbrunnen-tourismus.ch
www.lauterbrunnen.ch; www.lauterbrunnen-tourismus.ch

Bike Shops
Imboden Bike Werner: 3822 Lauterbrunnen; Phone: 033 8552114.

Sightseeing
The area's top site by far is the Trummelbach Falls,. Here, waterfalls gush inside a mountain and carry glacier melt from the nearby Eiger, Monch, and Jungfrau mountains. It is open daily from 9 a.m. to 6 p.m. The cost is 10 CHF.

Luggage Transfers
Taxi Interlaken Wyss Helmut: Bahnhofplatz; Lauterbrunnen; Phone: 033 8555555.

Swiss mountain biking is unlike its American counterpart. While some routes traverse rough, off-road terrain, a fair percentage follow coarsely paved farm roads.
Jerry Soverinsky

GRINDELWALD TO LAUTERBRUNNEN
ROUTE NOTES

Day 3: Grindelwald to Lauterbrunnen

Three words of advice for visitors to Lauterbrunnen: Take a camera. As if rocky, vertical cliffs bookmarking the village aren't dramatic enough, throw in dozens of gushing waterfalls, and you've got one of the most beautiful settings imaginable. It's another five-star cycling day. You begin today's ride along Grindelwald's *Top Ten* number 5 up to Grosse Scheidegg. This is a steep climb, but not too severe. Along the way, lock your bike at the Hotel Wetterhorn (mountain hotel) and hike/walk to the Oberere Grindelwaldgletscher. These are magnificent ice caves, and the visit will break up your steep climb to Grosse Scheidegg.

From Grosse Scheidegg, there's a (mainly) paved road leading to the Reichenbach Falls, made famous from Sherlock Holmes. The falls are in Meiringen, a good lunch spot.

From Meiringen, head to Giessbach via Unterbach on a relatively flat road. Head next for Giessbachfall. Under clear conditions, Giessbachfall is a great visit (as well as the very old Hotel Giessbach).

From Giessbachfalls, head to Bonigen and on to Wilderswil. On the way to Bonigen, feel free to stop for a swim in the Brienzer See.

From Wilderswil, the road to Lauterbrunnen (via Zweilutschinnen) follows both paved and gravel roads along the river and forests. You'll notice on your main map (Berner Oberland) that there are two paths from Zweilutschinnen to Lauterbrunnen. Both include similar terrain and you can cycle along either side of the river.

Summary

	Km	Altitude Change (meters)
Grindelwald-Grosse Scheidegg	12	928
Gr. Scheidegg-Meiringen	14	1,367
Meiringen-Giessbachfall	9	135
Giessbachfall-Bonigen	10	200
Bonigen-Wilderswil	5	-
Wilderswil-Lauterbrunnen	10	270
TOTAL:	60	-

Background Notes
Where Am I?
Country: Switzerland
Region: Bernese Oberland
Canton: Bern
City: Griesalp

Tourist Information
Griesalp is a tiny hamlet and doesn't maintain its own tourist office. Contact the Kiental office, a few miles down the road for information.
Verkehrsverein Kiental
Dorfstrasse
Kiental 3723
Phone: 033 676 10 10
Fax: 033 676 1354
ferine@kiental.ch
http://www.kiental.ch/

Bike Shops
The closest shop is in Reichenbach, 9 miles away: **Ryter Zweiradcenter**, Frutigenstr. 89; Phone: 033 6762448.

Luggage Transfers
Gerber Taxi: Phone: 033 6762929.

LAUTERBRUNNEN TO GRIESALP
ROUTE NOTES

Day 4: Lauterbrunnen to Griesalp
The Road

Today's ride concludes with a 28 percent, 2-kilometer grueling climb up to Griesalp—along a *paved* road. And if you've never seen a 28 percent grade along a *paved* road, it's a scary sight.

The first time that I encountered the road,[5] I was driving the support vehicle for one of my company's trips. I approached the base (much like a parent might approach a mosh pit) and thought I better not. It looked like a roller coaster ride, and it seemed far too steep for my company's van. Just then, the manager from the Griesalp hotel happened to be coming down the mountain, and she stopped to chat when she saw me. I told her that I wasn't sure if my van was powerful enough to make the climb, and she asked to see its driver's manual.

She leafed through the manual's pages, studied the motor diagrams, occasionally peered under the chassis of the van to check things out . . . and she said, quite simply, "I think it can make it." And then she was off, on her way to some errand in Bern.

I *think* it can make it (emphasis supplied). I kept repeating it in my head: I *think* it can make it. I *think* it can make it. Not really the reassurance that I was looking for, but at that point, one of my group's participants, Linda (not her real name),[6] arrived at the base, and she looked at the climb and told me, "I'm gonna need a lift." She was unaware of my apprehension about tackling the climb with my van.

"Okay," I said tentatively. "Let's do it."

"They're really cute, Jerry, but why are you showing me pictures of your family? Let's just go," she asked. We'd been parked at the base for several minutes and my stalling had run its course. I took a deep breath, shifted the van into first gear, and started the climb.

The first turn comes after about 100 yards, so around the 40-yard mark, I'm psyching myself up, screaming every Japanese word I can remember from martial arts films, while trying to hold onto the steering wheel with my sweat-soaked hands. Just then, I see an Audi station wagon coming down the road (toward me), and it appeared that we would meet at the turn.

I thought to myself, okay, no problem, you can do this, the road is wide enough for two cars, not by U.S. standards of course, but we're in Europe, gotta adjust, gotta adapt . . .

As I approached the turn, the Audi came through it first, and it took a very sharp turn, so much so that it appeared to me that if I proceeded at my current pace, that I'd hit it. So reflexively, I tapped on my brakes and then . . . you guessed it . . . my van stalled.

Now, if you've never stalled a manual-shift cargo van jammed full of gear in the middle of a 28-percent-grade paved road that's littered with gravel, here's what happens: you start to slide downhill.[7] Actually, not so much slide as lurch. Lurch! Lurch! Lurch!

Thoughts raced through my mind: whatever happened to my sixth grade teacher, she was so pretty, wonder if she's seeing anyone . . . I stole bottle rockets from Bargain Town when I was seven, I wonder if that's why they went bankrupt later that spring . . . Did I watch enough TV, you know, quality shows, these past few years . . .

All the insecurities from a lifetime of decisions, they're immediately resurrected and brought to the forefront of your conscience. But there was no time for a stroll down memory lane. I needed to act.

---

[5] As a driver. I had visited the road twice before while researching the route.

[6] Her real name is Brook Shoane, 22 years old, architect grad student from Southfield, Michigan. Parents are Bernie and Michelle; siblings are Tom, Julius, and Allie (youngest).

[7] I must confess, just writing this story is making my hands sweat—probably because I can stand to lose a few pounds—but more likely because I remember vividly the fear that I felt that day.

"Linda, get out of the van!"

"Why, what's wrong?" she asked. She apparently didn't sense any imminent danger, thinking it reasonable that her support van was heaving downhill against the wishes of its driver. And if she wasn't yet alarmed, I certainly didn't want to cause her any undue concern.

"I need you to direct me!" I screamed. It was the best I could come up with under the pressure.

I need you to direct me. On a 6-foot-wide road that has no turnoffs, and I needed her to direct me. Well, guess what? She bought it.

"Okay, sure," she responded giddily, obviously tickled that I was seeking her assistance.

After several failed attempts, I somehow managed to restart my van's engine and navigate the remainder of the road. I reached the hotel, my t-shirt thoroughly soaked. ("Why are you sweating so much, Jerry?" Linda asked, as I helped her carry her suitcase to her room. "Dunno," I answered.)

After my group arrived, I had one of my guides drive me to the bottom of the road, for I wanted—no, needed—to cycle the ascent forcefully, you know, really bring the mountain to its knees. I needed to attack the thing, make it pay for the fear that it caused me earlier that day.

So I cycled the entire climb without the use of a triple chainring. That's right: the entire 2-kilometer, 28-percent grade with no granny gear. But that wasn't all. As I'm cycling, I pull out my video camera and start taping my ascent. One hand on my handlebars, one hand taping the ascent. And I'm swearing at the road as I'm cycling, especially at the loose bits of gravel that are strewn everywhere.

"You mother f _ _ _ _ _ _ road, you steep f _ _ _ _ _ _ road . . . " You know, typical road-slander stuff. And then I start taunting it, "You're not so steep, look, I'm taping you, I'm videotaping you and only riding with one hand, what do you say to that, huh, road? Huh? Road? Road? Road?!!!!"

But as I reached the top and dismounted my bike, a sudden wave of emotions swept over me. I scurried ten feet or so back down the mountain and respectfully massaged the last long stretch of pavement that leads to the top. Tears streaking down my cheeks, I collapsed into a spent heap of raw emotion, embracing the road not as its enemy, but as its reverent ally.

I was no longer sweating, no longer rehashing the harrowing drive from earlier that day, or the vengeful cycling ascent that I had completed moments earlier. They were byproducts of a lifetime of misunderstood public works projects, countless failed attempts to comprehend the natural miracle that is a 28-percent paved road.

I picked myself up, swept away the gravel that was clinging affectionately to my shirt, and walked toward my hotel. I nodded my head knowingly, fully aware of what I had accomplished that day—the understanding and insight that one gains from truly recognizing what it is to be a road.

And I sensed that the road understood this achievement too; it really appreciated this transference of knowledge and acceptance, for just as I was a foot or so from the top, I tripped on some loose gravel.

I smiled, winked at the road, a mutual understanding that the journey had come to its respectful conclusion. There would be no more vans that night. There would be no more bicycles.

There would be . . .

. . . just . . .

. . . the road.

And so I headed for the bar and got really drunk.From Lauterbrunnen, retrace the path to Wilderswil (from Grindelwald-Lauterbrunnen ride). From Wilderswil, cycle over the Rugen hill to Leissigen. Along the way, you'll cycle along the Thunersee, and for a short while you'll be along the main road (there's a bike path, just be careful for traffic). In Leissigen, turn to the **LEFT** and head uphill to Aeschi where you'll enjoy a wonderful view overlooking the lake and mountains. You'll pass Krattigen along the way.

From Aeschi, cycle along a small trail to Mulenen and then on to Reichenbach. From Reichenbach, you can follow the paved road (very little traffic) all the way to Kiental; or detour first to Kien and then bike along very tiny trails (and a much steeper ascent) via Aris to Kiental. **NOTE:** *You'll be following the latter route tomorrow.*

From Kiental, you'll follow a paved road to Tschingelsee. The last two miles to Griesalp are extraordinarily steep, a 28 percent grade. Follow the road all the way to the top to reach the Griesalp hotels.

Summary

	Km	Altitude Change(meters)
Lauterbrunnen-Wilderswil	10	270
Wilderswil-Leissigen	10	50
Leissigen-Aeschi	12	300
Aeschi-Reichenbach	10	220
Reichenbach-Kiental	16	260 (up and down)
Kiental-Griesalp (STEEP)	8	460
TOTAL:	66	-

Background Notes
Where Am I?
Country: Switzerland
Region: Bernese Oberland
Canton: Bern
City: Kandersteg

Tourist Information
Kandersteg Tourism
Postfach 81
Kandersteg 3718
Phone: 033 675 80 80
Fax: 033 65 80 81
info@kandersteg.ch
www.kandersteg.ch

Bike Shops
The closest shop is in Frutigen, 8 miles away: **Veloschopfli Zurcher,** Kanderstegstr. 18; Phone: 033 6713646.

The Swiss mountain biking itinerary reaches into the most spectacular areas of the country, filled with dramatic, awe-inspiring scenery.
Jerry Soverinsky

Some of your Grindelwald layover rides will lead you to Kleine Scheidegg, the site of the 1975 Clint Eastwood thriller, *The Eiger Sanction. Grindelwald Tourism*

Luggage Transfers

Wandflug Andre: Kanderstegstr.; Blausee-Mitholz;
Phone: 033 6712377.

GRIESALP TO KANDERSTEG
ROUTE NOTES

Day 5: Griesalp to Kandersteg

At the end of today's ride, do yourself a huge favor and continue cycling to the Oechinensee, a glacial lake that is absolutely magnificent. Park your bike and grab a cappuccino at the nearby mountain café, a great way to relax and enjoy your natural surroundings.

Today's route is fairly easy with long descents. Be careful riding down from Griesalp. It's very steep and the road can be littered with gravel.

In Kiental, turn off to the **LEFT** and ride a steep downhill, crossing the gorge and ascending through forests until you reach a main road. Turn **RIGHT** downhill, pass the few houses of Aris, and cycle to Kien. Cycle over the Kander river and follow it up to Frutigen (good food stop). Carry on the main road to Kandersteg as far as the big railroad bridge. From here, turn **RIGHT** and follow the side street to Blausee. At the sign "Blausee," turn **LEFT** until you come to the main road. Turn **LEFT**, and you'll soon reach the Blausee entrance. After a visit to the lake, retrace your path to the "Blausee" sign and turn **LEFT** to encounter the steepest climb of the day, all the way to Kandersteg.

Summary

	Km	Altitude Change (meters)
Griesalp-Frutigen	22	604
Frutigen-Blausee	8	97
Blausee-Kandersteg	7	280
TOTAL	37	981

Background Notes
Where Am I?
Country: Switzerland
Region: Bernese Oberland
Canton: Bern
City: Adelboden

Tourist Information
Adelboden Tourism
Adelboden 3715
Phone: 033 673 80 80
Fax: 033 673 80 92
info@adelboden.ch
www.adelboden.ch

You'll need a quality mountain bike to maneuver the steep daily climbs along the route. The more gears, the better. *Grindelwald Tourism*

Bike Shops
Inniger Fritz: Bodenstr. 1; Phone: 033 6732260.
Buschlen Garage: Schlegelistr. 1; Phone: 033 6732460.

Luggage Transfers
ABC Funk Taxi: Landstr. 124B Hirzboden; Phone: 033 6732848.
Taxi Bandi: Landstr. 145; Phone: 033 6731515.

The Oeschinensee near Kandersteg is the most extraordinary glacial lake I've ever seen (and I've seen four). On the far side of the picture sits a mountain restaurant, an ideal place to enjoy a late afternoon cappuccino while reviewing your day's itinerary. *Kandersteg Tourismus*

KANDERSTEG TO ADELBODEN
ROUTE NOTES

Day 6: Kandersteg to Adelboden
Today's ride is not as difficult as some of the others on this tour, and you can make a detour to the Thunersee for some water sport activity. Otherwise, when you reach Adelboden, continue with the extension up to Engstligenalp with a cable car excursion. It's a wonderful area for a mid-afternoon hike or walk, and the mountain restaurant serves light lunches.

From Kandersteg, it's a quick downhill to Frutigen. Shortly before you reach the big railroad bridge, turn **LEFT** onto a footpath that leads to the Old Adelboden Road. When you reach the road, turn **LEFT**, and you'll then embark on a long and steep ascent toward Elsigbach. After a short way further, you'll cycle steep, rolling hills for the duration, all accompanied by wonderful views. Follow signs to Adelboden.

NOTE: For an extension, you can follow signs to Unter dem Birg/Engstligenalp as you approach Adelboden. Just after you make this turn, you'll follow the hiking trail along the Engstligen river to the end of the valley. You'll find a cable car station here and you can take a ride up to Engstligenalp for some late-afternoon hiking.

Summary

	Km	Altitude Change (meters)
Kandersteg-Frutigen	12	373
Frutigen-Elsigbach	8	800
Elsigbach-Adelboden	7	250 (up and down)
TOTAL:	27	1000 (approximate)

This is a typical mountain biking road along your Swiss route. It's nothing too technical to navigate. In most cases, it's hard-packed dirt. *Kandersteg Tourismus*

Background Notes
Where Am I?
Country: Switzerland
Region: Bernese Oberland
Canton: Bern
City: Lenk

Tourist Information
Lenk Tourism
Tourist Center
Lenk 3775
Phone: 033 733 31 31
Fax: 033 733 20 27
info@lenk.ch
www.lenk.ch

Bike Shops
Velosport Morger: Oberriedstr. 5; Phone: 033 7333424.

ADELBODEN TO LENK
ROUTE NOTES

Day 7: Adelboden to Lenk
Today's ride to Lenk is another ho-hum alongside snow-capped mountains and breathtaking Alpine Landscapes. Look carefully for detour to the seven fountains, a very worthwhile stop at the end of your ride.

Begin by following signs to Geils; it's almost all uphill and on paved road. From Geils to Hahnenmoos, it's a winding and open road. At the top of the Hahnenmoospass, in addition to wonderful vistas, you'll find a well-equipped mountain restaurant.

The first part of the ride down from Hahnenmoos is along a steep, gravel road. The remainder, from Buhlberg to Lenk, is mostly paved.

From Lenk, you can make a great side-trip to the Simmenfalls and on to the famous "seven fountains." This is a steep uphill, but very worthwhile. It's easy to find your way to the Simmenfalls, but you'll need to ask directions once there for the ride up to the seven fountains because the trail is poorly marked.

Summary

	Km	Altitude Change (meters)
Adelboden-Geils	10	329
Geils-Hahnenmoos	5	204
Hahnemoos-Buhlberg-Lenk	10	889
Lenk-Simmenfalls-	22	600 (up and down)
Seven fountains		
TOTAL	22-plus	

LOW COUNTRIES

Cycling in Holland and Belgium is an absolute joy (did I just write that?). The endless miles (kilometers to locals) of bike paths reach into the most remote parts of both countries and afford cyclists the opportunity to intimately explore almost any area without motorized support.

Mechanical assistance is ubiquitous, even in the smallest towns, where local fiets winkels (magasin de velo in southern Belgium) stock the most contemporary components.

Goede reisen and bon voyage!

Cycling Overview

Cycling in Holland and in most parts of Belgium reminds me of a word that I used when I was in grade school: *cinchy*. And it is cinchy, except . . .

There's always exceptions, right? Sure, the Holland route in this section is very, very flat (maybe 10 meters maximum of altitude climb at any one stretch), but the wind can make some of the rides tough. The wind is unpredictable, too.

I've cycled the North Sea route both north and south, and encountered headwinds in both directions.[57] But the winds weren't nearly as bad as those along the Southwestern peninsulas (see *Amsterdam to Bruges* section), which were absolutely brutal. Overall, winds along these two trips haven't posed too much of a problem for my guests.

I've hosted cyclists of all abilities on these two trips. One woman in her seventies couldn't remember how to apply brakes when she arrived in Amsterdam, and she finished every ride. A 50-pound, 7-year-old boy who arrived with his father did just fine on his department store-quality bike (he was great, but the bike was in constant need of repair).

The second half of the Belgium tour, from Brussels to Han sur Lesse, is not flat. In fact, it's pretty hilly, and what I consider rolling terrain. If you're able to cycle the rides on the first half of the trip, you'll be in fine shape to handle the extra hills during those last few riding days. Especially because the beer in that region is really good.

Climate

You can cycle both the Holland and Belgium tours from April through October. The spring and fall extremes will bring heavier rains and cooler temperatures, but that just makes the genever (Dutch gin) all the more welcome.

I usually offer these tours in June, July, and August, when the temperatures are traditionally the most agreeable (see individual tour entries for average monthly temperatures). However, tourist crowds are also at a peak during those months, so you'll need to consider the CF.[58]

---

[57] And in one freak instance, simultaneously.
[58] Claustrophobic factor.

Moments earlier, these two cyclists asked the motorist in this passing vehicle whether their cycling form was enviable. When the answer was affirmative, they were understandably upbeat.
Jerry Soverinsky

Combining Tours

When you finish the Holland tour in Delft, convenient train service can shuttle you to Bruges in just over 3 hours for about 28 Euros (http://www.ns.nl/international/international.cgi?International/Tickets/Buying+Tickets+and+Passes). Expect to pay a surcharge to carry your bike on the Dutch and Belgian trains, which currently is 12 Euros. You need to make sure that the train you've selected will transport bikes (there are restrictions depending on departure times).

Currency

Both Holland and Belgium have adopted the Euro ( ), so it's kinda like traveling between Ohio and Indiana (except, of course, that Indiana has Pop-a-Shot at its interstate rest stops, while Belgium has beer).

Special Notes

English is widely spoken along both itineraries, but the last few days in Belgium (after you leave Brussels) will take you through some towns where you may have to hone your pointing skills[59].

You'll hear Dutch/Flemish (same language) throughout Holland and the northern part of Belgium, and French from Brussels through Han sur Lesse.

Travel Advice

You'll have wasted a terrific gastronomic opportunity if you don't sample the *gevulde koeken* while in Holland. These mashed almond masterpieces shame even the strongest Chips Ahoy! Cookies. You can never eat just one.

The ubiquitous blue bike path sign, as found in Holland and Belgium—a welcome friend throughout your journey.
Jerry Soverinsky

[59] The best way I've found to practice pointing: Watch *The Price is Right* models. They're really pretty, too!

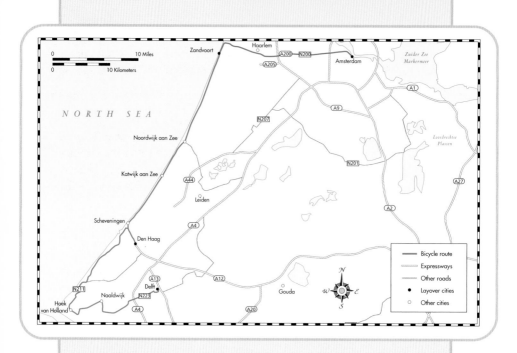

Quick Holland Tour

For pure cycling enjoyment and cultural diversity, Holland is the perfect destination. Beginning in Amsterdam, you can spend several days wandering its bustling network of canals and admiring centuries-old architecture in a sophisticated, cosmopolitan environment.

The biking is enjoyable for cyclists of all abilities. You'll parallel the North Sea Coast for much of the tour and follow dedicated biking paths along wild heather and sand dunes, never more than a few hundred yards from the sea. You'll end the Dutch portion in Delft, one of Holland's most charming cities, renowned for its pottery.

Tourist Information

Prior to departure, download information from the Netherlands Board of Tourism's website: www.visitholland.com. The website is comprehensive and even delves into such topics as liquor laws and school holiday schedules through 2099. You can also make contact via email at info@goholland.com.

Under the individual daily itineraries, you'll notice reference to local VVVs.[60] These are the tourist information offices, present in towns of almost any appreciable size, that are immensely helpful and provide comprehensive tourist brochures and candy.

When to Go

I've cycled through Holland from mid-March through late October. It rains pretty often throughout the year, though more so before and after the summer months. I've traveled to Holland in December and January, and while it would have been possible to cycle, the winds and rains would have made for a miserable trip.

Below is what you can expect for weather.

AMSTERDAM[61]

MONTH	AVERAGE HIGH (°F)	AVERAGE LOW (°F)	AVERAGE PRECIPITATION (IN)
JANUARY	41	34	3.1
FEBRUARY	42	32	1.7
MARCH	48	37	3.5
APRIL	53	40	1.5
MAY	61	46	2.0
JUNE	66	52	2.4
JULY	69	55	2.9
AUGUST	70	55	2.4
SEPTEMBER	64	51	3.2
OCTOBER	57	46	4.1
NOVEMBER	48	39	3.0
DECEMBER	44	36	2.

Arrival and Departure
Air

Amsterdam's Schiphol Airport is a convenient travel hub, no matter your starting point (yes, yes, even Dubuque, Iowa). The airport maintains an extensive website at http://www.schiphol.nl/ where you'll find tons of information to help plan your arrival and departure.

Public and Private Transportation

Public transportation throughout Holland is excellent and inexpensive. Trains depart from the airport toward central Amsterdam and cost €3 for the 19-minute

[60] Very, very, vixen-ish.
[61] From http://www.usatoday.com/weather/climate/europe/netherla/wamstrdm.htm.

The start of every Belgian work-day is punctuated by three cyclists and five pedestrians crossing a bridge. *Ghent Tourist Office*

journey: www.ns.nl. For your return from Delft, you'll pay €7.40 for the 40-minute trip.

Alternatively, you can book ahead with Schiphol Travel Taxi, a shared taxi service that offers transfers to and from the airport and any city in Holland. Cost for the communal taxi to downtown Amsterdam is €22, and the cost for a ride from Delft back to Schiphol is €29. Its website is very helpful, and they quote fares from any postal code in Holland: http://www.schiphol.nl/schiphol/taxi/stp_travel_stt1.jsp.

Bike Rental

Dutch bikes are typically not your $1,000 sleek U.S. models to which you might be accustomed. Rather, the majority are 3-speed, steel (translation: heavy), bomb-proof models that will be perfectly adequate for the flat cycling along this itinerary.

Amsterdam's VVV provides a detailed listing of all local rental shops (http://www.holland.com/amsterdam/gb/geninfo/travelinfo/bikeren.html). Click on *Travel Information* and then *Bike Rental Information* to direct you to the proper page. Prices start at €30 a week for the most basic models, and you'll be required to return your bike to the shop at the end of your rental period.

Cycling Notes

If you're a first-time Holland cyclist, be patient for the unique bicycle signage that is omnipresent, but a bit tricky to learn. You'll come to love the word *fietspad*—Dutch for *bike path* but curiously, French for *strudel*—a miraculous network that weaves its way into the deepest corners of the country.

Signs won't assign road names to the paths that you follow. Rather, they'll only point in the direction of neighboring towns. If this feels a bit imprecise, it's . . . well . . . because it is. The sheer thrill of cycling on dedicated bike paths for miles on end without motor traffic more than compensates for this very minor confusion.

"What's a windmill?" your daughter asks when you arrive for your family's Dutch cycling trip. "It's a—a—well, it blows wind, dear," you say, struggling for an answer. "But what's it do?" she demands, peppering you further for an answer. "Anyone for pannekoeken?" you ask, deftly changing the subject. And you head for the nearest restaurant, glad to indulge yourself in the savory Dutch treats.

Jerry Soverinsky

In very short order, you'll cycle enthusiastically along the fietspads, wondering why your town can't introduce a similar system, stopping occasionally for pannekoeken at seaside cafés, shouting "Goede morgen"[62] to passing Dutch cyclists, inhaling the fragrant bouquets of the much-in-bloom tulips, before calling home and speaking to your kids who want to know what presents you've bought them.

Amsterdam Tourist Information

I recommend spending at least two full days sightseeing in Amsterdam prior to setting out on your bike. Contact the Amsterdam VVV for full tourist details:

Amsterdam VVV
Stationsplein 10
Amsterdam 1012
Phone: 020 201 88 00
Fax: 020 625 28 69
info@amsterdamtourist.nl
www.visitamsterdam.nl/gb/

I also cover Amsterdam tourism in more detail under Tour 15, the North Sea Coast to Amsterdam.

Maps

Good: Michelin #211, Rotterdam-Apeldoorn-Maastricht; 1:200,000. This map covers the entire tour but omits bike paths.

Excellent: ANWB publishes bike maps (fiets kaarten) of the various regions of Holland. You can purchase the appropriate North Holland map at http://basic.anwb.nl/basic/sh_a571318.htm.

---

[62] Good morning.

I advise you to take the Michelin map, because you can buy the ANWB maps when you arrive in Holland. They're available at most local VVVs.

Lock Your Bike—
and then Hope for the Best

You'd think that the Dutch, whose bikes outnumber cars 7:1,[63] wouldn't present a bicycle theft problem, since almost every Dutch person owns one. But alas, my friend, you'd be very wrong, and probably thirsty, too.

During one of my first visits to Amsterdam, I was sightseeing at midday on a busy street when a man drove his motor scooter up to a bicycle that was locked to a parking meter. In less than 30 seconds, the man extracted a tiny saw from his jacket pocket, hacked off the flimsy lock, and toted the bike away.

I always advise my company's participants to bring steel u-locks and to secure their bikes whenever they leave their bikes unattended, even if they run into a store for a soda. This has proved modestly successful, but I remember one participant who had locked her bike to a tree, only to return from a leisurely lunch to a fallen tree and no bike.

Like they say, if you can't find an octogenarian carrying a miniature dog in his front bicycle basket in a North Sea town, you can't find an octogenarian. *Jerry Soverinsky*

[63] Made-up statistic.

Background Notes
Where Am I?
Country: Holland
Province: Noord-Holland
City: Zandvoort

Tourist Information
VVV Zuid Kennemerland
(covers Haarlem, Zandvoort,
and Ijmuiden)
Schoolplein 1
Zandvoort 2042
Phone: 023 5712262
Fax: 023 5717003
pr@vvvzk.nl; info@vvvzk.nl
www.vvvzk.nl

Bike Shops
Lukon Tweewielers: Kochstraat 8; Phone: 023 5716504.
Versteege Wielersport: Haltestraat 31; Phone: 023 5714499
www.versteegewielersport.nl.
Martijn's Fietsenhoek: Tolweg 6; Phone: 023 5714484.

Sightseeing
Today's ride is relatively easy, and you'll pedal through Haarlem en route to
Zandvoort and the North Sea Coast. Haarlem, better known as the birthplace
of Frans Hals, was founded in the tenth century and remains one of my favorite
city stops in North Holland. It maintains a beautiful city center with wonderful cafés, shops, and restaurants. Among the sites, check out the Grote Kerk (fifteenth-century church), Grote Markt (central square), Frans Halsmuseum, and
Teylers Museum. You can find detailed sightseeing information for Haarlem at
http://www.vvvzk.nl/.

Zandvoort was once a popular fishing village but is now home to miles of
beautiful North Sea beachfront. Even if the weather is inappropriate for swimming, it's still wonderful to take an invigorating walk close to the rugged shoreline
of the North Sea.

Test your gaming luck at the Holland Casino, the city center gambling hall.
Just remember to wear leather shoes and bring your passport.

Circus Zandvoort (Gasthuisplein 5) includes a cinema and theatre.

Circuitpark Zandvoort is a famous racing circuit track where the Formula 1
Grand Prix was held until 1985.

Restaurants

Finding somewhere to eat in Zandvoort is never a problem. Check out the beachfront boulevard or main street in town, where there are plenty of bistros, pub-style restaurants, and fish restaurants.

Luggage Transfers

Zandvoort Taxicentrale: Stationsplein 1; Phone: 023 5712600.
Business Taxi: Keesomstraat 189; Phone: 06 53968229.

AMSTERDAM TO ZANDVOORT
ROUTE NOTES

Day 1: Amsterdam to Zandvoort

Today's ride is flat, flat, flat, and leads you through the Dutch market town of Haarlem en route to Zandvoort, a holiday seaside resort. You'll take long walks along its sandy beach, and perhaps enjoy a stroopwaffel cookie and strong "kopje koffie"[8] at an outdoor cafe.

Distance: 37 kilometers

Lunch Stop: Haarlem or Zandvoort.

Directions (km): Route begins from the corner of Tesselschadestraat and Nassaukade (S100), at the Marriot Hotel. Cycle north along Nassaukade (or the S100 ring road).

0.7: Cross a small bridge and stay on the bike path (you're following the S100 until you reach the S103).

3.0: You reach the S103/ S104. Cross this intersection and turn **LEFT**, cycling toward Ring A10/ Den Haag/ Haarlem. The red and white bike signs will also point to Geuzenveld/ Haarlem. Cycle parallel to the S103 toward Haarlem.

5.0: The bike path switches sides of the road. Continue following red and white bike signs toward Geuzenveld/ Halfweg/ Haarlem.

7.6: Begin following the S104 toward Geuzenveld/ Halfweg/ Haarlem.

12.0: Halfweg. Continue following red and white bike path signs to Haarlem.

12.6: The S104 will become the A200.

13.7: Follow red and white bike signs toward Haarlem 5.

19.3: Follow the red and white bike signs toward Centrum/Bloemendaal/Zandvoort to the **RIGHT**.

19.4: Continue following the same red and white signs (Centrum/ Bloemendaal/ Zandvoort) to the **LEFT**. Turn **LEFT** and keep a lookout for more red and white signs.

20.2: Follow the red and white signs toward Centrum/Bloemendaal/Zandvoort to the **LEFT**. This will bring you into the older part of Haarlem.

20.3: Turn **RIGHT**, following the same signs (Centrum/Bloemendaal/Zandvoort).

20.4: You're in the center of Haarlem. After sightseeing, begin following signs toward Bloomendaal/ Zandvoort. You'll be paralleling the N208 and the road signs will read Haarlem(North)/ Bloomendaal. Continue toward Bloomendaal 2/Zandvoort 11.

25.7: Turn **LEFT**, following the red and white bike signs toward Bloomendaal/Zandvoort 10/Aerdenhout 6/Heemstede 6.

25.9: Bloomendaal. Just ahead, follow blue road signs toward Bloomendaal an

[8] Cup of coffee.

Zee/Overveen/Zandvoort, veering to the **LEFT**.

26.6: Turn **LEFT** toward Bloomendaal an Zee/Overveen/Zandvoort.

27.6: Turn **RIGHT** onto the N200 toward Bloomendaal/Zandvoort.

33.0: The North Sea is in view. As the bike path (and road) veers **LEFT**, you'll be able to see Zandvoort, too. Cycle with the North Sea to your right and you're now on the LF1A bike path.

35.2: Zandvoort.

36.1: You'll see the Palace Hotel directly in front of you and the bike path will veer **LEFT** (on the side of the road) away from the sea and into town.

36.4: Turn **LEFT** onto Zeestraat.

36.6: Turn **RIGHT** toward VVV.

36.9: Turn **LEFT** onto Schoolstraat. You're at the VVV and Zandvoort's center.

Background Notes

Where Am I?

Country: Holland
Province: Zuid-Holland
City: Den Haag

Tourist Information

The Hague Visitors and
Convention Bureau
Nassaulaan 25
Den Haag 2514
Phone: 070 361 8888
Fax: 070 361 5459
info@vvvdenhaag.nl
www.denhaag.com

Many Dutch towns hold a weekly Kaasmarkt, or cheese market, throughout the summer. It's a great place to purchase fresh, local varieties from knowledgeable vendors. *Jerry Soverinsky*

Bike Shops

Tons in Den Haag. Here are
a few of the 57:
Bruin Fietsen: Badhuisstraat 65; Phone: 070 354228.
Clasen Rijwielhandel: Pippelingstrat 30; Phone: 070 3682680;
www.tweewielerspecialist.nl.
Bert's Wielershop: Betje Wolffstraat 215; Phone: 0703661010.

You'll need a good sense of direction to find your way through the larger Dutch cities. Their maze-like network of canals—while richly adding to the charm of the cities—can be maddeningly difficult to navigate. *T.I.P. Delft*

Sightseeing

Originally a medieval fishing village, Scheveningen developed in the nineteenth century as one of Europe's most fashionable beach resorts. Den Haag (The Hague or Gravenhage), where the Dutch government is based, is an elegant city with tree-lined avenues and extensive parks.

    Scheveningen

Built in 1887, the Kurhaus is one of Europe's grandest hotels.

The Sea Life Centre provides a glimpse of North Sea marine life (Strandweg 13, Scheveningen).

Den Haag

The Old Town building dates to the fifteenth century.

Unless you've got young children in tow, skip **Madurodam** (175 Haringkade), a miniaturized Dutch village/playground.

Binnenhof is the Dutch Parliament. Guided tours are available Monday through Saturday from 10 a.m. to 4 p.m. and Sunday from 10 a.m. to 4 p.m. in July and August only.

Marvel at works by Rembrandt, Vermeer, and Frans Hals at **Mauritshuis**.

Groenmarkt is the central square in Den Haag.

Grote Kerk (or Sint-Jacobskerk) is a fifteenth-century church.

Royal Picture Gallery Mauritshuis (8, Korte Vijverberg) features seventeenth-century Dutch artists. It is open Tuesday through Saturday from 10 a.m. to 5 p.m. and Sunday from 11 a.m. to 5 p.m.

Restaurants

There are several modestly priced restaurants along Scheveningen's Pier that provide five-star views of the North Sea.

For an authentic Indonesian Ricetable dinner, try Raden Mas at Gevers Deynootplein 125 (Phone: 354 54 32).

For fresh fish, visit De Bomschuit at 15 Strandweg (Phone: 355 0280).

Traditional Dutch specialties can be found at De Hoogwerf (20 Zijdelaan, Den Haag; Phone: 347 5514).

Luggage Transfers

Hofstad Taxicentrale: Forellendaal 430; Phone: 070 3462626; www.hofstadtax.nl.

Achttax BV: Zwetstraat 97; Phone: 070 3839696; achttax.bv@12move.nl.

HTC Taxicentrale; Rijswijkseweg 127; Phone: 070 3907722; www.htmc.nl.

ZANDVOORT TO DEN HAAG
ROUTE NOTES

Day 2: Zandvoort to Den Haag

Today's ride follows the dedicated North Sea bicycle path almost exclusively, leading you along gently rolling hills of wild heather and sand dunes. You'll pass the exciting Dutch holiday seaside town of Noordwijk en route to Den Haag, perhaps stopping at a secluded North Sea farmhouse for Dutch pannekoeken (pancakes). I almost always include one full layover day in Den Haag, especially during summer when the Scheveningen beachfront is so welcoming.

Distance: 40 Kilometers

Lunch Stop: Noordwijk, or any of the other North Sea towns.

NOTE: Follow the LF1A, which leads south. Do not follow the LF1B, which heads north.

Directions (KM):

0.0: From the front doors of the VVV, turn **LEFT**. Just ahead, turn **RIGHT** onto Louis David Straat. Just ahead at the roundabout, take the second exit off of the roundabout onto Krocht Gasthuis.

0.4: Turn **LEFT** and follow the main road to the LF1A.

1.9: Turn **RIGHT** onto the bike path (LF1A), which you'll follow all the way to Scheveningen/Den Haag. Look for the small, concrete posts that are placed intermittently along the LF1A path.

11.0: Marine Radio Station Noordwijk is to the right. Veer **LEFT** with the LF1A. You'll pass dozens of signs, but you'll always follow the LF1A.

16.8: Turn **RIGHT** following the LF1A toward Strand 0.3/Noordwijk a/Zee 1.1 Katwijk a/Zee 8.3.

17.0: Continue following the LF1A toward Katwijk a/Zee 8.2/Noordwijk a/Zee 1.

17.9: You'll pass a sign for the town limits of Noordwijk, continue **STRAIGHT**.

23.8: Katwijk, another good town for a rest. To continue your ride, follow the sea through the town until you find the LF1A. You'll see signs toward Wassenaarse Slag 4/Wassenaar 8/Scheveningen 13/Den Hagg 15.

35.4: Continue following LF1A signs.

39.5: Scheveningen.

Background Notes
Where Am I?
Country: Holland
Province: Zuid-Holland
City: Delft

Tourist Information
Delft Tourist Information Point
Hippolytusbuurt 4
2611 HN Delft
Phone: 015 215 40 51.
www.delft.nl

Bike Shops
Karlas Fietsen: Bartokpad 4; Phone: 015 2572545.
De Fietsenmaker: Geitenkamp 1; Phone: 015 2615969.

Sightseeing
The town's main church, **Nieuwe Kerk,** is a fourteenth-century Gothic church that lies just off its central square (**Markt**).

When you arrive at a Dutch city for the first time, head straight for the Maarkt, the focal point of the town, which is surrounded by shops, restaurants, and cafes. *T.I.P. Delft*

City boat tours depart Koornmarkt daily between 9:30 a.m. and 6 p.m. from mid-March to the end of October.

Oude Kerk is a thirteenth-century church and it is also a worthwhile stop.

Restaurants

I love the Hotel de Emauspoort (see *Accommodations*), and their dinner presentations are outstanding. You'll also find dozens of intimate cafés along the central square and its surrounding streets.

DEN HAAG TO DELFT
ROUTE NOTES

Day 3: Den Haag to Delft

You'll spend the first half of today's ride again along the North Sea Coast, perhaps savoring a lazy lunch at a Hoek van Holland cafe. You'll pedal anxiously for Delft, a charming Dutch village that still retains much of its medieval atmosphere.

Distance: 46 kilometers

Lunch: Hoek van Holland

Directions (km): From the VVV, follow your Scheveningen map to reach the corner of Houtrust Weg and Pluvierstraat. It will be almost 7 kilometers to cycle from the Scheveningen VVV to the LF1A beachside path.

6.9: Follow the LF1A to Hoek Van Holland 16. You'll also see signs for Kijkduin 2.8/Ter Heijde 9.2/Hoek Van Holland 16.

7.8: Continue **STRAIGHT** for Kijkduin 2.2.

9.9: Turn **LEFT** toward Kijkduin 0.3/ Hoek Van Holland 14.

10.3: The Atlantic Hotel will be on your right. Follow the LF1A **RIGHT** toward Monster 5/Ter Heijde 5/Hoek Van Holland 13.

14.6: Turn **LEFT** toward Ter Heijde 2.2/Monster 1.7/Hoek Van Holland 9.3.

16.9: Monster.

20.7: Keep following LF1A signs.22.9: Turn **RIGHT** on the LF1A toward Centrum 2/Harwich Ferry 2/Camping Strand 2. Next, take an immediate **LEFT** on the LF1A toward Rotterdam 32/Centrum 2/Harwich Ferry 2. Cross the road and continue following signs to Centrum 2/Harwich Ferry 2. Follow signs toward the Centrum.

23.7: Turn **LEFT** toward the Centrum1/Harwich Ferry 1. Immediately after this, turn **LEFT** toward the Centrum 1/Harwich Ferry 1.

24.4: Straight ahead is the main street in Hoek van Holland, a great lunch spot.

When you're ready to continue to Delft:

Begin at the post office in the center of Hoek Van Holland. Follow Prins Hendrikstraat to the LF1B (not LF1A), pointing to Rotterdam/Den Hagg/Strand. You'll enter a wooded area. Just ahead, follow the LF1B to the **RIGHT** toward Rotterdam/Den Hagg. Turn **LEFT**, following signs to the LF1B.

26.1: Follow the LF1B Noordzee Route to the **RIGHT**.

26.4: You'll leave the wooded area and just ahead will be a parking lot. Go through the parking lot and follow signs to the LF1 Noordzee Route, toward Rotterdam/Den Hagg.

26.8: Continue toward Naaldwijk 6/'s-Gravenzande 3. There will be a Q8 gas just ahead of you.

27.9: Turn **RIGHT** toward Naaldwijk 5/Delft 18/Maassluis 12.

Many Dutch towns seal off their central areas from motorized traffic. These four brown vertical posts delineate a pedestrians-only zone, a thoughtful gesture that makes sightseeing that much more worry-free. *T.I.P. Delft*

28.7: Continue **STRAIGHT** to Naaldwijk 5/Delft 17.

29.6: Go **LEFT** toward Naaldwijk 4/'s-Gravenzande 1.

30.6: Follow signs toward Naaldwijk 3/Delft 16 on Naaldwijk Straat.

33.1: Continue **STRAIGHT** toward Delft 14.

35.1: Turn **LEFT** following the bike sign toward Maassluis 7/Rotterdam 26/Westerlee-de Lier 3/Delft 12.

35.6: Reach Westerlee-de Lier and continue straight on the bike path.

37.2: Go **STRAIGHT** toward Delft 9.

37.7: Continue **STRAIGHT** toward Den Hoorn 6/Delft 9 (red and white sign). Continue following signs to Delft.

43.5: Turn **LEFT** toward Den Hoorn 1/Delft 3. As you cross a road, veer **RIGHT** toward Doorgaand Verkeer. Follow signs toward Den Hoorn 1/Delft 2.

43.7: Den Hoorn.

44.3: Cross a bridge toward Delft.

45.3: Delft.

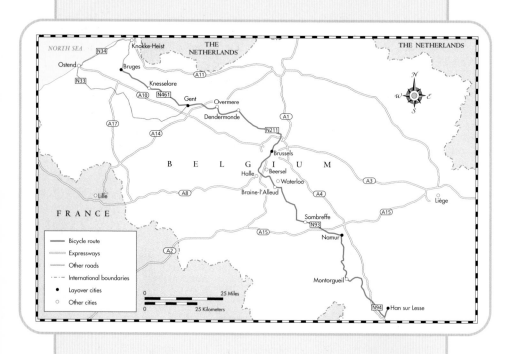

The Best of Belgium
Tents for Sale

I love traveling to Belgium.[64] The people are friendly, the beer is good, tourist pricing is reasonable, and you always leave with a hilarious story that somehow always ends with the catchphrase "it was a very dumb thing to do."

In 1993, I was finishing a three-month stay in Europe where I had guided a dozen or so cycling trips, the majority which stayed at campgrounds. I supply the tents for all of my company's camping-style trips, and the 27 I was transporting at the end of that summer had seen better days. In fact, I knew that for my company's 1995 programs, I'd need to buy new tents, and I was trying to decide what to do with the old ones.

While I was in a Bruges camping store, the manager overheard me talking and he offered to buy the tents later that night. He told me to meet him back at the store at 10 p.m., when the owner would inspect my inventory. He seemed eager and very serious, so I couldn't imagine the downside.

---

[64] I used to love it even more, when Sabena was still around and offered direct flights from Chicago to Brussels. Man, they brewed a damn good cup of coffee!

My friend Lori was visiting my trip at the time. I told her about the potential sale and asked her to drive into town later that night with me. She agreed, but when we arrived at the store, only the manager was there. He said that the owner would be meeting us "a few minutes outside of the city." Okay, I thought, no big deal, so we followed the manager out of the city.

Bruges is not a big city, and you're quickly outside its city center in minutes. Which should give you some relative understanding that after 25 minutes of driving and following the Belgian store manger along tiny, rural roads, we were indeed far away from my group. And very far away from anywhere recognizable.

Around 10:45 p.m, we arrived at an isolated Belgian farm (I'm pretty sure we were still in Belgium).

"Jer, this doesn't look good," Lori said, her voice cracking with nerves (Lori's a great gal, but brave she's not).

"They're Belgians, don't worry," I replied. "They owe us big time."

As we pulled up to the farm, an albino Belgian man—think *Deliverance* meets Antwerp—approached the store manager's car that had arrived moments earlier. I strained to hear what the two were saying, but not knowing Flemish, it wouldn't have mattered anyway.

The store manager exited his car and motioned for me to pull my truck behind the barn. That's *behind* the barn, as in out of sight from the road.

"Jer, what the hell?" Lori said.

This isn't good, I thought to myself, but then the store manager waved his arm faster and faster.

"No, it's okay, Lor. Look, he's waving his hand faster."

So I followed him. And then, for some strange reason, the *Deliverance* theme started playing in my head.

"Do-do-do-do-do-do-do-do-do . . . "

As we pulled the car behind the barn, in addition to the store manager and the albino Belgian, there were three other men standing around drinking beer. The banjo music was now deafening.

"Do-do-do-do-do-do-do-do-do . . . "

I exited my car tentatively and told Lori to remain seated, a request to which she had no intention of objecting. I heard her lock my door after I got out of the van, and was relieved that she was taking independent safety precautions (that's sarcasm, but as the saying goes: "When in Belgium, watch your own back.").

And then miraculously, thankfully, incredibly, astoundingly—you pick the word—the men indeed only wanted to purchase the tents. Which they did at a sum I accepted without negotiation.

As Lori and I returned to our Bruges campground later that night, I thanked her for accompanying me, and we headed straight for a nearby bar, where we

Belgium remains a less than enthusiastic tourist destination for Americans, which is puzzling to me. They have a diverse collection of culturally rich cities filled with picturesque, centuries-old buildings and tourist facilities that are modestly priced. Suit yourself, people, stay at home. More beer for me. *Ghent Tourist Office*

blew the entire tent sale sum—roughly $60 in Belgian currency—on extra strong beer.

As we sat at the bar finishing our third blue-label Chimay, we reflected on a night that we were relieved had ended uneventfully. Still, I thought to myself as I asked the bartender for another round of beers, following that man into the countryside . . . it was a very dumb thing to do.

Tourist Information

I've had a strong relationship with the people at the Belgian Tourist Office since I started my company over 13 years ago. They're some of the most knowledgeable people (about Belgium—I've no idea if they can answer algebra questions) who go to any extreme to assist with your travel needs to Belgium.

You can visit their website at www.visitbelgium.com, or else contact them at the addresses below:

U.S.
Belgian Tourist Office
780 Third Avenue, Suite 1501
New York, NY 10017
Phone: (212) 758-8130
Fax: (212) 355-7675
info@visitbelgium.com

U.K.
Tourism Flanders-Brussels
Flanders House
1a Cavendish Square
London W1G OLD
Phone: 020-7307-7730
Fax: 020-7307-7731
Email: office@visitflanders.co.uk

When to Go

I've cycled through Belgium from mid-March through late October, but it's pretty cold and rainy during those outside months. I prefer May through September—the temperatures are mild and rarely too hot, even during the summer. Take decent rain gear along because Belgium does receive its share of rainfall, as you can see from the chart below.

BRUSSELS[65]

MONTH	AVERAGE HIGH (°F)	AVERAGE LOW (°F)	AVERAGE PRECIPITATION (IN)
JANUAR.	42	34	3.2
FEBRUARY	42	33	2.0
MARCH	49	38	3.2
APRIL	55	40	2.1
MAY	63	47	2.9
JUNE	67	52	2.9
JULY	72	56	2.3
AUGUST	72	55	1.7
SEPTEMBER	66	52	2.7
OCTOBER	58	46	3.3
NOVEMBER	48	39	2.4
DECEMBER	44	36	2.7

[65] From http://www.usatoday.com/weather/climate/europe/belgium/wbrussel.htm.

Arrival and Departure
Air and Public Transportation
Brussels Zaventem Airport is a popular European hub, and your agent should have little trouble finding you a round-trip flight from your North American or U.K. starting point. The airport maintains a good English-language website with a lot of helpful travel information (www.brusselsairport.be).

TO BRUGES
Trains run from the airport via central Brussels to Bruges in 90 minutes and cost €11.60 (http://www.b-rail.be), and it will be €9 more if you're bringing a bike. Taxis throughout Belgium charge on average €2 per kilometer, and expect to pay roughly €200 for the one-hour trip.

FROM HAN-SUR-LESSE
If you'd like to take advantage of the substantial public transportation cost savings, you'll need your hotel to help arrange a short transfer to Jemelle, 6 miles from Han, and site of the nearest train station. From there, it's a 2-hour journey back to Zaventem and the total one-way trip will set you back only €13.60 (http://www.b-rail.be), and €9 more for your bike.

If time is tight and you need a private transfer, you'll pay €200 to €230 for the 60 to 75 minute trip. **Ardennes Taxi:** Rue du Poteau 28; Rochefort; Phone: 084 21 34 18.

Bike Rental
There are at least 5 shops and hotels in Bruges that rent bicycles, all ranging from €5 to €9 per day (ask for weekly discounts):

Railway station: Phone: 050 38 58 71.

'**t Koffieboontje, Hallestraat 4:** Phone: 050 33 80 27; Hotel_Koffieboontje@unicall.be; http://www.hotel-koffieboontje.be/.

Eric Popelier, Mariastraat 26 : Phone: 050 34 32 62.

De Ketting, Gentpoortstraat 23: Phone: 050 34 41 96.

Snuffel Sleep-In, Ezelstraat 47- 49: Phone: 050/33.31.33; info@snuffel.be; http://www.snuffel.be/.

Cycling Notes
Like its Dutch neighbor to the North, Belgium is very much a bike-friendly country. There are bike paths, or at least broad shoulders, where you'll feel comfortable cycling everywhere. You'll also find well-equipped bike shops liberally sprinkled throughout the country, enabling you to cycle reassured that professional assistance is always nearby.

Maps
Michelin #213, *Bruxelles-Oostende-Liege*; 1:200,000; and Michelin #214, *Mons-Dinant-Luxembourg*; 1:200,000.

Bruges
I detail Bruges information under Tour 16, Amsterdam to Bruges. In the meantime, if you're having trouble flipping pages, here's the essential contact information:

Bruges VVV
Burg 11
Bruges 8000
Phone: 050 44 86 86
Fax: 050 44 86 00
toerisme@brugge.be
www.brugge.be/toerisme/en/index.htm

I recommend spending at least one full day sightseeing in Bruges.

Background Notes
Where Am I?
Country: Belgium
Region: Flanders
Province: East Flanders
City: Gent

Tourist Information
Ghent Tourist Office
Predikherenlei 2
Gent 9000
Phone: 09 225 36 41
Fax: 09 225 62 88
toerisme@gent.be
www.visitgent.be

Bike Shops
Wheels: Burgsesteenweg 97; Phone: 093 297061.
Janssens: Wolfputstraat 182; Phone: 092515828.
Eric Fietsatelier: Pieter Van Vyncktstraat 37; Phone: 092266115.

Sightseeing

There are many popular sites in Gent. The **St. Baaf's Cathedral** dates from the fifteenth century, and **St. Niklaaskerk** (St. Nicholas Church) is a thirteenth-century church.

Take a glass elevator to the **Belfry's** roof for great views of the city. There are tours daily every 30 minutes from 10 a.m. to 4:30 p.m.

The **boat trips** around Gent's waterways depart from the Korenlei daily from 10 a.m. to 7 p.m.

Gravensteen, the castle of the counts of Flanders, resembles an old battleship. It's located at Sint-Veerpleplein and is open daily from 9 a.m. to 6 p.m.

Motorboat rentals are a great way to see Gent. Call Minerva at 09 221 8451 for information.

For a **guided walking tour, contact** Gidsenbond van Gent at 09 233 0772.

Restaurants

For dinner, **Marco Polo** (Serpentstraat 11, 09 225 04 20) serves great Italian food.

One of the city's most renowned restaurants is **Jan Van den Bon** (Kon. Leopold II, Phone: 09 221 9085), which serves a variety of contemporary dishes with regional ingredients.

Gent? Where's Gent? It's stop number two along your Belgium itinerary, a beautiful city overflowing with character and bustling with activity, both day and night.
Ghent Tourist Office

Luggage Transfers

BC Limo: Heernislaan 55; Phone: 09 2242010; info@bclimo.be.
V-Tax: Stapelplein 82; Phone: 09 2223323; info@v-tax.be.

BRUGES TO GENT
ROUTE NOTES

Day 1: Bruges to Gent

Today's ride visits the heart of the Flanders region and gives you the opportunity to visit dozens of interesting small towns and villages along the way. You'll spend the night in Gent, a historically rich town with outstanding architecture and a lively central-downtown area.

Distance: 43 kilometers

Lunch Stop: Knesselare.

Directions (km): 0.0: Start from the Novotel at the corner of Katelijnestraat and Oude Gentweg. Turn **RIGHT** onto Oude Gentweg.

> 0.7: At Gentpoortstraat, turn **RIGHT** and head over the bridge. You'll then cross over the Buiten Gentpoortvest (a major road marked R30). After you cross this larger road, you'll be on the N337 (Gen. Lemanlaan). Continue **STRAIGHT** on the N337 following signs to Knesselare and Assebroek. There will be a bike path along the right side.
>
> 3.5: The bike path crosses the street. Continue along the N337.
>
> 8.4: Oedelem. Continue following signs to Knesselare on the N337.
>
> 15.2: Knesselare.
>
> 16.4: Cross the N44 and join the N461 (**STRAIGHT** ahead) toward Ursel 4/Eeklo 13.
>
> 21.2: As you leave Ursel, you'll come to a stop sign. Continue **STRAIGHT** on the N461.
>
> 24.9: You'll see Jubilar de Sportsman pub on your right; turn **RIGHT**. Continue following signs to Hansbeke, taking a **LEFT** just ahead on Spinhout Straat.
>
> 29.9: As you reach Hansbeke, cross a white bridge. Continue into town and just before you cross the train tracks, turn **LEFT** (30.4 kilometers). Stay on the N461.
>
> 32.9: Continue over a bridge, and when you reach a stop sign at 33.6, turn **RIGHT** toward Drongen 7.
>
> 37.8: Veer **RIGHT** onto the Antoon Catrie Straat.
>
> 41.3: Turn **LEFT** onto the N466.
>
> 41.8: At a roundabout, continue **STRAIGHT** on the N466.
>
> 42.7: Cross a large bridge and enter Gent.

Background Notes
Where Am I?

Country: Belgium
Region: Brussels
City: Brussels

Tourist Information
Brussels Tourist Information
Town Hall
Grand Pl.
Brussels 1000
Phone: 02 513 89 40
Fax: 02 513 82 20
tourism@brusselsinternational.be
www.brussels.be;
www.brusselsinternational.be

Bike Shops
Cyclo Fietsatelier: Rue de Flandre;
Phone: 02 4276290.
Cicli Fransman: Rue Fransman;
Phone: 02 5139555.
Maison du Velo: Chaussee de
Louvain 341; Phone: 02 7420745.

Arrive early at your Belgian destination
and opt for a boat ride. Both Bruges
and Gent offer several guided tours.
Ghent Tourist Office

Sightseeing
One glance at your Brussels map reveals a confusing arrangement of streets that run in every direction. The city's two loosely delineated regions are Lower Town, where most of the sights are located; and Upper Town, the area where Belgian Royalty is the focus. The Lower Town is the area east of the main North/South Street, Boulevard Adolphe Max.

For an architectural tour, contact **ARAU** (rue du Midi 2) at 513 47 61 for information.

Brussels' most popular sight is the **Mannekin Pis** (Rue de l'Etuve and rue du Chene), a bronze statue of a boy urinating. If you venture out near the Gare du Nord, you'll find many people replicating the act.

The Grand Place, the central meeting point in Brussels, is a magnificent market square surrounded by some of Brussels' most outstanding architecture.

Cathedrale Saint-Michel et Sainte-Gudule (Parvis Ste.-Gudule) is a wonderful cathedral; its construction began in 1226. It's open daily from 7 a.m. to 6 p.m.

Belgian Comic Strip Museum (also called Centre Belge de la Bande Dessinne) is largely a result of the popular Belgian strip Tintin, who has become a national hero in Belgium. This museum houses Tintin and works from over 25,000 cartoons (Rue des Sables 20). It's open Tuesday through Sunday from 10 a.m. to 6 p.m.

Galeries St. Hubert is Europe's first indoor arcade, and it was built in 1847. There are many upscale cafes and restaurants inside, as well as fashionable boutiques.

Restaurants

Some of the most popular restaurants are the **Aux Vieux Bruxelles** (Rue Saint Boniface), for mussels; **In't Spinekopke** (Jarrdin aux Fleurs 1) for traditional Belgian dishes; and **'t Kelderke** (Grand Place 15) for people watching, owing to its enviable location in the central market square.

Luggage Transfers

De Langhe: Rue des Faines 170; Phone: 02 2429550; andre@limousines-delanghe.be.

Air Auto BVBA: Steenokkerzeelstraat 96; Phone: 02 7206838; airauto@pandora.be.

GENT TO BRUSSELS
ROUTE NOTES

Day 2: Gent to Brussels

You'll next cycle to Brussels, one of Europe's most exciting cities. Whether wandering its bustling streets, sipping coffee at an outdoor cafe in the Grote Markt, or visiting one of its interesting museums, your time here will be one of your tour's highlights.

Be especially careful cycling in and out of Brussels. It's a busy city, with motorized traffic zipping through its winding streets.

Distance: 67 kilometers

Lunch Stop: Dendermonde.

Directions (km): From Vogelmarkt (center of Gent):

Follow Vogelmarkt as it changes to Brabantdam; continue following signs to the R40.

1.0: At a roundabout, take the third exit toward R40 Strads Ring/Dampoort on Nieuwebosstraat. The road will become cobblestone, follow it around and you'll come to Tweebruggenstraat and then cross over a bridge. Continue **STRAIGHT** and you'll be on Kasteellaan (there will be a bike path on the right).

1.7: Turn **LEFT** toward Lokeren on the N70 and Zell on the N445.

2.4: As you reach a roundabout, follow signs to the N445 and Destelbergen. Go under a bridge then continue to the right on the N445. Continue on the N445 and you are out of Gent. Follow the blue signs **RIGHT** to Zele and Laarne on the N445.

10.5: You pass over the highway.

18.5: Overmere; follow signs **RIGHT** for Uitbergen and Aalst.

21.5: Uitbergen; follow signs to Wichelen 2; as you enter Wichelen (23.5 km), turn **LEFT** for Dendermonde on the N416.

32.3: Dendermonde. Follow signs **LEFT** for Dendermonde. Just ahead (33 km), turn **LEFT** for Andere Richtingen.

As you pass through the area, head for Brussels on the N41 and Mechelen on the N17.

36.3: Turn **RIGHT** for Lebbeke on the N41 and Brussels on the N47.

40.2: Go **LEFT** for Lebbeke on the N47.

41.4: Turn **LEFT** toward the church, then **RIGHT** at Broed and Banket (Jules Buck Street).

41.5: Turn **LEFT** onto Laurierstraat; the road becomes Opwijkstraat.

43.3: Opwijk.

46.5: You reach a roundabout after crossing a bridge; follow signs for Brussels and Vilvoorde. At the next roundabout, continue **STRAIGHT** for Brussels and Vilvoorde.

49.0: Turn **LEFT** for Merchtem 2.

50.7: Merchtem. As you head through the town (lots of markets), turn **RIGHT** for Brussels 15 on a blue sign. Ahead 100 yards, make another **LEFT** for Brussels 15. Keep following signs to Brussels and Wemmel.

As you reach Wemmel, head toward for Brussels. As you approach Brussels, follow signs for Centre/Centrum.

64.5: You reach the basilica. Pass the roundabout and go through the park area just to the right of the tunnel. After the park area, continue **STRAIGHT** onto Leopold Laan II. You'll pass the Golden Tulip Hotel on your left and then the Rogier subway stop. You're now at Adolphe Max Laan and at the tip of the heart-shaped road that encircles central Brussels.

Background Notes

Where Am I?

Country: Belgium
Region: Walloon
Province: Namur
City: Namur

Tourist Information

Office du Tourisme de Namur
Hotel de Ville
Namur 5000
Phone: 081 24 64 44
Fax: 081 24 71 28
tourism@ville.namur.be
www.ville.namur.be; www.namur.be

Bike Shops

Parmentier Cycles: Ave. du Transvaal 85; Phone: 081 744408.
Saitta Cycles: Ave. de la Plante; Phone: 081 220314.

Sightseeing

Namur is located at the meeting of the Sambre and Meuse rivers, with its imposing citadel overlooking the Sambre. Be sure to visit its old town, which is centered around Marche aux Legumes.

Tresor Hugo d'Oignies houses a collection of crosses and religious artifacts produced by Brother Hugo d'Oignies for the nearby Oignies monastery during the thirteenth century (Rue Billiart 17). It's open Tuesday through Saturday from 10 a.m. to 12 p.m. and 2 p.m. to 5 p.m; and Sunday from 2 p.m. to 5 p.m.

The **Archaeologique Museum** (Rue du Pont) contains Roman antiquities from the Namur region. It's open Tuesday through Friday from 10 a.m. to 5 p.m., and Saturday and Sunday from 10:30 p.m. to 5 p.m.

Namur's most popular site by far is its **Citadelle** (Route Merveilleuse 8),. which was attacked dozens of times over the centuries and provides tourists with great views of Namur and the surrounding Ardennes. You can reach the top by cable car or foot. It's open daily from 11 a.m. to 5 p.m.

Restaurants

The city's most acclaimed restaurants are **Bietrume Picar** (16 Tienne Maquet) and **La Petite Fugue** (5 Pl. Chanoine Descamps). Both restaurants serve contemporary food in intimate settings.

Luggage Transfers

GMD Taxi: Pl. de la Station; Phone: 0473 883803.
Taxi Services SA: Rue de l'Abbaye 2; Phone: 081 742656.

Hostel travelers are easy to spot. Only on a deserted street, with a 40-pound knapsack tugging at her neck, could this traveler find the energy to pull out a sketch pad. Wait until she corners you later and tells you her life story. Oy-vey. It's a steep price to pay for sex in a bathroom. *Ghent Tourist Office*

BRUSSELS TO NAMUR
ROUTE NOTES

Day 3: Brussels to Namur

Be careful leaving Brussels (I always like to depart early in the morning to beat traffic), and when you're safely outside the city limits, pedal anxiously for Waterloo. You'll want to learn all about the famous 1815 battle. The view from the top of the Butte du Lion provides a strategic view of the former battleground. You'll spend the night in Namur, a charming town perched at the junction of the Sambre and Meuse rivers

Distance: 80 kilometers

Directions (km): 0.0: Begin from St. Michel Cathedral at the corner of Rue d'Assaut and Rue du Bois Sauvage. Follow Rue d'Assaut to the end of the street and bear **RIGHT.** Make an immediate **LEFT** down Wolvengracht in the direction of De Brouckere; pass the main street and turn **LEFT** down rue de Laeken/Lakensestraat; the street becomes Poissonniers Visverkopers; keep going **STRAIGHT** for Mons and you are now on Rue Van Artevelde.

1.7: You cross the major ring road; continue **STRAIGHT**.

3.0: The road will bear **RIGHT**, continue following signs toward Ring (the sign is just ahead).

3.7: Turn **LEFT** toward Ring. Just ahead, follow signs again toward Ring.

9.4: Veer **RIGHT** toward St. Pieters Leeuw's centrum, then continue **STRAIGHT**. This will be just after passing a Texaco gas station on your right.

12.6: Turn **LEFT** toward Halle/Ruisbroek (at traffic light).

13.8: Turn **RIGHT** toward Halle 5.

15.9: Turn **LEFT** toward Sint Genesius Rode/Huizingen/Buizingen.

20.1: Dworp.

22.2: Alsemberg (town limit sign) and continue following signs to Alsemberg centrum/ St. Genesius Rode 1.

23.7: Stop sign; turn **RIGHT** toward Eigenbrakel. Just ahead, there will be a traffic light at a major intersection. Turn **RIGHT** and cycle uphill past the large department store, Vastiau Godeau.

28.3: Braine L' Alleud. Continue to Braine L' Alleud centrum.

29.7: At the Shell gas station on your left, veer **LEFT** toward Nivelles/Waterloo (on a blue sign).

30.6: Begin following signs to Butte du Lion and Waterloo.

30.8: Small roundabout; exit toward Waterloo and Butte du Lion.

31.3: Veer **RIGHT** toward Nivelles and Butte du Lion.

31.7: Another small roundabout; exit toward Nivelles/Butte du Lion.

33.1: The parking lot for the Butte du Lion will be on the right and just past it will be the visitor's center.

33.2: Leaving the visitor's center, turn **RIGHT** out of the parking lot. Just ahead, turn **RIGHT** toward Charleroi 33/Genappe 9 onto the N5.

43.6: Turn **LEFT** toward Villers la Ville.

49.3: Reach Villers la Ville and the Abbaye (worthwhile visit). Turn **RIGHT** toward Tilly 5.

49.4: You'll cycle under a small arched way building and then veer **RIGHT**.

49.6: Turn **RIGHT** toward Villers la Ville 1.5/Tilly.

56.2: Turn **LEFT** to Namur on the N93. Follow the N93 all the way to Namur. The road can get busy, so be careful.

60.3: Veer **LEFT** with the road to Namur 21. Continue following signs to Namur on the N93.

79.9: Namur.

Background Notes
Where Am I?
Country: Belgium
Region: Walloon
Province: Namur
City: Han sur Lesse

Tourist Information
Han sur Lesse Tourist Information
Pl. Theo Lannoy
Han sur Lesse 5580
Phone: 084 37 75 96
Fax: 084 37 75 76
han.tourisme@euronet.be
www.tourismerochefort.be/contacts_fr.htm (shared website)

Bike Shops
Nearest shop is in Rochefort, 5 miles away:
Cycle Sport: Rue de Behogne 59; Phone: 084 21 32 55.

Sightseeing
Dinant is a great spot for lunch. In addition to many restaurants and markets, there's also a citadel.

Han sur Lesse, a charming, quaint town in the Meuse Valley is famous for its Grottes de Han, caves that were discovered over 150 years ago. In order to view the caves, you'll ride a tram to the caves' entrance. Guides will then lead you through a network of dimly lit chambers and

Can't make it in Troy, Michigan? Come to Belgium, where even the most talentless people can find an audience.
Ghent Tourist Office

stalagmites. The entire trip takes about 90 minutes, and it is open daily from 10 a.m. to 5 p.m.

The Wildlife Reserve, a 625-acre park filled with native animals, is located nearby and is open daily from 10 a.m. to 5 p.m.

Also nearby is Lavaux-Sainte Anne, where you can visit Chateau de Lavaux Sainte Anne, a twelfth-century castle. It's open daily from 9 a.m. to 6 p.m.

Restaurants

There's not a huge variety of restaurants in town, and my groups usually eat at hotel restaurants. **Ardennes 2** serves French dishes at modest prices. Try **Henry IV** (59 Rue Chasseurs Ardennais) for simple Belgian meals.

NAMUR TO HAN SUR LESSE
ROUTE NOTES

Day 4: Namur to Han sur Lesse
Your last day's ride winds through the peaceful Ardennes, finishing in Han-Sur-Lesse, a sleepy town with an extensive network of underground grottoes.
Namur to Han sur Lesse: 65 kilometers
Directions (km): 0.0: Start from the southern edge of Avenue de la Gare, the street bordering the central station. Head east and just ahead, the road will bear **RIGHT**. Continue on Rue Rogier toward Dinant/Jambes.

1.0: Roundabout; head toward Marches 46/Jambes.

1.3: Enter Jambes and at a roundabout, turn onto the N947 toward Yvoir 21/Jambes.

3.6: Follow signs to Dinant and Yvoir.

7.1: Dave.[9] Continue on the N947.

9.5: Lustin.

13.8: Turn **RIGHT** toward Yvoir 6.

15.2: Reach Godinne and the road will bear **RIGHT** under a narrow bridge.

16.5: Veer **RIGHT** toward Dinant/Yvoir.

19.2: Reach Yvoir and continue **STRAIGHT**. Follow signs toward Dinant on the N92.

20.8: Turn **RIGHT** toward Dinant 7.

25.6: Dinant (good lunch spot).

27.2: Turn **LEFT** onto the N948 toward Spontin 11/Lisogne 5/Loyers 3.

27.4: Turn **RIGHT** toward Lisogne/Thynes 7.

34.4: Turn **RIGHT** toward Ciney and Sorinnes (great picnic spot).

35.4: Turn **LEFT** by a small sign for the Circuit Charlemagne.

36.4: Stop sign; turn **LEFT**, then an immediate **RIGHT** to Foyndame 3/Eglise de Monumentale.

38.1: Foy de Notre Dame, then the road will bear **LEFT** around the Eglise de Monumentale.

[9] Curiously, named after Tom.

Just after the road bears left, turn **RIGHT** toward Dinant/Neufchateau/Celles 3.

39.6: Stop sign; turn **LEFT** toward Celles 2/Veves, continuing to follow the Circuit Charlemagne.

40.8: Continue toward Neufchateau 62/Rochefort 22/Houyet 10.

47.6: Continue on the N94 to Neufchateau 56/Han sur Lesse 18/Beauraing 17/Rochefort 17.

51.6: Cross over the E411 highway.

52.0: Villers; continue following signs to Han sur Lesse 14.

60.0: Continue **STRAIGHT** on the N94 toward Han sur Lesse 8.

60.8: Turn **LEFT** toward Han sur Lesse/Ave et Auffe/Rochefort.

62.0: Ave; continue **STRAIGHT**.

63.6: Auffe.

64.4: Han sur Lesse.

MULTI-COUNTRY ITINERARIES AND CONNECTING TOURS
Stomach Of Darkness

It could have been any number of factors that caused Lori Beekman[66] to projectile vomit that hazy July morning in 1994. An impromptu soccer game—or football as they called it at our German campground—sent a wildly kicked ball into her lower abdomen the evening before. The weather had also been near heat wave levels for several days. And I was all too aware that my fifth annual Bratwurst Festival could have played a role. I mean, let's face it. How do you really know when the white ones are fully cooked?

Lori was perfectly willing to wait out her discomfort, patiently expecting and hoping that her symptoms would subside. But when she coughed up what resembled to be a small piece of lung, I persuaded her that we should visit a hospital.

At just barely 20 years old and away from her native Vermont for the very first time, Lori was reluctant. After all, she had never been to a German hospital. And in this sleepy German village, we were miles—make that kilometers—from the nearest big city. But her small piece of lung was soon followed by an unmistakable piece of esophagus, and while I'm no doctor, I know that when internal organs surface outside the body, it's time for a check-up.

The campguard—not such an endearing title for the manager of a German campground—told us about a klinic—that's clinic with a "k" if you're not reading along—10 minutes by car from our campsite. Informing my group that I'd meet up with them later that night, I drove deep into the Mosel hills with Lori in search of medical attention.

The banks of the Mosel Valley are lined with vineyards, an impossible patchwork that clings to every rock and crevice along its steep banks. Eastern European immigrants are the main source of labor for their upkeep, and in mid-July, they dot the trails that wind up from the river, busily attending to the monotonous task of staking vines. As my cargo van slugged its way up the hills, the workers eyed me suspiciously, wondering what reason I could possibly have for invading their usually tranquil workspace. Or so I thought. Turns out I'd been driving with the parking brake engaged, and it was making an annoying grinding noise to all within earshot. Stupid car.

Now if you've never visited a German klinic—that's clinic with a "k", once again—I highly recommend it. Not for the medical attention; heavens, no. But they all—well, this one did—have the most delightful gardens out front. Lilacs, daffodils, roses, and carnations. It's a veritable bounty of summer-time life! I turned to Lori and gave her the "not bad" look. You know, when you nod and half-cock your head and then raise your eyebrows in a sign that you're pleasantly

---

[66] Not Lydia Bronfman's real name.

Don't get me wrong, I love traveling through Britain. But come on, folks! A diaper, flannel shirt, and rubber boots? Just wait until your kid turns 16. Talk about self-esteem issues. *Jerry Soverinsky*

surprised. "Not bad," I said to her. Good, I was verbalizing in sync with my thoughts. We were now parked directly in front of the klinic's entrance.

I turned to her for a response, and she looked terrified. "What?" I asked. "There," she pointed, at the klinic's front door. And there, before our eyes, in this tiny German hamlet in the upper reaches of the Mosel Valley, was a garden full of amputees—all wearing white Birkenstock sandals. Irrespective of age, they were in wheelchairs, on crutches, all sitting lifeless, congregating near the klinic's front door. And all wearing white Birkenstock sandals. This was no time for skepticism. Lori was in pain and needed medical attention, but I could sense her uneasiness.

"What?" I asked, "The amputees? Not so unusual," I lied, trying to keep my best reassuring game face on.

"It's not that, it's the white Birkenstocks," she said, obviously panicked.

I paused, trying to absorb what I, too, thought to be a valid concern.

"I'm kidding, idiot" she said, a reassuring sign that her sense of humor was not totally lost. "You f_ _ _ _ _," I playfully responded, lightly slugging her shoulder. And we entered the klinic.

You should know that my German is quite efficient if I'm speaking with a two-year-old child who has no knowledge of the German language. But if I'm speaking with a two-year-old child who understands German, he tends to squint his eyes and

Classic England. *Jerry Soverinsky*

laugh as if I'm playing a game. In a hospital setting, my German is called "broken English." But several years ago, I taught myself a trick in order to communicate in foreign countries. I phrase everything in the form of a yes-no question, enabling me to pick up at least the answer to my question. Anything that I'm able to understand after that is just, well, distracting.

Thankfully, the klinic's admitting agent/secretary/cook/nurse, Monika—that's now clinic with a "k" and Monica with a "k"—spoke broken German in response to my broken English, so Lori and I were able to gain entry into an "examination room" and wait for a doctor. I'd never before seen a stone floor in a hospital, and apparently, Lori hadn't, either. "Very European," I assured Lori with a wink. "You f _ _ _ _ _," she shot back, playfully slugging my arm. In any event, it had a nice view of the garden out front.

After several minutes, Monika reappeared, this time with Dr. Wolffe. That's Wolffe with a "w" but pronounced like a "v." Dr. Wolffe was an imposing man in his fifties with hands the size of pizzas. He spoke only German, so Monika became our translator. Broken English to broken German to German. I smiled and nodded perceptively. "This must be how things work at the U.N.," I said aloud, curiously verbalizing my internal thoughts once again.

The Luxembourg to Frankfurt itinerary passes through several lively Bavarian-like towns, each more festive than the last.
Jerry Soverinsky

"What?" asked a panicked Lori.

"Nothing," I said, and then resumed explaining Lori's history to Monika. I continued to stutter and struggle for several minutes, trying to explain Lori's symptoms in German. I drew pictures, re-enacted the soccer game and bratwurst festival, even made moaning signs. After several minutes, I sensed that Monika understood. And I was right, as she turned to Dr. Wolffe and said simply, *"Ihr magen."* Her stomach.

One thing you immediately notice in a German klinic—after the flower entrance, the amputees, and the white Birkenstocks—is that they dispense with the formal accoutrements of U.S. hospitals. They're not spending taxpayer dollars on examination gloves, hospital gowns, antiseptic, or other extraneous items. Rather, they ensure that their vending machines are all fully stocked. So before Lori could protest, Dr. Wolffe had taken off Lori's t-shirt and bra, pressed on her stomach, and after Lori moaned, "Oww," formed his diagnosis. But he had to wait to relay the information to Monika, who would then relay it to us, because at that moment, one of the double-arm-amputees was having trouble opening the front door and was lightly banging his head against the glass, so she excused herself momentarily while she went to assist him. When she returned, Dr. Wolffe rattled off a few words to Monika and then exited the room. Monika began wheeling Lori out the door, following him. Incidentally, it's very difficult to wheel a 40-year-old gurney on a stone floor.

"What's going on?" I asked Monika. "Where are you taking Lori?" And just so you're up to speed, that's now shirtless and braless Lori, who's mortified that I've seen her breasts.

"It's her . . . how do you say . . . appendix. Appendix," Monika answered.

"Her appendix! What are you talking about?"

Lori was equally scared and I didn't attempt to falsely reassure her. It appeared that she was being wheeled down for stomach surgery. She was petrified and needed assistance.

After the British Connecting Tour, you'll board a ferry in Harwich that will transport you (and your bike) to Holland. As for the ship, take along some Dramamine. North Sea waters can get rough. *Jerry Soverinsky*

I blocked the pathway of the gurney and forced Monika to stop the procession. "You can't take out her appendix." I was nervous and fumbling for a reason. Monika looked at me, expectantly. "It's the only useless tissue emanating from her bowels!" I fudged a little, trying to recall my high school biology. I hoped I was close.

Lori looked at me in horror, tears streaking down her cheeks. "That's the best you can do?"

"Dr. Wolffe is our best doctor," Monika countered, thinking that this lofty accolade could persuade us, but I wasn't having any of it, so Monika and I argued back and forth for several minutes. When it appeared that we were at a standstill, I decided to buy more time.

"One of the amputees is falling," I interjected, pointing to the garden. Monika hurried away to assist.

I looked at Lori. "Okay, first, flirty girl, put your shirt on," I said, tossing her the rumpled t-shirt underneath the gurney. "And second, I'm no doctor, but if you'd like a second opinion, I'll be glad to drive you to Frankfurt. We're about 90 minutes away. I'm sure there's an American-type hospital there."

Lori decided to call her mother, and her mother implored me to take her to Frankfurt. Well, not exactly in those words. It was more like, "If you don't get my daughter to a f _ _ _ _ _ _ twentieth-century hospital, I'll sue your [insert your favorite male anatomy part here] off." Lori's mother made a persuasive argument—much more so than did Monika—so we decided to leave the klinic.

Why do cricket players wear slacks?
Jerry Soverinsky

As Lori finished getting dressed, Monika was now back from assisting the amputees and Dr. Wolffe was now returning to inquire about the delay. I explained to Monika that Lori's mother insisted we get a second opinion, but please not to be offended. I decided not to wait for Dr. Wolffe's reaction to the translation, because when Monika was relaying the information to him, I grabbed Lori's hand and told her to quickly leave.

I yelled my most sincere *"danke schön"* to Monika and Dr. Wolffe, and Lori and I drove to Frankfurt where we found a reputable hospital. After a blood test and ultrasound, the U.S.-trained resident diagnosed Lori as having the flu and reassured her that a full recovery was expected within 48 hours.

He was right. Two days later, Lori was back drinking beers with our group at another German campground and playing soccer. Football. Whatever.

Cycling Overview

The tours in this section cover a broad range of cycling challenges. As a very rough guide, here's what you can look for in the various tours:

Tour	Appropriate Cycling Level (Beginner-Expert)
Connecting England with Continental Europe	Advanced Beginner and above
North Sea Coast to Amsterdam	All levels
Paris to Luxembourg	Advanced Beginner and above
Luxembourg to Frankfurt	All levels (modest climbs during one ride)
Swiss and Italian Lakes	Intermediate and above
Vienna to Prague	Intermediate and above

These are the standards I use for distinguishing the cycling levels:

Appropriate Cycling Level	Easy to spot at a health club because . . .
Beginner	Refers to exercise bike as "pedal machine"
Advanced Beginner	Refers to Beginners as "losers"
Intermediate	Starts every sentence with "I . . ."
Advanced Intermediate	Stops in front of every mirror
Expert	Starts every sentence with "No, Lois was my 5th wife . . ."

Climate and When to Go

All of the tours in this section can be comfortably cycled mid-spring through early fall. That's a generalization, so please see the individual tour descriptions for a listing of the average daily temperatures.

Combining Tours

Combining this section's tours is easy and affordable.

Connecting England with Continental Europe can be preceded by **England's Cotswolds** (requires a short train ride from Stratford to Colchester: 4 hours, £37, www.nationalrail.co.uk) and followed immediately by **The North Sea Coast to Amsterdam** (no interruptions, no transfers necessary) which can be followed immediately by **Amsterdam to Bruges** (no interruptions, no transfers necessary).

Amsterdam to Bruges: a 2 hour and 30 minute train ride and 71 (http://www.b-rail.be/) will bring you to Paris, where you can cycle the **Paris to Luxembourg** and then **Luxembourg to Frankfurt** itineraries. From Frankfurt, a 7 hour and 30 minute train ride at roughly $114 (www.raileuropecom) will bring you to Lugano, the start of the **Swiss and Italian Lakes** tour (you can also join **The Best of Switzerland** and **Switzerland Mountain Bike Challenge**, which both start very close to Lugano).

From Como, an 11-hour train ride and a little over $110 (www.raileurope.com) will bring you to Vienna, the start of the **Vienna to Prague** tour.

Zagats London gave this a 2.
Jerry Soverinsky

Currency

All of the countries under this section, except England, Switzerland, and the Czech Republic, have adopted the Euro (€). The United Kingdom uses the Pound Sterling (£).

Switzerland uses the **Swiss Franc** (SFr or CHF), and the official currency of the **Czech Republic** is the **Czech Crown** *(koruna),* abbreviated Kc or CZK

Colchester Castle is a renowned Essex destination that features a rich collection of Colchester's history. *Colchester Borough Council, U.K.; www.visitcolchester.com*

Tourist Information

For tours 14, 15, 16, and 19, I've already provided the main tourist information links earlier in the book. I'll include links to each city's tourist office under the appropriate day's ride. The rest of the main tourist information centers, covering tours 17, 18, and 20, are as follows:

LUXEMBOURG: http://www.ont.lu/

U.S.

17 Beekman Place

New York N.Y. 10022

Phone: 001 212 935 88 88

Fax: 001 212 935 58 96

luxnto@aol.com

U.K.
122, Regent Street
GB - LONDON W1B 5SA
Phone: 0044 (0) 20 7434 2800
Fax: 0044 (0) 20 7734 1205
tourism@luxembourg.co.uk

GERMANY: http://www.germany-tourism.de/
U.S.
German National Tourist Office
122 East 42nd Street, 52nd Floor
New York, N.Y. 10168-0072
Phone: (212) 661 72 00
Fax: (212) 661 71 74
gntonyc@d-z-t.com
U.K.
German National Tourist Office
Nightingale House
P.O. Box 2695
London W1A3TN
Phone: (020) 7317 0908
Fax: (020) 7317 0917
gntolon@d-z-t.com

AUSTRIA:
http://www.austria-tourism.at/
U.S.
Austrian Tourist Office, Inc.
120 West 45th Street, 9th Floor
New York, NY 10036
Phone: (212) 944 6885
Fax: (212) 730 4568
travel@austria.info
U.K.
Austrian National Tourist Office
14 Cork Street
 London W1N 3NS
Phone: (020) 762 90 461
Fax: (020) 749 96 038
info@anto.co.uk

CZECH REPUBLIC: www.visitczechia.cz; www.czechcenter.com; http://www.czechcentre.org.uk/home.html.
U.S.
Czech Tourism USA
1109 Madison Avenue *(at 83rd Street; subway 4, 5, 6 to 86th Street)*
New York, NY, 10028
Phone: (212) 288-0830, ext. 105, 101
Fax (212) 288-0971
travelczech@pop.net
U.K.
Czech Centre London
13 Harley Street
London W1G 9QG
Phone: 0207 307 5180
Fax: 0207 323 3709
info@czechcentre.org.uk

Special Notes

All of this section's tours combine multiple cultures. What does this mean for you, the traveler? For most of you, it'll be an opportunity to discover in intimate detail, and in a relatively short period of time, a kaleidoscope of diverse landscapes and captivating cultures. You'll be transported to places you've dreamed about for years and seen only on long-winded CNN reports, where you'll interact with locals in an atmosphere of congeniality and respect, who in turn will shower you with admiration for the effort and determination you've shown in your adventurous travel approach.

And if you're a college student choosing the hostel route, it means you'll be eating a lot of Ramen noodles, saving the bulk of your travel reserves for beer and strip clubs.

Travel Requests

When crossing the North Sea on the **Connecting England with Continental Europe** tour, ask your Sea Link ferry staff if they ever found my neck pillow. It cost me $20 and I know I left it on the ship sometime between 1992 and 1996.

When cycling the Paris to Luxembourg tour, see if Claudette's still in charge at the roadside frituur (french fry truck) just before Vouziers. If so, remind her to fix the noisy muffler on her Renault. Really annoying!

And to the organ grinder on the Charles Bridge in Prague—that's not a dog, it's a large rat. And anyway, it's dead.

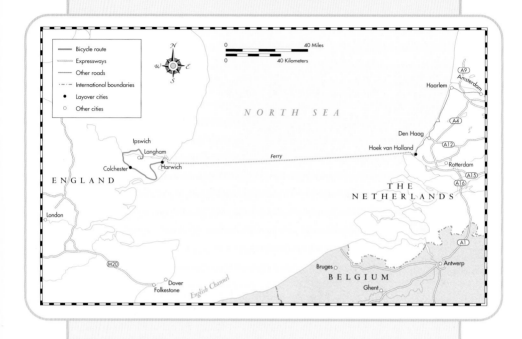

Connecting England with Continental Europe

Are you finished with the Cotswolds trip and want to begin cycling in Holland? Rather than board a no-frills London flight to Amsterdam, you can cycle to the North Sea coast, enjoying an extra couple of days winding through hedge-lined British lanes.

Your British cycling brings you first to Colchester, the oldest town in England, which dates to the Iron Age. You'll find Roman walls, Norman castles, a Victorian town hall, and Dutch-style houses, as well as a surprisingly modern downtown shopping district. After a few cycling days in the East Anglia region, you'll cross the North Sea en route to the Netherlands (Holland). You'll end the tour in Hoek van Holland, an intimate Dutch port town.

Arrival and Departure

Air

For this tour, your arrival airport city will be London and your departure airport will be Amsterdam. See Tours 3 and 12 for detailed information on those airports.

To and From the Airport
TO COLCHESTER
Taxi: There are hundreds of taxis outside of every London airport (and at least 14 outside the Bristol terminal). If you're starting from London, a taxi to Colchester will be steep: at least $200 at today's exchange rate.

Alternatively, if you want to arrange a private car or van for the journey, Motion Europe can help with the planning. Motion Europe: Phone: 020 762 99777; Fax: 020 762 99333; Email: Mail@motion-europe.com.

Train: From the London airports, high-speed trains regularly service Colchester. Check out http://www.nationalrail.co.uk for details on your specific itinerary. Approximate times and prices are as follows:

Departure Airport	Duration	Cost (pounds)
Stansted	0h59	28
Gatwick	2h08	23
Heathrow	2h05	31

FROM HOEK VAN HOLLAND
Taxi: Book ahead with Schiphol Travel Taxi, a shared taxi service that offers transfers to and from the airport and any city in Holland. Budget €29 for the 1-hour transfer (http://www.schiphol.nl/schiphol/taxi/stp_travel_stt1.jsp).

Train: Efficient Dutch trains connect Hoek van Holland with Amsterdam's Schiphol Airport in 80 minutes for €11.20 (www.ns.nl).

Bike Rentals
If renting a bike is a requirement for your European trip, this particular itinerary is not for you. Because you're starting and ending in two different countries separated by the North Sea, the time and expense that you'll incur returning a rental bike to London will far outweigh its cost.

Cycling Notes
Left in London, right in Holland. That is, you're cycling on the left side of the roads in England, and the right side in continental Europe.

Tourist Information
First-time visitors to England should allow at least three full days for sightseeing in London prior to cycling. Contact the London Tourist Board for information to assist your visit:

Visit London
1 Warwick Row
London SW1
Phone: 020 7932 2000

Fax: 020 7932 0222
enquiries@visitlondon.com
www.visitlondon.com

Maps
Ordnance Survey Landranger #s 155, 168, 169; 1:50,000. These will cover the entire region in England. See Tour 15 for maps covering Holland.

Temperatures and Rainfall

LONDON[67]

MONTH	AVERAGE HIGH (°F)	AVERAGE LOW (°F)	AVERAGE PRECIPITATION (IN)
JANUARY	45	36	2.4
FEBRUARY	45	36	1.4
MARCH	51	38	2.0
APRIL	55	41	1.7
MAY	62	47	1.8
JUNE	68	52	1.8
JULY	72	56	1.8
AUGUST	72	56	1.7
SEPTEMBER	66	52	1.7
OCTOBER	58	46	2.9
NOVEMBER	51	40	1.8
DECEMBER	47	38	2.3

COLCHESTER LOOP RIDE
ROUTE NOTES

NOTE: The route begins from Langham, a village 8 miles north of Colchester. After checking into your Colchester hotel, ask your concierge to hire a taxi to transport you to the starting point.
Distance: 27 miles
Directions (miles): 0.0: Start at the Shepherd and Dog pub. Facing the front of the pub, head **RIGHT**.
 .9: Go **RIGHT** to Dedham at a T-intersection.
 1.5: Langham Hall entrance is on the left; continue **STRAIGHT**.
 2.0: Turn **LEFT** to Ipswich 11, and Stratford St. Mary 1 (right is Colchester 6.5);
 2.2: Just ahead, follow signs **RIGHT** to Dedham.
 3.1: B1029 intersection: Turn **LEFT** to Ipswich on High Street; you'll enter Dedham (food, banks, markets).
 3.4: Turn **LEFT** onto Mill Lane.

[67] From http://www.usatoday.com/weather/resources/climate/worldcli.htm#l.

4.5: There's large church on the left; turn **LEFT** to Stratford St Mary 0.5, Higham 1.5 (straight ahead is Colchester 8). You'll pass under the A12; just past it, turn **RIGHT** to Higham (not straight to Stratford St. Mary).

5.3: Intersection; go **STRAIGHT** to Higham (right points Green Lane; to the left points Stratford St Mary).

5.9: Intersection; turn **LEFT** to Stoke and Sudbury on the B1068 (right is East Bergholt on the B1068).

7.2: Thorington Street (pub in town).

9.2: In Stoke by Nayland, turn **LEFT** on Church Street/B1087 toward Nayland.

10.8: Pass through town (Nayland) heading toward Colchester (A134); there are markets in Nayland.

11.3: At the A134 intersection, cross over and turn **RIGHT** and quick **LEFT** to Burres.

12.7: Turn **LEFT** to Bures 3 and Sudbury 8.

15.7: Just past the church, there is a grocery store (Central Stores). Follow the B1508 left to Colchester 9 (an obscured sign).

18.0: As you enter Wormingford, turn **RIGHT** to Fordham.

21.9: Turn **LEFT** to West Bergholt on Heath Rd.

22.5: Continue **STRAIGHT** to West Bergholt; the road curves left.

23.2: At an intersection (unmarked), turn **RIGHT**.

24.1: A bridge goes over the highway, over which you can walk your bike; turn **LEFT** on the other side of the bridge; you are on a residential street; you pass the National Westminster bank before you reach the A604.

24.8: Turn **LEFT**. Follow the roundabout to Lexden.

26.5: At a roundabout, go **STRAIGHT** for Town Centre, Hythe.

26.6: Turn **LEFT** at a traffic light for Town Centre; you are on Head Gate.

26.7: The road becomes Head Street. You're in the center of town.

Background Notes
Where Am I?
Country: England
Region: East of England
County: Essex
City: Colchester

Tourist Information
Colchester TIC
1 Queen St.
Colchester CO1
Phone: 01206 282920
Fax: 01206 282924
vic@colchester.gov.uk
www.colchesterwhatson.co.uk

Bike Shops

Colchester Cycle Stores: 50, St. Johns St.; Phone: 01206 563890.
Action Bikes: 24 Crouch St.; Phone: 01206 541744.
Cycle King: 46A East St.; Phone: 01206 867756.
Halford's: Cowdray Ave.; Phone: 01206 763725.

Sightseeing

While in Colchester, be sure to visit the **Roman Walls,** a mile-plus stretch of architecture that survived the town's Roman occupation centuries ago.

Colchester's **Norman Castle** dates from the eleventh century, and tours of its underground cellar are offered daily.

The Dutch Quarter, off High Street, was the settlement quarter for sixteenth and seventeenth-century Flemish refugees.

The **Clock Museum** (Trinity Street) is housed in a restored, late fifteenth-century house, and admission is free. It's open Monday through Saturday from 10 a.m. to 1 p.m. and from 2 p.m. to 5 p.m.

Walking Tours are given daily June through September at 2 p.m. and 11 a.m. on Sundays from the Tourist Information Office at 1 Queen Street.

Restaurants

You'll find plenty of moderately priced choices around High Street, especially typical pub fare.

Luggage Transfers

A1 Taxis: Cowdray Ave.; Phone: 01206 5466777.
Silver Carriage Company: Lexden Rd.; Phone: 01473 313000.
Micraline Minicabs: 17 Osborne St.; Phone: 01206 544244.

COLCHESTER TO HARWICH
ROUTE NOTES

Day 2: Colchester to Harwich

Today's ride winds through more British lanes en route to Harwich, a busy town notable for its North Sea connections. Enjoy an early lunch in Clacton, a seaside town with a bustling shopping district.

Distance: 43 miles

Directions (miles): 0.0: Begin from the Colchester Mill Hotel, just east of the Tourist Information Center on East Street. Turn **LEFT** out of hotel. You are on East Street.

    0.1: There is a small roundabout; bear **RIGHT** as you pass through it.

    0.2: You reach another roundabout; straight ahead is Harwich (A120); to the right is The Hythe.
        Go **STRAIGHT**.

0.3: Double roundabouts; straight ahead is Manningtree and the A137; to the right is Clacton on the A133; turn **RIGHT** (it also points to the University).

0.9: Follow signs to Clacton and the A133.

1.1: As you turn **LEFT**, signs point to Clacton on the A133.

1.9: Turn **RIGHT** to St. Osyth on the B1027.

2.4: Turn **LEFT** to Clacton and St. Osyth on the B1027.

13.5: At a roundabout, turn **RIGHT** onto the A133 toward Clacton, a good place for lunch and sightseeing.

14.8: Visit the pier for lunch. When you're ready to continue your ride to Harwich, follow signs to Holland-on-Sea, Frinton on Sea, and the B1032.

16.2: Once in Holland-On-Sea, follow signs for Frinton and Walton on the B1032.

19.2: Follow the B1032 until you reach the B1033 intersection. Turn **LEFT** on the B1033 toward Thorpe-le-Soken 3.

21.7: When you reach Thorpe-le-Soken, continue **STRAIGHT** along the B1033 to Weeley 2.

22.5: Turn **RIGHT** on the B1035 to Manningtree 8, and Tendring 3.

31.5: Turn **RIGHT** for Mistley 1 on the B1352 .

32.2: **RIGHT** to Mistley on the B1352

34.3: Turn **LEFT** for Ramsey and Harwich on the B1352 (Strangers' Home Inn). You're heading for Harwich and Parkeston Quay.

39.2: Ramsey. A few hundred yards ahead, bear **LEFT** for Manningtree.

39.4: Follow the roundabout **STRAIGHT** on the B1352 to Dovercourt 2, not left toward the A120.

40.5: Continue **STRAIGHT** to Dovercourt and Harwich.

41.4: Continue **STRAIGHT** to Harwich.

41.8: You go past a BP gas station.

42.2: Harwich.

Background Notes
Where Am I?
Country: England
Region: East of England
County: Essex
City: Harwich

Tourist Information
Harwich TIC
Iconfield Park, Parkeston
Harwich CO12
Phone: 01255 506139
Fax: 01255 240570
Harwich@eetb.info
www.harwich.net/tic.htm

Bike Shops
Harwich Radio & Cycle Supplies: 69 Church St.; Phone: 01255 502278.
HS Howlett & Son: 15 Kingsway, Dovercourt; Phone: 01255 503599.

Sightseeing
Clacton-on-Sea has one of the largest piers in Europe (over 6 acres). A seaside town, it has a large beach and pier-based amusement park.

In **Walton-on-the-Naze**, a short detour from Clacton, visit The Naze, an open grassland of 137 acres on the edge of 70 foot cliffs.

A short ride from Manningtree, the Mistley Place Park Environmental and Animal Rescue Centre is a parkland of 25 acres with wildlife habitats and views across the Stour Valley. It's open daily from 10 a.m. to 6 p.m.

Restaurants
Harwich's most notable restaurant is Harbourside (The Quay, 01206 241212), a moderately priced stop that serves fresh seafood.

Luggage Transfers
NOTE: You'll want to arrange with one of the companies below to meet you at the Stena Line ferry with your luggage for the North Sea crossing. You'll board the ship with your bike and luggage, and work with a Hoek van Holland taxi (plenty are waiting at the port) upon your Holland arrival.
Harwich Taxis: Haven House; Phone: 01255 551111;
www.harwichtaxis.com.
Starlings Taxis: 113 High St.; Phone: 01255 503000.

HARWICH TO PARKESTON QUAY
ROUTE NOTES

Day 3: Harwich to Parkeston Quay (England); ship to Hoek van Holland (Holland)
You'll begin the day with a 2-mile ride from Harwich to Parkeston Quay, the launching point for the Harwich-Hoek van Holland ferry route.

The North Sea crossing is operated by Stena Line, which offers a few travel options for its three- to six-hour crossings. For current sailing information, check out http://www7.stenaline.co.uk. For reservations and information, call 08705 707070 from within the U.K., or +44 1233 647022 from everywhere else. Summer fares for one passenger and bicycle begin at £33.

Distance: 2 miles
Directions (miles): 0.0: Start on the Main Road at the corner of Portland Avenue. Cycle west.
    0.6: At the roundabout, turn **RIGHT** to Parkeston and Tourist Information.
    0.9: At the next roundabout, head toward Parkeston on the A136. As you cycle around the roundabout, follow signs for Hoek of Holland and Passenger Ferries.
    1.4: At the roundabout near the Shell Station, follow the signs for a car ferry.

Background Notes
Where Am I?
Country: Holland
Province: Zuid-Holland
City: Hoek van Holland

Tourist Information
Hoek van Holland VVV
Prins Hendrikstraat 265
Hoek van Holland 3151
Netherlands
Phone: 0174 310080; Fax: 0174 310083
HvH@rotterdam-marketing.nl
www.hoekvanholland.nl/vvv

Bike Shops
Burg Fietsspecialist: Prins Hendrikstraat 235; Phone: 0174 382318.

Sightseeing
Hoek van Holland is a charming seaside town whose main street is Prins Hendrikstraat. An evening walk along the Strand (beach) is a perfect way to end your day.

Restaurants
My favorite Hoek van Holland restaurant is **Roma Antica** (Prins Hendrikstraat 182), an intimate Italian ristorante with an owner who prepares fresh, traditional meals at modest prices.

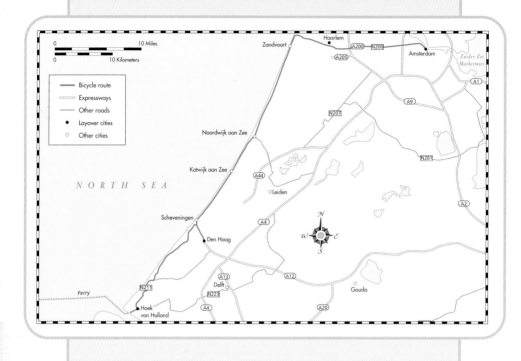

THE NORTH SEA COAST TO AMSTERDAM

This is technically not a multi-country tour, but my presumption is that you'll begin your trip in London, cycle Tour 14, and then continue with this tour at least until Amsterdam. Much of the planning details for the route are listed under Tour 12, so references are given when appropriate to avoid repeating the information.

Arrival and Departure
Air
See Tour 12 for detailed information on Amsterdam's Schiphol Airport (http://www.schiphol.nl/), your arrival and departure airport.

Taxi and Public Transportation
TO HOEK VAN HOLLAND
Taxi: Schiphol Travel Taxi, a shared taxi service that offers transfers to and from the airport and any city throughout Holland, will charge €29 for the 1-hour transfer: http://www.schiphol.nl/schiphol/taxi/stp_travel_stt1.jsp.
Train: Efficient Dutch trains connect Hoek van Holland with Amsterdam's Schiphol Airport in 80 minutes for €11.20 (www.ns.nl).

FROM AMSTERDAM
Train: You'll pay €3.10 for the 16-minute train ride from Amsterdam's Centraal Station to Schiphol. Alternatively, taxis are nominally quicker and will cost €25 to €35.

Bike Rentals
See Tour 12 for detailed information on renting a bike in Amsterdam. Prices start at €30 a week for the most basic Dutch models
(http://www.holland.com/amsterdam/gb/geninfo/travelinfo/bikeren.html).

Cycling Notes
See Tour 12 for detailed cycling notes for Holland.

Tourist Information
More than likely, you'll arrive from England and spend the night in Hoek van Holland. The lively port town operates a very helpful VVV that can reserve hotel rooms.

    Hoek van Holland VVV
    Prins Hendrikstraat 265
    Hoek van Holland 3151
    Phone: 0174 310080
    Fax: 0174 310083
    HvH@rotterdam-marketing.nl
    www.hoekvanholland.nl/vvv/

Holland is the mecca for cycling. Its collection of fietspadden (bike paths) is demonstrable proof of the Dutch commitment to cycling-as-a-way-of-life.
Jerry Soverinsky

Maps
Good: Michelin #211, *Rotterdam-Apeldoorn-Maastricht*; 1:200,000. This map covers the entire tour, but omits bike paths.

Excellent: ANWB publishes fiets kaarten (bike maps) of the various regions of Holland. You can purchase the appropriate North Holland map at http://basic.anwb.nl/basic/sh_a571318.htm.

Temperatures and Rainfall

AMSTERDAM[68]

MONTH	AVERAGE HIGH (°F)	AVERAGE LOW (°F)	AVERAGE PRECIPITATION (IN)
JANUARY	41	34	3.1
FEBRUARY	42	32	1.7
MARCH	48	37	3.5
APRIL	53	40	1.5
MAY	61	46	2.0
JUNE	66	52	2.4
JULY	69	55	2.9
AUGUST	70	55	2.4
SEPTEMBER	64	51	3.2
OCTOBER	57	46	4.1
NOVEMBER	48	39	3.0
DECEMBER	44	36	2.0

Background Notes
Where Am I?
Country: Holland
Province: Zuid-Holland
City: Den Haag

Tourist Information
The Hague Visitors
and Convention Bureau
Nassaulaan 25
Den Haag 2514
Phone: 070 361 8888
Fax: 070 361 5459
info@vvvdenhaag.nl
www.denhaag.com

Bike Shops, Sightseeing Restaurants, Accommodations, Cycling Notes
See Tour 12 for detailed background
information about Den Haag.

Like his American counterparts, the Dutch Good Humor man peddles his product to an enthusiastic populace. You should see the five-year-olds clamor for cheese wheels when he rings his bell. *Jerry Soverinsky*

[68] From http://www.usatoday.com/weather/climate/europe/netherla/wamstrdm.htm.

Dutch towns are labyrinths of canals, bridges, and cobblestone streets; inviting atmospheres that make any cycling vacation time well-spent. *T.I.P. Delft*

HOEK van HOLLAND TO DEN HAAG
ROUTE NOTES

Day 1: Hoek van Holland to Den Haag
Today's ride is a perfect introduction to North Sea riding. You'll cycle past miles of pristine, ocean-front beaches en route to Den Haag, capital of the Netherlands and a bustling, seaside city.
Distance: 25 kilometers
Directions (km): From the center of Hoek van Holland, follow the LF1B signs. Less than one mile later, you reach the Hoek van Holland campground and the beginning of the North Sea path. Continue along the LF1B, and look carefully for the LF1B signs whenever you reach a town or village.
    8.5: Monster (shops, markets).
    15.1: Kijkduin (shops, markets).
    22: The southwestern edge of Den Haag.

Background Notes
Where Am I?
Country: Holland
Province: Noord-Holland
City: Haarlem

Tourist Information
VVV Zuid Kennemerland
Stationsplein 1
Haarlem 2011
Phone: 023 5313506
Fax: 023 534 0537
info@vvvzk.nl
www.vvvzk.nl

Bike Shops
Jansen Cronje Fietsen: Generaal Cronjestraat 160; Phone: 023 5256125.
Fietsenstalling: Botermarkt 3; Phone: 023 5321193.

Sightseeing
Haarlem, better known as the birthplace of Frans Hals, was founded in the tenth century and remains one of my favorite city stops in North Holland. It maintains a beautiful city center, with wonderful cafés, shops, and restaurants. Among the sites, check out the **Grote Kerk** (fifteenth-century church, which is open Monday through Saturday from 10 a.m. to 4 p.m), **Grote Markt** (central square), and the **Frans Halsmuseum** (62 Groot Heiligland) that features a collection of famous "Haarlem School" painters' works. It's housed in a seventeenth-century courtyard building and is open Tuesday through Saturday from 11 a.m. to 5 p.m. and Sunday from 12 p.m. to 5 p.m.

Teylers Museum (Spaarne 16) first opened its doors in 1784 and is the oldest Dutch museum, which displays famous works of Western European artists. It's open Tuesday through Saturday from 10 a.m. to 5 p.m. and Sunday from 12 p.m. to 5 p.m.

Restaurants
Haarlem hosts dozens of top-quality restaurants. Among the more popular are **Het Stille Water** (19, Oostkolk) and **de Eetkamer van Haarlem** (45 Lange Veerstraat) for diverse continental fare; and **Napoli** (1 Houtplein) for quality Italian.

Luggage Transfers

A1 Business Class Taxi: Laan van Angers 194; Phone: 023 5407420; www.a1taxi.nl.

O-Tax BV Taxi Centrale: Mollerusweg 1; Phone: 023 5123456; www.jandewitautocars.com.

DEN HAAG TO HAARLEM
ROUTE NOTES

Day 2: Den Haag to Haarlem

Today's ride continues along the LF1B North Sea path, an idyllic trail that weaves its way along massive sand dunes and wild heather, never straying more than a few 100 yards from the North Sea. You'll spend the night in Haarlem, a medieval city that graciously incorporates both the old and new into its lively downtown Centrum.

Distance: 54 kilometers

Lunch Stop: Noordwijk; Katwijk; Zandvoort.

Directions (km): Continue along the LF1B (see yesterday's directions). You'll pass Wassenaar, Katwijk, Noordwijk, and Zandvoort.

About 3 kilometers into your ride, you'll see signs for Meijendel 4km. This makes a worthwhile stop and detour (pancake house in a nature area).

As you pass through Katwijk, the path is sometimes brick.

After Katwijk, Noordwijk is 4 kilometers away. Follow the road along the shore the rest of the way. Once you reach Noordwijk, follow signs for the LF1B. Head in the direction of Zandvoort and Haarlem.

Through Zandvoort, if you miss the LF1B signs, follow signs to Haarlem and Amsterdam. When you reach Heemstede, follow signs to Haarlem and Alkmaar, not the N201 to Centrum, Amsterdam, Den Haag, and Utrecht.

As you reach Haarlem, follow signs to the Centrum. You reach Haarlem at 54 kilometers.

Background Notes
Where Am I?

Country: Holland

Province: Noord-Holland

City: Amsterdam

European locals find it endearing when they find you passed out on their side streets.

Jerry Soverinsky

As you leave Gouda, en route to Willemstad, you'll pass Kinderdijk, the largest concentration of windmills in Europe (19). The mill at the far right is operable and open for tours. *Jerry Soverinsky*

Tourist Information
Amsterdam VVV
Stationsplein 10
Amsterdam 1012
Phone: 020 201 88 00
Fax: 020 625 28 69
info@amsterdamtourist.nl
www.visitamsterdam.nl/gb/

Bike Shops
Beter Fietsen: Zaanstraat 148; Phone: 020 6817555;
www.beterfietsen.nl.
Zijwind Fietsenmakerij; Ferdinand Bolstraat 168; Phone: 020 6737026.
Freewheel Fietsenmakerij: Akoleienstraat 7;
Phone: 020 6277252.

Forgot your tent? Many Dutch campgrounds provide rustic cabins, a cheap alternative to hotels. *Jerry Soverinsky*

Sightseeing

Allow at least two days to explore Amsterdam and its sites.

Anne Frank Huis (263 Prinsengracht) is where Anne Frank wrote her famous diary. It's open 9 a.m. to 5 p.m. Monday through Saturday, and 10 a.m. to 5 p.m. on Sunday.

The former home of Rembrandt is now the **Museum Het Rembrandthuis** (4 Jodenbreestraat) and is open Monday through Saturday from 10 a.m. to 5 p.m. and Sunday from 1 p.m. to 5 p.m.

Rijksmuseum (42 Stadhouderskade) is one of Amsterdam's best and features extensive collections of Rembrandt and other Dutch painters. Tours are given at 11 a.m. and 2:30 p.m. Otherwise, you can walk through yourself from 10 a.m. to 5 p.m. daily.

More than 200 works of Van Gogh are on display at the **Van Gogh Museum** (7 Paulus Potterstraat). It's open daily from 10 a.m. to 5 p.m.

Joods Historich Museum and Joods-Portugese Synagoge (Jonas Daniel Meijerplein) is open 11 a.m. to 5 p.m.

Nieuwe Kerk (New Church) and Oude Kerk (Old Church). The Old Church is the oldest building in Amsterdam, and it is open from 11 a.m. to 5 p.m. Monday through Saturday and 1 p.m. to 5 p.m. on Sunday. The New Church is open from 11 a.m. to 5 p.m.

Restaurants

There are hundreds of restaurants from which to choose. For traditional Indonesian rijstaffel, try **Puri Mas** (Lange Leidsedwarsstraat 37-41) and **Sama Sebo** (P.C. Hoofstraat 27).

Castell Barbecue (Lijnbaansgracht 252-254) offers steaks and seafood.

Piet de Leeuw (Noorderstraat 11) is a fun beer and steak place in a casual atmosphere.

D' Vijff Vlieghen (Spuistraat 294) is my personal favorite. It's an upscale (expensive) restaurant that serves wonderful Dutch dinners in a historic building.

HAARLEM TO AMSTERDAM
ROUTE NOTES

Day 3: Haarlem to Amsterdam

You'll cycle today along a flat, nondescript bike path that plows its way toward Amsterdam (some travelers elect to take the train from Haarlem to Amsterdam, eliminating the rather drab suburban scenery), one of Europe's most exciting cities. I recommend spending at least two full days sightseeing here, taking in the many sites and attractions within the city limits.

Distance: 24 kilometers

Directions (km): From the center of Haarlem, follow bike path signs to Amsterdam. You'll eventually cycle on the path that runs parallel with the A5/N5 road. It's a straight ride, but the path will stop and start as you enter towns. Keep following the bike path signs to Amsterdam.

Eventually, the A5/N5 becomes the S103. Stay on the S103 until you reach the S100.

20: Downtown Amsterdam. The S103 continues to the VVV, if you need to purchase a map and find directions to your hotel.

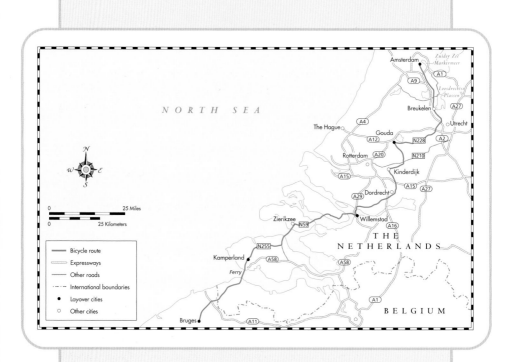

AMSTERDAM TO BRUGES

While the terrain on this trip is almost entirely flat, it's not always an easy cycling itinerary because the daily distances are fairly long and the wind can slow your progress considerably.

The tour begins and ends in major cities, which is perfect for those seeking culture and nightlife. However, for several days in between, you'll be cycling through very quiet, rural landscapes devoid of significant sightseeing attractions, but perfect for those who want to interact with locals in an unspoiled and generally off-the-beaten-path region.

Arrival and Departure
Air
See Tour 12 for detailed information on Amsterdam's Schiphol Airport (http://www.schiphol.nl/) and Brussels' Zaventem Airport (www.brusselsairport.be), your arrival and departure airports.

To and From the Airport

TO AMSTERDAM

Train: You'll pay €3.10 for the 16-minute train from the airport to Amsterdam's Centraal Station. Alternatively, taxis are nominally quicker and will cost €25 to €35.

FROM BRUGES

Trains run from Bruges station to Zaventem Airport in 90 minutes and cost €11.60, and €9 more if you're bringing a bike (http://www.b-rail.be). Taxis throughout Belgium charge on average €2 per kilometer, so expect to pay roughly €200 Euros for the one-hour trip.

Bike Rentals

See Tour 12 for detailed information on renting a bike in Amsterdam. Prices start at €30/week for the most basic Dutch models:
http://www.holland.com/amsterdam/gb/geninfo/travelinfo/bikeren.html.

Cycling Notes

See Tours 12 and 13 for detailed cycling notes for Holland and Belgium.

Maps

Good: Michelin #211, *Rotterdam-Apeldoorn-Maastricht*; 1:200,000; and Michelin #212, *Brugge-Rotterdam-Antwerepen*; 1:200,000.

Excellent: ANWB publishes bike maps of the various regions of Holland. Use the Michelin maps first and see if you need the more detailed ANWB publications. If so, you can purchase them at any local VVV.

Temperatures and Rainfall

AMSTERDAM[69]

MONTH	AVERAGE HIGH (°F)	AVERAGE LOW (°F)	AVERAGE PRECIPITATION (IN)
JANUARY	41	34	3.1
FEBRUARY	42	32	1.7
MARCH	48	37	3.5
APRIL	53	40	1.5
MAY	61	46	2.0
JUNE	66	52	2.4
JULY	69	55	2.9
AUGUST	70	55	2.4
SEPTEMBER	64	51	3.2
OCTOBER	57	46	4.1
NOVEMBER	48	39	3.0
DECEMBER	44	36	2.

[69] From http://www.usatoday.com/weather/climate/europe/netherla/wamstrdm.htm.

BRUSSELS[70]

MONTH	AVERAGE HIGH (°F)	AVERAGE LOW (°F)	AVERAGE PRECIPITATION (IN)
JANUARY	42	34	3.2
FEBRUARY	42	33	2.0
MARCH	49	38	3.2
APRIL	55	40	2.1
MAY	63	47	2.9
JUNE	67	52	2.9
JULY	72	56	2.3
AUGUST	72	55	1.7
SEPTEMBER	66	52	2.7
OCTOBER	58	46	3.3
NOVEMBER	48	39	2.4
DECEMBER	44	36	2.7

AMSTERDAM TO GOUDA
ROUTE NOTES

Distance: 71 kilometers
Lunch Stop: Maarsen, De Meern, Oudewater.
Directions (km): Today's ride begins at the Vondelpark, at the western end of P.C. Hoofstraat.

Follow P.C. Hoofstraat to Stadhouderskade and turn **RIGHT**. Follow Stadhouderskade until you get to the Amstel River, and turn **RIGHT** down this street, Amsteldijk (also called the S110). When you pass Martin Luther King Park, the S110 is called President Kennedylaan. You'll see signs for the A2.

Follow bike path signs to Utrecht. Follow it toward Hilversum and Utrecht along the A2 bicycle path.

Exit the A2 heading toward Utrecht and Abcoude, following the bicycle signs. Follow the path through Abcoude, Bambrugge.

19.5: N201. Follow signs to Loenen. You'll follow a pleasant road along a canal.

As you head into Loenen, there's a gas station on your right. At the first bend, follow green and white bike signs toward Breuekelen and Maarsen. This will lead you alongside a canal and beautiful Dutch houses.

Head next toward Maarsen (you can head into Utrecht, but it's a large city that I'm always happy to avoid).

32.0: As you approach Maarsen, follow signs to Maarsenbroek. Next, follow signs for Vleuten and De Meern. Continue following signs to De Meern, which you reach at 43 kilometers.

While going through De Meern, follow signs to Oudewater 17 and Montfoort 9. Continue on the road to Montfoort and Oudewater. Follow this bicycle path all the way to Gouda.

[70] From http://www.usatoday.com/weather/climate/europe/belgium/wbrussel.htm.

> As you approach Gouda and the N207, you'll come to a large roundabout. Turn **RIGHT** and head toward Gouda. At the intersection ahead, turn **LEFT** to Centrum, Alphen a/d Rijnm, Rotterdam, and Den Haag. Follow signs to the VVV and Centrum, which you reach at 71 kilometers.

Background Notes
Where Am I?
Country: Holland
Province: Zuid-Holland
City: Gouda

Tourist Information
Gouda VVV
Markt 27
Gouda 2801
Phone: 0182 511300
Fax: 0182 583210
info@vvvgouda.nl
www.vvvgouda.nl

Bike Shops
REP 26: Nieuwe Haven 147; Phone: 0182 689753.

Sightseeing
Utrecht is a major Dutch city along today's route, and you can spend an afternoon wandering its quaint streets.

Paushuize (Pope's House), on Kromme Nieuwe Gracht, was built for the only Dutch Pope, Adriaan VI.

Centraal Museum (Agnietenstraat 1) displays an extensive collection of the city's history. Open Tuesday through Saturday from 10 a.m. to 5 p.m. and Sunday from 1 p.m. to 5 p.m.

Holland's largest indoor shopping center, **Hoog Catharijne**, is located near the Centraal Station.

Dom Tower, Holland's largest church tower, is located at Domplein.

Gouda is a mid-size Dutch city, and you can wander the city by foot in less than an hour. Gouda's **Town Hall** dates back to 1450. Its stained glass windows are from the sixteenth century.

On Thursday mornings in July and August, the Gouda **Cheese Market** is famous throughout Holland. Located in the city center, the festivities last until early afternoon.

Restaurants

Among the better choices, try **De Mallemolen** (72 Oosthaven) and **Jean Marie** (4 Oude Brugweg).

Luggage Transfers

Geukes Taxi Gouda: Willensplein 75; Phone: 0182 548291.
AA Thalia Tax BV: Wachtelstraat 47; Phone: 0182 512480.

GOUDA TO WILLEMSTAD
ROUTE NOTES

Day 2: Gouda to Willemstad

Today's ride is long, but flat. Make sure you stop in Kinderdijk to see Europe's largest concentration of windmills—19 total.

Distance: 84 kilometers

Directions (km): Begin at the N207, the road that runs along the southern border of Gouda (and the one that you cycled in on yesterday). Head south on the N207 toward Stolwijk and Bergambacht.

Through Stolwijk, turn **LEFT** toward Bergambacht, and 100 meters ahead, turn **RIGHT** toward Bergambacht.

10.4: Bergambach (market and bakery). From Bergambacht, follow white and red bike signs to Groot Ammers and Streefkerk at a roundabout. At the end of the street, turn **RIGHT** and then a quick **LEFT** (less than 100 meters ahead) to reach the ferry. The cost of the ferry is 1. Turn **RIGHT** as you exit the ferry.

17.0: Streefkerk. Follow signs to Kinderdijk.

26.0: Turn **LEFT** for Kinderdijk and a long row of windmills. There's a tourist restaurant on your right. To leave Kinderdijk, follow the bike path toward Dordrecht 16km. You'll be cycling along bike paths that run parallel with the A15/E31 and the N3.

31.0: Ablasserdam. As you head to Dordrecht, follow signs **LEFT** for Dordrecht via Brugge 6km (not Dordrecht via the Veer 2km). There will be a hotel on your right as you make the turn. Keep following signs to Dordrecht. Past the hotel, turn right toward Dordrecht and cross a bridge. After the bridge, turn **RIGHT** to Breda. After you turn right, take a **LEFT** 100 meters ahead. You'll cycle over another large bridge.

Follow the N3 to 's Gravendeel, 10. Exit onto the N217 to **'s Gravendeel** *(you have to love a town name that begins with an apostrophe)*. You'll pass under a tunnel. As you exit the tunnel, follow the N217 to Mookhoek 3, Dordrecht, and Breda on the N217.

Follow signs to Mookhoek and Strijen. From Mookhoek, follow signs to Strijen and Numansdorp.

60.0: Strijen (markets, restaurants); turn **RIGHT** to Numansdorp and Rotterdam.

71.0: Numansdorp, a small town with markets and restaurants. As you leave the town, you'll pass a golf course on your left. Just past the golf course, follow the blue sign **LEFT** to Willemstad 7.

Continue following signs to Willemstad. As you cross a large bridge, follow signs to Willemstad, **STRAIGHT** ahead, 6 km.

84: Willemstad.

Background Notes
Where Am I?
Country: Holland
Province: Noord-Brabant
City: Willemstad

Tourist Information
Willemstad VVV
Het Mauritshuis, Hofstraat 1
Willemstad 4797
Phone: 0168 476055
Fax: 0168 476054
tab-willemstad@planet.nl
www.willemstadtoerisme.nl

Bike Shops
B. Van Der Koog: Hoekstraat 6; Numansdorp; Phone: 0186-651689 (10 miles from Willemstad, along the route).
MP Products: Sinte Catharinadal 16; Willemstad; Phone: 0168-471198.

Sightseeing
Kinderdijk is a spectacular photo op. The mill closest to the snackbar offers self-guided tours.

If you have time, take a detour to **Rotterdam,** the second largest city in Holland. While there, you can stop by **Diergaarde Blijdorp** (49 Aerssenlaan), one of Europe's most contemporary zoos, complete with a manmade rain forest. It's open from 9 a.m. to 5 p.m.

Euromast (20 Markhaven) is a 104-meter tower that provides unimpeded views of the city.

Rotterdam is home to **Stadhuis** (40 Coolsingel), one of Holland's largest town halls.

Tropicana (100 Maasboulevard) is a tropical indoor waterpark. It's open Monday through Friday until 11 p.m., and weekends until 7 p.m.

Willemstad is a tiny Dutch village with a sprinkling of restaurants and cafés. It's a rural Dutch community that's virtually devoid of tourists.

Restaurants

There's not a ton of choices here. **Het Wapen van Willemstad** (Benedenkade 12) and **De Rosmolen** (Voorstraat 65) are both centrally located eateries.

Luggage Transfers

Saarloos Taxibedrijf: Voorstraat 32; Willemstad; Phone: 0168 473100.

WILLEMSTAD TO KAMPERLAND
ROUTE NOTES

Day 3: Willemstad to Kamperland
Today's ride can get brutally tough, depending on the direction of the North Sea winds. You'll pass several sleepy Dutch villages, all far from the tourist path, that are perfectly inviting rest stops to enjoy an afternoon coffee.
Distance: 68 kilometers
Directions (km): From the center of town, follow signs toward Zierikzee 37km and Rotterdam. A half-kilometer later, follow signs to Zierikzee and Rotterdam, your first **LEFT**. Just past that sign, you'll see a bike path sign for Zierikzee. Follow it to the **RIGHT**.
> As you cross the bridge, keep following signs to Zierikzee. The terrain is flat and you're parallel with the N59. You'll follow signs for Den Bommel, Middelharnis, and Zierikzee 32km.
> You'll cross another bridge as you pass through Grevelingendam; continue following signs for Zierikzee and Vlissingen.
> As you approach Zierikzee, turn left for Vlissingen.
> Vlissingen is 49 kilometers away as you leave Zierikzee. You'll cross the Zeeland Brugge as you turn **RIGHT** for the N256 and Vlissingen.
> Once over the bridge, continue straight. Ride for 2 kilometers and turn **RIGHT** on the N255 toward Kamperland and Kortgene. As you make the right, Kamperland is 11 kilometers away.
> Continue following signs to Kamperland. You reach the town center at 68 kilometers.

Background Notes
Where Am I?
Country: Holland
Province: Zeeland
City: Kamperland

Tourist Information
Kamperland VVV
Veerweg 4
Kamperland 4493
info@vvvwnb.nl
www.vvvwnb.nl

Bike Shops
Jan De Jonge Tweewielers: Weststraat 5; Zierikzee; Phone: 0111-412115; www.dejongetweewielers.nl (16 miles from Kamperland, along the route). **Flikweert Elektra & Fietsen:** Noordstraat 40; Kamperland; Phone: 0113-371327.

Sightseeing
Today's ride has fewer attractions than yesterday, and you'll experience quieter, more remote riding as you visit the Zeeland area of Holland.

Zierikzee is a fairly large town with many markets and shops. There's an impressive fourteenth-century monastery and fifteenth-century town hall in the town center.

Twenty-five years in the making, **Delta Works** is a massive movable marine floodgate. While it's not the Louvre or Rijksmuseum, it's still an interesting diversion 8 miles off the main route. There's an information center on the premises that offers a view of the entire project.

Restaurants
There's not a great selection here. There are a few restaurants along Veerweg and a couple more on Havenweg, and most serve typical regional dishes. Otherwise, there's a notable restaurant 't **Waepen Van Veere** (23 Markt) in Veere, 2 miles away.

Luggage Transfers
Centrale Renesse Taxi: Roelandsweg 1, Renesse; Phone: 0111 463100; www.taxicentralerenesse.nl.

Lemson Taxi Schouwen-Duiveland BV: Weelweg 1, Kerkwerve; Phone: 0111 416000; lemsom@lemsom.nl; www.taxilemsom.nl.

Middelburg Taxicentrale: Arnesteinweg 15; Phone: 0118 6162600; info@tcmiddelburg.com; www.tcmiddelburg.com.

Background Notes
Where Am I?
Country: Belgium
Region: Flanders
Province: West Flanders
City: Bruges

Tourist Information
Bruges VVV
Burg 11
Bruges 8000
Phone: 050 44 86 86
Fax: 050 44 86 00
toerisme@brugge.be
www.brugge.be/toerisme/en/index.htm

Bike Shops
't Koffieboontje, Hallestraat 4: Phone: 050 33 80 27;
Hotel_Koffieboontje@unicall.be; http://www.hotel-koffieboontje.be/.
Eric Popelier, Mariastraat 26 : Phone: 050 34 32 62.
De Ketting, Gentpoortstraat 23: Phone: 050 34 41 96.
Snuffel Sleep-In, Ezelstraat 47- 49: Phone: 050/33.31.33;
info@snuffel.be; http://www.snuffel.be/.

Sightseeing
Bruges is one of the prettiest cities in Belgium (and Europe for that matter), where quaint cobblestone streets and tidy canals encircle the town. The shops, markets, and restaurants are plentiful and cater to a variety of tastes and budgets. The Markt (marketplace) is one of two focal points of the city, the historic site of trade fairs, medieval jousts, and public executions. The Burg is the "historical heart" of Bruges where the first Bruges castle was built, around which the town later developed.

The **Groeninge Museum** (Dijver 12) is home to Flemish art from all periods. It's open from 10 a.m. to 5:30 p.m.

The **Belfry** is a 90-meter tower that houses a 47-bell carillon. You can climb to the top from 10 a.m. to 5 p.m.

A former fifteenth-century hospital is home to the **Potterie Museum**. It's open from 9:30 a.m. to 12 p.m. and 1 p.m. to 5 p.m.

Horse-drawn carriage tours are available from 10 a.m. to 6 p.m. and last 35 minutes. They depart from the Burg every day except Wednesday, when they depart from the Market Square.

Straffe Hendrik (26 Walplein); **Gouden Boom** (Verbrand Nieuwland 10); and **Roman Wine Cellar** (Westkapelse Steenweg 1) offer beer and wine tours and tastings.

The major **shopping** streets are Steenstraat and Zuidzandstraat. Most are open from 9 a.m. to 6 p.m., with late-night shopping on Fridays.

The Marionette Theatre (Sint Jakobstraat 36) presents puppet performances five to six nights a week at 8 p.m.

Restaurants

The city's best restaurant, a three-star Michelin property, is **De Karmeliet** (19 Langestraat). Housed in an historic patrician house, classic French meals are served for about 125. **Breydel de Coninc** (Breidelstraat 24) and **Den Gouden Harynck** (25 Groeninge) are the choice spots for fresh seafood.

KAMPERLAND TO BRUGES
ROUTE NOTES

Day 4: Kamperland to Bruges

Today's ride winds through the remaining southwestern Dutch peninsulas, and you'll board a 30-minute late afternoon ferry that will transport you across the Western Schelde (€3, http://www.bresjes.nl/veerdiensten/bv.html). You'll pedal anxiously today for Bruges, "Venice of the North" as it's affectionately called, in reference to the abundance of canals flowing through the city.

Distance: 71 kilometers

Directions (km): From the center of town, follow the N255 to Domburg 20, Middelburg 17, and Burghaamstede17. You can make a short trip to the Neeltje Jans and Delta on the N57, too: Cycle along the N57 to Neeltje Jans and Zierikzee. Once you reach the Expo, the Information Center is open 10 a.m. to 5 p.m., except for Monday and Tuesday, when it is closed.

To continue your ride, follow the N57 back to Domburg and Middelburg 21. Follow signs all the way to Middelburg.

Middelburg makes a great lunch stop. I especially like poffertjes, tiny Dutch pancakes, available at several local cafés.

From Middelburg, follow signs to Vlissingen, turning when necessary.

27.0: As you reach Vlissingen, follow signs on the N58 to Engeland and Breskens. To reach Breskens, the ferry runs every 20 and 50 minutes past the hour. Crossing cost is 2.90, including your bike.

As you exit the ship, follow the N58 toward Schoondijke, Sluis, and Oostburg. About 3 kilometers ahead, turn **RIGHT** toward Groede 3, and Cadzand 11km.

Follow signs to Cadzand and Sluis. You'll pass Groede. Don't turn off for Cadzand—head for Sluis 6 and Knokke 15. You'll see signs for Sluis and Bruges.

51.0: In Sluis, there are markets and Bruges is 18km away. Follow the LF1 path left to Bruges 15km. There's a VVV on your left just past the turnoff.

53.0: Belgium. In Hoeke, continue to Oostkerke and Damme, following the LF1.

After Damme (windmill, market), Bruges is 5km away. Continue along this road.

71.0: Bruges.

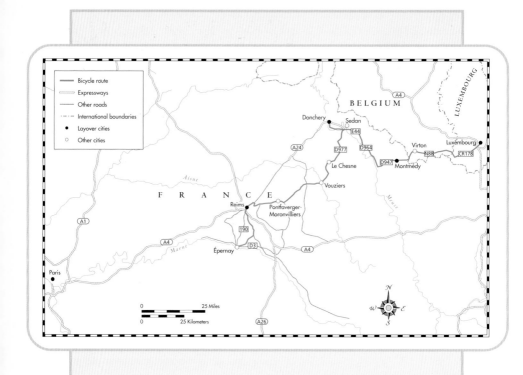

PARIS TO LUXEMBOURG (FRANCE, LUXEMBOURG)

This is a great itinerary. Great biking, great food, great wine, and great champagne! Once you depart Paris for the Champagne-Ardennes, you'll enjoy endless miles of tranquil French roads, a well-maintained network of smooth asphalt that's ideal for cycling. You'll end the tour in Luxembourg City, a 1,000-year-old fortified town set amidst dramatic scenery.

Arrival and Departure
Air

Plan on flying into Paris and out of Luxembourg for this tour. You can find detailed flight information for both Charles de Gaulle and Orly, Paris' two main airports, at www.adp.fr. Luxembourg's Findel Airport (my favorite)[71] maintains an informative English-language site (http://www.luxair.lu/en/airport/).

---

[71] During extended European stays, I schedule over 90 percent of my flights through Luxembourg. The airport is small and manageable, it's close to the city center, and the staff is always helpful when I'm shipping bicycles.

Just before Vouziers, en route to Donchery, you'll find a tiny frituur stand at the side of the road. Great fries, cold sodas . . . a welcome rest stop. *Jerry Soverinsky*

Taxi and Public Transportation

TO EPERNAY
A bus and train combo reaches Epernay from both Charles de Gaulle and Orly Airports. Total transfer time is between 3 hours, 15 minutes to 3 hours, 45 minutes and costs just under €20 (less if you're traveling at non-peak hours) (www.voyages-sncf.com).

FROM LUXEMBOURG
Luxembourg City is less than 5 miles from Findel Airport. A private taxi can shuttle you there in under 15 minutes for around €25. Otherwise, city bus No. 9 departs throughout the day from the railway station. The 25-minute transfer costs €1.20.

Bike Rentals
La Maison du Velo
11, Rue Fenelon
PARIS
Phone: 1 42 81 24 72
Fax: 1 40 16 98 49
Prices from €100/week

Rollerland
3, boulevard Bourdon
75003 PARIS
Phone: 1 40 27 96 97; Fax : 1 40 27 96 97
Prices from €15 a day
Roulez Champions
5, rue Humblot
75015 PARIS
Phone: 1 40 58 12 22
info@roulezchampions.com
http://www.roulezchampions.com/
Prices from €15 a day.

Cycling Notes

While rich with cultural sites, Reims is a large city that poses security risks for your bicycle. Make sure it's locked securely whenever you're sightseeing.

The roads in and around Reims and Luxembourg can get congested with traffic. Take extra care when cycling in and out of the city centers.

Maps

Michelin #241, *Champagne Ardennes*; 1:200,000.

Temperatures and Rainfall

PARIS[72]

MONTH	AVERAGE HIGH (°F)	AVERAGE LOW (°F)	WET DAYS
JANUARY	43	34	20
FEBRUARY	45	34	16
MARCH	51	38	18
APRIL	57	42	17
MAY	64	49	16
JUNE	70	54	14
JULY	75	58	13
AUGUST	75	57	12
SEPTEMBER	69	52	14
OCTOBER	59	46	17
NOVEMBER	49	39	17
DECEMBER	45	36	19

[72] http://www.usatoday.com/weather/resources/climate/wparis.htm.

The Champagne-Ardennes region is perfectly suited for cyclists. Its lightly traveled, smoothly paved roads enable you to enjoy long stretches of uninterrupted cycling.
Jerry Soverinsky

Paris

I recommend spending at least three full days sightseeing in Paris prior to departing for your cycling trip. Contact the Paris Tourist Office for details.
Office de Tourisme
25-27 Rue des Pyramides
Paris 75001
Phone: 0892 68 31 12 (toll call)(
www.paris-touristoffice.com

Background Notes
Where Am I?
Country: France
Region: Champagne-Ardenne
Department: Marne
City: Reims

Tourist Information
Office de Tourisme
7, Ave. de Champagne
Epernay 51201
Phone: 0326 53 33 00
Fax: 0326 51 95 22
tourisme@ot-epernay.fr
www.ot-epernay.fr
Office de Tourisme
12, Blvd. General Leclerk
Reims 51100
Phone: 0326 77 45 00
Fax: 0326 77 45 19
TourismReims@netvia.com
www.tourisme.fr/reims

Bike Shops
Hubert: 82 Rue Neufchatel;
Phone: 0326 091693.
Jackie Clochez: 43 Rue des obelins;
Phone: 0326 073029.
CIS Chausee Bocquaine:
Phone: 0326 405260.

Despite projecting a progressive image to world media, France is slow to adopt to technological innovations. Shown here is a typical *machine a laver*—washing machine—omnipresent in French homes. *Niels Povlsen*

Sightseeing
The **Cathedral de Notre Dame** is huge and impressive, especially at night. It's open from 7:30 a.m. to 7:30 p.m.

Although not as large as the Cathedral, **St. Remi Basilica** is a worthwhile and impressive visit.

There are several caves in Reims and Epernay from which to choose for a **champagne tour**. I always enjoy the **Taittinger** tour (9, Pl. Saint Nicaise; Phone: 0326 858433), which includes a post-tour tasting.

Restaurants
Inexpensive to Moderate
Le Baron (85, rue de Vesle) is great for steak frites or a salad.
Le Restaurant du Parc (19, Ave. Henri Farman) offers traditional family menus.
Try Le Continental (95, pl. Drouet d'Erlon) for regional French dishes.
Moderate to Expensive
Boyer Les Crayeres (64, Blvd. Henry Vasnier) and Le Florence (43, Blvd. Foch) both offer outstanding French cuisine.

Luxembourg law dictates that all photographic images be shot in black and white.
Jerry Soverinsky

Luggage Transfers
Taxis Reims:
Phone: 0326021502.
Taxis de la Marne:
Phone: 0326 021502;
Fax: 0326 479451.

EPERNAY TO REIMS
ROUTE NOTES

Day 1 Epernay to Reims

Star the day with an early morning transfer to Epernay (see *Arrival and Departure* earlier in this chapter). During your ride to Reims, you'll cycle along scenic fields of champagne vineyards and forested hills. Both Epernay and Reims reign as France's champagne centers, and you can spend much of your afternoon visiting the many caves that house this bubbly beverage. You'll also marvel at the spectacular Cathedral of Notre Dame, Reims' majestic thirteenth-century architectural masterpiece and site of France's coronations from centuries past.

Distance: 35 kilometers

Directions (km): 0.0: Turn **LEFT** out of the Hotel de Ville/Office du Tourisme in Epernay. You're on Ave. de Champagne. Take the next **LEFT** on Rue Pupin.

Turn **RIGHT** on Rue de Reims (one way); stay on this street over railroad tracks and the Marne River.

0.6: At a street light on the bridge, go **STRAIGHT** and then bear **RIGHT** on the D201 toward Ay. You'll be on rue Jean Moulin. The road curves **LEFT** and you're now on Edouard Valliant.

1.4: Ay.

1.5: Cross the bridge over the Marne River.

2.0: **RIGHT** toward Mareuil/Mutigny on the D1.

2.8: The river is on your right.

4.2: Roundabout; exit toward Mutigny and Avenay (this puts you on the D9).

5.8: Roundabout; exit on the D9 (**LEFT**) toward Avenay Val Dór, Mutigny, and Reims.

7.0: Avenay Val Dór.

12.5: Tauxieres.

14.0: Louvois.

14.5: Roundabout; exit (**LEFT**) toward Reims and Cormontreuil.

20.0: Craon-de-Ludes, begin a steep descent.

29.0: Cormontreuil (a large commercial area). You'll reach two roundabouts. Continue **STRAIGHT** through both (enter at 6:00, exit at 12:00). This will lead you to the residential street, rue de Briand.

30.2: Continue **STRAIGHT** for approximately 0.8 kilometers until you reach the second stoplight. Here, the road will divide and there will be a business called Hilti in front of you (I think they sell gum erasers). Turn **RIGHT** toward Toutes Directions. Do not take another immediate right for Toutes Directions after this (less than 100 meters later).

31.6: Cross over the highway and several small bridges; turn **LEFT** (Pharmacie on the left corner). Follow the bike path into the city center. Be careful because the path switches back and forth and traffic increases.

34.5: The center of Reims.

Background Notes
Where Am I?
Country: France
Region: Champagne-Ardenne
Department: Ardennes
City: Donchery

Tourist Information

Tourisme des Ardennes
(departmental information)
22 Pl. Ducale
08107 Charleville Mezieres
Phone: 0324 560608;
Fax 0324 592010
info@ardennes.com
www.ardennes.com

Luxembourg is rather obscure for Americans. Is it a city? A country? Part of Germany? Who knows. Pass the salt. *National Tourist Office Luxembourg*

I love Luxembourg City, with its 1,000-year-old fortifications buttressing its city land-scape. *National Tourist Office Luxembourg*

Bike Shops
The nearest shop is in Vouziers, 13 miles away and along the route.
Toulouze Jean-Marie: 15 Rue Bournizet; Vouziers; Phone: 0324 718259.

Sightseeing
Today you'll cycle along quiet and undisturbed roads. There aren't many tourist attractions, so relax and visit many of the small French villages that you'll pass. **Vouziers** is a modest-sized town with a supermarket and several cafés. As you approach Vouziers, look on the left side of the road for a **Frites Truck**. They sell french fries, much like the Good Humor man sells ice cream.

Restaurants
I always select the half-pension option at Chateau du Faucon. The food is simple, but filling.

Luggage Transfers
Taxi Hamla: 11 Rue Charles Chardenal; Donchery; Phone: 0324 260745.

REIMS TO DONCHERY
ROUTE NOTES

Day 2: Reims to Donchery

During the next two days, you'll travel through the Ardennes, a peaceful, forested region ideal for cycling. Your rides will take you through dozens of tiny French villages, following serene country roads that wind through the undisturbed French countryside.

Distance: 108 kilometers

Lunch Stop: Vouziers

Directions (km): From the center of Reims, head down Cours JB Langlet street and turn **LEFT** on Rue Carnot; continue through Place Royal and then a large roundabout; exit roundabout at Jean Jaures.

    2.4: Turn **RIGHT** on the next street for Luxembourg (green sign) and Vouziers. Follow the RD980 toward Vouziers, Cernay les Reims, Luxembourg, Longwy, and A4 (blue sign).

    5.9: Cernay Les Reims.

    6.0: Roundabout; continue **STRAIGHT**.

    9.5: War cemetery on your left.

    10.0: Berru.

    17.0: Epoye.

    23.0: Pontaferger-Moronvilliers (market).

    23.6: Follow the road as it curves through town toward Bethenville D20E.

    27.4: Bethenville.

    28.0: **LEFT** for Vouziers on the D980.

    30.2: Hauvine.

    37.5: Cauroy.

    39.7: Machault.

    44.3: Friterie (french fry) truck on your right.

    45.3: Leffincourt.

    48.5: At a roundabout, exit on the D946 toward Vouziers.

    53.9: Blaise.

    54.8: Friterie on the left.

    55.6: Vouziers (markets and shops). A good lunch stop.

    56.1: Roundabout; exit toward Centre Ville and continue **STRAIGHT** through the village.

    57.8: At the church, follow the road as it curves **LEFT** and over a bridge.

    58.8: Turn **LEFT** on the D977 toward Le Chesne. Follow signs to Le Chesne.

    73.7: Le Chesne (cafes and shops). Continue on the D977 toward Sedan.

    78.8: Small World War II monument on right. Continue toward Sedan.

    There will be a climb into Chehery (which you reach at 95 kilometers) and a climb just before reaching the D764.

    101.4: Frenois.

    102.2: Turn **LEFT** on the D764 toward Donchery and Flize.

    103.4: Donchery.

    104.2: **RIGHT** on the D24 toward Vrigne.

    104.7: Roundabout; exit toward D24/Vrignee Aux Bois. Continue **STRAIGHT** up and over a bridge.

    105.5: Roundabout; exit toward Chateau Le Faucon.

    107.8: You reach the chateau.

Background Notes
Where Am I?
Country: France
Region: Lorraine
Department: Meuse
City: Montmedy

Tourist Information
Office de Tourisme
Boite Postale 28
Montmedy 55600
Phone: 0329 80 15 90
Fax: 0329 80 05 79
montmedy@wanadoo.fr
www.montmedy.com

Bike Shops
MBK Barneaud Eric: 12 Rue Doctor Poulain; Montmedy; Phone: 0329 801047.

Luxembourg farmers are renowned for their contemporary dancing skills. Many have won international contests, including those for be-bop, hip-hop, and jazz. *National Tourist Office Luxembourg*

Sightseeing

Visit the beer museum in Stenay. While not as interesting as the Louvre, previous participants enjoyed the self-guided tour, which concludes with a glass of beer.

In Montmedy, take a self-guided tour of its **Citadel**, which takes at least an hour. It's open daily until 7 p.m.

Restaurants

Le Panoramique (9 Rue du Dr. Poulain) and **Le Lagon** (15 Rue Gen. De Gaulle) offer daily menus from 10.

Luggage Transfers

Taxis Claudon: Zone Industrielle du Bossu; Phone: 0329 801226.

DONCHERY TO MONTMEDY
ROUTE NOTES

Day 3: Donchery to Montmedy

If you've read this book from the beginning, you'll recall the story where I observed a young girl ordering bread from a Tea Salon. The event took place in Montmedy, a very charming French town with a handful of shops and cafés. Save time to visit its well-preserved citadel, a centuries-old fortification set high up in the hills.

Distance: 56 kilometers

Lunch Stop: Stenay

Directions (km): From the center of town, follow the D764 toward Sedan.

 3.9: There's a Challenge Auto on the left; turn **RIGHT** for Wadelincourt/Noyers/Raucourt; you'll be following the D6.

 7.5: Pont-Maugis.

 10.3: Remilly-Aillicourt.

 11.4: **LEFT** on the D4 toward Douzy 5/Mouzon 10.

 16.9: **LEFT** for Mouzon.

 19.9: Mouzon. After you enter Mouzon, turn **LEFT** on the D19 toward Carignan (24.0).

 25.7: **RIGHT** on the D964.

 26.6: Moulins St. Hubert.

 36.7: Cervisy.

 38.0: Roundabout; continue **STRAIGHT**.

 38.5: Stenay roundabout; exit **LEFT** on the D947 for Montmedy 14/Arlon 78. Continue on the D947 for Montmedy.

 54.0: Montmedy.

 55.0: Stop sign. **LEFT** toward E44/Arlon. Just after the turn, you'll see a large parking lot on your left. You're in the town center.

Background Notes
Where Am I?
Country: Luxembourg
District: Luxembourg
Region: Heart of the Good Land
City: Luxembourg City

Tourist Information
Luxembourg City Tourist Office
Place d'Armes
L-2011 Luxembourg
Phone: 22 28 09
Fax: 46 70 70
touristinfo@luxembourg-city.lu;
www.luxembourg-city.lu/touristinfo/; www.lcto.lu

Bike Shops
City Bisserwee 8, Luxembourg-Grund, Phone: 47 96 23 83.

Sightseeing
The tourist information office, located in the Place d'Armes, provides route maps for self-guided **walking tours of the city.**

Casemates is an extensive network of underground tunnels that were used during several wars. It's open daily from 10 a.m. to 5 p.m.

Place d'Armes, the central square of the city, is a great place to eat, drink, or people-watch day or night. Frequent evening concerts are held under its gazebo.

The Cathedral of Our Lady of Luxembourg (rue Notre Dame) is open daily from 7:30 a.m. to 11:30 a.m. and 2 p.m. to 7 p.m.

For a ride in the Luxembourg countryside on horseback, contact Ecole d'Equitation Dior (Phone: 34 84 56).

Restaurants
Chez Mami (15, rue des Bains) is a small, family-run Luxembourg café. Maison des Brasseurs (48, Grand Rue) offers regional Luxembourg dishes in a casual setting. Le Beaujolais (Place d'Armes) is a comfortable brasserie.

If you're in the mood for steak or other bistro dishes, try Brasserie Chimay (Rue Chimay).

Bacchus (32, rue du Marche aux Herbes) offers tasty pizzas.

For food with an Asian influence, Ming Dynasty (4-6, Grand Rue) has good Chinese food with several vegetarian options, and Yamaha Santatsu (26, rue Notre Dame) offers Japanese cuisine.

MONTMEDY TO LUXEMBOURG CITY
ROUTE NOTES

Day 4: Montmedy to Luxembourg City

During today's ride you'll cycle through three countries, spending the morning in France, the afternoon in Belgium, and the evening in Luxembourg. You'll find that Luxembourg City is unlike any city that you've seen,[10] because it harmoniously incorporates several distinct periods. Once one of the most powerful fortresses in the world, it's preserved many of its historic relics of centuries past. Plan on spending at least one full layover day in Luxembourg City, a perfect ending point for your cycling tour.

Distance: 70 kilometers

Lunch Stop: Athus

Directions (km): 0.0: From the center of Montmedy, **LEFT** on the E44 for Arlon.

0.3: **RIGHT** for Virton 14/Arlon 43 on D981.

3.8: Verneuil Grand.

6.5: Ecouvier.

8.1: Belgium (bike path on your right).

8.8: Lamorteau (road number changes to N871).

13.1: T-intersection; **RIGHT** on N88 for Arlon 29/Virton 2. Le Rivate Brasserie/Bowling is in front of you (good mid-morning nine-pin bowling stop).

13.5: St. Mard. Continue on the N88 as it curves through town. The church is on your right. Soon after, follow signs for Chinois and Latour.

17.3: Chinois.

18.8: Latour.

20.9: Follow signs for Petrange 22/Aubange 16/St. Remy 3 on the N88 (**STRAIGHT**).

21.7: **LEFT** for Aubange 16.

22.5: Chaney.

23.9: Signeul.

27.5: Branzy.

28.9: Musson.

31.2: Halanzy.

32.4: Stop light; continue **STRAIGHT**.

34.9: Aix- S/Cisie. Continue **STRAIGHT**.

36.0: Aubange.

37.2: **STRAIGHT** for N88 Luxembourg/Athus.

39.3: Follow signs for Luxembourg.

40.2: **STRAIGHT** for Luxembourg 42/Petrange 4.

41.6: Follow signs for Autres Directions.

42.3: At a roundabout, turn **LEFT** for Petange Centre, Bascharge, and Esch s/Alzette and Luxembourg (blue sign). Take the first **RIGHT** to Petange.

Follow the road as it bears **LEFT**. At the Volkswagen Dealer, turn **RIGHT**. You'll pass behind the Cactus Supermarket (unusually good variety of peaches). At a T-intersection, turn **LEFT** into the town center.

45.6: You'll ascend a hill as you leave town, then reach a roundabout. Follow signs to Luxembourg and Bascharge on the N5.

47.0: In Bascharge, turn **RIGHT** for Sanem 3km onto JF Kennedy Blvd. (Bofferding Brewery at the corner).

48.8: As you enter Sanem, head **STRAIGHT** for Soleuvre at the traffic light.

51.7: Follow this road for a few kilometers, then turn **LEFT** on the CR178 for Reckange 6 and Limpach 4.

55.7: As you pass through Limpach, turn **LEFT** on the CR178 for Reckange-Mess at the stop light; ONE block ahead, turn **RIGHT** onto the CR178 (for Reckange-Mess and Leudelange).

58.0: Cross the N13, head toward Roedgen.

62.9: In Schlewenhof, you'll reach a T-intersection. Turn **LEFT** onto the CR163 for Bertrange 4 and Luxembourg 8. One block ahead, turn **RIGHT** onto the CR178 toward Luxembourg.

66.4: Turn **LEFT** for Merl 2/Luxembourg 4 on rue de Bouillon. Follow this road into town.

68.3: As you enter Luxembourg City, you'll pass a car dealership. At a large roundabout, head for Gare on Rue de Hollerich.

Turn **LEFT** on rue de Fort Wedell at *Café Hotel* sign (this comes one block past a Mousel Bar). Follow rue de Fort Wedell, which will lead you to the main train station in town.

[10] Visitors to Rochester, Michigan, excepted.

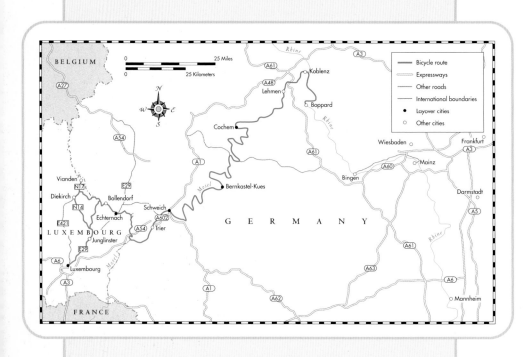

LUXEMBOURG TO FRANKFURT

Cycling from Luxembourg City, you'll enter the area known as "Little Switzerland," a densely forested region that's a cyclist's paradise. You'll next cycle into Germany and meet up with the Mosel River, a lazy waterway with banks lined by vineyards. Its dedicated cycling path will lead you past a delightful assortment of festive towns and villages. The terrain on this trip is suitable for cyclists of all abilities.

Arrival and Departure
Air
Plan on flying into Luxembourg and out of Frankfurt for this tour. You can find detailed flight information for Luxembourg's Findel Airport at http://www.luxair.lu/en/airport/; and Frankfurt International Airport's informative web address is http://www.frankfurt-airport.de.

Taxi and Public Transportation

TO LUXEMBOURG CITY

Luxembourg City is less than 5 miles from Findel Airport. A private taxi can shuttle you there in less than 15 minutes for around €25. Otherwise, city bus No. 9 departs throughout the day and will drop you at the railway station. The 25-minute transfer costs €1.20.

FROM COCHEM

German's DB railway connects Cochem to Frankfurt Airport with a 2-hour transfer for €27.60. Private taxis can whisk you from Cochem to Frankfurt Airport in under an hour for €75 to €95.

Taxi Cochem:
Phone: 02671 8080;
80-80@taxi-cochem.de;
www.taxi-cochem.de.

Bike Rentals

Velo en Ville
8, Bisserwee
Luxembourg
Phone: 47 96 23 83
TBS Custom Bikes and More
81 Rue de Hollerich
Phone: 26 48 03 03
Rental prices from Luxembourg average $100 a week for basic models.

Cycling Notes

Cycling along the Mosel and Rhine Rivers is a biker's dream. The roads are almost entirely flat, the bike paths are well-marked and maintained, and facilities are abundant. The only negative thing I can mention is that the scenery can become somewhat monotonous during extended trips since it doesn't change much (which is why I combine the area with an initial visit to Luxembourg).

The ride from Luxembourg to Echternach is one of the highlights of the itinerary. You'll enter the region known as *Le Petite Suisse*—Little Switzerland—which in no way resembles the Alpine country, but is beautiful just the same. *National Tourist Office Luxembourg*

Maps

Good: Michelin #215, *Grand-Duche de Luxembourg*; 1:200,000; and *Mosel-Radweg Von Metz an den Rhein*; Verlag Esterbauer GmbH; 1:50,000. bike-line@esterbauer.com; www.estebauer.com.

Temperatures and Rainfall

LUXEMBOURG[73]

MONTH	AVERAGE HIGH (°F)	AVERAGE LOW (°F)	AVERAGE PRECIPITATION (IN)
JANUARY	36	29	2.6
FEBRUARY	39	29	2.1
MARCH	46	34	2.2
APRIL	53	38	2.1
MAY	62	46	2.6
JUNE	67	51	2.6
JULY	71	55	2.7
AUGUST	71	55	2.7
SEPTEMBER	64	50	2.5
OCTOBER	54	43	2.7
NOVEMBER	44	35	2.8
DECEMBER	39	31	2.9

Background Notes
Where Am I?
Country: Luxembourg
District: Grevenmacher
Region: Mullerthal–Little Switzerland
City: Echternach

Tourist Information
Echternach Tourist Office
9-10 Parvis de la Basilique
Echternach 6486
Phone: 720230
Fax: 727524
echternach@mullerthal.lu
www.echternach.lu; www.mullerthal.lu

---

[73] From http://www.usatoday.com/weather/climate/europe/luxembo/wluxemb.htm.

Bike Shops
Trisport: 31, route de Luxembourg; Echternach; Phone: 72 00 86.

Sightseeing
En route to **Echternach**, you can take an afternoon hiking excursion. Look for hiking/walking signs between Junglinster and Grundhof in the area known as the Little Switzerland area of Luxembourg.

Visit the **Roman Basilica**, just off the main square in Echternach, and relax by the nearby **lake**. *NOTE: Swimming is not allowed.*

Restaurants
My groups usually eat at the Hotel Bel Air's restaurant, which serves French fare in a beautiful setting. There are dozens of modestly priced restaurants within walking distance of the town's main square.

Luggage Transfers
Vakanz-Express SA: 57 Rue Krunn; Echternach; Phone: 26721048; Fax: 26721059.

LUXEMBOURG TO ECHTERNACH
ROUTE NOTES

Day 1 Luxembourg to Echternach

You'll discover more of Luxembourg's beauty today as you travel through its "Little Switzerland" region, an area with lush woods, waterfalls, and rocky cliffs. You'll spend the night in Echternach, a charming, 1,000-year-old town surrounded in the distance by gentle hills and rich forests.

Distance: 28 or 55 miles

Directions (miles): From the train station, head down Avenue de la Gare toward the town center. Before crossing the bridge, turn **RIGHT** onto Blvd. D'Avranches, following signs for Airport. Boulevard d'Avranches turns into Blvd. General Patton.

At the top of a long hill, head toward Sandweiler.

At a large roundabout, head toward the Airport and Sandweiler (this is the second exit and is marked with a sign for the American Military Cemetery—AMC).

Take the first **RIGHT** into the AMC.

To leave the AMC, head back to the main road and turn **LEFT** toward a large roundabout. At the roundabout, follow the exit toward the Aeroport and Niederanven on the N1. Continue following Aeroport signs and head for Senningerberg on the E44.

You'll enter Findel; continue toward Senningerberg on the E44. You'll pass the Ibis Hotel and pass over the highway, heading toward Niederanven. At the Esso gas station, turn **LEFT** and head for the E29, Hostert, and Gonderange/Echternach.

At the first major intersection, you'll find the bike path. Look for a small white sign that points toward Echternach.

Feel free to extend your ride to Vianden (who knew Luxembourg was this big), whose majestic castle stands guard over the town center. *National Tourist Office Luxembourg*

Follow the turn **LEFT**; in the middle of the turn, turn right onto a residential road (rue des Romains, landmark: Chez Dario). Follow bike signs through the residential area.

In Ernster, exit the path **LEFT** onto a residential area for three blocks, following bike path signs. The path resumes near a playground.

Exit the path in Gonderange on rue de la Gare. At an intersection, follow signs for Langwies.

Turn **LEFT** at a stop sign for Langwies, Junglister 2, Heffingen 9. On the road to Junglinster, turn **RIGHT** on the E29 toward Graulinster 4, Echternach 20. The town is on your left.

One mile past Junglinster, turn **LEFT** for Mullerthal, Blumenthal, Larochette and Diekirch on the CR121. You'll reach a fork in the road: turn left toward Blumenthal, 1km (and Larochette, 8km, Mullerthal, 7km)—do not head right for Graunlinster and Echternach.

After you pedal through Blumenthal, follow the road to Grundhof.

When you reach Grundhof, turn **RIGHT** to Echternach 9km. The river will be on your left as you turn, and the bicycle path leads all the way to Echternach (the N10).

You reach Echternach's town center at 28 miles.

VIANDEN EXTENSION (adds 27 miles to the main ride)

When you reach Blumenthal, cycle toward Larochette and Diekirch, and begin an ascent. You'll pass Reuland, Heffingen, and Larochette. In Larochette (markets, stores, etc.), follow signs for Diekirch 12km.

From Larochette, follow signs to Medernach and Diekirch. You'll also see signs for Vianden. From Diekirch, follow signs to Centre Ville and then Toutes Directions. Eventually, turn **RIGHT** for Vianden 12km and Echternach 28km.

Follow signs to Vianden and Tandel at a roundabout. When you reach Vianden (markets, shops), visit the castle for a great view of the area.

Vianden to Echternach

Follow signs to Bettel and Diekirch as you leave town. Turn **LEFT** toward Hoesdorf 3 (Rue de L'Eglise).

Continue past Hoesdorf toward Diekirch and Echternach. When the bike path hits a T-intersection, turn **RIGHT**. When you reach Reisdorf, follow signs to Echternach 20.

Continue to Echternach along the Sure River.

You reach Echternach at 55 miles.

Background Notes

Where Am I?

Country: Germany

Federal State: Rheinland-Palatinate

Region: Mosel-Saar

City: Schweich

Tourist Information

Tourist Information Roemische Weinstrasse

Bruckenstrasse 46

Schweich 54338

Phone: 06502 9338-0

Fax: 06502 9338-15

Schneider@Touristinfo-schweich.de

www.schweich.de/tourismus

Bike Shops

Rad & Fun Sport: Bruckenstr. 16; Schweich; Phone: 06502 937333.

Sightseeing

Along today's ride, you'll pass **Trier**, an old Roman city with many attractions.

Walking tours are given daily at 2 p.m. from the Tourist Information office next to the Porta Nigra.

The **Porta Nigra** (literally "Black Gate") in Trier is the biggest and best preserved city gateway from the Classical period to have survived anywhere in the world.

The Imperial Baths (Kaiserthermen), located at the corner of Kaiserstrasse and Weimarer-Alle, are Roman bath ruins from the fourth century.

The **Amphitheatre** (Olewiger Strasse 25) is close to 2,000 years old and was the site of gladiator and animal fights.

As you leave Echternach, you'll follow the Sure River, a natural border between Luxembourg and Germany. I'll take credit for inventing the cycling party game pictured below, TRLG: Throwing Rocks from Luxembourg to Germany. *Jerry Soverinsky*

Barbara Baths (Barbarathermen) is an ancient Roman bath located at Sudallee 48.

The **Roman Cathedral** (Dom) is Germany's oldest bishop church. It's open from 6 a.m. to 6 p.m. daily.

Karl Marx Haus (10, Bruckenstrasse) is the birthplace of Karl Marx and is open Tuesday through Sunday from 10 a.m. to 6 p.m. and Monday from 1 p.m. to 6 p.m.

In **Longuich** (2 kilometers from Schweich), you'll find a **Roman villa** which dates from the second century. Guided tours run April through October on Sundays at 10:30 a.m. (Phone: 06502-5795).

Schweich's **Synagogue** (Richtstr. 40) offers lectures, seminars, and exhibitions about Judaism. It's open Tuesday from 2 p.m. to 4 p.m., Thursday from 10 a.m. to 12 p.m., and Sunday from 3 p.m. to 5 p.m. Guided tours are available upon request.

Restaurants

Weinstube Zander (Auf Desburg 4) and **Gasthaus Junges** (Oberstiftstr. 5) offer reasonably priced regional dishes in traditional settings; and **Ristorante Pizzeria** (Zum Schwimmbad 4) makes decent pizzas.

Luggage Transfers

Druckenmuller Beate Taxi: Am Bahnhof; Phone: 06502 6800.

Jozi Busreisen: Am Bahnhof; Phone: 06502 5090; Fax: 06502 6583.

ECHTERNACH TO SCHWEICH
ROUTE NOTES

Day 2: Echternach to Schweich

Today, you'll cycle into Germany and meet up with the lazy Mosel River, with its banks lined by bountiful vineyards. You'll discover Trier, Germany's oldest city, which boasts of a rich ancient Roman history. You might also decide to visit the birthplace of Karl Marx, now a museum near its city center. You'll spend the night in Schweich, a quaint German town on the banks of the Mosel.

Distance: 28 miles

Lunch Stop: Trier

Directions (miles): Cycle toward the Sure River until you meet the bike path, which you'll follow away from Grundhof and toward Wasserbilig.

> Look for bicycle path signs: White signs with a green bicycle and "*piste cyclable de la basse Sure.*" Follow alongside the N10 road to Wasserbilig, which is in Luxembourg.

> You can cross over into Germany at Moersdorf and then follow the river to the Wasserbilig/German border, or cycle all the way to Wasserbilig on the Luxembourg side. Either way, keep following the Sure River. While in Germany, you may also see bicycle path signs that say "*Sauertalradweg.*"

> If you cross over in Moersdorf, look for signs to Mesenich and Wasserbilig. Note that after Moersdorf, the bike path ends, so you'll follow the N10 road to Wasserbilig (following signs to Trier, too). Eventually, you'll hit a fork pointing right to Luxembourg and left to Trier along the Sauertalradweg. Follow the road to Trier. As you cycle through Langsur, you'll cross into Germany; 200 yards later, you meet the Mosel bike path (*Moselradweg*)

CYCLING ALONG THE MOSEL RIVER

> *The Moselradweg, or Mosel bicycle path, will lead you almost the entire way to Cochem. Be patient and constantly on the lookout for bicycle path signs, especially as you enter and leave a town (the paths frequently detour).*

> Follow the bicycle path into Trier. You'll be cycling along the B53 road whenever the path ends. You reach Trier after 25 miles. Follow the signs to Centrum to sightsee. Be careful locking your bike—theft is high here.

> To continue to Schweich from Trier's center, follow signs to the Moselradweg. When you reach the path, the river should be on your right.

> In Pfazel, the bike path ends. Follow green bike signs to Ehrang and the Moselradweg. Stay on the Moselradweg with the river to your right. The road will curve; wind under the road and you'll see a green bike sign to Schweich.

You reach Schweich at 28 miles.

Background Notes
Where Am I?
Country: Germany

Federal State: Rheinland-Palatinate

Region: Mosel-Saar

City: Bernkastel-Kues

You'll cycle next into Germany, following a well-marked cycle path along the Mosel River. The charming towns and villages make ideal overnight destinations.
Jerry Soverinsky

Tourist Information

Mosel-Gaste Zentrum
Gestade 6
Bernkastel-Kues 54470
Phone: 06531-4023
Fax: 06531-7953
info@bernkastel.de
www.bernkastel.de/index2.html

Bike Shops

Berger Radsport: Saarallee 1;
Bernkastel-Kues;
Phone: 06531 915750.
Fun Bike Team Fahrradfachgeschaft: Schanzstr. 22; Bernkastel-Kues;
Phone: 05631 94024.

Sightseeing

While in Bernkastel-Kues, check out the **Landshut castle ruins**, high above the city.

Several **river cruises** of varying length depart from the riverfront. Contact **Mosel Route Guides** (Goldbachstr. 52; Bernkastel-Kues; Phone: 06531 8222; michels@germanline.com; www.germanline.com/member/michels.htm) for information.

Restaurants

My groups usually eat at the **Hotel Zur Post**'s restaurant, which offers a good value for its half-pension options. Other local favorites include **Binz** (1 Markt) and **Baren** (9 Schanzstr.), which serve traditional German dishes.

Luggage Transfers

Edringer Hans Taxi: Burgstr. 51; Bernkastel-Kues; Phone: 06531 8149.
Priwitzer Thomas Taxi: Cusanusstr. 37; Bernkastel-Kues; Phone: 06531 96970.

SCHWEICH TO BERNKASTEL-KUES
ROUTE NOTES

Day 3: Schweich to Bernkastel-Kues

The next two bicycling days follow the Mosel River, allowing you to experience first-hand the dozens of charming, quaint towns that line its gentle banks. You can visit 500 year old castles, sample fresh delicacies from local bakeries, and enjoy homemade wine at local wineries.

Distance: 32 miles

Lunch Stop: Any of the Mosel villages along your route.

Directions (miles): Follow the Moselradweg the entire way to Bernkastel.

- Cycle in the direction of Koblenz and Bernkastel-Kues. If you follow the Moselradweg, you'll be cycling along the B53 road whenever the path ends.
- As you reach Thornish, it will appear that the path ends. There will also be a small café to your right. Continue past a chicken coop, then turn **LEFT**. This will bring you to a larger road and the green bike path signs.
- After passing Piesport, veer **RIGHT** in front of a Neukauf Supermarket. This will bring you to the 53 road and a bridge. The green and white signs will give you two options to reach Bernkastel: The better one is to turn left over the bridge (if you continue straight, the path becomes dirt).
- As you cross the bridge, there will be a steep exit to Bernkastel on the left. Be careful. If you do not choose to take it, then you can continue on this road along the shoulder.
- Stay on the road until Kesten then veer left into town and follow signs for Lieser. As you enter Lieser, you'll see a sign for Bernkastel on your right. You're approximately 4km from Bernkastel.
- As you leave Lieser, follow the bike path and signs to Bernkastel. You reach the town center at 32 miles.

Background Notes
Where Am I?

Country: Germany
Federal State: Rheinland-Palatinate
Region: Mosel-Saar
City: Cochem

Tired of cycling? Feel free to hop on a Mosel ferry, perhaps sipping a beer while taking in your picturesque surroundings.

Jerry Soverinsky

Tourist Information

Touristiche Informationen Verkehrsamt Cochem
Enderplatz 1
Cochem 56812
Phone: 02671 6004-0
Fax: 02671 6004-44
verkehrsamt.cochem@lcoc.de
www.cochem.de

Bike Shops

There's one bike shop in Cochem, but they stole several hundred dollars from me in 2002 (true story). If you need a shop, I advise visiting nearby Treis-Karden, 7 miles away:
Bike Store: Haupststr. 34; Phone: 02672 912250.

Sightseeing

Along the ride to Cochem, you'll pass several quaint Mosel towns. Stops in **Traban-Trabach, Zell/Mosel, Alf,** and **Bullay** are particularly worthwhile. Make sure to visit **Beilstein,** a romantic German town that makes a perfect lunch spot. Climb to the top of Burg Metternich for great views of the valley.

While in **Cochem**, visit **Reichsburg Cochem**, a huge castle perched high above the town. It's open from 9 a.m. to 5 p.m.

Restaurants

I like restaurant-hunting in Cochem. There's something in every taste category, even decent Chinese. Among the local favorites, try **Am Hafen** (4 Uferstr.) and **Brixiade** (13 Uferstr.) for regional dishes.

BERNKASTEL-KUES TO COCHEM
ROUTE NOTES

Days 4 and 5: Bernkastel-Kues to Cochem; Cochem Layover Ride

Had enough of endless vineyards, quaint Mosel towns, and lively wine bars? Hopefully not, since you've got more in store today, as you ride to Cochem.

I detail a Cochem century ride, one of the flattest and easiest 100-mile routes you'll ever tackle. Note that the cycling along the Rhine River bike path is choppy at points, and the route through Koblenz is confusing

Bernkastel-Kues to Cochem Route Notes
Distance: 52 miles
Lunch Stop: Traban-Trabach, Beilstein.

Directions (miles): Cross the Mosel to the Kues side of the river; after two miles, you'll reach Wehlen. Cross over the river, following the green Moselradweg signs toward Traban-Trabach. Always follow the green Moselradweg signs to the next town along today's route: Rachig, Erden, Traban-Trabach.

After Traban-Trabach, follow signs to Enkirch and then to Punderich. Sometimes the bike path ends and you'll follow the main road.

Cross over the river in Zell and follow a bike lane parallel with the road. Cross over again to Beilstein when you see the Beilstein 7km sign. Follow this road, the L98, into Cochem (a good bike shoulder here), which you reach after 52 miles.

Germany is home to the bratwurst, a spicy sausage that's served with sauerkraut. My camping groups traditionally hold a gala Bratwurst Festival and locals have become enamored with my barbecuing skills.
Jerry Soverinsky

COCHEM LAYOVER RIDE
ROUTE NOTES
A CENTURY RIDE ALONG THE MOSEL AND RHINE

Distance: 100 miles

Directions (miles): Follow signs from the town center along the river to Koblenz 49km. Cycle north with the river to your right. You're following the B49 road to Koblenz, and there's a large shoulder. About seven miles ahead, you can follow the B49 as it crosses the Mosel and heads to Koblenz, or you can continue along the left side and the 416 to Koblenz and Lof.

Continue along the 416 if you want to visit Burg Eltz, a worthwhile afternoon stop.

Follow the B416 to Koblenz, Metternich, and Leutzel.

Follow the road into Koblenz. Eventually, follow the B-9 road that heads south to Boppard and Mainz along the Rhine River. To reach the B-9 road, turn **RIGHT** on Hohenfelderstrasse near the center of town, next to a church.

Follow the B-9 to Boppard (good lunch stop). Be careful riding along the Rhine because the path is much choppier than the Moselradweg. From Boppard, backtrack along the B-9 and follow it back to Koblenz and then to Cochem.

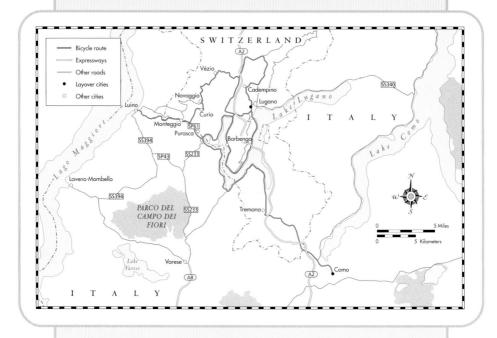

SWISS AND ITALIAN LAKES:
Lugano & Como (Switzerland, Italy)

Did you ever eat a ton of chocolate ice cream and feel like you couldn't eat any more, but you found some Oreo cookies and shoved a few in your mouth, just because? And then lying on your couch a few minutes later, bloated like a pig, feeling like you couldn't fit another crumb in your mouth, you tell your girl-friend to bring you a can of macadamia nuts that you bought last month telling yourself that they'd be for company, while knowing all along they'd find their way into your gluttonous yap-hole before too long? No? Well, I have.

You'll love Lugano and Como. They're idyllic retreats that hold court on their respective lakes, beckoning all who come to meander their cosmopolitan streets, while tempting you subconsciously to wander off and play in their impressive collection of bordering mountains.

You'll begin the trip in Lugano, based in the Ticino area of Switzerland. Its palm trees, warm breezes, and Mediterranean-like climate create a harmonious blend of Swiss and Italian cultures.

Your last day's ride brings you to Como, a centuries-old retreat for artists, and an ideal base for further cycling.

Arrival and Departure
Air

Lugano Airport in nearby Agno lies less than 5 miles from the center of Lugano. The major commercial carrier into Lugano, Swiss Airlines, may not be on your frequent flyer program's partner list, so you may fare better flying into Milan's Malpensa Airport, 55 miles away. This will be your departure airport, anyway (Como is 56 miles from Malpensa), so you might strike a better deal flying roundtrip into Milan. Either way, here are the airports and their links:

Lugano Airport
Via Aeroporto
6982 Agno, Switzerland
Phone: 0 91 610 11 11
Fax +41 0 91 610 11 00
airport@lugano.ch
www.swiss.com
Milan's Malpensa Airport
http://www.sea-aeroportimilano.it/Eng/Malpensa/

Taxi and Public Transportation
TO LUGANO

If you're flying into tiny Lugano City Airport, there's a shuttle bus that makes frequent city runs throughout the day to Lugano (Shuttle Bus Sagl, Phone: 91 967 60 30, airport@shuttle-bus.com, www.shuttle-bus.com). The cost is 10 CHF for the one-way transfer.

Otherwise, a taxi ride is a steep 40 CHF (you're still in Switzerland, remember).

If you're flying into Malpensa, Malpensa Shuttle operates multiple Malpensa-Lugano transfers for 30. Malpensa Shuttle, Via Zorzi 41, CH-6902 Lugano-Paradiso, Phone: 0994 88 80,

busexpress@csa-97.ch; www.busexpress.com/shuttle.asp.

A taxi from Malpensa to Lugano can range from €60 to €95.

FROM COMO

Bus SPT offers service from Como to Milan. The one-hour journey costs €13 (http://www.sptcomo.it/servizi/malpensa2.asp).

A taxi from Como to Malpensa airport will cost €60 to €95:

Radiotaxi Lario: Via Anzani Francesco 52; 031 2772; **Taxi Como**: Piazzale S. Gottardo; Phone: 031 271000.

Bike Rentals

Switzerland offers one of the best and most efficient bike rental systems in Europe. You can pick up a city, mountain, or child's bicycle at one of over 100

rail stations throughout Switzerland and return it to any of the other participating stations. Lugano's station offers several models. Expect to pay 30 CHF
per day (http://www.rentabike.ch/).

Cycling Notes

The roads in and out of Lugano are almost always congested. Pay extra attention
because traffic can move quickly, too.

The same goes for Como. It's a beautiful city and you'll be tempted to
stare off into the distant mountains as you cycle into the city, but please keep
your eyes focused on the road.

Maps

Kummerly + Fry's *Holiday Map Tessin*; 1:120,000; and Euro Cart's *Carte Delle
Zone Turistiche i Laghi*; 1:100,000.

Temperatures and Rainfall

LUGANO[74]

MONTH	AVERAGE HIGH (°F)	AVERAGE PRECIPITATION (IN)
JANUARY	37	2.6
FEBRUARY	40	2.6
MARCH	45	4.5
APRIL	52	6.0
MAY	59	7.7
JUNE	66	7.1
JULY	71	6.5
AUGUST	69	7.2
SEPTEMBER	63	6.8
OCTOBER	54	7.2
NOVEMBER	45	5.3
DECEMBER	39	3.1

Background Notes
Where Am I?

Country: Switzerland
Region: Ticino
Canton: Ticino
City: Lugano

[74] From http://www.worldclimate.com/cgi-bin/grid.pl?gr=N46E008.

Ticino's surroundings are a perfect balance of land and sea. And brush up on your high school Italian, for despite its Swiss location, it's Italian-speaking territory here. *Ticino Tourism*

Tourist Information
Lugano Official Tourist Office
Riva Albertolli 5
Lugano 6900
Phone: 091 913 32 32
Fax: 091 922 76 53
info@lugano-tourism.ch
www.lugano-tourism.ch; http://www.lugano.ch/turismo/welcome.cfm

Bike Shops
Casa Del Ciclo: Via Trevano 46; Phone: 091 9723234.
Ponti Bici Sports: Via Cantonale; Phone: 091 9945008.
Alberto Bike Store: Via Cantonale; Phone: 091 9464464.

Sightseeing
The **Parco Civico** is Lugano's largest park and the site of the Casino and Villa Ciani art museum.

There is no shortage of churches in Lugano. Here you'll find the **Cathedrale of San Lorenzo** (Via Cattedrale) and **Church of St. Mary of the Angels** (Piazza Luini).

Churches play a central role in the lifestyle of the Ticinese (Ticinians? Ticiners?), and their churches often enjoy the most enviable spots within their cities. *R. Gerth, Ticino Tourism*

Nearby is the **Schmid Museum** (Contrada Pro 22, in Bre), former home of architect Wilhelm Schmid, which displays his work and writings. It's open Wednesday through Sunday from 1:30 p.m. to 5 p.m.

Villa Favorita in Castagnola, which is open Friday through Sunday from 10 a.m. to 5 p.m., contains one of Europe's greatest private art collections, which belongs to Baron Hans Heinrich Thyssen Bornemiszza.

Take a funicular to **Monte San Salvatore**, which provides visitors great views over the Swiss and French Alps. Departures are from 9 a.m. to 6 p.m.

If **water sports** are your thing, you can rent rowboats, sail boats, and motorboats from Circolo Velico (Foce Cassarate; Phone: 971 09 75). Scuba enthusiasts should call on **Lugano-Sub** (G. Bucher, corso Elvezia 3; Phone: 994 37 40). Contact **Club Nautico-Lugano** at Via Calloni 9 (Phone: 649 61 39) for waterskiing.

Restaurants

Lugano's most acclaimed restaurant is **Principe Leopoldo** (5 Via Montalbano), which serves classic French dishes from 135 CHF. Also try **Scala** (29 Via Nassa) and **Osteria Calprino** (28 Via Carona) for traditional Ticino dishes.

Luggage Transfers

Euro Taxi: 091 9412424.
Nuovo Taxi: 091 9931616.
Blue Taxi: 091 9711212.
Super Taxi: 091 9715757.

LUGANO LOOP RIDES
ROUTE NOTES

Days 1-4: Lugano Loop Rides

If the trains weren't so darned efficient and expensive, you'd swear that Lugano was in Italy. Almost everyone is speaking Italian and the architecture closely resembles what's found in Lombardy and Tuscany. But as I said, the trains are all punctual and ridiculously pricey, so you'll figure something's fishy, and then when a local storekeeper spits on your Euros and demands Swiss Francs . . . well, that's when it'll hit you: You're in Switzerland.

These four rides are presented in no particular order. These are all great routes, some easy, some difficult—but please be careful entering and leaving Lugano because traffic there can be brutal. **Distance:** 49 kilometers

Directions (km): Directions for all four rides begin from the intersection of Via Zorzi and S. P. Pambio, at the western edge of Lugano-Paradiso.

Cycle down S. P. Pambio and make a **RIGHT** on Via Geretta.

0.5: Follow the green highway signs **LEFT** on Via S. Salvatore. At the end of the street, turn **LEFT** for Bellinzona and Ponte Tresa. Get in the far right lane and just ahead, turn **RIGHT** for Bellinzona, Ponte Tresa, and the airport.

1.1: Turn left for Ponte Tresa, the campground, and the airport. You're on Via Antonio Riva.

2.2: Traffic light; turn **LEFT**. Immediately after the turn, follow signs to the **RIGHT** for Varese, Ponte Tresa, and Agno. You start a downhill at 2.3 kilometers. Ride along the bike path whenever possible. Keep following signs for Ponte Tresa.

4.9: Agno. As you pass through the area, turn **LEFT** for Ponte Tresa. Keep following signs for Ponte Tresa, but when you reach Caslano, there is a bikes/pedestrians-only path that will take you around the tiny peninsula.

10: Ponte Tresa. Follow signs to Luino.

11.9: You see a sign for Luino 18km. Follow signs to Luino and Fornasette for the next eight miles.

18.4: You start an uphill en route to Fornasette. You'll pass Italian customs.

21.2: The outskirts of Luino. Continue downhill until you reach the lake and center of Luino, at 23.5. This makes a good lunch spot.

You can retrace your path or follow the road parallel with this back toward Ponte Tresa.

Lugano Loop Ride #2 Route Notes

Distance: 31 kilometers

Directions (km): From ride #1, above: Just past the airport and railroad tracks, turn **RIGHT** for Locarno, Bioggio, and Bellinzona.

6.5: Serocca D.

7.3: Bioggio; follow signs for Bellinzona and Lugano.

8.1: Stoplight; head for Lugano. You pass over the highway at 8.6.

You are following the path through Cadempino, Lamone, Taverne, Origlio (uphill), Carnago, Tesserete (21.1km). From here, you can continue with sharp climbs to Bidogno and Val Colla; or head back to Lugano, via Lugaggia, Ganobbio, Massagno, and then back to Lugano. You're heading downhill en route to Lugano, following blue signs. As you reach Lugano, follow signs to centro. You reach the center at 31 kilometers.

Lugano Loop Ride #3 Route Notes

NOTE: *This is a very challenging ride.*

Distance: 51 kilometers

Directions (km): 5.0: Set out as per ride #1. You reach Agno at 5 kilometers. Past the airport, follow signs to Ponte Tresa. As you pass through Magliaso, turn **RIGHT** for Pura. The turn comes just as you reach Caslano.

> 9.2: Pura. As you reach the post office, make the sharp **LEFT** toward Ponte Tresa.
>
> 10.1: A small fork; follow the white sign to Ponte Tresa.
>
> 12.0: T-intersection with no signs; turn **RIGHT**.
>
> 12.2: Purasca. You pass Barico; just ahead (.4km), bear **RIGHT** for Novaggio and Croglio.
>
> Next, you'll head for Castelrotto (careful for sharp turns), Biogno, Bedigliora, Banco (head toward Curio when you reach this town, not Astano), Curio, Novaggio, Miglieglia, Breno, Fescoggia (head toward Arosio), Vezio (Lugano is 14 kilometers away), Mugena, Arosio, (turn right for Gravesano), and Gravesano. From here, follow signs for Lugano.
>
> 35.0: T-intersection past Gravesano; turn **RIGHT** for Lugano.
>
> 35.3: At the roundabout, follow signs for Manno and Ponte Tresa; you'll next pass through Bioggio, Agno, and the airport; and then head back to Lugano.
>
> 41.0: Airport turnoff.
>
> 51: Lugano.

Lugano Loop Ride #4 Route Notes

Distance: 32 kilometers

Directions (km): Follow the same route out of town toward Agno as per previous days' directions.

> 3.6: You pass underneath the highway.
>
> 4.4: Turn **LEFT** for Morcote and Figino.
>
> 7.9: Carabietta. You'll next pass through Casoro, Figino, Morcote, and Vico Morcote.
>
> 16.7: Turn **LEFT** for Vico Morcote and Carona (a very sharp turn); you're heading uphill.
>
> 18.7: Vico Morcote. Keep heading uphill toward Carona and Lugano. You reach the top at 22.4.
>
> 23.6: Carona. You'll next pass Carabbia, then Pazzallo.
>
> 29.8: Paradiso. Head toward Paradiso Centro as you're heading downhill.

You return to your starting point at 32 kilometers.

Background Notes
Where Am I?

Country: Italy
Region: Lombardy
Province: Como
City: Como

Don't let the breezy demeanor of these cyclists fool you. This is challenging cycling terrain, suitable for strong riders only.
Ticino Tourism

Tourist Information
Azienda di Promozione Turistica del Comasco
Piazza Cavour 17
Como 22100
Phone: 031 33001 11
Fax: 031 26 11 52
lakecomo@tin.it
www.lakecomo.org

The Swiss dabbled briefly in experimental punishments. This very rare fourteenth-century photo showcases a group of petty thieves, who were spared the guillotine, and were forced to march through the streets clad in red tights, copper breastplates, and feather boas. *Ticino Tourism*

Bike Shops

Rullo Bike: Via Grandi Achille 17;
Phone: 031 263025.
Riccardi: Via Diaz Armando 90;
Phone: 031 260105.
Martinelli Franco: Viale Lecco 95;
Phone: 031 264417.

Sightseeing

Even if you find yourself in a drunken stupor, you can't miss the **Duomo**, a beautiful marble church that combines Gothic and Early Renaissance styles.

A few steps away is San Fidele Square, where you'll find **Church of San Fidele,** its Romanesque basilica. Also nearby is the **Casa del Faxcio**, a twentieth-century palace built to house Italy's 1939 fascist government.

For swimming, visit **Lido Villa Olmo**'s (Phone: 57 09 68) sandy beach. It's open from 10 a.m. to 6 p.m. daily.

Restaurants

Try **Il Solito Posto** (9 Via Lambertenghi) and **Crotto del Lupo** (17 loc. Card. Via Pisani Dossi) for modestly priced regional specialties.

LUGANO TO COMO
ROUTE NOTES

Day 5: Lugano to Como

Como, at the base of several mountain passes leading into Italy, has been a desirable city since the Middle Ages. It began a rich silk trade in the sixteenth century, which continues today (Como produces about one-third of the world's silk). Como's Centro Sotrico, enclosed by twelfth-century walls, presents a rich collection of medieval churches and lively piazzas.

If you'd like to extend your trip in Como and you're jonesin' for some more bikin', the tourist office publishes a collection of mountain bike rides in the Lake Como region.

Distance: 56 kilometers

Directions (km): Continue to Agno as in the previous days and head then toward Ponte Tresa. You reach Ponte Tresa at 11 kilometers. Follow the road through the town en route to Varesse until you pass through customs. Just ahead, turn **LEFT** for Brusimpiano and Porto Ceresio on the SP61. Follow the bike path whenever possible.

18.7: Keep following the lake toward Porto Ceresio. Eventually, cross over into Switzerland near Brusino Arsizio. You next pass through Riva S. Vitale, and up the road, turn **RIGHT** toward Rancate and Stabbio.

Follow signs all the way to Rancate; you head uphill until you reach the town at 34.8 kilometers. Follow signs next toward Ligornetto as you pass through Rancate.

You'll next pass Genestrerio, Novazzano, Chiasso, and eventually see signs toward Como. Be careful for traffic. Follow blue signs, not green highway signs.

49.1: Italy. Follow centro signs for Como. You reach the town center at 56 kilometers.

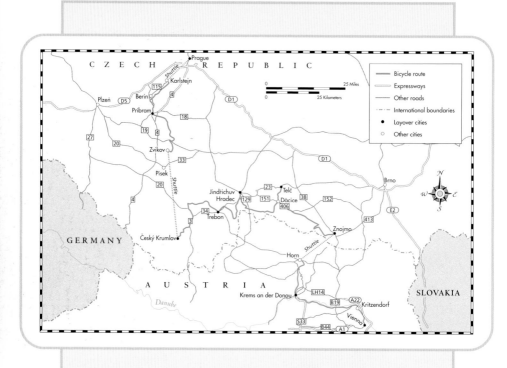

VIENNA TO PRAGUE (Austria, Czech Republic)

The route between Vienna and Prague is a cyclist's dream. The majority of the itenerary follows well-marked cycle paths, the locals are exceptionally considerate to your physical journey, and the towns and villages along your route are filled with rich, cultural gems that beckon your perusal.

This was a new tour for my company in 2003, and it was met with enthusiastic reviews. Much of the cycling is along the Greenways bicycle route, a wondrous trail that weaves through the area's most impressive and important sites. The rolling terrain is challenging and you should be at least an intermediate cyclist to attempt it because public transportation lifts are inefficient.

Arrival and Departure
Air
You'll want to fly into Vienna and out of Prague for this trip, which is an easy task because both cities' airports are served by major airlines.

Be on the lookout for Viennese aristocrats, whose chauvinistic and caste-system ideals are anachronistic pinings of a lost generation.
Niels Povlsen

Vienna Schwechat Airport
Phone: +43 1 7007 0
http://english.viennaairport.com/
Prague Ruzyne Airport
Phone: +420 220 113 314
http://www.csl.cz/en/frames.htm

Taxi and Public Transportation
TO VIENNA
Vienna's Schwechat Airport (say it four times quickly while chewing crackers) lies 11 miles east of the city center.

Buses run throughout the day and cost €5.80 for the 20-minute transfer. Trains run from the airport to Vienna Mitte or North stations in 30 minutes and cost €5.85.

A taxi from the airport to central Vienna costs €30 to €35.

FROM PRAGUE
Buses depart for Ruzyne Airport every half-hour from 5:30 a.m. until 9:30 p.m. from Namesti Republiky. The 25-minute journey costs 90 CZK.

Taxi fares are based on zones, and the total price to the airport will range from 120 to 870 CZK. Have your hotel staff pre-arrange the hotel and confirm the price before you depart.

Bike Rentals
I rent all bikes for this tour from a reliable Vienna shop, Pedal Power:
Pedal Power
Ausstellungsstraße 3
A-1020 Vienna
Phone: 0043 1 729 72 34
Fax: 0043 1 729 72 35
office@pedalpower.at
www.pedalpower.at

One-day rentals cost €27, but there are generous discounts if you rent by the week. Pick up and delivery services are also available.

Like the German Mosel, the Austrian Danube offers travelers the opportunity for relaxing cruises. *Niels Povlsen*

Cycling Notes

The Czech Republic poses the only significant language barrier among all countries mentioned in this book. Even in the tourist industry, few people speak English fluently, and you may be frustrated trying to find assistance and facilities when you need them.

For practical arrangements, I urge you to keep your contacts to a minimum. I always work with CZ Eurotour when bringing groups to the Czech Republic because their knowledge of the country and its tourism contacts has saved me tons of time and expense. They can book all your hotels, arrange for your luggage transfers, and even get you to and from the airport. Ask for Jaromir, he does great work.

CZ Eurotour
Dolejsi 69
398 06 Mirovice
Czech Republic
Phone: +420 604 538 023
Fax: +420 362 831 298
info@czeurotour.com
www.czeurotour.com

Luggage Transfer Notes

I urge you to have CZ Eurotour make your luggage transfer arrangements (if your hotel cannot do it for you). The majority of taxi drivers in the Czech Republic, even those in Prague, do not speak English, and your phone call will therefore be an exercise in futility. For this reason, I will omit the luggage transfer section from each of the daily itineraries.

Maps

Freytag & Berndt's *Osterreich 2000 Wien Niederosterreich, Die Strassenkarte*; 1:200,000. This map will cover your Austria cycling.

They're difficult to find outside the Czech Republic, but the Shocart Active Turisticka Mapa series (1:100,000) are the best I've found. You'll use #s 207-210, 213-218—a lot of maps, I know—but they're cheap, about $2 per map at today's exchange.

Temperatures and Rainfall

VIENNA[75]

MONTH	AVERAGE HIGH (°F)	AVERAGE LOW (°F)	WET DAYS
JANUARY	36	27	21
FEBRUARY	39	28	17
MARCH	49	35	19
APRIL	57	41	19
MAY	67	49	18
JUNE	72	55	20
JULY	77	59	18
AUGUST	77	59	16
SEPTEMBER	69	53	15
OCTOBER	57	43	15
NOVEMBER	44	35	20
DECEMBER	39	30	22

PRAGUE[76]

MONTH	AVERAGE HIGH (°F)	AVERAGE LOW (°F)	AVERAGE PRECIPITATION (IN)
JANUARY	34	24	0.8
FEBRUARY	36	25	0.7
MARCH	46	32	1.0
APRIL	54	36	1.4
MAY	64	45	2.3
JUNE	69	51	2.7
JULY	72	54	2.6
AUGUST	73	53	2.5
SEPTEMBER	65	48	1.6
OCTOBER	54	39	1.2
NOVEMBER	41	32	1.1
DECEMBER	36	28	0.9

[75] From http://www.usatoday.com/weather/climate/europe/austria/wvienna.htm.
[76] From http://www.usatoday.com/weather/climate/europe/czechrep/wprague.htm.

Czech Republic Phone Numbers

Phone numbers, especially city codes, change rapidly in the Czech Republic. Check the website

http://phonebook.quick.cz/index.php?fce=10&VYMAZFORM=on&id=1

(English page) for an updated search engine of Czech numbers.

Vienna

Spend as much time as you like sightseeing in Vienna prior to your departure. I recommend at least two full days. The Vienna Tourist Office can provide you with tons of helpful information:

Vienna Tourist Office
Obere Augartenstrasse 40
Vienna 1025 Austria
Phone: 01 21 114
Fax: 01 216 84 92
info@info.wien.at
www.info.wien.at; www.vienna.info

Background Notes
Where Am I?

Country: Austria
Province: Niederoesterreich
Region: Danube-Lower Austria
City: Krems an der Donau

Tourist Information

Verkehrsburo Krems
Undstrasse 6
Krems 3500
Phone: 02732 82676
Fax: 02732 70011
Austropa.krems@verkehrsbuero.at
http://www.krems.info

Your Czech cycling begins in Znojmo, where you're bound to find traditional Czech music at select local restaurants. *Niels Povlsen*

You'll find the Czech people to be some of the warmest in Europe. Despite encountering few English-speaking locals, you're sure to receive a friendly nod from fellow cyclists. *Niels Povlsen*

Bike Shops

Radstudio Krems: Hafnerplatz; 3500 Krems; Phone: 02732 81880.

Rund ums Rad: Steiner Landstraße 103; 3504 Krems-Stein; Phone: 02732 71071.

Sightseeing

The **Klosterneuburg Abbey** is a magnificent medieval abbey. It's open Monday through Friday from 9 a.m. to 6 p.m., and Saturday and Sunday from 10 a.m. to 5 p.m.

Krems' main sites include the **Steiner Gate** (1480) with its baroque tower; and the **Weinstadt Museum Krems** (Kornermarkt 14), a Gothic Dominican abbey-turned-museum, which includes the works of Martin-Johann Schmidt. The admission fee is €3 and is open Wednesday through Sunday from 1 p.m. to 6 p.m.

Restaurants

Local favorites include **Gasthof Klingerhuber** (Wienerstrasse 2), **Hotel-Restaurant Alte Post** (Obere Landstrasse 32), **Gastehaus Fam. Einzinger** (Steiner Landstrasse 82), and **Zum Goldenen Engel** (Wienerstrasse 41).

VIENNA TO KREMS
ROUTE NOTES

Day 1: Vienna to Krems

You'll begin the cycling portion of your trip along the Danube river, following a well-marked riverside bike trail that meanders past castles, medieval villages, and latticed vineyards. You'll cycle through Klosterneuberg, an old market town that houses a twelfth century abbey. You'll end your ride in Krems, a delightful 1,000-year-old town teeming with winding cobbled streets and a focal point for Riesling wine production.

Distance: 76 kilometers

Lunch stop: Tulln
Directions (km): 0.0: Leave Vienna along the bike path on the south side of the Donau Kanal, following bicycle path signs to Klosterneuberg.

14.0: Klosterneuberg. Follow signs to Stift to visit the abbey. To continue to Krems, follow bicycle path signs to Tulln.

17.5: Kritzendorf. Head toward Hoflain an der Donau

20.5: Hoflain an der Donau; head toward Greifenstein.

23.0: Greifenstein.

30.0: Muckendorf a.d. Donau; head toward Oberaigen.

33.0: Oberaigen; head toward Tulln.

38.0: Tulln, a good lunch stop. Head toward Kronau.

42.5: Kronau.

44.5: Langen-Schonbichl.

46.5: Pischelsdorf.

48.0: Kleinschonbichl; head toward Zwentendorf a.d. Donau.

49.0: Zwentendorf a.d. Donau.

68.0: Hollenburg. Head toward Krems.

76.0. The cycle path circles and takes you over a bridge into Krems. Follow signs into the city center, which you reach at 76 kilometers.

Background Notes
Where Am I?
Country: Czech Republic
Region: South Moravia
Province: Jihomoravsky Kraj
City: Znojmo

Tourist Information
Tourist Information Centre Znojmo
Obrovoka ul. 10
Znojmo 669 01
Phone: 515 2225 52
Fax: 515 22 25 52
znojemsko@bravissimo.cz; tic@beseda.znojmo.cz
www.znojmo.cz/index3.html

Bike Shops
Cyklosport Suler, Horni Namesti 8.

Sightseeing

Znojmo's castle dates from the eleventh century, and today it houses the **South Moravian Museum**, a military shrine. The admission is 20CZK and the museum is open Tuesday through Sunday from 9 a.m. to 4 p.m.

For 35 CZK, you can climb to the top of the **Town Hall Tower** and take in great views of the surrounding countryside. It's open daily from 8:30 a.m. to 4 p.m.

Don't miss the **Znojemske Podzemi**, fourteenth-century catacombs used in wars past. It's open daily from 9 a.m. to 4 p.m., and admission is 40 CZK.

Restaurants

La Casa Navarra (Kovarska 10), **Na Ceske** (Dolni Ceska 6), and **Astor** (Kollarova 4) are all great restaurants to visit.

KREMS TO HORN
ROUTE NOTES

Day 2: Krems to Horn; transfer to Znojmo

You'll head north from the Danube to the Lower Austria region of Niederosterreich, passing first through Langenlois (Austria's largest wine town), and perhaps stopping for lunch at Rosenburg to visit its beautiful Renaissance castle. After reaching Horn, you'll need to arrange for a taxi (see Luggage Transfer notes earlier in the chapter) to bring you across the Czech border to Znojmo, a thirteenth-century town combining Gothic, Renaissance, and Baroque houses.

Krems to Horn Route Notes (transfer from Horn to Znojmo required)
Distance: 45 kilometers (to Horn)
Directions (km): The bike path is well-marked all the way to Rosenberg.

- 8.0: On the crossroad on the left, follow the blue cycle path.
- 8.5: Gobelsburg; head toward Langenlois.
- 11.0: Langenlois; head toward Zöbing.
- 14.0: Zöbing; head toward Schönberg-Neustift.
- 15.5: Schönberg-Neustift; head toward Schönberg am Kamp.
- 17.5: Schönberg am Kamp; head toward Stiefern.
- 20.0: Stiefern; head toward Oberplank.
- 27.5: Buchberg am Kamp; head toward Zitternberg.
- 28.5: Zitternberg; head toward Gars am Kamp.
- 30.0: Gars am Kamp; head toward Stallegg.
- 33.5: Stallegg; head toward Rosenburg.
- 35.0: Rosenburg; head toward Altenburg.
- 39.0: Altenburg; head toward Frauenhofen.
- 43.0: Frauenhofen; head toward Horn.
- 45.0: Horn; transfer to Znojmo via public or private transport.

The perimeters around many Czech towns are rather drab and industrial, thanks to the Communist decorating touches of the 1960s and 1970s. As you draw closer to the town centers, you'll discover a delightful collection of centuries-old historic buildings. We're about halfway to one town center in this photo.
Niels Povlsen

Background Notes
Where Am I?
Country: Czech Republic
Region: South Moravia
Province: Jihomoravsky Kraj
City: Telc

Tourist Information
Town Information Centre
Namesti Zachariase z Hradce 10
Telc
Phone: 567 112 407
Fax: 567 112 403
www.telcsko.cz

Bike Shops
Ralsport: Namesti Zachariase z Hradce.
Cyklo Steidler: Namesti Zachariase z Hradce.

Sightseeing
En route to Telc, you'll pass **Vranov Castle**, a beautiful fourteenth-century baroque chateau. It's open Tuesday through Sunday from 9 a.m. to 6 p.m.

Telc, a Renaissance-looking town, was rebuilt in the seventeenth century after it was ravaged by a fire. **Zachariás of Hradec Square** is the focal point of the city.

Telc is also home to a fourteenth-century castle, which is open Tuesday through Sunday from 9 a.m. to 5 p.m.

Restaurants

Restaurant Na Zamecke: Namesti Zachariase z Hradce 1.

ZNOJMO TO TELC
ROUTE NOTES

Day 3: Znojmo to Telc

Today's ride begins with a stop at Vranov nad Dyji, and its seventeenth-century Baroque castle. You'll next cycle through the Vranov National Park en route to Telc, an UNESCO (United Nations World Heritage Site) historical town and South Moravian gem with a splendid town square and Renaissance castle.

Distance: 74 kilometers

Lunch stop: Vranov nad Dyji.

Directions (km): 0.0: From the Hotel Prestige in Znojmo, turn **LEFT** at the gas station on Prazska. Take the fourth right (Haristska). Count the streets because you won't see a sign.

Stay on this road and follow well-marked signs. You're heading first toward Masovice.

7.3: Masovice; head for Podmoli;

9.6: Podmoli; head for Lukov.

12.0: Lukov; head for Horni Breckov.

15.3: Horni Breckov; **LEFT** at the church and then **RIGHT** 300 meters later toward Lesna.

17.3: Follow road 398 **LEFT** toward Vranov nad Dyji (you can skip the loop to Vranov nad Dyji by turning **RIGHT** toward Jemnice along the 408 road).

17.7: Follow road 398 toward Vranov nad Dyji.

22.0: Vranov nad Dyji.

After visiting the castle, to continue your ride:

Descend from the castle and turn **LEFT** at the bottom of a hill.

Begin a steep ascent and turn **RIGHT** following bike path and #48 signs.

Follow the bike path signs through the park. Do not cross the metal bridge.

Turn **RIGHT** at the bridge, following bike path signs. Continue on this small road.

At an intersection with a café, turn **RIGHT** and begin a long climb, following bike path #48.

Turn **LEFT** at the top of the hill.

At your next crossroad, turn **LEFT** and follow signs for villages along the 408: Sumna (28km), Stitary (31km), Zalesi (35km), Desov (42km), Slavikovice (47km) and Jemnice (51km). Follow signs from here to Dacice.

62.0: In Dacice, turn **RIGHT** to Kostelni Vydri.

Between Kostelni Vydri and Telc, there are several small turns that don't appear on even the most detailed maps. You can follow Telc signs, which lead you to the 406.

74.0: Once you reach Telc, head for the church towers and you'll find the central square.

Background Notes
Where Am I?
Country: Czech Republic
Region: South Bohemia
Province: Jihocesky kraj
City: Jindrichuv Hradec

Tourist Information
Informacni Stredisko
Panska 136/I
Jindrichuv Hradec 37701
Phone: 331 363 546
Fax: 331 361 503
info@jh.cz
www.jh.cz

Bike Shops
P+V, Cykloservis: Namesti Miru 8 / I.

Sightseeing
About 7 miles into your route, you'll reach **Slavonice**, a thirteenth-century town and former staging post en route to Vienna. Check out the two market squares and Renaissance houses.

   Jindrichuv Hradec Castle dates from the thirteenth century and is a fine example of Gothic and Renaissance influences.

Restaurants
Krcma u Jachyma: Dobrovskeho 1 / I.
U Papousku: Na Prikopech 188 / II.

TELC TO JINDRICHUV HRADEC
ROUTE NOTES

Day 4: Telc to Jindrichuv Hradec
Today's ride is a treasure trove of thirteenth-century Czech villages. You'll pass first through Slavonice, a thirteenth-century town distinguished by its extraordinary Gothic and Renaissance housing. Next, it's on to Landstejn, where you'll get a peek at its thirteenth-century Romanesque castle ruins. Finally, you'll finish your ride in Jindrichuv Hradec, a fortified town dominated by its Gothic castle, the third largest structure of its kind in the Czech Republic.

Distance: 66 kilometers

Directions (km): 0.0: Start in Telc at the Hotel cerny. With the hotel at your back, turn **RIGHT**; go out of the square and through the next gate; turn **RIGHT**. Follow signs for Kostelni Myslova.

    3.7: Kostelní Myslová.

    5.5: Zadní Vydrí; turn **LEFT** toward Kostelní Vydrí.

    6.5: Turn **RIGHT** toward Kostelní Vydrí.

    8.5: Kostelní Vydrí turn. Turn **RIGHT** toward Pec. At a yield sign just after Kostelni Vydri, follow cycle path #16; first **LEFT,** then **RIGHT**.

    9.3: Continue **STRAIGHT** (unsigned, but you're heading toward Pec).

    10.8: At a crossroad, continue **STRAIGHT** (unsigned, but you're heading toward Pec).

    11.6: At a crossroad, continue **STRAIGHT** toward Pec-road No. 406.

NOTE: *EXTREME CAUTION—You should get off your bike and walk down a slope at this intersection (where you cross road No. 151).*

    12.9: At a crossroad, continue **STRAIGHT** toward Pec.

    14.2: Pec. Continue **STRAIGHT** toward Dolní Bolíkov-road No. 406.

    17.0: Dolní Bolíkov; follow road No. 406.

    19.2: Continue **STRAIGHT** toward Slavonice-road No. 406.

    21.2: Slavonice; follow signs to Staré Mesto-road No.152.

    28.5: Staré Mesto p./Land; turn **RIGHT** toward Landstejn.

    31.5: Landstejn (visit castle ruins); to continue, follow signs to Nová Bystrice.

    36.3: At a crossroad, turn **RIGHT** to road No. 152.

    42.3: Nová Bystrice. Follow signs to Smrena, then right at the bar.

    46.6: Novy Vojírov.

NOTE: *From here, you're following cycle path #1009 to cycle path #32.*

    48.6: Lhota. At a crossroad, turn **RIGHT** toward Sedlo.

    50.2: Sedlo; after 500 meters turn **RIGHT** at a crossroad.

    52.9: At a crossroad, turn **LEFT**; road No. 149.

    53.6: At a crossroad, turn **RIGHT** toward Nová Ves.

    54.3: Nová Ves. You're on cycle path #32.

NOTE: *The path is dirt from Nova Ves until Dolni Zdar.*

    57.2: Malíkov n/Nezárkou.

    58.9: At a crossroad, **STRAIGHT** on cycle path # 32.

    59: Dolní zdár. Turn **RIGHT** onto cycle path #32.

    60.8: Horní zdár. Continue on cycle path #32.

    63.4: Lisny Dvur. Continue on cycle path #32.

    65.6: Jindrichuv Hradec.

The Czech Republic has literally thousands of miles of public cycling paths, a network that reaches into the country's very best sites and attractions. *Niels Povlsen*

Background Notes
Where Am I?
Country: Czech Republic
Region: South Bohemia
Province: Jihoresku kraj
City: Trebon

Tourist Information
Tourist Centre
Masarykovo Namesti 103
Trebon 37901
Phone: 384 721 169
Fax: 384 721 356
info@iks.tbnet.cz
www.trebon-mesto.cz

Bike Shops
Velkoservis Kocanda: Taboritska 61.

The terrain in the Czech Republic is challenging, with rolling hills along almost every ride. Because public assistance can be difficult to coordinate, you should be a capable cyclist before setting out on your own. *Niels Povlsen*

Sightseeing
Trebon Castle, a beautiful Renaissance castle, is open Tuesday through Sunday from 9 a.m. to 12 p.m. and 1 p.m. to 5 p.m. The cost of admission is 30 CZK.

Weather permitting, you might also visit **Rbnik Svet** on the south side of the Old Town. It's a small lake that rents windsurfers and other watersport equipment.

Restaurants
Hotel and Restaurant Zlata Hvezda (Masarykovo Namesti 107) and **Billy Konicek:** (Masarykovo Nam. 97) offer traditional Czech dishes.

If you're in the mood for Italian, check out **Pizzeria Mecando** (Zamek 112).

JINDRICHUV HRADEC TO TREBON
ROUTE NOTES

Day 5: Jindrichuv Hradec to Trebon
You'll cycle today to the thirteenth-century fortified town of Trebon, which was awarded spa rights under its former Communist rule.
Distance: 61 kilometers
Directions (km): 0.0: From Jindrichuv Hradec, head to Lísny Dvur.
2.2: Lísny Dvur; turn **LEFT** toward Horní Zdár and Viden onto cycle path No. 32 (the path is dirt for about 1 kilometer).

4.8: Horní Zdár; follow signs to Dolní Zdár.

6.6: Dolní Zdár; follow signs to Horní Lhota.

7.8: Horní Lhota; follow signs to Lásenice.

10.1: Lásenice; turn **LEFT** toward címer onto road No. 149.

13.0: Stankov; turn **RIGHT** onto cycle path No. 32.

17.9: Turn **RIGHT** onto cycle path No. 322.

29.7: Stankov; turn **RIGHT** toward Chlum u Trebone onto cycle path No. 322.

32.7: Chlum u Trebone; follow signs to Lutová onto cycle path No. 1011.

36.6: Lutová; follow signs to Stríbeec onto cycle path No. 1035.

42.5: Stríbeec; follow signs to Stará Hlína onto cycle path No. 1035.

47.5: Stará Hlína; follow signs to Presek onto cycle path No. 1035.

54.5: Continue **STRAIGHT** onto cycle path No. 1034.

56.0: Presek Bridlice; follow signs to cycle path No. 1034.

58.8: Bridlice; follow signs to Trebon.

60.3: Trebon.

Background Notes
Where Am I?
Country: Czech Republic
Region: South Bohemia
Province: Jihocesky Kraj
City: Cesky Krumlov

Tourist Information
Tourist Service
Rooseveltova 28
Cesky Krumlov 38101
Phone: 337 712 853
Fax: 337 711 900
tourist.service@unios.cz
www.ceskykrumlov-info.cz

Bike Shops
HM Sport Plus: Modlitba Jan, Slupenecka 85.
Diablo Sport: Urbinska 187.

Sightseeing
Námesti Péemysla Otakara II, the town's main square, is one of Europe's largest main squares.

You can also visit **Krumlov Castle**, a fourteenth-century, Renaissance-style castle. It's open Tuesday through Sunday from 9 a.m. to 12 p.m. and 1 p.m. to

5 p.m. The admission is 150 CZK.

Restaurants

Rybrska Basta Jakuba Krcina (Kajovska 54) offers wonderful seafood.

U Pisare Jana (Horni 151) and **Restaurant Gotika** (Horni 48) are also good choices for local dishes.

TREBON TO CESKY KRUMLOV
ROUTE NOTES

Day 6: Trebon to Cesky Krumlov

Your ride today begins with a stop in Hluboka and its 141-room castle, affectionately referred to as the "Pearl of South Bohemia." You'll pedal anxiously for your evening destination, Cesky Krumlov, one of the prettiest towns in all of Bohemia and another UNESCO city. Feel free to visit its thirteenth-century castle and garden.

Distance: 63 kilometers

Directions (km): 0.0: Trebon; head toward Bridlice.

1.5: Bridlice; turn **LEFT** toward Dunajovice following cycle path No. 122.

5.7: Dunajovice.

8.0: Horní Slovenice; cycle along the pond (Dvoriste) following cycle path No. 122.

10.6: Continue following cycle path No. 122.

18.2: Turn **RIGHT** following cycle path No.122 (road No.146).

19.0: Kolmy (road No. 146).

19.3: Turn **RIGHT** toward Lhotice-road No.146.

20.8: Turn **RIGHT** toward Lhotice-road No.146.

21.5: Lhotice.

23.0: Continue **STRAIGHT** to Hluboká-road No. 146.

25.4: Continue **STRAIGHT** to Hluboká-road No. 146.

28.5: Hluboká; follow cycle path No. 12 toward Bavorovice.

32.0: Bavorovice; follow cycle path No. 12 along the Vlatava river to Ceske Budejovice.

38.3: ceské Budejovice (good lunch stop). To continue, follow cycle path No. 12 to Borsov nad Vltavou.

45.3: Borsov nad Vltavou; follow signs to Kamenny Újezd.

48.2: Kamenny Újezd; follow signs to Rancice.

50.1: Rancice; follow signs to Opalice.

51.7: Opalice; follow cycle path No. 12 toward Radostice.

52.7: Radostice; follow cycle path No. 12 toward Záluzí.

53.3: Turn **RIGHT** toward Záluzí following cycle path No. 12.

53.2: Záluzí (still on cycle path No. 12); follow signs to Stekre.

54.4: Stekre; follow signs to Zlatá Koruna.

55.9: Zlatá Koruna (still on cycle path No. 12); follow signs to Srnin.

56.9: Turn **LEFT** toward Srnín.

57.5: Turn **LEFT** toward Srnín.

58.6: Srnín; follow signs toward Prísecná.

59.9: Prísecná; follow road No. 39 to Cesky Krumlov.

63.0: Cesky Krumlov.

Czech signage is prominent and easy to spot—even if you can't understand the message. *Niels Povlsen*

Background Notes

Where Am I?
Country: Czech Republic
Region: Central Bohemia
Province: Stredocesky kraj
City: Pribram

Tourist Information
Information center (housed in the local library)
Library Jana Drdy
Namesti T.G.Masaryka 156
261 80 Pribram
Phone : 318 622 384
Fax : 318 628 179
icko@kjd.pb.cz;
knohovna@kjd.pb.cz
www.kjd.pb.cz

Bike Shops
Jizdni Kola: Sici stroje, Plzenska 76
   Kobra Sport: Kpt. Olesnickeho 51

Sightseeing
The **Zvíkov Castle** was built as a royal castle in the thirteenth century. It's open Tuesday through Sunday from 9 a.m. to 5:30 p.m.

   Orlík Castle, a neo-Gothic style castle from the thirteenth century, has a magnificent interior. It's open Tuesday through Sunday from 9 a.m. to 5 p.m.

   When you're near Pribram, check out the Mining Museum (Hornicke Muzeum), a shrine to the area's mining past, in the southwestern suburb of Brezove Hory. It's open Tuesday through Sunday from 9 a.m. to 3 p.m.

   Also visit **Svata Hora** (Holy Mountain), home to one of the largest pilgrimage churches in the country. You can reach the shrine from a covered stairway that begins on Dlouha Street. It's open daily from 8:30 a.m. to 5 p.m.

Restaurants
My groups eat at **Hotel Modry Hrozen.** The restaurant serves filling Czech dishes for a very reasonable half-pension supplement (about $6 at today's exchange).

CESKY KRUMLOV TO PRIBRAM
ROUTE NOTES

Day 7: Cesky Krumlov to Pribram

Begin the day with a private transfer to Zvikov, bypassing a relatively uninteresting stretch of terrain. You'll then cycle to Orlik and its thirteenth-century castle, a wonderfully restored estate set amidst a lush forest. You'll finish your ride in the pilgrimage town of Pribram.

Distance: 58 kilometers

Directions (km): 0.0: Start in the Zvíkovské Podhradí parking area; head toward Kucer.

3.6: Continue **STRAIGHT** toward Milevsko (Sobedraz).

5.0: Turn **LEFT** toward Sobedraz.

7.8: Sobedraz; head toward Kostelec nad Vltavou.

9.6: Turn **LEFT** toward Kostelec nad Vltavou.

11.6: Continue **STRAIGHT** toward Orlík nad Vltavou.

14.2: Zdákov bridge.

16.2: Orlík nad Vlatvou; retrace your route toward Kostelec nad Vltavou.

18.2: Zdákov bridge.

20.8: Turn **LEFT** toward Voltyrov, Zahorany 6, Prehr, Orlik 17.

22.3: Turn **LEFT**.

26.1: Continue **STRAIGHT** toward Voltyrov.

27.9: Voltyrov; turn **RIGHT** toward Klucenice.

29.5: Klucenice; turn **LEFT** toward Koubalova Lhota, Prehrada Orlik 7.

30.7: Turn **LEFT** at the café.

32.0: Koubalova Lhota; follow signs to Klenovice.

33.0: Klenovice; follow signs to Solenice.

34.7: Turn **LEFT** for Prehrada 2.

38.1: Orlík dam; continue **STRAIGHT** to Solenice.

39.6: Turn **RIGHT** toward Solenice (180-degree turn).

40.6: Solenice; head toward Horní Hbity.

45.7: Turn **LEFT** toward Horní Hbity.

46.9: Horní Hbity; continue toward Jablonná.

48.1: Jablonná; head toward Príbram.

53.4: Continue straight toward Príbram on road No. 118.

57.6: Príbram.

Background Notes
Where Am I?
Country: Czech Republic
Region: Praha
Province: Stredocesky
City: Prague

Tourist Information

Prague Information Service
Betlemske Namesti 2
Prague 11698
Phone: 012 444
info@czechtourism.cz; tourinfo@pis.cz
www.prague-info.cz

Sightseeing

There are tons of sites to see in Prague. See http://www.prague-info.cz/a/prague/aplan.html for a comprehensive listing of attractions.

Prague Castle is the official residence of the Czech president and is an extraordinary complex, worthy of at least a 3 to 4 hour visit. It's open daily from 9 a.m. to 5 p.m., and admission is 120 CZK.

Charles Bridge is one of the finest medieval bridges in Europe and dates from the fourteenth century.

The **National Gallery's** (Narodni Muzeum, Vaclavske Nam. 68) dramatic structure fooled the Communists during their 1968 invasion. They thought it was a government building and fired on it. It's open daily from 9 a.m. to 5 p.m., and admission is 70 CZK.

The **State Jewish Museum** manages all of the Jewish landmarks within Prague, including the Ceremonial Hall, Old Jewish Cemetery, Old-New Synagogue, Pinkas Synagogue, Klaus Synagogue, Maisel Synagogue, and Spanish Synagogue. The admission to all of the museum parts is 300 CZK. It's open Sunday through Thursday from 9 a.m. to 6 p.m. and Friday from 9 a.m. to 5 p.m.

If you're interested in Jewish history, you can also contact Wittmann Tours. Sylvie Wittmann offers programs within Prague's Jewish Quarter and the countryside. The tour to Terezin, a World War II concentration camp, is a remarkable educational trip. Contact Sylvie at (2) 222 524 72 or cell (0603) 42664. The tours range from 3 to 7 hours and cost from 600 CZK.

Wenceslas Square is one of Prague's three main historic squares.

Restaurants

Pubs, or *hospody*, offer inexpensive Czech dining options. Some of the best are **Pivnice Radegast** (Templova 2, open 11 a.m. to 12 a.m.), **Restaurant U Cizuku** (Karlovo Nam. 34, open 10 a.m. to 10 p.m.), and **U Medvidku** (Na Perstyne 7, open until 11 p.m).

If you'd rather dine in a traditional restaurant, try **Café Restaurant Louvre** (Czech food, Narodni Trida 20, open until 11 p.m.), **Klub Architektu** (Czech food, Betlemske Nam. 5a, open until 12 a.m.), and **Radost FX Café** (Vegetarian, Belehradska 120, open 11:30 a.m. to 4:30 a.m).

And finally, moderate to expensive choices include **Le Café Colonial** (French, Siroka 6, open until 1a.m.; Phone: 02 2481 8322), **Ostroff** (Italian, Strelecky Ostrov 336, open daily until 10:30 p.m.; Phone: 02 2491 9235), and **Kampa Park** (Seafood, Na Kampe 8b, open until 1a.m.; Phone: 02 5753 2685).

Prague Castle's grandeur is heightened by a daily parade of military guards, whose exhibition far surpasses similar displays, such as the one at London's Buckingham Palace. *Niels Povlsen*

PRIBRAM TO PRAGUE
ROUTE NOTES

Day 8: Pribram to Prague
You'll cycle first to the dramatic fourteenth-century castle of Karlstejn, a spectacular estate set in a remarkable, fairytale-like setting of forests and vineyards, perched high atop a hillside. From there, you'll need to arrange for a transfer to Prague because the cycling between Karlstejn and Prague is unsafe. Plan on spending at least two to three full sightseeing days in Prague, one of my favorite cities.

Distance: 39 kilometers

Directions (km): 0.0: Príbram; follow signs to Hlubos.

    7.0: Hlubor; follow road No. 118 to Cenkov.

    10.5: Cenkov; follow road No. 118 to Bestín.

    13.3: Turn **RIGHT** to Bestín onto road No. 115.

    16.9: Bestín; head toward Hostomice.

    19.4: Hostomice; follow road No. 115 toward Skripel.

    21.8: Skrípel; follow road No. 115 toward Osov.

    22.8: Turn **LEFT** (unmarked).

    23.0: Turn **RIGHT** toward Osov (road No. 115).

    23.4: Osov; follow road No. 115 toward Osovec.

    24.0: Osovec; follow road No. 115 to Vízina.

    25.0: Vízina; follow road No. 115 to Skuhrov.

    28.7: Skuhrov; follow road No. 115 to Hate.

    30.1: Hate; follow road No. 115 to Hodyne.

    31.0: Hodyne; follow road No. 115 to Svinare.

    32.0: Svinare; turn **LEFT** toward Zadní Trebán (Liten).

    32.6: Turn **RIGHT** toward Zadní Trebán.

    35.6: Zadní Trebán; continue **STRAIGHT** and follow the road as it curves left. Head toward Karlstejn.

    36.4: Turn **LEFT** behind the bridge to Karlstejn-road No. 116.

    36.7: Turn **LEFT** to Karlstejn-road No. 116.

    38.5: Karlstejn.

From Karlstejn, you'll need to arrange a transfer to Prague. See Luggage Transfer section for information.

PART 3

FINAL CONSIDERATIONS

PAINT THE LINES TOUR

For those who want to combine physical activity with European civic-minded-ness, the internationally renowned and very festive *Schilder De Lijnen Tocht*—Paint the Lines Tour—is a perfect acclimation to European cycling. And as all great Dutch stories do, this one traces its roots to a lazy government worker, his Belgian mistress, and far too much genever (Dutch gin).

It was January 1952 when Jan Van de Groop, an employee with the Dutch Highway Association (DHA), was assigned the unenviable task of painting the highway median stripe from Rijswijk to Schiedam, along what is now the A4-Highway. Typical of Western European bureaucracies of the time period, the Dutch government wired the 4,000 Dutch guilders (roughly $2,000) into his ABN savings account, instructing him to purchase supplies from local distributors and complete the 15-kilometer stretch of road within 12 years.

For some perspective on pricing, in 1952, the average Noord Brabaant house cost 2,254 guilders,[77] so the 4,000-guilder stipend was a powerful temptress for the gregarious de Groop (he was well known on the local club scene and a very generous tipper, especially for a Dutchman). By 1964, the figure had remained relatively stable and had increased to only 2,300 guilders.[78]

De Groop wasted little time pilfering the government's highway funds, and by 1954, the entire 4,000 guilder balance had been spent on song requests to local DJs.

Skip ahead to December 1963, the month before the DHA's project deadline. De Groop was feeling the strains of his fiscal irresponsibility, and he was a clinical alcoholic by even the loosest standards (Irish). His dubious behavior had crept into his personal life, and he was regularly seen entertaining an Antwerp coed on Den Haag trams.

---

[77] From *Historical Dutch Housing Costs for Dummies*, page 2.
[78] Ibid, page 3.

An Azerbaijan cyclist prepares his bike for his seventh Paint the Lines Tour. "Yakstu mofel yeshtu poma," he responds, when asked what he likes best about the annual event. Amen to that. *Jerry Soverinsky*

December 25, 1963, Christmas Day.

Snow blanketed the forested landscape of Steenvoorde, De Groop's hometown. Jan hadn't been sober in nearly a month, and his wife and three children had departed days earlier for Breda, to spend the holidays with strangers.

"Six days to go," he thought to himself, as he massaged the shoulders of his Belgian concubine, Miek. "I'm in trouble." He placed his head in his hands and wept, shaking violently with convulsive spasms.

Miek giggled but said nothing, for she had no sound advice, owing to the fact that she was dumb. As the hour approached seven, she bid him adieu.

"I'm bored, Jan," she said, walking her bicycle delicately across his front room (Jan was fiercely proud of the linoleum that he personally installed, and he was adamant that no one would ride a bicycle across it). She wedged her flowing corn rows into her thick, wool cap, and she kissed Jan goodbye.

"*Goeden nacht,*" she said softly. Good night.

As she exited the front door, she inadvertently knocked over the lone paint can that Jan had bought, his futile purchase that he hoped might stretch for the duration of his road project.

"My linoleum!" he cried, watching helplessly as a bright marigold puddle seeped into the floor's foundation. "Jeepers!"

Miek was unaware of the spillage, for besides her thick, wool cap that muffled external sounds, she was, alas, still dumb.

Jan ran for the door and called after Miek, but she was pedaling away, thinking about penguins.

"My floor! My floor!" he shrieked into the still night, to no one in particular, but everyone in general. "Why can't you be more careful!"

But Miek was now gone, coasting effortlessly down his street, whistling an obscure song that a neighbor would later swear sounded like jazz. Jan watched helplessly as she moved further away, a sharp, gold line emanating from her rear wheel, affixing itself to the street.

"Miek!" he cried, one last attempt to bring order to an untenable situation. "Miek!!!"

If you wanna meet the mayor in Bullay, Germany, you gotta go through this woman first. *Jerry Soverinsky*

He fell to his knees, contorting his body into a fetal-like state, writhing with the pain of opportunities lost. He glanced one last time after Miek, her angelic figure gliding toward the horizon, the bright yellow paint from her rear wheel tracing a reminder of relationships lost. He shook his head solemnly, the painful demise slowly making its presence felt.

"But what's this, could it be?" he thought to himself numbly, as he rubbed his eyes and stood, carefully evaluating the bright streaks of yellow that adorned his street.

"The paint," he began, "the paint that touched her tires, she's painting a line, she's painting a line . . ."

He stumbled forward, the effects of his drinking disturbing his balance, but determined to follow the line.

"The line!" he cried, wheezing as he barreled his way down the street, tracing its contours sensually with his forefinger. "The line!!!"

His balance improved and he was now rushing down the street with a resolve that had carved its purpose from a lifetime of failures, laughing and dancing hysterically with passion.

"The line! The line!"

Half a kilometer away, the line was still noticeable and strong, and he stopped, exhausted, releasing his body into a spent heap on the barren pavement. He was laughing—or was it crying?—with a force that once again brought spasms to Jan's withered body.

"The line!!!!!!!"

It's been said that the best ideas are born from awareness,[79] and this could easily be the epitaph on Jan's tombstone, except that he's not yet dead and hasn't left burial instructions.

"I must get the people to help paint the lines, only then will I complete my task on time," he mumbled to himself, with an intensity that reeked of newborn confidence. Less than 48 hours later, after an intensive marketing campaign, Jan's efforts had paid off, for he had miraculously attracted hundreds of locals who were

Cycling over train tracks takes special care.
Jerry Soverinsky

---

[79] I said it, in order to provide a convenient transition.
[80] A junior college in Limburg still offers the 4-credit "Christmas of '63" as a core class in its marketing program.

Guys, do everyone a favor and leave your tank tops at home. *Cork-Kerry Tourism*

eager to "paint the lines" as Jan had promised in his ubiquitous shopping center circulars.

"Come paint the lines and drink beer!" was his catch phrase, a line that would be used endlessly in Dutch university marketing classes for decades to come.[80]

December 31, 1963. The Rijswijk Convention Center parking lot.

It was a beautiful winter day, the air crisp and the sky blue. By 9:45 a.m., Jan had counted 300 beer-crazy Dutchmen and their faithful bicycles, all eager to help "paint the lines" from Rijswijk to Schiedam, the lone rewards being a bottomless mug of Heineken and congratulations by Jan for a job well done.

The event was remarkably successful, and despite some stray green paint blotches near the tiny hamlet of Schilpluiden,[81] Jan's roadwork project was completed by 2:00 p.m.—on time and on budget.[82]

The festivities at the finish line in Schiedam lasted well into the New Year. In addition to overflowing kegs of Heineken, someone had the foresight to bring pretzels, and a true party tradition had begun.

Today, almost 40 years later, the ritual continues. The tour was opened to all members of the EC in 1975, and to "Cyclists of the World," as its television campaign blared in 44 countries, in 1979.

In fact, despite political tensions and a weak global economy, 2003 saw roughly 21,000 eager cyclists, from near and far, "Paint the Lines" from Rijswijk to Schiedam. The youngest was a 4-day-old infant from Beijing, who was pulled in a trailer by a very proud father (and nursed en route by a very tired mother), and the oldest, a 112-year-old woman from Ottawa adorned in 70 Canadian patches.

And standing proudly by the finish line in Schiedam was Jan, with his Belgian mistress, Miek, a tight wool cap encasing the wispy strands of gray hair that had long since replaced her corn rows. She was smiling but saying nothing, for she was, alas, still dumb.

They were handing out glasses of Heineken to all who finished, and Jan was congratulating one and all for a job well done.

Author's Note: For more information on **Schilder De Lijnen Tocht**, *contact me directly at* info@cbttours.com.

---

[81] Rumor spread that it was a Frenchmen who had infiltrated the tour, attempting to create havoc by introducing a non-primary color. This has never been substantiated and has been relegated to local myth.
[82] Conditions for the free beer stated that riders needed to bring their own paint, a modest requirement for the paint-crazy Dutch.

Essential Language

While you'll be able to find your way comfortably through Europe without knowledge of a foreign language, you'll enhance your International Experience if you equip yourself with a few important phrases. I've found the ones below to be the bare minimum necessary to ensure effortless communications. For your target country, consult the website http://www.worldlanguage.com and select the language that you need (French, German, Dutch, Italian, Czech—they're all there).

At the airport/On an airplane:

Do you have any seats next to people who [shower/ use deodorant]?

Is the decimal point on these price tags in the correct position?

What's with all the Adidas sweatsuits?

What do you mean, keep my voice down?

In a Restaurant

No, seriously, what am I eating?

I said coffee, not espresso. Oh, this is coffee? Sorry.

What do you mean, "A coat and tie?" That's ridiculous, I didn't bring one.

At a Hotel

What channel's CNN?

Oh? You don't allow your guests to take silverware from the breakfast room? My bad.

No ice machines? That's ridiculous.

And have her bring a plunger, too.

At a Hostel

What do you mean, "Put on my shoes?" It's a kitchen, for heaven's sake!

Would you like to have sex in the [shower/game room/dining hall/manager's office/bathroom]?

I'll trade you an apple for some rice.

I'd like to report a theft.

At a Museum/While Sightseeing

Lines, shmines. I'm an American. Let me through.

(While banging on museum entrance door) I know you're closed, but I came all the way from Texas! Hello?! I see you!

"Vahehi or vehetzi shmi, lech levo morai techin. Orehai tzion barech eetam. O-techam verey, ohev tishlav, vehetzi, vehetzi Europey otech yevu barah yevarelechah moshieav trurah." Enjoy your trip and travel safely. *Kandersteg Tourismus*

How fabulous! Look how fabulous! Isn't that fabulous?!

Can I get a different headset? This one's covered with ear wax.

Interacting With Locals

Please remove your [hands/feet/tongue] from my wife's [elbow/buttocks/cheek/breasts].

That's not my leg.

Are you litigious?

Glossary

In any 400-page book, there are bound to be words that escape your normal usage. Here's my guide to those words and phrases most frequently misunderstood.

Alp Horn: traditional Swiss instrument used to frighten wildlife.

Bag Pipes: traditional Scottish instrument used to frighten people.

Bicycle: see *turshlot*.

Belgian beer: eighth wonder of the world.

Belgian chocolate: ninth wonder of the world.

Belgium: what's left if you take the mountains out of Switzerland.

British beer: see *under-chilled*.

Dutch: secondary language taught in schools throughout Holland.

Euro: clever abbreviation for *European*.

Four-star Italian hotel: Swiss youth hostel.

France: see *forgetful, ungrateful*. Adj. *French*. Antonym: happy.

Gelato: tenth wonder of the world.

Helmet: vital protective headgear for American cyclists; decorative planter used by Europeans.

Italian coffee: eleventh wonder of the world.

Lycra shorts (for men): silly.

Lycra shorts (for women): smart.

Mortadella factory tour: effective method for converting carnivores to vegetarians.

Parisian taxi: see *deathmobile, coffin, killing machine, life remover*.

Peat: what's left if you remove the pubs from Ireland.

Swiss neutrality: see *bogus, anachronistic, charade, hoax*.

Turshlot: Cro Magnon for *bicycle*. See also *turshlov* (Eastern Mediterranean variant).

Whiskey: Irish spirit, consumed whenever Guinness tap is dry.

Whisky: Scottish spirit, consumed whenever possible.

Closing Words

As I write these words, my athletic Dutch lady-friend is massaging my feet, we're trying to stay awake watching a James Ivory film, nibbling foie gras petit fours, washing them down with steins of German beer, the strains of Placido Domingo wafting from my stereo, while gazing at the brilliant Irish landscape in a picture that's hanging on my Nevada trailer-home wall.

Life is good.

But, oh, how much sweeter the massage would feel if I were on a North Sea beach, watching the film in a West End Cineplex, eating dinner at a Quartier Latin café, quenching my thirst at a Bavarian beer hall, listening to a live performance at Milan's Opera House, and breathing in the invigorating sea air at the Cliffs of Moher.

Life is better.

Wherever your passions may lead, may you experience all that Europe has to offer, from its heavenly French croissants to its majestic Alpine peaks, and from its scrumptious Dutch gevulde koeken to its golden Tuscan sunsets.

Vahehi or vehetzi shmi, lech levo morai techin.[83]

National shall not lift up sword against Nation.

Orehai tzion barech eetam.

Neither shall Man learn how to knit.

O-techam verey, ohev tishlav, vehetzi, vehetzi Europey . . .

For when traveling to Europe . . .

. . . otech yevu barah . . .

. . . do not forget . . .

. . . yevarelechah moshieav trurah.

. . . your asthma medication.

Enjoy your trip and travel safely.

—*Jerry Soverinsky*
Chicago, Illinois
January 2004
jerry@cbttours.com

---

[83] Ancient blessing, transliterated text.

About the Author

Jerry Soverinsky has been guiding and developing European cycling trips since 1985. He started his own company, CBT Tours (www.cbttours.com), in 1989 while he was a law school student. Since then, he has hosted travelers from 49 U.S. states (come on, North Dakota!) and 14 countries on his European tours.

Soverinsky is a graduate of Chicago's Second City Training Center and has been a recent contributor to *Adventure Cycling* and NationalLampoon.com.

Jerry lives in Chicago and dates women who like men who drink chocolate milk.

Feel free to write him directly with comments about this book or our nation's poaching laws at jerry@cbttours.com or jecbt@hotmail.com.

TYPE	NAME	ADDRESS	PHONE	FAX

IRELAND & SOUTHWEST COAST ACCOMMODATIONS NOTES

I don't recommend camping in Ireland. Irish campgrounds are mostly caravan parks, and the abundant rain along the southwest coast makes camping uncomfortable.

CASTLETOWNBERE

TYPE	NAME	ADDRESS	PHONE	FAX
2-star hotel	Cametringane Hotel	Castletownbere, Co. Cork	(027) 70379	(027) 70506
B&B	Island View B&B	Castletownbere, West Cork	(027) 70415	
B&B	Old Presbytery	Castletownbere, Brandy Hall	(027) 70424	(0)27 70420
B&B	Rodeen Country Home		(027) 70158	
Hostel	Harbour Lodge Hostel	Castletownbere, West Cork	(027) 71043	(027) 71983

KENMARE

TYPE	NAME	ADDRESS	PHONE	FAX
5-star hotel	Sheen Falls Lodge	Kenmare, Co. Kerry	064 41600	064 41386
3-star hotel	Riversdale House	Kenmare, Co. Kerry	064 41299	064 41075
B&B	The Coachman's Inn	Henry St.; Kenmare	064 41311	064 41311
Hostel	Failte Hostel	Shelbourne St.; Kenmare	064 42333	064 42466
Campground	Ring of Kerry Camping	Kenmare, Co. Kerry	064 41648	064 41631

KILLARNEY

TYPE	NAME	ADDRESS	PHONE	FAX
5-star hotel	Hotel Europe	Killarney, Co. Kerry	064 31900	064 32118
4-star hotel	Great Southern Torc	Killarney, Co. Kerry	064 31262	064 31642
3-star hotel	Eviston Hotel	New Street, Killarney	064 31640	064 33685
B&B	Crystal Springs	Ballycasheen Cross, Killarney	064 33272	064 35518
Hostel	Neptune's Hostel	New Street, Killarney	064 35255	064 32310
Campground	Killarney Flesk	Muckross Rd., Killarney	064 31704	064 35439

DINGLE

TYPE	NAME	ADDRESS	PHONE	FAX
4-star hotel	Dingle Skellig	Dingle	066 9150200	066 9151501
4-star guesthouse	Heaton's	The Wood, Dingle	066 9152288	066 9152324
3-star hotel	Benner's Hotel	Main Street, Dingle	066 9151638	066 9151412
B&B	Doonshean	Garfinney, Dingle	066 9151032	
Hostel	Ballintaggart	Dingle	066 9151454	066 9151412
Campground	Ballintaggart	Dingle	066 9151454	066 9151412

TRALEE

TYPE	NAME	ADDRESS	PHONE	FAX
4-star hotel	Ballygarry House	Killarney Rd., Tralee	066 7123322	066 7127630
3-star hotel	Abbey Gate Hotel	Main St., Tralee	066 712 9888	066 712 9821
B&B	The Willows	5 Clonmore Terr., Tralee	066 712 3779	
Hostel	Collis Sandes	Oak Park, Tralee	066 7128658	066 7128658

KILKEE

TYPE	NAME	ADDRESS	PHONE	FAX
3-star hotel	Kilkee Bay Hotel	Kilrush Rd., Kilkee	065 9060060	065 9060062
2-star hotel	Ocean Cove	Kilkee Bay, Kilkee	065 6823000	065 9083123
B&B	Murphy's	1 Marine Parade, Kilkee		065 9056026

DOOLIN

TYPE	NAME	ADDRESS	PHONE	FAX
3-star hotel	Ballinalacken Castle	Coast Rd., Doolin	065 7074025	065 7074025
B&B	Harbour View	Boherbui House, Doolin	065 7074154	065 7074935
Hostel	Paddy's	Fisher St., Doolin	065 7074006	065 7074421

EMAIL	WEB	PRICE (per-person, 1/2 twin, Euros)
info@camehotel.com	http://www.camehotel.com/	40-50
islandview@iolfree.ie	http://www.islandviewhouse.com/	20-23
marywrigley@tinet.ie	http://www.midnet.ie/oldpresbytery/index.htm	20-25
rodeen@utvinternet.ie	http://www.welcome.to/rodeen/	32
bearalodge@eircom.net	www.bearainfo.com/accommodations/hostel/harbourlodge.htm	12+
info@sheenfallslodge.ie	www.sheenfallslodge.ie	130 to 750
riversdale@eircom.net	www.riversdalehousehotel.com	45 to 100
info@thecoachmans.com	www.thecoachmans.com	25-35
failtefinn@eircom.net	http://www.neidin.net/failtehostel/	12-16
info@kerrycamping.com	www.kerrycamping.com	8+
sales@kih.liebherr.com	http://www.killarneyhotels.ie/europe/contact.html	90-500
res@killrney-gsh.com	www.gsh.ie	75+
evishtl@eircom.net	http://www.killarney-hotel.com/	39-69
crystalsprings@eircom.net	http://www.crystalspringsbnb.com/	30-40
neptune@eircom.net	www.neptuneshostel.com	11-35
killarneylakes@eircom.net		8+
dsk@iol.ie	www.dingleskellig.com	60-200
heatons@iol.ie	www.heatonsdingle.com	40-85
benners@eircom.net	www.bennershotel.com	55-102
doonsheanview@eircom.net	http://homepage.eircom.net/~doonsheanview/	26.50-30
info@dingleaccommodation.com	www.dingleaccommodation.com	12.50-27.50
info@dingleaccommodation.com	www.dingleaccommodation.com	11+
bllygarry@eircom.net	www.ballygarry.com	95
abbeygat@iol.ie	www.abbeygate-hotel.com	55-80
2thewillows@eircom.net	www.thewillowsbnb.com	30
colsands@indigo.ie	www.colsands.com	15+
info@kilkee-bay.com	www.kilkee-bay.com	40-49
reservations@lynchotels.com	www.oceancovehotel.com	35
	acantrel@gofreeindigo.ie	32
ballinalackencastle@eircom.net	www.ballinalackcastle.com	80-100
kathlen@eircom.ie	www.harbourviewdoolin.com	30
doolinhostel@eircom.net	www.kingsway.ie/doolinhostel	15+

TYPE	NAME	ADDRESS	PHONE	FAX

SCOTLAND'S HIGHLANDS

NAIRN

TYPE	NAME	ADDRESS	PHONE	FAX
4-star hotel	Newton Hotel	Inverness Rd., Nairn	01667 453144	01667 454026
3-star hotel	Windsor Hotel	16 Albert St., Nairn	01667 453108	01667 456108
2-star hotel	Braeval Hotel	Crescent Rd., Nairn	01667 452341	
Campground	Camping Nairn	Delnies Wood, Nairn	01667 455281	

GRANTOWN-ON-SPEY

TYPE	NAME	ADDRESS	PHONE	FAX
4-star hotel	Auchendean Lodge	Dulnain Bridge	1479 851 347	1479 851 347
3-star hotel	Garth	Castle Road	1479 872 836	1479 872 116
2-star hotel	Ben Mhor	53-57 High St.	1479 872 056	1479 873 537
B&B	Birchwood B&B	12 Rowan Park, Carrbridge	1479 841 393	1479 841 393
Hostel	Ardenbeg Bunkhouse	Grant Rd.	1479 872 824	1479 873 132
Campground	Caravan Park	Seafield Avenue	1479 872 474	

BRAEMAR

TYPE	NAME	ADDRESS	PHONE	FAX
3-star hotel	Invercauld Arms	Braemar	01339 741 605	01339 741 428
B&B	Craiglea	Hillside Dr.	013397 41641	013397 41641
Hostel	Braemar YH	Glenshee Rd.	013397 41659	013397 41659
Campground	Invercauld Caravan	Glenshee Rd.	013397 41373	

PITLOCHRY

TYPE	NAME	ADDRESS	PHONE	FAX
4-star hotel	Green Park	Clunie Bridge Rd.	01796 473248	01796 473520
3-star hotel	Fishers Hotel	Atholl Rd.	01796 472000	01796 473949
2-star hotel	Bridge of Tilt	Blair Atholl	01796 481333	01796 481335
B&B		Kinnaird, Pitlochry	01796 470100	
Hostel	Pitlochry YH	Konckard Rd.	01796 472308	
Campground	Faskally Camping		01796 472 007	

ENGLAND'S COTSWOLDS

British B&Bs, as mentioned in the introduction section, are not your typical Vermont-adultery-weekend-type. Well, some are, but others are not. Many bedrooms lack private facilities and are in desperate need of renovation. If you've found what you think to be too good a deal, it probably is too good to be true. Double-check to ensure that you'll be receiving what you expect. Camping in the Cotswolds is very pleasant. The story below is my experience from London camping. There is a difference.

BATH

TYPE	NAME	ADDRESS	PHONE	FAX
5-star hotel	Royal Crescent	16 Royal Crescent	01225 823333	01225 339401
4-star hotel*	Bath Priory	Weston Rd.	01225 331922	01225 448276
3-star hotel	Abbey Hotel	North Parade	01225 461603	01225 447758
2-star hotel*	Royal Hotel	Manvers St.	01225 463134	01225 442931
B&B	Avon Guest House	1 Pulteney Gardens	01225 313009	01225 313009
Hostel	City of Bath YMCA	Broad St. Place	01225 325900	01225 462065
Campground	Newton Mill Camping	Newton Rd.	01225 333909	

MALMESBURY

TYPE	NAME	ADDRESS	PHONE	FAX
3-star hotel*	King Arms	High St.	01666 823383	01666 825327
3-star hotel	Old Bell	Abbey Row	01666 822344	01666 825145
2-star hotel	Mayfield House	Crudwell	01666 577409	01666 577977
B&B	Widley's Farm	Sherston	01666 840213	01666 840156
Campground	Burton Hill	Arches Ln.	01666 826880	01666 826880

EMAIL	WEB	PRICE
		(per-person, 1/2 twin, Euros)
	www.morton-hotels.com	61-96
windsornairnscotland@btinternet.com	www.windsor-hotel.co.uk	42.50
ian@braeval-hotel.co.uk	www.braeval.co.uk	26-30
		11+
hotel@auchendean.com	www.auchendean.com	39-48
reception@garthhotel.com	www.garthhotel.com	27-35
christine@benmhorhotel.co.uk	www.benmhorhotel.co.uk	30+
normanwhitehall@lineone.net		17-20
enquiries@ardenbeg.co.uk	www.ardenbeg.co.uk	8.5+
gm.inv@barbox.net	www.shearingsholidays.com	25-40
Craigleabandb@btopenworld.com	www.craigleabraemar.com	20+
braemar@syhga.org.uk	www.syha.org.uk	10+
	www.threegreenpark.co.uk	32
fishers@crearhotels.com	www.british-trust-hotels.com	20-40
		26-41
jj.Moville@talk21.com	www.smoothhound.co.uk/hotels/movile	22-25
		12+
		8+
reservations@royalcrescent.co.uk	www.royalcrescent.co.uk	90-165
bathprioryhotel@compuserve.com	www.thebathpriory.co.uk	115-160
ahres@compasshotels.co.uk	www.compasshotels.co.uk	63-70
info@royalhotelbath.co.uk	www.royalhotelbath.co.uk	38-48
		25-28
reservations@bathymca.co.uk	www.bath-org/ymca/index	12
newtonmill@hotmail.com	www.campinginbath.co.uk	5-12
kingsarmshotel@malmesburywilts.freeserve.co.uk	www.kingsarmshotel.info	20-4
info@oldbellhotel.com	www.oldbellhotel.com	34-95
reception@mayfieldhousehotel.co.uk	36-49	
		20-35
audrey@burtonhill.co.uk	www.burtonhill.co.uk	8-10

TYPE	NAME	ADDRESS	PHONE	FAX

BURFORD

TYPE	NAME	ADDRESS	PHONE	FAX
4-star hotel	Burford House	99 High St.	01993 823151	01993 823240
3-star hotel	Bay Tree Hotel	Sheep St.	01993 822791	
Unrated	Old Bell Foundry	45 Witney St.	01993 822234	01993 824704
B&B	St. Winnow	160 The Hill	01993 823843	
Campground	New Inn	Burford OX7 6SD	01993 830827	

STOW-ON-THE-WOLD

TYPE	NAME	ADDRESS	PHONE	FAX
4-star hotel	Fosse Manor Hotel	Stow/Cheltenham	01451 830354	01451 832486
3-star hotel	Unicorn Hotel	Sheep St.	01451 830257	01451 831090
2-star hotel	Gate Lodge	Stow Hill	01451 832103	
B&B	Pear Tree Cottage	High St.	01451 8321210	

STRATFORD-UPON-AVON

TYPE	NAME	ADDRESS	PHONE	FAX
5-star hotel	Alveston Manor	Clopton Bridge	0870 400 8181	01789 414095
4-star hotel	Billesley Manor Hotel	Billesley, Alcester	01789 279955	01789 764145
3-star hotel	Swan's Nest	Bridgefoot, Stratford	0870 400 8183	01789 414547
Hostel	YHA Stratford	Hemmingford House	0870 770 6052	0870 7706053

DORDOGNE & SOUTHWEST FRANCE

BORDEAUX

There are loads of campgrounds and hotels in almost every price category, but book early, especially if you're heading over in the summer. Popular hotels tend to fill quickly.

SARLAT-LA-CANEDA

TYPE	NAME	ADDRESS	PHONE	FAX
3-star hotel	Hotel de Selves	93, Ave. de Selves	0553 31 50 00	0553 31 23 52
2-star hotel	Hostellerie Couleuvrine	1, Pl. de la Bouquerie	0553 59 27 80	0553 31 26 83
Campground	Camping Les Perieres	Les Perieres	0553 59 05 84	0553 28 57 51

ROCAMADOUR

TYPE	NAME	ADDRESS	PHONE	FAX
3-star hotel	Hotel Beau Site	Cite Medievale	0565 33 63 08	0565 33 65 23
2-star hotel	Hotel Lion D'Or	Cite Medievale	0565 33 62 04	0565 33 72 54 contact@lio
B&B	Domaine de Lagardelle	0565 33 44 03	0565 33 44 03	info@lagardelle.com
Campground	Relais du Campeur		0565 33 63 28	0565 33 69 60

CAHORS

TYPE	NAME	ADDRESS	PHONE	FAX
4-star hotel	Chateau de Mercues	46090 Mercues	0565 20 00 01	0565 20 05 72
3-star hotel	Hotel de France	252, Ave. Jean Jaures	0565 35 16 76	0565 22 01 08
2-star hotel	L'Escargot			
B&B	Anne-Marie Charazac	Pasturat	0565 31 44 94	0565 31 41 99
Campground	Quercy-Vacances	Le Mas de la Combe	0565 36 87 15	0565 36 02 39

FIGEAC

TYPE	NAME	ADDRESS	PHONE	FAX
4-star hotel	Chateau du Viguier	Rue Emile Zola	0565 50 05 05	0565 50 06 06
3-star hotel*	Hotel du Pont d'Or	2 Ave. Jean Jaures	0565 50 95 00	0565 50 95 39
2-star hotel	Hotel des Bains	1, Rue du Griffoul	0565 34 10 89	0565 14 00 45
Dorm	Gite DLV Romaine	6, Ave. de Toulouse	0565 34 21 94	
Campground	Les Rives du Cele	Le Surgie	0565 34 59 00	0565 34 83 83

ACCOMMODATIONS

EMAIL	WEB	PRICE
		(per-person, 1/2 twin, Euros)
stay@burfordhouse.co.uk	www.burfordhouse.co.uk	55+
bookings@cotswold-inns-hotels.co.uk	www.cotswold-inns-hotels.co.uk	73+
barguss@ukgateway.net		28+
b&b@stwinnow.com	www.stwinnow.com	25
		10+
		40-61
reception@birchhotels.co.uk	www.birchhotels.co.uk	23+
		20+
peartreecottage@btinternet.com		23+
sales.alvestonmanor@macdonald-hotels.co.uk	www.macdonald-hotels.co.uk	50+
bookings@billesleymanor.co.uk	www.billesleymanor.co.uk	55+
sales.alvestonmanor@heritage-hotels.co.uk	www.heritage-hotels.co.uk	35+
stratford@yha.org.uk	www.yha.org.uk	12+
hotel@selves-sarlat.com	www.selves-sarlat.com	38+
lacouleuvrine@wanadoo.fr	www.la-couleuvrine.com	30+
les-perieres@wanadoo.fr	www.campings-dordogne.com/les-perieres	18
hotel@bw-beausite.com	www.bw-beausite.com	43-53
.com	www.liondor-rocamadour.com/	31-60 (per room)
	www.lagardelle.com	19
le.comphostel@wanadoo.fr	http://www.rocamadour.com/us/campings/index.htm	10+
mercues@relaischateaux.com	www.relaischateaux.com/mercues.fr	75-125+
hdf46@hoteldefrance-cahors.fr	www.hoteldefrance-cahors.fr	20-35+
		19-30+
gitescharazac@hotmail.com		14-20
quercyvacances@wanadoo.fr		10+
hotel@chateau-viguier-figeac.com		86-117
contact@hotelpontdor.com	www.hotelpontdor.com	35-57
	www.hoteldesbains.com	26-36
		10-15
	www.domdesurgie.com	10+

TYPE	NAME	ADDRESS	PHONE	FAX

COTE D'AZUR & SOUTHERN FRANCE

Coursegoules is a tiny village and Fayence is a fairly small town, so don't expect a wide assortment of hotel choices. On the other hand, if you can do without the mundane frills that go with the more luxurious properties you'll do just find at these towns' family-run establishments. They all seem to gush with personal attention and warmth, which more than compensates for their modest facilities.

COURSEGOULES

TYPE	NAME	ADDRESS	PHONE	FAX
2-star hotel	Auberge de L'Escaou	06140 Coursegoules	0493 59 11 28	0493 59 13 70
Campground	Camping St. Antoine	06140 Coursegoules	04 93 59 12 36	

FAYENCE

TYPE	NAME	ADDRESS	PHONE	FAX
3-star hotel	Les Oliviers	Quatier la Ferrage	0494 76 13 12	0494 76 08 05
2-star hotel	Auberge Fontaine	Route de Frejus	0494 76 07 59	0494 76 07 59
Unrated	La Sousto	4, Rue du Paty	0494 76 02 16	
Campground	Le Parc	Quartier Trestaure	0494 76 15 35	0494 84 71 84

MOUSTIERS SAINTE MARIE

TYPE	NAME	ADDRESS	PHONE	FAX
4-star hotel	Bastide de Moustiers	Sud Village	0492 70 47 47	0492 70 47 48
3-star hotel	La Ferme Rose	Rte. Ste. Croix	0492 74 69 47	0492 74 60 76
2-star hotel	La Bonne Auberge	Rte. De Castellane	0492 74 66 18	0492 74 65 11
Campground	Le Vieux Colombier	Qtr. St. Michel	0492 74 61 82	

ST. MAXIMIN LA STE. BAUME

TYPE	NAME	ADDRESS	PHONE	FAX
3-star hotel	Hotel de France	Ave. Albert 1er	0494 78 00 14	0494 59 83 80
2-star hotel	Le Plaisance	20, Pl. Malherbe	0494 78 16 74	0494 78 18 39
B&B	Mme. Marie Cinelli	522, Ch. Pet. Royal	0494 78 16 73	
Campground	Le Provencal	Rte. De Mazagues	0494 78 16 97	0494 78 0022

AIX-EN-PROVENCE

TYPE	NAME	ADDRESS	PHONE	FAX
4-star hotel	Chateau de la Pioline	260, Rue Guillaume	0442 52 27 27	0442 52 27 28
3-star hotel	Amdeus	Montee d'Avignon	0442 23 20 99	0442 21 27 29
2-star hotel	Arquier	Rte. D. Pet. Moulin	0442 24 20 45	0442 24 29 52
Campground	Airotel Chantecler	Val St. Andre	0442 161 184	

LOIRE VALLEY

The turn-by-turn directions each begin from expensive chateaux properties, but you can still cycle the identical itineraries and stay at less expensive hotels. Below are several alternate lodging choices:

EVENING 1:

TYPE	NAME	ADDRESS	PHONE	FAX
4-star	Chateau Rochecotte	Sint Patrice, Langeais 37130	0247 96 16 16	0247 96 90 59

ALTERNATE NEARBY LODGING:

TYPE	NAME	ADDRESS	PHONE	FAX
Three-star	Errard Hosten	2 Rue Gambetta, Langeais	0247 96 82 12	0247 96 56 72
Two-star	La Duchesse Anne	10 Rue De Rours, Langeais	0247 96 82 03	0247 96 68 60
Camping Municipal		Access N2152, Langeais	0247 96 85 80	0247 96 69 23.

EVENINGS 2-4:

TYPE	NAME	ADDRESS	PHONE	FAX
Four star	Chateau d'Artigny	Montbazon 37250	0247 34 30 30	0247 34 30 39

ALTERNATE NEARBY LODGING:

TYPE	NAME	ADDRESS	PHONE	FAX
Three-star	Domaine de la Tortiniere	10, route de Ballan, Montbazon	0247 34 35 00	0247 65 95 70
	Camping La Grange Rouge *	37250, Montbazon	0247 26 06 43	0247 26 03 13

*Open May 1 through September 15

EMAIL	WEB	PRICE (per-person, 1/2 twin, Euros)
	www.hotel-escaou.com	30
		8+
Hotel.Oliviers.fayen@free.fr	www.hotel.Oliviers.fayen.free.fr	
bernard.Martin80@wanadoo.fr		26-36
hotel.sousto@wanadoo.fr		22-29
		7+
contact@bastide-moustiers.com	http://www.bastide-moustiers.com/Bastide/	115-140
infos@le-colombier.com	http://perso.wanadoo.fr/soleil2/iris/	30-68
labonneauberge@post.club-internet.fr	http://perso.club-internet.fr/lbauberg/	25-35+
camping.vieux.colombier@wanadoo.fr	ttp://perso.wanadoo.fr/camping.vieux.colombier/etranger/principale_en.htm	8+
	http://www.hotel-de-france.fr/	38
		28-31
		20
camping.provencal@wanadoo.fr		8+
info@chateau-la-pioline.fr	www.chateau-la-pioline.fr	120-205
hotelamadeus@ten.fr	ix-en-provence.com/hotelamadeus	30-60
arqui-hr@easynet.fr		36-43
resaix@aixenprovencetourism.com		8-15+
Chateau.rochecotte@wanadoo.fr	www.chateau-de-rochecotte.fr	125-800+
info@errard.com		150-175
		140-185
artigny@wanadoo.fr	www.artigny.com	80-147
domaine.tortiniere@wanadoo.fr	http://www.tortiniere.com/	64-155.

TYPE	NAME	ADDRESS	PHONE	FAX

IL MUGELLO

Except for Florence, don't expect a broad variety of hotel choices along this route. What you'll find are family-run properties whose owners will take an immediate interest in your bicycle adventures, and who will ensure that all of your needs are enthusiastically met and exceeded.

PALAZZUOLO SUL SENIO

TYPE	NAME	ADDRESS	PHONE	FAX
3-star hotel	Locanda Senio	Borgo dell'Ore 1	055 8046485	055 8046019
2-star hotel	Europa	Via M. Pagani 2/4	055 8046011	
1-star hotel	Biagi	Via Roma 55	055 8046064	
B&B	Le Panare	Lozzole 6	055 8046346	
Campground	Visano	Via Faggiola 19	055 8046106	

TREDOZIO

TYPE	NAME	ADDRESS	PHONE	FAX
2-star hotel	Albergo Caverna	Loc. Monte Busca	0546 943941	
B&B	Torre Fantini	Via S. Michele, 47	0546 943403	
Campground	Camping Le Volte	Via S. D. Acquisto, 2	0546 943161	

VICCHIO

TYPE	NAME	ADDRESS	PHONE	FAX
3-star hotel	Viola Campestri	Via di Campestri 19	055 8490107	055 8490108
1-star hotel	Antica Porta Di Levante	Piazza V. Veneto 5	055 844050	
B&B	Farnetino	Via Pirlaciano 53	055 8497372	
Campground	Vecchio Ponte	Via Costoli 16	055 8448306	055 579405

RUFINA

TYPE	NAME	ADDRESS	PHONE	FAX
3-star hotel	La Speranza	Via Piave 14	055 8397027	055 8397028
2-star hotel	Da Marino	Via Forlivese 21	055 8397030	055 8398567
B&B[1]	Fattoria I Busini	Via Scopeti 12	055 8397809	055 8397004

ITALY'S TUSCANY

GREVE-IN-CHIANTI

TYPE	NAME	ADDRESS	PHONE	FAX
3-star hotel	Giovanni da Verrazzano	Piazza Matteotti 28	055 8546098	055 853648
2-star hotel	Da Omero	Via G. Falcone	055 850716	055 850495
B&B	Casa Nova	Via Uzzano 30	055 853459	055 853459
Hostel	Villa San Michele	Via Casole	055 851034	055 851034

SAN GIMIGNANO

TYPE	NAME	ADDRESS	PHONE	FAX
4-star hotel	Relais Santa Chiara	Via G. Matteotti 15	0577 940701	0577 942096
3-star hotel	La Cisterna	P. della Cisterna	0577 940328	0577 942080
1-star hotel	Latini	Loc. Steccaia	0577 945019	0577 945022
Campground	Il Boschetto	Loc. Santa Lucia	0577 940352	0577 941982

SIENA

TYPE	NAME	ADDRESS	PHONE	FAX
5-star hotel	Grand Hotel	Banchi Di Sopra 85	0577 56011	0577 5601555
4-star hotel	Villa Scacciapensieri	Scacciapensieri 10	0577 41441	0577 270854
3-star hotel	Ai Tufi	Massetana Rom. 68	0577 283292	0577 284076
2-star hotel	Cannon D'Oro	Montanini 28	0577 44321	0577 280868
1-star hotel	La Perla	Delle Terme 25	0577 47144	
B&B	Il Colombaio	Strada di Renaccio	0577 378064	0577 223708
Campground	Colleverde	Scacciapensieri 47	0577 280044	0577 333298

ACCOMMODATIONS

EMAIL	WEB	PRICE
		(per-person, 1/2 twin, Euros)
info@locandasenio.it	www.locandasenio.it	62-75
	www.italiaabc.it/az/europah	32
albergo.biagi@libero.it	www.paginegialle.it/hotelbiagi	21-24
lepnare@tin.it	www.lepanare.it	31-50+
		8-15+
albergo.monte.busca@comunic.it		20-23
caffe-letto.torre.fantini@comunic.it		22-24
camping.le.volte@comunic.it		8-15+
villa.campestri@villacampestri.it	www.villacampestri.it	91+
		31+
farnetino@tiscalinet.it	www.farnetino.com	34-40
info@campingvecchioponte.it	www.campingvecchioponte.it	14+
lasperanza@caramail.com	www.tiscalinet.it/grazzini	37
		22-28
villabusini@libero.it	www.ibusini.com	50+
info@verrazzano.it	http://www.verrazzano.it	51-59
casprini@cdaomero.com		39-48
info@casanova-laripintura.it		36-45
info@villasanmichele.it	www.villasanmichele.it	18+
rsc@rsc.it	www.rsc.it	75-135
lacisterna@iol.it	www.hotelcisterna.it	45-60
latini@dada.it	http://www.ristorantelatini.com/	35-38
bpiemma@tiscalinet.it		
continental@royaldemeure.com	www.ghcs.it	155-305
villasca@tin.it	www.villascacciapensieri.it	90-118
aitufihotel@tin.it	www.tufihotel.it	48
info@cannondoro.com	www.cannondoro.com	52
		35
		52+
campingsiena@sienaturismo.toscana.it		8+

TYPE	NAME	ADDRESS	PHONE	FAX
PIENZA				
3-star deluxe	Chistro di Pienza	Corso Rossellino 26	0578 748400	0578 748440
3-star hotel	Corsignano	Via D Madonnina	0578 748501	0578 748166
2-star hotel	Albergo Rutiliano	Via D. Madonnina 18	0578 749408	0578 749409

ITALY'S UMBRIA

TYPE	NAME	ADDRESS	PHONE	FAX
PERUGIA				
5-star hotel	Brufani Palace	Piazza Italia 12	075 5732541	075 5720210
4-star hotel	Gio Arte e Vini	Via R. D'Andreotto	075 5731100	0755731100
3-star hotel	Barone	Via Tuderte 20	0755837650	075 5837651
2-star hotel	Morlacchi	Via Tiberi 2	075 5720319	075 5735084
Hostel	Della Gioventu	Via Bontempi 13	075 5722880	075 5739449
Campground	Il Rocolo	Str. Fontana d. Trinit	075 5178550	075 5178550
TODI				
4-star hotel	Hotel Bramante	Circ. Orvietna 48	075 8948381	075 8948074
3-star hotel	Hotel Villa Luisa	V. Ang. Cortesi 147	075 8948571	075 8948472
B&B	Old Roses	Voc. Maiola	075 8944644	
TREVI				
4-star hotel	Antica Dimora	Piazza della Rocca	0742 385401	0742 78925
3-star hotel	Trevi Hotel	Via fantosati	0742 780922	0742 780772
2-star hotel	Albergo Il Pescatore	Via Chiesa Tonda	0742 784833	0742 78483
1-star hotel	Albergo La Cerquetta	Via Flaminia	0742 381 455	0742 381455
ASSISI				
4-star hotel	Grand Hotel Assisi	Via F.lli Canonichetti	075 81501	075 8150777
3-star hotel	Fontebella	Via Fontebella 25	075 812883	75 812941
2-star hotel	Alexander	P.tta Chiesa Nuova 6	075 816190	075 816190
1-star hotel	Bellavista	S. P. Campagna 140	075 8041636	075 80429492
B&B	Agricola Nizzi	Costa di Trex 65	075 813378	075 8043749
Campground	Fontemaggio	Via S. Rufino	075 813636	075 813749

BEST OF SWITZERLAND

No matter your budget or accommodations preference, you'll find an extensive assortment of lodging choices on every stop along this trip. Whether you'd like to pitch a tent at a rural campground or dine among royalty at deluxe five-star hotels, you'll find abundant choices along this route. If you're planning on camping, rates in Switzerland can get expensive—$20 or so at today's exchange—by the time you add in pitch fees and taxes.

TYPE	NAME	ADDRESS	PHONE	FAX
LUZERN				
5-star hotel	Grand Hotel National	Haldenstrasse 4	041 4190909	041 4190910
4-star hotel	Ambassador	Zurichstrasse 3	041 4188100	041 4188190
3-star hotel	Alpina	Frankenstrasse 6	041 2100077	041 2108944
2-star hotel	Schlussel	Franziskanerplatz 12	041 2101061	041 2101021
Campground	Lido Camping	Lidostrasse 19	041 370 2146	
BERN				
5-star hotel	Bellevue Palace	Kochergasse 3	031 3204545	031 3114743
4-star hotel	Allegro	Kornhausstrasse 3	031 339 5500	031 3395510
3-star hotel	Metropole	Zeughausgasse 26	031 3115021	031 3121153
2-star hotel	National	Hirschengraben 24	031 3811988	031 3816878
Campground	Camping Eichholz	Strandweg 49	031 9612602	031 9613526

EMAIL	WEB	PRICE
		(per-person, 1/2 twin, Euros)
ilchiostro@jump.it	www.relaisilchiostrodipienza.com	90-110
info@corsignano.it	www.corsignano.it	38-50
info@albergorutiliano.it	www.albergorutiliano.it	50-80
brufani@tin.it		216-305
hotelgio@interbusiness.it		50-100
barone@econet.it		45-65
		50-55
		24+
		9+
bramante@hotelbramante.it	www.hotelbramante.it	130-140
villaluisa@villaluisa.it	www.villaluisa.it	60-80
oldroses@hotmail.com	www.oldroses.supereva.it	31-38
hotelallarocca@libero.it	www.hotelallarocca.it	52-156
trevihotel@tiscalinet.it		80-105
		45-50
cercquetta@bcsnet.it		45
info@grandhotelassisi.com	www.grandhotelassisi.com	70-93
info@fontebella.com	www.fontebella.com	25-145
alexander@italyhotel.com	www.assisi-hotel.com	20-60
info@assisibellavista.it	www.assisibellavista.it	22-25
nizzi@nizzi.com	www.nizzi.com	26-65
		9.50+
info@national-luzern.ch	www.national-luzern.ch	185-310
ambassador@ambassador.ch	www.ambassador.ch	105-140
hotel@alpina-luzern.ch		80-108
		43-79
direktion@bellevue-palace.ch	http://www.bellevue-palace.ch	230-270
allegro@kursaal-bern.ch	www.allegro-hotel.ch	128-230
info@hotelmetropole.ch	www.hotelmetropole.ch	85-98
info@nationalbern.ch	www.nationalbern.ch	47-75
info@campingeichholz.ch	www.campingeichholz.ch	12+

TYPE	NAME	ADDRESS	PHONE	FAX

INTERLAKEN

TYPE	NAME	ADDRESS	PHONE	FAX
5-star hotel	Victoria Jungfrau	Hoheweg 41	033 8282828	033 8282880
4-star hotel	Metropole	Hoheweg 37	033 8286666	033 8286633
3-star hotel	Carlton	Hoheweg 92	033 8223821	033 8220355
2-star hotel	Hotel Blume	Jungfraustrasse 30	033 8227131	033 8227194
B&B	Arnold's B&B	Parkstrasse 3	033 8236421	033 8233478
Hostel	Alplodge	Marktgasse 59	033 8224748	033 8232098
Campground	Manor Farm	Seestrasse 201	033 8222264	033 8222279

BULLE

TYPE	NAME	ADDRESS	PHONE	FAX
3-star hotel	Hotel les Alpes	Rue Nicolas Glass. 3	026 9129292	026 9129992
3-star hotel	Hotel le Rallye	Route de Riaz 16	026 9198040	026 9198044
B&B	Famille Rene Morel	Ch. D'Ogoz 24	026 9126878	

LAUSANNE

TYPE	NAME	ADDRESS	PHONE	FAX
5-star hotel	Beau Rivage	P. du Port 17	021 6133333	021 6133334
4-star hotel	Agora	Ave. Rond Point 9	021 6171211	021 6162605
3-star hotel	Alagare	Rue du Simplon 14	021 6179252	021 6179255
2-star hotel	De L'Ours	Rue du Bugnon	021 3204971	021 3204973
Hostel	Lausanne Guesthouse	Chemin des Epinettes	021 6018000	021 6018001
Campground	Camping de Vidy	Chemin du Camping	021 6225000	021 6225001

SWITZERLAND MOUNTAIN BIKE CHALLENGE

GRINDELWALD

TYPE	NAME	PHONE	FAX
5-star hotel	Regina	033 8548600	033 8548688
4-star hotel	Eiger	033 8543131	033 8543130
3-star hotel	Central Hotel Wolter	033 8543333	033 8543339
3-star hotel	Bernerhof	033 853 1021	033 853 4646
2-star hotel	Lauberhorn	033 8531082	033 8531571
Hostel	Jugendherberge	033 8531009	033 8535029
Campground	Gletscherdorf	033 8531429	033 8533129

LAUTERBRUNNEN

TYPE	NAME	PHONE	FAX
3-star hotel	Schuten	033 8552032	033 8552950
2-star hotel	Oberland	033 8551241	033 8554241
B&B	Schutzenbach	033 8551268	033 8551275
Campground	Camping Jungfrau	033 8562010	033 8562020

GRIESALP

TYPE	NAME	PHONE	FAX
NR	Hotel Berghaus	033 6761231	033 6761242
NR	Berggasthus Golderli	033 6762192	033 6762192

KANDERSTEG

TYPE	NAME	PHONE	FAX
5-star hotel	Royal Park Hotel	033 6758888	033 6758880
4-star hotel	Doldenhorn	033 6758181	033 6758185
3-star hotel	Adler	033 6758010	033 6758011
2-star hotel	Alpina	033 6751246	033 6751233
Campground	Rendezvous	033 6751354	033 6751445

ADELBODEN

TYPE	NAME	PHONE	FAX
4-star hotel	Hotel Beau-Site	033 6732222	033 6733333

EMAIL	WEB	PRICE (per-person, 1/2 twin, Euros)
interlaken@victoria-jungfrau.ch	www.victoria-jungfrau.ch	265-360
mail@metropole-interlaken.ch	www.metropole-interlaken.ch	125-180
info@carlton-interlaken.com	www.carlton-interlaken.com	80-120
hotel-blume@tcnet.ch	www.hotel-blume.ch	35-75
arnolds@bluewin.ch		40-50
info@alplodge.com	www.alplodge.com	19-45
manorfarm@swisscamps.ch	www.manorfarm.ch	15+
hotel@alpesgruyere.ch	www.chhotel.ch	80-100
lerallye@worldcom.ch	http://www.hotel-lerallye.ch/	49-67
rene_morel@bluewin.ch	http://www.mypage.bluewin.ch/bnbmorel	49
info@brp.ch	www.brp.ch	230-380
agora@fhotels.ch	www.fassbindhotels.com	90-129
info@alagare.com	www.alagare.com	70-170
masseria@bluewin.ch		70-88
info@lausanne-guesthouse.ch	www.lausanne-guesthouse.ch	29-50
info@campinglausannevidy.ch	www.clv.ch/ANG/default.htm	20+
info@grandregina.ch	www.grandregina.ch	205-260
hotel@eiger-grindelwald.ch	www.eiger-grindelwald.ch	105-170
wolter@grindelwald.ch	www.grindelwald.ch/wolter	85-115
bernerhof@grindelwald.ch	www.bernerhofhotel.ch	165-205
hotel-lauberhorn@grindelwald.ch	www.hotel-lauberhorn.ch	70-80
grindelwald@youthhostel.ch	www.youthhostel.ch/grindelwald	27-51
info@gletscherdorf.ch	www.gletscherdorf.ch	12+
info@hotelschuetzen.com	www.hotelschuetzen.com	55-90
info@hoteloberland.ch	www.hoteloberland.ch	60-80
info@schutzenbach-retreat.ch	www.schutzenbach-retreat.ch	15+
info@camping-jungfrau.ch	www.camping-jungfrau.ch	21+
		65
		60+
royal@rikli.com	www.royalkandersteg.ch	150-190
doldenhorn@compuserve.com	www.waldhoteldoldenhorn.com	105+
chaletadler@bluewin.ch	www.chalethotel.ch	85-90
alpinakandersteg@bluewin.ch	www.alpina-online.ch	50-60
rest-rendez-vous@bluewin.ch		15+ (approx.)
hotelbeausite@bluewin.ch	www.hotelbeausite.ch	85-120

TYPE	NAME	ADDRESS	PHONE	FAX
3-star hotel	Hotel Bristol		033 6731481	033 6731650
2-star hotel	Hotel Kreuz		033 6732121	033 6732152
Campground	Camping Bergblick		033 6731454	033 6733352

LENK

TYPE	NAME	ADDRESS	PHONE	FAX
5-star hotel	Lenkerhof Alpine		033 7363636	033 7363637
4-star hotel	Hotel Simmenhof		033 7363434	033 7363436
3-star hotel	Betelberg		033 7363333	033 7363330
2-star hotel	Alpina		033 7331057	033 7333898
Campground	Hasenweide		033 7332647	033 7332973

LOW COUNTRIES

ZANDVOORT

TYPE	NAME	ADDRESS	PHONE	FAX
4-star hotel	Golden Tulip	Burgemeester v. Al.	023 5760760	023 5719094
3-star hotel	Amare	Hogeweg 70	023 5712202	023 5714374
2-star hotel	Astoria	Dr. CA Gerkestraat	023 5714550	023 5712840
1-star hotel	Casa Blanca	Oosterparkstraat 83	023 5714007	
Campground	De Branding	Blvd. Brnaart 30	023 5713035	023 5719283

DEN HAAG

TYPE	NAME	ADDRESS	PHONE	FAX
5-star hotel	Steigenberger Kurhaus	Gevers Deynootplein	070 4162636	070 4162646
4-star hotel	Bilderberg Europa Hotel	Zwolsestraat 2	070 4169595	070 4169555
3-star hotel	Badhotel Scheveningen	Gevers Deyn. 15	070 3512221	070 3555870
2-star hotel	Hotel Albion	G. Deynootweg 118	070 3557987	070 3555970
Hostel	Hotel Scheveningen	Gevers Deynootweg	070 3547003	070 3547003
Campground	Kijkduinpark	M. Vrijenhoeklaan	070 4482100	

DELFT

TYPE	NAME	ADDRESS	PHONE	FAX
4-star hotel	Hotel de Ark	Koornmarkt 65	015 2157999	015 2144997
3-star hotel	Hotel de Emauspoort	Vrouwenregt 9	015 2190219	015 2148251
1-star hotel	Hotel 'T Raedthuys	Markt 38	015 2125115	015 2136069
Campground	Delftse Hout	Koortlaan 5	015 2130040	015 2131293

BELGIUM

GENT

TYPE	NAME	ADDRESS	PHONE	FAX
4-star hotel	NH Gent	Kon. Albertlaan 121	09 2226065	09 2201605
3-star hotel	Astoria	Achilles Mussch. 39	09 2228413	09 2204787
2-star hotel	Trianon II	Voskenslaan 34	09 2204840	09 2204950
1-star hotel	Monasterium P.Ackere	Oude Houtlei 56	09 2692210	09 2692230
B&B	Atlas	Rabotstraat 40	09 2334991	
Campground	Strandgebouw	Zuiderlaan 5	09 2668170	09 2668174

BRUSELLS

TYPE	NAME	ADDRESS	PHONE	FAX
5-star hotel	Radisson SAS	47, Fosse aux Loups	02 2192828	02 2196262
4-star hotel	Crowne Plaza Brussels	107 rue de la Loi	02 2301333	02 2300326
3-star hotel	Forum Hotel	2, Ave. Haut Pont	02 3403400	02 3470054
2-star hotel	Albert Hotel	27 Rue Royale	02 2179391	02 2192017
Hostel	Youth Hostel	Rue de l'Elephant 4	02 4103858	02 4103905

ACCOMMODATIONS

EMAIL	WEB	PRICE
		(per-person, 1/2 twin, Euros)
bristol@bluewin.ch	www.bristol-adelboden.ch	98-150
hotel@kreuz-adelboden.ch	www.kreuz-adelboden.ch	33-89
bergblick@bluewin.ch	www.bergblick.ch	15+
welcome@lenkerhof.ch	www.lenkerhof.ch	245+
simmenhof@bluewin.ch	www.simmenhof.ch	100-150
reception@sporthotelbetelberg.ch	www.sporthotelbetelberg.ch	88-99
alpina_lenk@bluewin.ch	www.lenk.ch/mini/alpina/html	60-75
	www.camping-hasenweide.ch	10+
info@gtzandvoort.goldentulip.nl	www.goldentulip.nl	60-80
hotel.amare@wxs.nl	www.travel.to/amare	30-64
		43-59
		19-35
		10+
info@kurhaus.nl	www.kurhaus.nl	138-157
europa@bilderberg.nl	www.bilderberg-europa-hotel.nl	109-150
info@badhotelscheveningen.nl	www.badhotelscheveningen.nl	68-92
		33-42
		25
		12+
hotel@deark.nl	www.deark.nl	60+
info@emauspoort.nl	www.emauspoort.nl	43+
		20-30
info@delftsehout.nl	www.delftsehout.nl	12+
nhgent@nh-hotels.be	www.nh-hotels.com	60-87
info@astoria.be	www.astoria.be	33-50
info@hoteltrianon.be	www.hoteltranon.be	31-40
info@monasterium.be	www.monasterium.be	61
atlasb.en.b@pandora.be		29
reservaties.blaarmeersen@gent.be		9+
sales.brussels@radissonsas.com	www.radissonsas.com	138
brussels@gc.com	www.crowneplaza.com	107-110
forumrt@hoteles-catlonia.es	www.hoteles-catalonia.es	83
info@hotelalbert.be	www.hotelalbert.be	38
	www.laj.be	16+

TYPE	NAME	ADDRESS	PHONE	FAX
NAMUR				
4-star hotel	Chateau de Namur	Ave. de l'Ermitage	081 729900	081 729999
3-star hotel	Beauregard	Ave. B. Moreau	081 230028	081 241209
2-star hotel	Hotel de Flandre	Pl. de la Station	081 231868	081 228060
B&B	Mme. Fernande	Ch. De Dinant	081 220026	
Hostel	Auberge de Jeunesse	Rue Felicien Rops 8	081 223688	
Campground	Les Treiux	Les Tris (Malone)	081 445583	
HAN SUR LESSE				
4-star hotel	Ardennes 2	Rue des Grottes 6	084 377220	084 378062
3-star hotel	Hotel Stradella	Rue d'Hamptay 61	084 378064	084 340990
B&B	Andre Ph.	Chemin de Prele 7	084 366801	
Campground	De La Lesse	Rue du Grand Hy	084 377290	

MULTI-COUNTRY ITENERARIES

TYPE	NAME	ADDRESS	PHONE	FAX
COLCHESTER				
3-star hotel	Butterfly Hotel	Colchester CO7	01206 230900	01206 231095
3-star hotel	George Hotel	116 High St.	01206 578494	01206 761732
3-star	Rose and Crown	East Street	01206 866677	01206 866616
B&B	Four Sevens Guest Hose	28 Inglis Rd.	01206 546093	01206 546093
Campground	Colchester Camping	Cymbeline Way	01206 545551	01206 710443
HARWICH				
3-star hotel	The Pier	The Quay	01255 241212	01255 551922
2-star hotel	Hotel Continental	28 Marine Parade	01255 551298	01255 551698
B&B	Woodview Cottage	Wrabness Rd.	01255 886413	
Campground	Dovercourt Camping	Low Rd.	01787 281027	

NORTH SEA COAST TO AMSTERDAM

TYPE	NAME	ADDRESS	PHONE	FAX
HOEK VAN HOLLAND				
2-star hotel	Hotel Kuperduin	Prins Hendr. 193	0174 383068	0174 388091
B&B	Pension Seinpad	Seinpad 21	0174 385652	
Hostel	August Retismahuis	Nieuwelands. 160	0174 382560	
Campground	Camping H. v. Holland	Wierstraat 100	0174 382550	
HAARLEM				
4-star hotel	Golden Tulip Lion d'Or	Kruisweg 34-36	023 5321750	023 5329543
2-star hotel	't Carillon	Grote Markt 27	023 310591	023 5314909
1-star hotel	Joop's Innercity Hotel	Oude Groenmarkt	023 512 5300	023 5359549
Hostel	Stayokay Hostel	Jan Gijzenpad 3	023 5373793	023 5371176
Campground	De Liede	Lie Oever 68	023 5358666	023 5404613

AMSTERDAM TO BRUGES

TYPE	NAME	ADDRESS	PHONE	FAX
AMSTERDAM				
5-star hotel	Radisson SAS	Boeing Ave. 2	020 6553131	020 6553100
4-star hotel	Park Hotel	Stadhoudersk. 25	020 6711222	020 6649455
3-star hotel	Hotel Nova	NZ Voorburg. 276	020 623 0066	020 627 2026

EMAIL	WEB	PRICE
		(per-person, 1/2 twin, Euros)
chateau.namur@province.namur.be		63+
hotel.beauregard@skynet.be	www.diamond-hotels.com	38-56
hotel.flandre@skynet.be		27-43
		23-45
ajnamur@skynet.be		13-15
camping.les.trieux@skynet.be		8-12+
hoteldesardennes@skynet.be		38
lastradella@skynet.be		35
huguette.evrard@belgacom.be	www.han-chambres.be	20
han.tourisme@tiscali.be		7+
colbutterfly@lineone.net	www.butterflyhotels.co.uk	37-50
		47-60
info@rose-and-crown.com	www.rose-and-crown.com	35-42
calypsod@hotmail.com		23-28
enquiries@colchestercampingco.uk	www.colchestercamping.co.uk	7+
info@thepieratharwich.co.uk	www.milsomhotels.co.uk	45-80
hotconti@bt.com	www.hotelcontinental-harwich.co.uk	33-45
anne@woodview-cottage.co.uk	www.woodview-cottage.co.uk	24
info@escapetothebeach.co.uk	www.escapetothebeach.co.uk	
		38
information@pension.seinpad.nl	http://www.pension.seinpad.nl/uk/uk_index.html	33-35
augustreitsma@nivon.nl		12+
http://www.campinghoekvanholland.nl/		8.20+
reservations@hotelliondor.nl	www.goldentulip.nl	71-80
		29-36
joops@multiweb.nl		22-28
haarlem@njhc.org		15-23
		8+
info@amszq.rdsas.com	www.radissonsas.com	137
info@parkhotel.nl	www.parkhotel.nl	124-200
novahotel@wxs.nl	www.bookings.nl/hotels/nova	50+

TYPE	NAME	ADDRESS	PHONE	FAX
2-star hotel	AMS Hotel Holland	PC Hoofstr. 162	020 6831811	020 6160320
Hostel	City Hostel	Zandpad 5	020 5898993	020 5898955
Campground	Vliegenbos	Meeuwenlaan 138	020 6368855	020 6322723

GOUDA

3-star hotel	Campanile	Kampenringw. 39	0182 535555	0182 571575
2-star hotel	't Trefpunt	Westhaven 46	0182 512879	0182 585186
2-star hotel	De Keizerskroon	Keizerstraat 11	0182 528096	0182 511777
Campground	Elzenhof[2]	Broekweg 6	0182 524456	

WILLEMSTAD

2-star hotel	Het Wapen Willemstad	Benedenkade 12	0168 473450	0168 473705
B&B	Mrs. Cooman	P. van Oldenb.	0168 473177	
Campground	Bovensluis	Oostdijk 22	0168 472568	0168 472064

KAMPERLAND

3-star hotel	Hotel Kamperduin	Patrizjenlaan 1	0113 371466	0113 376030
B&B	Pension d'Ouwe Smidse	Noordstraat 26	0113 372352	0113 373885
Campground	Camping de Molenhoek	Molenweg 69a	0113 371202	

BRUGES

4-star hotel	De Castillion	Heilige-Geestr.	050 343001	050 339475
3-star hotel	Grand Hotel Oude Burg	Oude Burg 5	050 445111	050 445100
2-star hotel	'T Koffieboontje	Hallestraat 4	050 338027	050 343904
1-star hotel	Uilenspiegel	Langestraat 2	050 346555	050 490206
Hostel	Int'l YH Europa	B. Ruzettl. 143	050 352679	050 353732
Campground	St. Michiel	Tillegemstraat 55	050 380819	050 380131

PARIS TO LUXEMBOURG

REIMS

4-star hotel	Boyer Les Crayeres	64 Bvd. H. Vasn.	0326 828080	0326 826552
3-star hotel	Kyriad Reis Centre	7 Rue Gen. Sarrail	0326 475080	0326 472420
2-star hotel	Best Hotel	Rue M. Hollande	0326 827210	0326 825517
1-star hotel	Saint Andre	46 Ave. J. Jaures	0326 472416	

DONCHERY

3-star hotel	Chateau du Faucon	08350 Donchery	0324 521001	0324 527156
B&B	Chateau Sautou	Bosseval	0324 527008	0324 527008

MONTMEDY

2*	Hotel du Chateau	2 Rue M. Bastie	0329 801274	0329 800543
Campground	La Citadelle	11 Rue Vauban	0329 801040	0329 801298

LUXEMBOURG CITY

5-star hotel	Hilton	12 Rue J. Engling	43781	436095
4-star hotel	City Hotel	1 Rue Strasbourg	2911221	291133
3-star hotel	Hotel Francais	14 Pl. d'Armes	474534	464274
Hostel	IYH Luxembourg	2, Rue Fort Olisy	226889	223360
Campground	Camping Kockelscheuer	22 Rte. Bettemb.	471815	401243

ACCOMMODATIONS

EMAIL	WEB	PRICE (per-person, 1/2 twin, Euros)
info@ams.nl	www.ams.nl	65
vondelpark@njhc.org	www.njhc.org/vondelpark	20+
		8+
		38
		29
		34
		8-10+
info@wapenvanwillemstad.nl	www.wapenvanwillemstad.nl	40
		24+
camping@bovensluis.nl		8-16+
kamperdu@zeelandnet.nl	www.hotelkamperduin.nl	53-63
ouwesmidse@zeelandnet.nl		25
molenhoek@zeelandnet.nl	www.demolenhoek.com	8+
info@castillion.be	www.castillion.be	58-125
grandhotel.oudeburg@skynet.be	www.diamond-hotels.com	55-85
hotel_koffieboontje@unicall.be	www.hotel-koffieboontje.be	31-75
		40
brugge@vjh.be	www.vjh.be	12.50
		6.2+
crayeres@relaischateaux.com	www.gerardboyer.com	152-244
		34-40
besthotel.reims@wanadoo.fr	www.besthotel.fr	27-33
		15-21
Faucon@faucon.fr	www.faucon.fr	39-46
		38+
		25
		3-8
rm_Luxembourg@hilton.com	www.hilton.com	82-186
mail@cityhotel.lu	www.cityhotel.lu	60-95
hfinfo@pt.lu	www.hotelfrancais.lu	63-70
luxembourg@youthhostels.lu		15.50
mail@camp-kockelscheuer.lu	www.camp-kockelscheuer.lu	7.50

TYPE	NAME	ADDRESS	PHONE	FAX

LUXEMBOURG TO FRANKFURT

ECHTERNACH

TYPE	NAME	ADDRESS	PHONE	FAX
5-star hotel	Eden Au Lac	Oam Nonnesees	728283	728144
4-star hotel	Bel Air	1 Rte. De Berdorf	729383	728694
3-star hotel	Hotel du Commerce	16 Pl. du Marche	720301	728790
2-star hotel	Hotel Aigle Noir	54 Rue de la Gare	720383	720544
Hostel	IYH Echternach	9 Rue A. Duchscher	720158	728735
Campground	Camping Officiel	5, Rte. Diekirch	720272	26720847

SCHWEICH

TYPE	NAME	ADDRESS	PHONE	FAX
2-star hotel	Hotel Leinenhof	Am Azertwald	06502 91860	06502 918640
Inn	Haus Grefen	Bruckenstr. 31	06502 92400	06502 924040
Campground	Zum Fahrturm	Manfr. Kreusch	06502 91300	06502 913050

BERNKASTEL-KUES

TYPE	NAME	ADDRESS	PHONE	FAX
4-star hotel	Hotel Moselpark	Im Kurpark	06531 5080	06531 508612
3-star hotel	Hotel Zur Post	Gestade 17	06531 96700	06531 967050
B&B	Gastehaus Port	Weingartenstr. 57	06531 91173	06531 91175
Campground	Campingpltz K W	Am Hafen 2	06531 8200	06531 8282

COCHEM

TYPE	NAME	ADDRESS	PHONE	FAX
4-star hotel	Moselromantik	Am Reilsb. 10	02671 97880	02671 3857
3-star hotel	Parkhotel v. Landenberg	Sehl. Anl. 1	02671 7110	02671 8379
B&B	Pension Gundert	Ravenestr. 34	02671 910224	02671 910224
Campground	Schausten Reif	Enderstr. 124	02671 7528	02671 1875

SWISS AND ITALIAN LAKES: LUGANO & COMO

The Lugano rides begin from the Lugano-Paradiso area on the western edge of the city. This has always been the starting point for my groups, since I find it much less congested than the streets around the central station. However, if you're not part of a large group, you may find the center more to your liking, as certainly most of the nightlife is focused there. Cycling from Lugano center to Lugano-Paradiso is a simple navigational matter.

LUGANO

TYPE	NAME	ADDRESS	PHONE	FAX
5-star hotel	Grand Hotel	Riva Paradiso 1	091 9859200	091 9859250
4-star hotel	Du Lac	Riva Paradiso 3	091 9864747	091 9864748
3-star hotel	Cristina Paradiso	Via F. Zorzi 28	091 9943312	091 9931568
2-star hotel	Dan	Via Dom. Fon. 1	091 9857030	091 9857031
Hostel	Hotel Montarina	Via Montarina 1	091 9667272	091 9660017
Campground	Golfo del Sole	Via Rivera 8	091 6054802	

COMO

TYPE	NAME	ADDRESS	PHONE	FAX
4-star hotel	Barchetta	Piazza Cavour 1	031 3221	031 302622
3-star hotel	Firenze	Piazza Volta 166	031 300333	031 300101
2-star hotel	Fontana	Via D. Fontana 19	031 271110	031 271110
B&B	Blulion	Via Valgidera 4	031 305894	
Hostel	Ostello Villa Olmo	Via Bellinzona 2	031 573800	031 573800
Campground	Camping International	Via Cecilio	031 521435	

EMAIL	WEB	PRICE
		(per-person, 1/2 twin, Euros)
hotel@edenaulac.lu	www.edenaulac.lu	56-86
belair@ptlu	www.belair-hotel.lu	51-80
chactour@pt.lu	www.hotelcommerce-echternach.lu	33-39
aiglnoir@pt.lu		22-28
echternach@youthhostels.lu		13.60
info@cmping-echternach.lu	www.camping-echternach.lu	8+
info@leinenhof.de	www.leinenhof.de	27-33
info@hotel-grefen.de	www.hotel-grefen.de	13-17
camping@kreusch.de	www.kreusch.de	7-12
info@moselpark.de	www.moselpark.de	59-90
Hotel-zur-Post-Bernkastel@t-online.de	http://www.hotel-zur-post-bernkastel.de/	40-72
weingutport@t-online.de	www.weingutport.de	20-25
rezeption@hotel-kessler-meyer.de	www.hotel-kessler-meyer.de	45-87
parkhotel-landenberg@t-online.de	www.castle-thorschenke.com/parkhotel	33-65
		23+
		8-12
info@edenlugano.ch	www.edenlugano.ch	90-138
dulac@dulac.ch	www.dulac.ch	67-95
info@cristina-paradiso.ch	www.cristina-paradiso.ch	30-50
dnlugano@yahoo.com	www.pibt.del/dan.htm	45
info@montarina.ch	www.montarina.ch	37+
info@golfodelsole.ch		12-18
info2@hotelbarchetta.com	www.hotelbarchetta.com	57-145
info@albergofirenze.it	www.albergofirenze.it	60
hotelfontana@iol.it	www.fontanahotel.net	40
blulion19@hotmail.com		25
ostellocomo@tin.it	www.ostellionline.org/ostello.php?idostello+368	13.50
		12+

TYPE	NAME	ADDRESS	PHONE	FAX

VIENNA TO PRAGUE

KREMS AN DER DONAU

TYPE	NAME	ADDRESS	PHONE	FAX
4-star hotel	Hotel Linblhuber	Wiener Str. 2	02732 86960	02732 8696050
3-star hotel	Donauhotel Krems	Edm. Hofb. 19	02732 87565	02732 8756552
2-star hotel	Hotel Kolping Krems	Ringstr. 46	02732 83541	02732 71121
B&B	Gasthof Wiener Brucke	Wienerstr. 2	02732 82143	02732 8214350
Hostel	Radfahrjugendherberge	Ringstr. 77	02732 83452	02732 5864153

ZNOJMO

TYPE	NAME	ADDRESS	PHONE	FAX
4-star hotel	Hotel Prestige	Prazska 669	515 224595	515 246621
3-star hotel	Hotel Dukla	Holandska 5	515 2273201	515 227322
Unrated	Hotel Karnik	Zelenaoska 25	515 226826	515 226826
B&B	Penzion Garni	Suchohrdelska 7	737 916000	515 222111

TELC

TYPE	NAME	ADDRESS	PHONE	FAX
3-star hotel	Hotel Celerin	Nam. Zachar z H.	066 724 3477	066 7213581
3-star hotel	Hotel U Cerneho Orla	Nam. Zach. Z. H.	066 7243220	066 7243221
3-star hotel	Hotel Pangea	Na Baste 450	066 7213122	066 7213265
Hostel	Volejbalove Kurty		567 243838	
Campground	Taboriste Lhotka	Horni Mrzatec	066 7317340	

JINDRICHUV HRADEC

TYPE	NAME	ADDRESS	PHONE	FAX
4-star hotel	Hotel Concertino	Nam. Miru 141	0331 362320	0331 362333
3-star hotel	Grand Hotel	Nam. Miru 165	0331 361252	0331 361251
2-star hotel	Hotel U Mesta Vidne	Nadrazni 203	0331 361639	0331 361640
B&B	Penzion Kapitan	Prazska 297	0331 362636	0331 363086

TREBON

TYPE	NAME	ADDRESS	PHONE	FAX
3-star hotel	Bertiny Lazne Trebon	Tylova 1	0384 754111	0384 721551
3-star hotel	Hotel Bohemia	U Sveta 750	0384 721394	0384 721396
3-star hotel	Hotel Bohemia & Regent	U Sveta 750		
Campground	Sport CentrumDoubi	Branna 108	0384 792895	0384 792999

CESKY KRUMLOV

TYPE	NAME	ADDRESS	PHONE	FAX
4-star hotel	Hotel Ruze	Horni 154	0380 772100	0380 713146
3-star hotel	Hotel Dvorak	Radnicni 101	0380 711020	0380 711024
B&B	Pension Ingrid	Kaplicka 194	0380 712337	
Hostel	Hostel Krumlov House	Rooseveltova 68	0380 711935	

PRIBRAM

TYPE	NAME	ADDRESS	PHONE	FAX
4-star hotel	Hotel Impuls	Brodska 140	0318 632045	0318 632046
4-star hotel	Hotel Modry Hrozen	Nam. TG M. 143	0318 628007	0318 628901
2-star hotel	Hotel Mineral	Marianska 431	0318 624402	0318 624463
B&B	Penzion Kunc I a II	Laz U Pribrami	0318 676319	0318 676319

PRAGUE

TYPE	NAME	ADDRESS	PHONE	FAX
5-star hotel	Hilton Prague	Pobrezni 1	0224 841111	0224 842378
4-star hotel	Arcotel Teatrino	Barivojova 53	0221 422111	0221 422222
3-star hotel	Anna	Budecska 17	0222 513111	0222 515158
2-star hotel	Hotel Sandra	Nad Opatov. 2140	02 7951621	02 7951621
B&B	Pension Museum	Mezibr. 15	02 96325186	02 96325188
Hostel	Advantage Hostel	Sokolska 11	0224 914062	0224 914067
Campground	Camp Dana Troja	Trojska 129	0283 850482	0283 850482